Chappaquiddick Speaks

Chappaquiddick Speaks

Bill Pinney

To Rochester

SECOND EDITION

Cover photo: Jack Hubbard

ISBN-13: 978-0-692-94376-2
Library of Congress Control Number: 2017913461

 Stormy Weather Press

For information and requests, please address
Stormy Weather Press
3242 Mary Street, PH3
Coconut Grove, FL 33133

About the Author

Bill Pinney was raised on Chappaquiddick and in Edgartown. He attended Columbia University in New York, graduating with a degree in philosophy in 1968. He was Editor/Publisher of the *Andean Times*, the English-language newspaper of Colombia, South America; Editor/Publisher of *This is Ontario* magazine in Canada; and a South American investigative reporter for the *Sunday Times* of London. His consuming interest is medieval history, with several books in the works since 1995. Bill has circumnavigated the world on his schooner, *Rachel J. Slocum*, and with his wife, Raquel, divides his time between his boat on the high seas, historical research in England and France, and home on Chappaquiddick.

Acknowledgements

Special thanks to Jim Crandall who was of great assistance explaining the intricacies of Kennedy's vehicle; Chappaquiddick resident Paul McDonough who helped with much of the early editing; Dr. Art Phinney who advised me on medical matters; Rick Cooper for his excellent graphics; Jonah Gouin for his technical photographic advice; Anna Jedrzejowski of Ryerson University and Chris Ward who went out of their way to locate Fred Ward's photos; crash analyst Bill Fischer who provided Inspector Kennedy's inquest accident sketch; Ann Floyd and Lynne Cameron who helped in so many ways and whose enthusiasm for the project was contagious; Vineyard insiders Chris Look, Steve Ewing, and Leslie Leland, the last who has become a good friend; John Farrar who has always offered his help and insights to every author who has investigated the incident, including this one; to my wife, Raquel, who not only started me off on this quest but encouraged me to continue with it when spirits were low; and most especially, to Kenneth Kappel who pointed the way; to Jack Hubbard, whose excellent photo collection was instrumental in confirming the author's theories; and to Dr. Rod Cross for his long-suffering patience, open mind, and brilliant physics.

Preface iv
Introduction vii

PART 1: BACKGROUND
Chapter 1. Ted Kennedy's Story 1
Chapter 2. Those Damn Witnesses… 7
Chapter 3. Other Oddities 17
Chapter 4. Uncertain Cause of Death 34

PART 2: NEW WITNESS
Chapter 5. Carol Jones – Her Eyewitness Account 38
Chapter 6. Affidavits 46
Chapter 7. Intimidation and Death Threats 52
Chapter 8. Huck Look 55
Chapter 9. Dike Bridge Theories 57
Chapter 10. Author's Involvement 61
Chapter 11. Kenneth Kappel 62
Chapter 12. Our Theory 66

PART 3: FORENSIC EVIDENCE
Chapter 13. Dike Bridge Channel 70
Chapter 14. Burst Bubbles 84
Chapter 15. Death of Mary Jo 90
Chapter 16. Blood Trail 94
Chapter 17. Crash Analysis 103
Chapter 18. Skid Marks 126
Chapter 19. Physics of the Accident (Dr. Rod Cross) 132
Chapter 20. Evidence of the Accident (Dr. Rod Cross) 157
Chapter 21. Technical Aspects (Dr. Rod Cross) 178
Chapter 22. From Speculation to Certainty 190

PART 4: ANALYSIS
Chapter 23. Questions with Answers 195
Chapter 24. The Mystery Man and Women 218
Chapter 25. Was There Another Woman Involved? 226
Chapter 26. The Relay 236
Chapter 27. The Reluctant Witness 246
Chapter 28. The Malms 250
Chapter 29. The Accident 259
Chapter 30. Dike Road and the Edgartown Channel 263

PART 5: AUTHOR'S OBSERVATIONS

Chapter 31. Rochester 273
Chapter 32. The Failed Autopsy 275
Chapter 33. The Kopechnes 278
Chapter 34. Joseph Gargan Jr. 282
Chapter 35. The BBC Documentary *Chappaquiddick* 285
Chapter 36. Look & Carol 291
Chapter 37. John N. Farrar 293

PART 6: THE REAL STORY

Chapter 38. How it Might Have Occurred 301
Chapter 39. Timeline 313
Chapter 40. The Unthinkable 320
Chapter 41. Alternative Possibilities 328
Chapter 42. Objections to Our Theories 349
Chapter 43. The Case for Ted Kennedy's Story 352

PART 7: SUMMARY

Chapter 44. The Boiler Room Girls 355
Chapter 45. Requiem for Edward Moore Kennedy 358
Chapter 46. Conclusion 360
Postscript 364

APPENDIX

Note 1: Torque Acting About a Pivot Point 366
Note 2: Air Flow from a Submerged Vehicle 366
Note 3: Impact Force on a Body & Head 368
Note 4: Flow Rate of Water from a Pond 369
Note 5: Formulas to Determine the State of the CM at Free Fall 370
Note 6: Door Structural Analysis (Cacciatore & Ochoa) 372
Note 7: Side Window & Front Windshield Structural Analysis (Ochoa) ... 378
Note 8: Roof & Front Windshield Structural Analysis (Ochoa) 383

INDEX

INDEX 392

From the Author

As I put this manuscript to bed there appear to be enthusiastic attempts to resurrect Ted Kennedy's image. A new Kennedy museum at the Kennedy Compound in Hyannis Port has a special room dedicated to Ted, our Democratic Party lauds his legacy, and a new political thriller movie is in the works purportedly suggesting that Kennedy's most grievous offence was not reporting the accident promptly. The theory these days, accepted by most, is that Kennedy was innocent of any serious wrong-doing. Either he was suffering from shock and should not be accountable for his actions, or Mary Jo drove off the bridge alone, or there was a real companion that Kennedy, Gargan, and Markham were attempting to protect all these years through some sense of old-fashioned chivalry, to the detriment of their reputations and careers. Except for a few old farts like me, the public indignation to the Chappaquiddick scandal, so passionate in 1969 and for a quarter century longer, seems to have all but disappeared.

Many friends have implored me not to write this book because of what it might do to the memory of a great man. "What's the point?" they ask me. "Think of all the good things he did. It was just an unfortunate mistake. No one cares about Chappaquiddick now. There won't be any interest. You're a Democrat, for God's sake!"

Before I put pen to paper I assured family and friends that if the science did not back up Carol's sighting, and what that sighting implied, I would abandon the effort. I had no wish to malign anyone's reputation if the evidence did not back up the accusation. But the forensic science and the medical evidence do back up the theory most strongly, and I'll hang my hat on the scientific method over wishful thinking or self-serving interest every time.

The Chappaquiddick incident is history, and these days attempts to ignore the historical record, or rewrite it, rarely succeed for long. I have been led by the evidence to accept that the underlying theory as set out in this book is true. As such I believe the truth has merit, and should be told.

Bill Pinney, March 2018

CHRONOLOGY

<u>1969</u>

July 18　　　　Sometime in the evening, Kennedy leaves Lawrence Cottage with Mary Jo Kopechne.

July 19　　　　Sometime in the early morning, Kennedy's Oldsmobile plunges off Dike Bridge into Poucha Pond. Mary Jo dies.

July 19　　　　At about 10:00 a.m., Kennedy gives a statement to Chief Arena at the Edgartown police station.

July 22　　　　Mary Jo Kopechne is buried in Larksville, Pennsylvania.

July 25　　　　Kennedy pleads guilty to leaving the scene of an accident and is given a two-month suspended sentence and a year's probation by Judge Boyle.

July 25　　　　Kennedy gives a nationally televised speech.

October 20-21　Judge Brominski presides over a hearing for the exhumation and autopsy of Mary Jo Kopechne.

December 10　Judge Brominski denies the exhumation and autopsy petition.

<u>1970</u>

January 5-8　Judge Boyle presides over a closed inquest in Edgartown.

February 18　Judge Boyle files his official report of the inquest findings.

April 6-7　　Leslie Leland, foreman of the grand jury, attempts to ascertain the facts of the accident but is thwarted by Judge Paquet.

April 29　　Inquest testimony is released to the public.

November 4　Kennedy is reelected to the Senate.

ii

CAST OF CHARACTERS

Joseph Kennedy	Edward Kennedy's nephew
David Burke	Administrative Assistant to Senator Kennedy
Stephen Smith	Kennedy's brother-in-law
Dun Gifford	Aide to Senator Kennedy
Dominick J. Arena	Police Chief, Edgartown, Massachusetts
Walter Steele	Dukes County Prosecutor, Martha's Vineyard
Edmund S. Dinis	District Attorney for the Southern District of Massachusetts
Armand Fernandes	Assistant District Attorney
George Killen	State Police Detective-lieutenant
Bernie Flynn	State Police Detective-lieutenant
James A. Boyle	Superior Court Judge, Dukes County Court, Massachusetts
Bernard C. Brominski	Judge, Luzerne County Court, Pennsylvania
Wilfred Paquet	Judge, Massachusetts Superior Court
Joseph Flanagan	Attorney for the Kopechnes
George Kennedy	Supervisor of the Massachusetts Registry of Motor Vehicles on Martha's Vineyard
John N. Farrar	SCUBA diver and head of the Search and Rescue Division of the Edgartown Volunteer Fire Department
Leslie Leland	Island pharmacist and foreman of the grand jury
Christopher "Huck" Look	Edgartown deputy sheriff
Dr. Donald Mills	Associate Medical Examiner, Martha's Vineyard
Dr. Robert Nevin	Chief Medical Examiner, Dukes County
Dr. Werner Spitz	Deputy Chief Medical Examiner for the State of Maryland
Dr. John McHugh	Director of the Massachusetts State Police Crime Lab
Eugene Frieh	Undertaker, Martha's Vineyard
Bill Fischer	Crash analyst
Robert Dubois	Crash analyst
Russell Peachey	Manager/part owner of the Shiretown Inn, Edgartown
Wilfred Rock	Gifford's pilot
Ross Richards	Yachtsman, Hyannis Port
Stan Moore	Automobile dealer and Edgartown Regatta participant
Tony Bettencourt	Owner of Dyke House
Sylvia Malm	Tenant of Dyke House in the summer of 1969
Sydney Lawrence	Owner of Lawrence Cottage
Foster Silva	Caretaker of Lawrence Cottage
Jared Grant	Chappaquiddick ferry owner in 1969
Richard Hewitt	Chappaquiddick ferry operator

Steve Ewing	Chappaquiddick ferry deckhand
Jon Ahlbum	Tow truck driver and owner of the Depot station, Edgartown
Douglas Batten	Ahlbum's assistant at the Depot station
Roderick "Roddy" Hoar	Owner of a missing rowboat, Chappaquiddick
Carol Jones	Witness on the evening of July 18
Nancy McDonald	Witness on the morning of July 19
Todd Ballou	Witness on the morning of July 19
Rochester	A Chappaquiddick dog

At the party:

Ted and his friends

Edward Moore Kennedy	Massachusetts senator (37, married)
Joseph Gargan Jr.	Lawyer and Ted Kennedy's first cousin (39, married)
Paul Markham	Lawyer and former US Attorney for Massachusetts (38, married)[1]
Charles Tretter	Lawyer and Kennedy aide (30, married)
Ray LaRosa	Kennedy campaign worker (41, married)
John Crimmins	Kennedy's part-time chauffeur (63, single)

Boiler Room Girls

Mary Jo Kopechne (28, single)
Rosemary "Cricket" Keough (23, single)
Esther Newberg (26, single)
Susan Tannenbaum (24, single)
Nance Lyons (26, single)
Mary Ellen Lyons (27, single)

---

[1] Many books have his age as 39. Hersh, Kennedy's biographer, says he was 38 when the incident occurred but 39 at the time of the inquest.

Preface

The Chappaquiddick incident of 1969 has been called "the most discussed traffic accident in history" and "the most brilliant cover-up ever achieved in a nation where investigative procedures are well-developed and where the principles of equal justice prevail." It is considered one of the great unsolved mysteries of twentieth-century America.

There have been 13 books written about the events at Dike Bridge.[1] In order of their publication date, these are:

Don Hastings, *The Ted Kennedy Episode*, Reliable Press, 1969
Jack Olsen, *The Bridge at Chappaquiddick*, Little, Brown & Co., 1970
Zad Rust, *Teddy Bare: The Last of the Kennedy Clan*, Western Islands, 1971
Robert B. Cutler, *You, the Jury*, self-published, 1973
Malcolm Reybold, *The Inspector's Opinion*, Saturday Review Press, 1975
Richard and Thomas Tedrow, *Death at Chappaquiddick*, Pelican Publishing Co., 1976
Robert Sherrill, *The Last Kennedy*, Dial Press, 1976
Larryann Willis, *Chappaquiddick Decision*, Better Books Publisher, 1980
Leo Damore, *Senatorial Privilege: The Chappaquiddick Cover-up*, Regnery Gateway, 1988
Kenneth Kappel, *Chappaquiddick Revealed: What Really Happened*, Shapolsky Publishers, 1989
James Lange and Katherine DeWitt, *Chappaquiddick: The Real Story*, St. Martin's Press, 1992
Leslie Leland and J. B. Shaffer, *Left to Die*, Strategic Book Publishing, 2009
Donald Nelson, *Chappaquiddick Tragedy: Kennedy's Second Passenger Revealed*, Pelican Publishing Co., 2016

These books detail the inconsistencies in Senator Edward Kennedy's statements and the testimony of his friends and lawyers who were with him in the evening and early morning of July 18 and 19, and of the cover-up that followed. They show all too clearly that Kennedy was given special treatment by Massachusetts police, judges, and government officials. A quick read of any one of them is a surrealistic journey through a theater of the absurd.

---

[1] Many other books have mentioned or analyzed the incident in passing. These include *Edward Kennedy and the Camelot Legacy*, James Burns, W.W. Norton & Company, 1976, pp. 163-173; *The President's Private Eye*, Tony Ulasewicz, MACSAM Publishing Company, 1990, pp 187-224; *The Gemstone File*, Stephanie Caruana, Trafford Publishing, 2006, pp. 77-80; and *Edward Kennedy: An Intimate Biography*, Burton Hersh, Counterpoint, 2010, pp. 344-380.

In the best and most forgiving light, Edgartown Police Chief Jim Arena was distressingly incompetent. State Police Detective Bernie Flynn acted behind the scenes as a Kennedy informer in the months leading up to the exhumation and inquest hearings. District Attorney Edmund Dinis walked a tightrope between actually doing his job as a prosecutor and trying to keep his Democrat friends happy to win reelection. The result was a lackluster effort that went nowhere. Walter Steele, the Dukes County prosecutor, did everything in his power to exonerate Kennedy, including intimidating those who tried to get at the truth. Judge Bernard Brominski, a self-professed Kennedy admirer who presided over the exhumation and autopsy hearing of Mary Jo, flew in the face of all case law and ruled against it. Massachusetts had requested the autopsy to establish the medical facts, yet Brominski dismissed their petition because it was unsupported by medical facts. Judge James Boyle, who presided over the Kopechne inquest, was so clearly on the side of Ted that it must have been embarrassing to the few who were allowed to attend. Boyle stacked the deck on the Kennedy side by establishing a set of ground rules that gave the prosecution no room to maneuver, even had they wanted to (which they clearly did not), then summarily dismissed or rejected much evidence and testimony that might suggest Kennedy and his friends were lying. Leslie Leland, who convened a grand jury to investigate the accident in spite of considerable pressure to walk away, was successfully stymied after only two days by Judge Wilfred Paquet, a militant Catholic, who was unable to conceal his outright hatred toward a person who had the audacity to buck the Kennedy machine. Several of Paquet's peers who reviewed the judge's conduct later were shocked and appalled and have accused him of tampering with a grand jury.

When you read over the testimony and evidence presented in this book it is important to remember that few government officials had any real interest in collecting evidence or interviewing witnesses. No one who stood up to the Kennedys in 1969 really had a chance. Alan Parker, son of the co-owner of the Shiretown Inn in Edgartown where Kennedy and several of his friends were lodged over that weekend, explained how things worked in those days: "A few days prior to testifying at the inquest my father was visited by two associates of the Kennedy clan who went through his testimony and made sure my father knew exactly what he was supposed to say. This was Massachusetts, after all, the Kennedy family's fiefdom. Anyone who did not toe the Kennedy line would not stay in business in that domain for very long."[1] Nelson cites secondhand testimony from Dorothy Crimmins, Judge Boyle's private secretary, describing "intense communications and directions coming down from Boston to control the whole [inquest] procedure."[2]

---

[1] http://blogs.canoe.com/parker/news/last-words-on-ted-kennedy-and-chappaquiddick/ and http://blogs.canoe.com/parker/?s=chappaquiddick&x=0&y=0
[2] *Chappaquiddick Tragedy*, p. 115

There are only three heroes in this story: John Farrar, the fire and rescue SCUBA diver who extricated Mary Jo from Kennedy's Oldsmobile; Huck Look, who observed the Oldsmobile between 12:40 and 12:45 a.m. on the early morning of July 19; and Leslie Leland, foreman of the neutered grand jury. These three refused to back down from the Kennedy team or go away. All three paid for it dearly with harassment, tax audits, and death threats. Their lives and the lives of their families were in jeopardy for many years after.

The only reason Kennedy and his team were ultimately unsuccessful in burying the story was because of a press who refused to quit and a national public that was far brighter than Kennedy realized. Most of the evidence that did come to light was due to the persistent digging of investigative reporters who were always far ahead of a police force and prosecution that were dragging their feet. I have talked to several people who have been under the impression that the press was in on the cover-up from the beginning. It just wasn't so. A few Massachusetts papers attempted to gloss over the story in the beginning, but once it had sunk its teeth into the obvious fabrications and inconsistencies in the senator's account the national press was tenacious and must be commended.

In this book it is not my intention to make an exhaustive study of all the evidence once more or to spend much time discussing the intricacies of the cover-up. For those interested, I believe the most thorough study will be found in *Senatorial Privilege*, followed by *Death at Chappaquiddick* and *Teddy Bare*. For sheer literary eloquence, nothing tops *The Last Kennedy*.

Instead, I will concentrate on the evidence recorded at the Kopechne inquest and elsewhere as it specifically relates to the testimony of Carol Jones, a new witness, who will relate what she saw on the night of July 18 to piece together a coherent story from what, heretofore, has been a confusing collection of inconsistencies.

In a personal interview, Joe Gargan, Ted Kennedy's cousin who was with Kennedy in the hours following the accident, told Leo Damore that he always feared a witness might appear one day to contradict the senator's story.[1] Gargan's fears have been realized. A new witness has finally stepped forward. At long last, *Chappaquiddick speaks.*

---

[1] *Senatorial Privilege*, p. 226

Introduction

This book is the result of a collaborative effort from two people who know Chappaquiddick well.

My great-grandparents began spending their summers on Chappaquiddick after my great-great-grandmother purchased what today is the Nicholas residence on the island in the 1890s. My grandfather purchased our present Chappaquiddick home nearby in 1925 and owned and farmed Sweetened Water Farm just outside Edgartown. My grandparents on both sides of the family lived in Edgartown year round when I was growing up, and my sister and I were raised on the Vineyard, spending the summers on Chappaquiddick and the winters in Edgartown.

The family spread, and since the early 1900s our extended family has always been the largest of any by far on the island of Chappaquiddick. In the summer we have counted more than 200 cousins at one time including, besides Pinney, these families who have been summer or year-round residents on Chappaquiddick for generations: Child, Bird, Bass, Gostenhofer, Turnbull, Phinney, Knight, Patterson, Getsinger, Tilghman, and Jones. Those cousins have been joined by more recent arrivals including Cook, Kidder, Burris, Morris, Lowenstein, Stone, Symmes, and Slade.

In *The Bridge at Chappaquiddick*, Jack Olsen paints Chappaquiddick as a private retreat for the wealthy and privileged. Pre-Kennedy, we were privileged all right. But if the island was private it was because few people wanted to live there. Chappaquiddick was known for its ticks, mosquitoes, poison ivy, and little else. Many on the Vineyard never made it over to Chappaquiddick in their lifetimes because they could see little point. Property was dirt cheap because no one wanted to buy.

There were some families on Chappaquiddick that were wealthy, of course, but those were mostly the exceptions. An uncle and a cousin were ministers just getting by, and my father survived by managing the Cooperative Dairy in Edgartown in between inseminating cows on the Vineyard and raising chickens on Chappaquiddick. There was no electricity at our Chappaquiddick home until I was six so we made do with kerosene refrigerators supplemented by pond ice purchased from the Jeffers. As young children we used outhouses instead of toilets and pages ripped from a Sears Roebuck catalog instead of toilet paper. We placed garbage in pits we dug ourselves on our own land. We rarely made any trips to Edgartown. We used old, rusted bicycles for everything. We lived in our bathing suits and rarely took baths. In spite of that, we wouldn't live anywhere else. Chappaquiddick was paradise for all of us. It was out-and-out *healthy*. That is, pre-Kennedy.

Post-Kennedy, the island is dotted with houses and the wealthy have moved in. Tourists clog the roads dressed in Spandex on their upmarket bicycles searching for "Kennedy Bridge" while inquisitive sightseers tramp through private property at will. It is impossible to know more than a fraction of the people these days. Many of the houses are built for show. The privacy that Olsen speaks of in *The Bridge at Chappaquiddick* is long gone, and so is the innocence.

Most of us were on Chappaquiddick on July 18, 1969, when Kennedy said he drove off Dike Bridge with Mary Jo Kopechne. Many of us, including Carol and her brothers and sisters, were at the Dike soon after they pulled Kennedy's Oldsmobile from the water. Carol's youngest sister, Maryann, set up a stand at the bridge and began selling lemonade, brownies, and chocolate chip cookies to the spectators. David Gostenhofer, an enterprising teenage cousin, operated a lucrative business at the ferry landing selling pieces of driftwood masquerading as bits of Dike Bridge to unsuspecting tourists. A reporter from the *Herald News* of Passaic, New Jersey, stayed at Carol's home for much of the time he was reporting the incident. We count a number of the principals who were interviewed by the reporters and authors who covered the story as friends, and we are personally acquainted with most of the others.

We have been reminded of those events each summer as we drive around the bend where Kennedy is supposed to have taken a wrong turn and driven off the bridge, and as the island population has mushroomed and trophy houses have sprung up everywhere, we have lived with the consequences. Not one of us has ever believed the story Kennedy and his team dreamt up in the days and weeks following the incident. Knowing Chappaquiddick as we do, it just never made sense.

Burton Hersh, Kennedy's biographer, claims the accident was "a fluke, over-reported and misunderstood hours after it happened, and now."[1] Hersh depicts the senator as a terrible driver who took a tremendous blow on the head and should not be held responsible for anything that ensued. In his recent book, *Edward Kennedy: An Intimate Biography,* Kennedy is portrayed as the victim of a terrible misunderstanding.

Well, maybe. But as Chappaquiddick insiders we think the evidence suggests otherwise and perhaps, after reading this book, you will, too.

---

[1] Burton Hersh, *Edward Kennedy: An Intimate Biography*, Counterpoint, 2010, p. 344. Hersh's analysis of the Chappaquiddick incident is predictable and disappointing – an unapologetic affirmation of Ted Kennedy's version of events and a condemnation of the army of reporters who "were roaming Martha's Vineyard, Chappaquiddick Island and Hyannis Port like starved wolves."

PART 1: BACKGROUND

1

Ted Kennedy's Story

Note: To those of us who live on Chappaquiddick, the spelling is Dike Road and Dike Bridge *but* Dyke House, *the last a spelling idiosyncrasy of the original owner, Tony Bettencourt. Chappaquiddick is frequently referred to as* Chappy. *The combined islands of Chappaquiddick and Martha's Vineyard are known as* the Vineyard.

Edgartown Regatta

𝓣he Edgartown Regatta on the island of Martha's Vineyard, Massachusetts, has been an annual event for decades. The Kennedys had been regular participants for more than 30 years and all three brothers had acquired well-deserved reputations for hell raising. Ted had visited the island as recently as the summer of 1968 during his period of mourning for his brother Robert, taking up a whole floor of the Harbor View Hotel in Edgartown.

The forty-seventh Edgartown Regatta was scheduled to begin on Friday, July 18, 1969. Ted Kennedy had entered a 25-foot Wianno Senior racing boat for the two-day event: the *Victura*. On this occasion, Kennedy and his party would be staying at the Shiretown Inn on North Water Street in Edgartown. Six young women known as the Boiler Room Girls, who had worked for Robert Kennedy as campaign workers before his assassination, were assigned lodging at the Katama Shores Motel just outside Edgartown. A small house, called Lawrence Cottage, had also been rented on the nearby island of Chappaquiddick to host a series of cookouts in the evenings after each race.

Chappaquiddick Island

Chappaquiddick Island is a sandy dot of land less than three miles wide, connected to Martha's Vineyard Island in 1969 by a single two-car ferry. In 1969, there was no land bridge between the two islands. Lawrence Cottage is located on School House Road, a half mile from a right-angle curve which forms a junction between Chappaquiddick Road heading west to the ferry, two and one-half miles away, and Dike Road, a dirt lane leading east seven-tenths of a mile to Dike Bridge. On the other side of Dike Bridge the road turns quickly to sand and the beautiful and secluded dunes of East Beach where Kennedy and his friends intended spending much of their time over the weekend swimming and sunbathing.

Kennedy's story

During the late morning and early afternoon of July 18, before the start of the first yacht race, Kennedy, Kennedy's chauffeur, four other married men, and six young, single women entertained themselves swimming and sunbathing on East Beach. From about 8:30 p.m. on July 18, the same twelve persons spent their evening relaxing at Lawrence Cottage. The group grilled steaks, drank sparingly, enjoyed light-hearted conversation intermixed with innocent dancing, and behaved themselves well.

At 11:15 p.m., a completely sober Ted Kennedy left the party at Lawrence Cottage in his 1967 Oldsmobile with an equally sober Mary Jo Kopechne to catch the ferry back to Edgartown. Kennedy said this was because Mary Jo had an upset stomach.[1] Confused because of his unfamiliarity with the Chappaquiddick roads, Kennedy made a sharp right turn onto the rough, narrow dirt road leading east to Dike Bridge and East Beach rather than following the banked paved road and directional sign to the left and west toward the ferry. At some point Kennedy realized this was a dirt road rather than a paved road but "did not think anything of it." Continuing at about 20 mph, he was suddenly aware of a bridge in front of him. Kennedy slammed on his brakes "a fraction of a second" before the car went over the side and into the water.

In the aftermath of the accident, Kennedy managed to escape the car but had "no idea in the world how." The current was fierce and he was swept down about 30 to 40 feet from the bridge, but he swam and waded back, stubbornly diving about seven or eight times "in the deep pond" in attempts to save Mary Jo. Exhausted from fighting the current to no avail, he rested for about 15 to 20 minutes on a bank, then jogged back to the cottage to get help. He did not see any lights on at any of the houses along the route.

Arriving back at Lawrence Cottage at precisely 12:15 a.m., Kennedy stood behind the rented white Valiant, the only other car available to the party that night, and asked Ray LaRosa, who was standing by the door to the cottage, to find his cousin Joe Gargan. He then sat down in the back seat of the Valiant until Gargan arrived. When Gargan had joined him he asked that he find Paul Markham. When Kennedy, Gargan, and Markham were all together in the Valiant, Kennedy told them that there had been a terrible accident and "we have to go."

In *The Inspector's Opinion*, Malcolm Reybold calls this exchange of messages between Kennedy, LaRosa, Gargan, and Markham, allegedly at 12:15 a.m., the *relay*. In the context of Carol Jones's eyewitness account, the *relay* is essential to an understanding of what actually must have occurred that night and will be discussed in more detail later in the book.

---

[1] Later, in a memoir published shortly before his death, Kennedy said that he and Kopechne decided to leave the party because they were both becoming emotional over the death of his brother Robert.

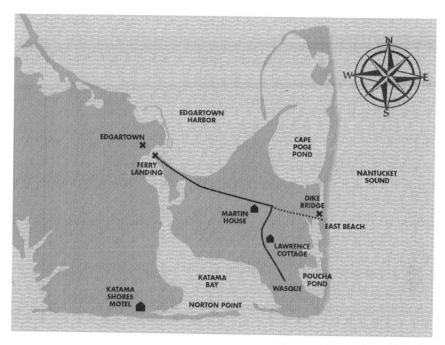

Chappaquiddick Island to the right, separated from the island of Martha's Vineyard (left) by the Edgartown Channel.

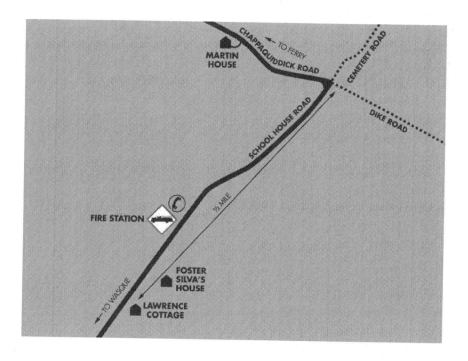

Kennedy, Markham, and Gargan then rushed to the bridge in the Valiant, arriving there at exactly 12:20 a.m. Kennedy rested on a bank while Markham and Gargan dove repeatedly in attempts to rescue Mary Jo or recover the body. They were ultimately unsuccessful, not even able to determine whether her body was still there. Neither Markham nor Gargan saw any lights at any of the nearby cottages, either.

All three then drove down to the Chappaquiddick ferry landing in the Valiant, with Markham and Gargan repeatedly advising Kennedy that he must report the incident immediately to the police. They arrived at the ferry landing about 1:40 a.m.

The group continued talking at the landing for a few minutes, but suddenly Kennedy dove impulsively into the water and swam back to the Edgartown side. Markham and Gargan were caught unawares but were unconcerned. The strong northerly set swept Kennedy more than a quarter of a mile to the beach at the Edgartown lighthouse where he finally managed to stumble out, grateful to be alive. Kennedy said he almost drowned a second time getting across. Kennedy then walked to his room at the Shiretown Inn in Edgartown, arriving there sometime before 2:00 a.m.

Disregarding the counsel of Markham and Gargan, Kennedy did not report the accident due to his "confused state" and because he "willed that Mary Jo still lived." Gargan and Markham, who returned to Lawrence Cottage around 2:00 a.m., did not report the accident either because they were under the impression that Kennedy would do this himself, and because Kennedy had asked them not to say anything to the others. Kennedy said this was because he was afraid the news might prompt the other Boiler Room Girls to attempt a needless and dangerous rescue.

At around 2:30 a.m., not being sure "whether it was morning or afternoon or night time," Kennedy showered and dressed, then went downstairs, complained about some noise, and asked for the time from "the room clerk." It was afterwards established that Kennedy spoke to the co-owner of the Shiretown Inn, Russell Peachey, and that the time was precisely 2:25 a.m.

At 7:00 a.m., Robert Samuel, a 22-year-old physical science teacher from New York, and Joseph Cappavella, his 15-year-old student, took the ferry over to Chappaquiddick for some fishing at East Beach. Walking back from the beach to the Dike to try their luck there, they discovered a car lying upside down in Dike Channel. Mrs. Malm, the woman renting Dyke House at the time, was notified of the accident and her call to the police station was logged at 8:20 a.m.; Chief of Police Arena arrived at the bridge by about 8:30 a.m.; and Tony Silva, Tony Bettencourt, Laurence Mercier, Robert Brougier, and John Farrar were on the scene at 8:45 a.m.[1]

---

[1] *The Bridge at Chappaquiddick*, pp. 110-113; *Senatorial Privilege*, pp. 4-6; exhumation testimony.

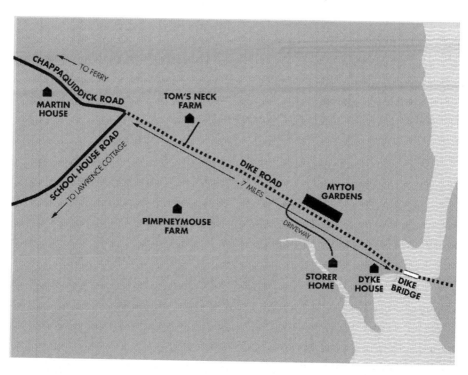

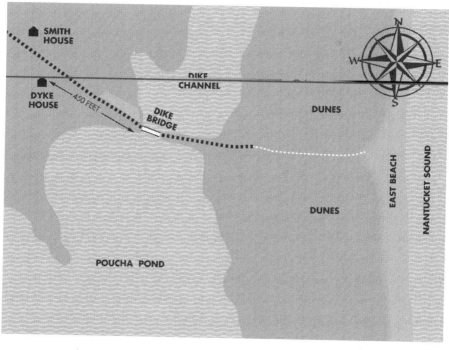

Meanwhile, Kennedy made a call from the public phone booth at the Shiretown Inn to his brother-in-law Stephen Smith soon after 8:00 a.m. Shortly after that, Kennedy met fellow racers Mr. Richards, Mrs. Richards, and Mr. Moore "very briefly," then Mr. Gargan, Mr. Markham, and Mr. Tretter at around 8:30 a.m. "just a few minutes after he met Mr. Moore probably."

Kennedy then took the ferry to Chappaquiddick to make a private call to a "dear friend Mr. Burke Marshall" because he felt that once he went to the police station he would "be involved in a myriad of details and I wanted to talk to this friend before I undertook that responsibility." Kennedy testified that these were the only two telephone calls he ever made.

Sometime before 10:00 a.m., after he "fully realized what happened," Kennedy "immediately" contacted the police. There, at the police station in Edgartown, Kennedy and Markham sat down to compose a short statement of less than 250 words affirming some of the above. Chief Arena left them in his office hard at work on their story, went back to the bridge to call off the search for more bodies and oversee the recovery of the Oldsmobile, and when he finally returned about an hour later the two still had not finished it.[1]

---

[1] *Senatorial Privilege*, pp. 19-23

2
Those Damn Witnesses...

Senator Kennedy's story, however, is belied by a number of witnesses who spoke up in the immediate aftermath. As many were intimidated later with harassment, and in some cases death threats, they might have wished they had not.

The Malms

ℳ rs. Malm, the woman renting Dyke House on the night of the incident 450 feet from Dike Bridge, told Chief Arena that she heard a car driving unusually fast over the road past her house in the direction of the bridge but had no idea of the time. Sylvia, Mrs. Malm's 21-year-old daughter who was reading by a window overlooking the bridge, later told Arena that she heard a car moving fast past their house in the direction of Dike Bridge. The daughter put the time as between 11:15 and 11:45 p.m. Mrs. Malm and her daughter both said they went to bed by midnight and heard nothing thereafter. Mrs. Malm said there was a light burning all night at the cottage.

Interviewed by the British Broadcasting Corporation (BBC) for their 1994 documentary *Chappaquiddick*, Sylvia, the daughter, said she was reading at the open window overlooking the bridge for about an hour and a half before she went to sleep at midnight. The car that drove past her house did not appear to have any problems, and "if there had been an accident with that car, or if the accident had actually occurred when I was awake, I am sure I would have heard it because my window overlooked the bridge, and at that time of night it was very quiet."

Mrs. Malm purchased the cottage in 1973 and died in 1996. In an interview with the author in 2014, Sylvia revealed that her mother had actually heard two other cars at the bridge that night after midnight. Jerry Jeffers, long time Chappaquiddick resident and owner of the Chappy Store, also said that Mrs. Malm told him she had heard two cars at the bridge after midnight.

Chris "Huck" Look

Huck Look, Edgartown Deputy Sheriff and a lifetime Vineyard resident, was a special police officer on a private detail duty at the Edgartown Yacht Club Regatta dance from 8:00 p.m. to 12:30 a.m. on the night and early morning of July 18 and 19. At the conclusion of the event, which was unusually peaceful, Look left the club at 12:25 a.m. and was dropped off on the Chappaquiddick side of the channel by the

Yacht Club launch at 12:30 a.m. to return to his wife at their rented cottage near Wasque. Entering his station wagon, which was parked at the landing, Look then proceeded toward home. Between 12:40 and 12:45 a.m. he arrived at the right-angle intersection to School House Road. Observing a car coming toward him, Look slowed down to a crawl because he knew cars tended to hug the left side of the road when coming around the curve and wanted to make sure they had enough space to pass.

Instead, the other vehicle slowed, continued straight into a narrow dirt lane called Cemetery Road, and stopped. Passing through his headlights, Look observed that the car was a dark sedan driven by a man with a woman in the front seat next to him, and something sticking up in the back seat – "a person, clothing, sweater, or pocketbook casting a shadow of some kind."

As the car began backing out of Cemetery Road, Look came to a stop on School House Road about 50 to 60 feet beyond the intersection. Thinking that the persons might need directions, Look got out and approached the vehicle. He was about 25 to 30 feet away when the car turned and drove off toward Dike Bridge at a moderate speed.

Look observed that the Massachusetts license plate on the sedan began with a letter L, then a 7, and ended with a 7. He distinctly remembered the plate number because seven was his lucky number and because, as he testified at the exhumation hearing, he did his usual "photostatic thing in his mind" as he had trained himself to do when observing license plates as a routine aspect to his job. Look thought the people might have observed his police uniform, badge, and whistle when the car's backup lights lit up the area as he was walking toward the car.

Look thought about going after the car but then reconsidered. They hadn't done anything illegal. So Look resumed his drive toward home but almost immediately met a man and two women doing a "conga dance" on the road. One woman was tall and the other short, and the man was short with curly hair. Stopping his car, Look asked if they needed a lift at that late hour. The tall woman said, "Shove off, Buddy, we aren't pick-ups." The man, however, assured Look that they were renting the cottage down the road and were OK. Look said he mentioned the "lost car" to his wife when he got home at precisely two minutes before one o'clock.[1]

The next morning, informed that a car had been found in the water of Poucha Pond, Look arrived at Dike Bridge at 9:00 a.m. As a black Oldsmobile sedan was pulled from the water with Massachusetts license number L78-207, Look told Officer Brougier, "Holy Jesus. I saw that car last night. It had a man and a woman in the front seat and another person or some kind of object sticking up in the back." Questioned immediately by Chief Arena about how sure he was, Look replied, "I'm positive. That's how sure I am."[2] At the exhumation hearing, Look said, "As soon as they

---

[1] *The Ted Kennedy Episode*, p. 16; *Senatorial Privilege*, p. 103
[2] *The Bridge at Chappaquiddick*, pp. 149-150

started to pull [the Oldsmobile] out and it became visible I went over and told Officer Brougier, 'Gee, that is the same car I saw last night.' "

Only 8 of 50 plates in Massachusetts beginning with L7 were later determined to have been issued to Oldsmobile-type vehicles in 1969. None of those vehicles were on the island of Chappaquiddick on the morning of July 19, except for Kennedy's Oldsmobile.[1]

At the inquest, Kennedy was asked if he ever returned to Dike Bridge after the accident shortly after 11:15 p.m.

Q: How many times did you go back to Dike Bridge that night?
Kennedy: Well, that was the only –
Q: After the accident, that was the only occasion?
Kennedy: The only time, the only occasion.

In their edition of August 1974, *McCall's* implored Kennedy to admit that he left the party after Look's sighting of the Oldsmobile (italics as they appeared in the article): "Whether or not he seeks the Presidency in 1976, a public and press that have always doubted the 'wrong turn' would welcome his candor if, even at this late date, he affirms that, yes, it *was* after midnight and he and Mary Jo *were* headed to the beach; that their going there was entirely innocent, but that the *appearance* of immorality was so inevitable that, in his grief and remorse about the accident itself, he despaired of answering that question straightforwardly at the time with any chance of being believed. If that were to happen, then perhaps the subject of Chappaquiddick could finally be closed."

Nevertheless, at the inquest and thereafter, Kennedy, Gargan, and Markham steadfastly maintained that Look was either mistaken or lying about observing the Oldsmobile in the early morning of July 19. In a November 6, 1974, letter to *Time* magazine, Kennedy wrote, "A 'most exhaustive investigation' of Sheriff Look's testimony is not required to reveal his fundamental contradictions and inaccuracies." Gargan told Damore in 1983, "How that incredible coincidence could have taken place with what Look says about the number plate and the color and style of the car, I don't know. I simply thought Look was wrong."[2]

On the other hand, Look told the *National Enquirer* on February 25, 1995, "I know what I saw that night. And I know I wasn't wrong. One of us lied – Ted Kennedy or me. I told the truth then, and I'm telling the truth now. There is no way I'll ever change my claim. It comes down to a matter of credibility. You either believe Kennedy, or you believe me."

---

[1] *Senatorial Privilege*, p. 380
[2] *Senatorial Privilege*, p. 226

Nancy McDonald

On December 18, private investigator J. E. Gautreau filed a report of an eyewitness, Nancy McDonald of Burlington, Vermont, a college student who worked as a waitress at the Harborside Inn in Edgartown. She and the assistant manager had walked to the Edgartown lighthouse beach around 12:30 a.m. on Saturday, July 19. They were seated on the dock when their attention was drawn to an American-style car traveling at a high rate of speed on the road leading to the ferry slip on Chappaquiddick, 350 yards away across the harbor. The car stopped at the landing and the lights were turned off, only 10 to 15 minutes before Huck Look saw Kennedy's car head down the road to Dike Bridge. They thought this strange, as they knew the ferry was no longer running at that hour.[1]

Todd Ballou

Damore says that *Sumatra,* Todd Ballou's Concordia yawl, was moored in the outer harbor close by the ferry channel for the regatta. A little before 2:00 on the morning of July 19, Ballou overheard a hushed conversation from "the forms of three persons" passing by in a boat that doused its lights and outboard motor. Then, a larger boat with a powerful engine left Edgartown, crossed the channel to a beach not far from the Chappaquiddick landing, and also shut off lights and motor. Ballou related, "At this point the small boat was drifting, pointed toward the beach and the larger boat. It seemed to be waiting, like somebody casing the area to see all was quiet." Five minutes later the small boat's motor started up again, lights were turned on, and it moved out of the harbor into the ferry channel.[2] However, Zad Rust, who also interviewed Ballou, said that the small motorboat, which was about 15 feet in length, approached a moored *sailboat* and then cut its lights and motor.[3]

Hastings relates that another witness had heard the sound of an outboard engine sometime after 1:30 a.m. but couldn't tell whether it came from the vicinity of the Edgartown Yacht Club "near where the ferry crosses" or from somewhere in the outer harbor "toward Cape Poge."[4]

The Manchester *Union Leader*'s investigative reporter Arthur E. Egan Jr. said that a powerboat was reported stolen that night. It was recovered at a dock less than 200 yards from the Shiretown Inn.[5]

Coincidentally, my father owned Concordia Boat Yard in 1969, the builder of Ballou's Concordia yawl. The yard is located in the small village of Padanaram, a part

[1] *Senatorial Privilege*, p. 341
[2] *Senatorial Privilege*, p. 263
[3] *Teddy Bare*, p. 83; p. 89
[4] *The Ted Kennedy Episode*, p. 54
[5] *The FBI Files, Mary Jo Kopechne (Chappaquiddick)*, Part 2, p. 76

of Dartmouth, Massachusetts, on Buzzards Bay, separated from the Cape and Hyannis Port by the Cape Cod Canal. *Sumatra* was stored and maintained at Concordia each winter, and my stepmother and her first husband, Breck Marshall, were very good friends of Todd and his wife, Pussy.

Long-term residents on the Vineyard were never fond of Kennedy after the events of that summer and this was especially so on Chappaquiddick. The island had been "discovered" and was never the same again. Hordes of tourists who were never interested in visiting Chappaquiddick before now descended daily in their rented bicycles to visit the scene of the crime and carry away pieces of the bridge as souvenirs. Busloads of gawking tourists were driven to "Kennedy Bridge" several times a day. The wait at the ferry line sometimes took an hour or more, even after a second three-car ferry was added. My father was disgusted and soon after gave his house on Chappaquiddick to my sister and me, rarely visiting the island again.

However, what was worse was that in the days immediately following the incident several Chappaquiddick residents were intimidated by Kennedy aides who threatened them with thinly veiled hints of tax audits if they spoke up with anything they might have seen that night. One of those residents was a cousin, and another a friend of my father.

Several years after 1969, one of Ted Kennedy's yachts sailed into Padanaram and the skipper asked if Concordia could do some routine repairs. My father bluntly told him his business was not welcome and that Kennedy's boat would have to get the hell off his dock, *"Now!"* The flabbergasted captain left with a red face, and my father noted with some satisfaction that he never saw that boat in Padanaram Harbor again.

Lansing Burns

Interviewed by Tony Ulasewicz, Lansing Burns, an employee of the Chappaquiddick Beach Club, said he heard suspicious noise near the club phones around 1:30 a.m. on the morning of July 19. After hearing activity twice, he went out to look but couldn't find anyone.[1] The Chappaquiddick Beach Club is located in the Edgartown outer harbor, about a quarter of a mile from the ferry landing, and has two long docks suitable for landing small boats.

Roddy Hoar

The Tedrows write that a boy on Chappaquiddick reported that his boat had been used the night of the incident and was tied back up in another place.[2]

---

[1] *The President's Private Eye*, p. 205
[2] *Death at Chappaquiddick*, p. 53

That boy was Roddy Hoar, a good friend of Carol's brother Peter. Ann Floyd, Roddy's sister, told me Roddy's rowboat had been used during that night and their mother reported it to the police after they heard Kennedy's claim that he swam the Edgartown Channel on the TV broadcast of July 25. Roddy said he found it tied with a landlubber's knot rather than the bowline he was accustomed to using and pulled up several yards away from where he had last left it. Although Roddy's rowboat could not have been the powerboat seen by Ballou, it might have been used to find it. Powerboats are tied up everywhere along the Edgartown waterfront and in 1969 they were rarely locked or chained.

Gargan told Damore, "There were no rowboats... I wish the hell there had been."[1] However, it was common knowledge to all teenagers living on Chappaquiddick that rowboats were always tied up and left unlocked near the ferry landing on both sides of the channel in the '60s. Ferry service stopped at midnight, and teenagers used these boats to cross back to Chappaquiddick after visiting the night spots in Oak Bluffs which stayed open to 1:00 a.m. No one seemed to mind, and the owners of the boats appeared resigned to it. In those days, nothing was locked, including houses. If you locked something up you were highly criticized for it.

As a young teenager in the '60s I used these boats all the time. All my cousins did too, including Carol's brothers. We were always very careful to leave any boats we borrowed carefully tied and neat and pulled up above the tide line. These rowboats were pulled up on the sand by their owners to the left and right of the ferry landing on the Chappaquiddick side, and pulled up on the small beach between the present Martha's Vineyard Shipyard store and the Seafood Shanty Restaurant on the Edgartown side just to the south of Memorial Wharf. As late as 2000, I must confess I used one of these boats to get back to Chappaquiddick with my nephew after a late night in Edgartown.[2]

I eventually owned my own rowboat and kept this tied to a post on the north side of the ferry landing on the Chappaquiddick side. Many mornings I found it tied up carefully on the Edgartown side. It didn't make much difference if there were oars in it – there were always oars to be found lying around somewhere or propped up against houses or porches. Oars were like cheap pens or reading glasses: always missing so you kept several pairs handy just in case. I always just smiled and rowed my boat back to Chappaquiddick. I enjoyed the exercise and the beautiful view of the boats in the harbor. And anyhow, why would I complain? That was how things worked in those days.

---

[1] *Senatorial Privilege*, p. 262
[2] When next I saw the boat it was attached to the dock with a shiny new padlock and chain, which I took to mean that perceptions were not the same in 2000 as they had been several decades earlier.

Unidentified Boiler Room Girl

In the first week following the incident, many of the Boiler Room Girls talked freely about the events of July 18 and 19. After the girls, as a group, refused to discuss the incident at all, many of the reporters got together to discuss what they had discovered. In comparing notes, a reporter related that one of the girls had told him that Kennedy returned to the cottage with the story that his car had run off the road and Mary Jo was sitting in it.[1]

The story was published by Hal Bruno in a September 1969 issue of *Newsweek*. "A guest at the party told friends that Kennedy had four or five drinks before leaving the cottage and that he was so stunned and incoherent when he returned that Gargan and Markham first believed that his car had merely run off the road somewhere and that Mary Jo was simply sitting in it."

This conflicts with the senator's story that he never entered the cottage after leaving with Mary Jo at 11:15 p.m. At the inquest he was asked, "Excuse me a moment. Did you go inside the cottage?" Kennedy replied, "No, I didn't."

Q: Was Mr. LaRosa aware of the accident?
Kennedy: No, he hadn't heard.
Q: No one else at the cottage was told of the accident?
Kennedy: No.

Why wasn't this girl named by the reporter? Perhaps because the information was given with the proviso that it was off the record. An investigative reporter cannot make a living without confidential sources, and if it ever becomes known that the identity of a confidential source has been revealed without permission, the reporter will never again be effective.

Unidentified Chappaquiddick witness

In the immediate aftermath of the incident, a Chappaquiddick witness was found who claimed to have been "near the cottage where the party was held." At about midnight on July 18, the witness had seen a car "pull away from the house," then park on the side of School House Road about 500 feet away. About 20 minutes later, the vehicle started up and proceeded toward the ferry. The witness said the vehicle then paused briefly at the Dike Road intersection before driving toward the Dike.[2]

---

[1] *The Bridge at Chappaquiddick*, p. 222
[2] *The Ted Kennedy Episode*, p. 3; pp. 53-54

Foster Silva

At the inquest, Kennedy and the Boiler Room Girls described the party at Lawrence Cottage as a dull affair with little drinking.

However, Foster Silva, the caretaker of Lawrence Cottage who lived next door about 100 yards away, said that at 10:00 p.m. the singing and laughing from the house was "damn loud." He tried to go to bed at midnight but couldn't sleep with all the noise. At 1:00 a.m. he was "pretty well damn fed up with the whole thing. It was a damn farce at that hour of the morning. If they had kept it up any longer I would have called the police." Dodie, Foster's wife, remarked to her husband, "Boy, they must be having a heck of a time. I hope they don't wreck the place." Their son John said, "There was yelling, music, and general sounds of hell raising." The Silvas said the party died down at around 1:30 a.m., but there was still a lot of talking going on at 2:30 a.m.[1]

Ross and Marilyn Richards, and Stan Moore

Although Kennedy testified he was up at around 8:00 on the morning of July 19, it was determined that he had borrowed a dime from the Shiretown receptionist and had made a call at the Shiretown public phone booth at 7:19 a.m. Although Kennedy testified that he met Ross Richards and Stan Moore only a few minutes before he met Gargan, Markham, and Tretter at 8:30 a.m., these men actually encountered a cheerful and chipper Ted Kennedy in the alley that separated the Shiretown Inn from the Colonial Inn at 7:30 a.m. Both said Kennedy was freshly shaven, dressed in clean yachting clothes for that afternoon's race, and appeared "normal in every way." Richards and Moore, joined 20 minutes later by Ross's wife, Marilyn, spent a half hour discussing boats, the weather, and other innocuous subjects. They all agreed to have breakfast together later in the morning. William Parker, co-owner of the Shiretown Inn, quoted Kennedy as saying, "Oh, what a lovely morning. How nice it is to be on this island. The boys here sure made a lot of changes."[2]

All testified that at no time did anyone see anything suspicious or alarming in Kennedy's behavior, until Gargan and Markham arrived at 8:00 a.m. Ross Richards told Detective-lieutenant John Dunn that Kennedy never mentioned Chappaquiddick at all.[3] At the inquest, Richards repeated, "There wasn't a word mentioned of Chappaquiddick."

---

[1] *Senatorial Privilege*, p. 105; *Death at Chappaquiddick*, p. 19; *The Last Kennedy*, pp. 199-200
[2] *The Ted Kennedy Episode*, p. 28
[3] *Senatorial Privilege*, p. 255

Edgartown Police Chief Dominick James Arena

Chief Arena's first impressions when meeting Kennedy, freshly shaven, clean, and with no visible signs of bumps, bruises, or scrapes after the accident: "I was far from being an expert, but I did have a certain training beyond that of the average lay person in the matter of accidents. The driver of the car would have to have taken a really hard blow to the head – the windshield on the driver's side was badly smashed in." Arena found it difficult to reconcile Ted Kennedy's appearance at the police station with that of the driver of a car in such an accident. "I found it hard to believe the senator had been in a major automobile accident. His face bore no traces of any marks. He never sat down or appeared in any kind of physical discomfort. If he had been injured, in shock, or confused, nothing of it lingered in our meeting, to my observation."[1] Edgartown Detective Dunn told Arena that Ross Richards had observed "no discomfort at all" while talking to Kennedy at the Shiretown Inn between 7:30 and 8:00 a.m.

Wilfred Rock

Interviewed by BBC investigators for their 1994 documentary *Chappaquiddick*, pilot Wilfred Rock said he received a call around 8:45 on the morning of July 19 from Dun Gifford, a Kennedy aide, to fly him from Nantucket to Edgartown. Gifford told Rock that Kennedy had been in an accident but was uninjured. Rock was asked to divert from his normal flight path and make a low pass over Dike Bridge. Rock said he flew over Dike Bridge at around 9:00 a.m., about a half hour after Chief Arena had arrived on the scene.[2] He remembered looking down and clearly seeing the submerged Oldsmobile silhouetted in the channel.

Rock said he was later asked to be interviewed by the *New York Times*. He said Gifford called him to see if he would mind meeting Kennedy's lawyers first. Rock agreed. He said Kennedy's lawyers wanted him to change his recollection to something he may have seen on a later flight. However, Rock said he could not be mistaken about when he received the call from Gifford or when he observed the Oldsmobile. His next flight was to Hyannis Port at 1:00 p.m., and that route took him nowhere near Chappaquiddick.

Dun Gifford, Rock's passenger and the man charged by the Kennedy team to fly the body of Mary Jo off the island at the earliest opportunity, was also interviewed by

---

[1] *Senatorial Privilege*, pp. 21-23
[2] The BBC said Rock flew over Dike Bridge "just after 9:00 a.m. at the latest, only moments *before* the salvage team arrived on the scene." This would be incorrect if Rock received his call at 8:45 a.m., as he stated. Chief Arena had arrived at the bridge by about 8:30 a.m. and Tony Silva, Tony Bettencourt, Laurence Mercier, Robert Brougier, and John Farrar were on the scene at 8:45 a.m.

the BBC. When told about Rock's recollection, Gifford appeared nonplussed, and very uncomfortable. He paused a long time, covered his mouth with his hands, then admitted sheepishly that he could not dispute his pilot's timeline. Asked again, he said he could not dispute it.

Prior to Gifford's admission, the assumption had been made that Kennedy's team called Gifford after Kennedy had reported the accident to the police. Both Damore and Hersh said that David Burke reached Dun Gifford at his vacation house on Nantucket Island at 10:30 a.m. and that Gifford landed at the Martha's Vineyard airport at 11:00 a.m.[1] Dun Gifford himself testified at the exhumation hearing that he heard of the death of Mary Jo "in the middle of the morning" on July 19, and when he landed on Martha's Vineyard he "engaged a taxi and had it take me to the funeral home." When asked whether the body of Mary Jo was there before he arrived, Gifford told the court, "Yes, it was." However, Rock's testimony means that Kennedy had made arrangements to fly Mary Jo's body off the island *before* he had crossed on the ferry from Edgartown to the Chappaquiddick side; *before* he was advised by Tony Bettencourt that his car was in the channel; *before* Kennedy observed the hearse driving to Dike Bridge; and *before* he had reported the accident to the Edgartown police. It also means that Gifford had arrived on the Vineyard at least a half hour *before* the body of Mary Jo Kopechne had arrived at the funeral home.

Nevertheless, at around 9:30 a.m., when Steve Ewing, the teenage ferry deckhand, took it upon himself to ask Kennedy and the others once more whether they were aware of the accident and the death of a young woman in Kennedy's car, the response was, "Yes, we just heard about it."

---

[1] *Senatorial Privilege*, p. 50; *Edward Kennedy*, p. 372

3
Other Oddities

Mary Jo Kopechne's purse and key

lthough Kennedy said that he and Mary Jo left to go back to Edgartown on an evening ferry, Mary Jo left her purse, including her driver's license and the key to her hotel room, at Lawrence Cottage. Mary Jo's parents, who remained convinced Kennedy was not to blame for their daughter's death, told *McCall's* in their edition of August 1974, "We don't understand why, if Mary Jo was going back to the motel, she left her pocketbook under the table in the cottage. That upset us terribly. We don't know the answer. It would not be like Mary Jo to forget her purse."

Injuries to Mary Jo

Kennedy was observed to have no injuries at all after the accident, but equally strange, the body of Mary Jo had no obvious injuries, either. The examination of Mary Jo's body at the scene by Dr. Mills was brief and superficial, but Mills took care to look for evidence of fractures and could not find any. Frieh, the undertaker, took more time examining the body and was surprised to find no fractures, marks, or bruises. The only injury he could find was a slight abrasion on a left-hand knuckle. The body of Mary Jo was prepared for burial at the Kielty-Moran Funeral Home in Plymouth, Pennsylvania. John Kielty, the funeral director, testified at the exhumation hearing that they found "no marks" on her body. Dun Gifford, the Kennedy aide who flew the body of Mary Jo to Pennsylvania, also testified at the exhumation hearing that he saw "no visible marks on the body of any sort" when John Kielty was preparing Mary Jo for viewing.

Farrar, the fire and rescue SCUBA diver, saw no marks or bruises on the body, but he did tell me in 2013 that he observed broken and torn fingernails with clear striations of blood at the fingertips. Farrar believes the broken fingernails were the result of Mary Jo clawing the carpet in the footwell of the Oldsmobile as she tried to find a way out.

It is necessary to point out that I have been unable to find a report of broken fingernails in any book, or in any newspaper or magazine article published from 1969 to today. Nor is it found in Farrar's own exhumation testimony, his inquest testimony, or in his radio interview in 1994. Farrar told me in 2013 that he had mentioned broken fingernails in numerous interviews, but he could not remember any specific book, newspaper, or magazine article that he could point me to.

According to Olsen, Dr. Mills had examined the nails with particular care at the scene and noticed that there was some slight foreign matter under them, but "the nails themselves were unbroken and nicely manicured."[1] David Guay, assistant undertaker who was tasked by Frieh to embalm the body before it left the Vineyard, was interviewed by the BBC in 1994. Guay said that they could find "no injuries, not even broken teeth or broken fingernails."

Blood evidence

State Police Detective Killen submitted the clothing that Mary Jo had worn at the time of her death to the state police chemistry lab in Boston. Testimony at the court hearing to rule on whether the body of Mary Jo would be exhumed for a belated autopsy indicated that ultraviolet light and a Benzidine test, performed first by Dr. Melvin Topjian, chemist, and then by Dr. John McHugh, had established blood "all over" the back of Mary Jo Kopechne's blouse and on the back of both sleeves. Unusually strong Benzidine reactions were also obtained on the outside rear collar area of the shirt.

When the Oldsmobile was finally examined several months after the incident, Dr. McHugh also discovered blood on the back seat.

Autopsy

Before 8:45 a.m. on July 19, Kennedy, or one of his friends, had called Dun Gifford, a Kennedy aide, to have the body of Mary Jo removed from the island even before he had talked to the police chief or Mary Jo's parents.

The body of Mary Jo was removed by the Kennedy team from the island of Martha's Vineyard to Wilkes-Barre, Pennsylvania, within 27 hours of the body being discovered. The Kennedys would have removed the body much sooner than this except for bad weather which kept the plane from flying. By the time Massachusetts District Attorney Edmund Dinis was considering ordering an autopsy on Sunday morning, State Police Lieutenant Killen told Dinis that the body had already left the Vineyard.[2]

Dinis petitioned the court of Luzerne County, Pennsylvania, to have the body of Mary Jo exhumed for an autopsy in August. Kennedy, who had no legal basis for opposing the autopsy, sent Cardinal Cushing, a longtime intimate friend who had appeared with him in a picture used as a publicity prop in his senatorial campaign of 1962, to make the case for him. Cushing told the Kopechnes it was their Christian duty

---

[1] *The Bridge at Chappaquiddick*, p. 144
[2] Dinis testified at the exhumation hearing that he requested the autopsy at 10:00 a.m. on Sunday from Lieutenant Killen of the state police but was told that that the body had already left the island. In fact, the body was still there due to bad weather that prevented flying.

to do all they could in their power to oppose the desecration of their daughter's body.[1] Gwen Kopechne told *McCall's* in September 1970 that at first they had welcomed the autopsy, but now they did not. Joseph Kopechne told the *Boston Herald Traveler* on August 7, "We'll do everything and anything we have to do in order to prevent an autopsy. They are not going to disturb our daughter." Dinis's request was vigorously opposed by the Kopechnes' lawyer, even though it was reasonably argued by Dinis that an autopsy could refute many of the unfavorable rumors and questions swirling around Kennedy at the time.

There were a number of reasons an autopsy should have been welcomed by Kennedy. It could have found that death did not occur by poisoning, strangulation, or manual suffocation, or indeed by any other form of homicide as many suspected. It would have lain to rest any suspicion of pregnancy. It could have found that Mary Jo did indeed succumb from drowning rather than by breathing her own carbon dioxide as Farrar, the SCUBA diver who recovered the body, has always maintained. It might have determined that the blood found on the back of her shirt and on the back seat of the Oldsmobile did not come from any wound to her head.

That is, the Kennedy team should have welcomed the result of an autopsy *if they had nothing to hide* and *if their stories were true*. But they did not welcome it. Their efforts prevailed, and the request for exhumation was denied.

Participation of Gargan and Markham

Gargan and Markham were never identified as participants until Kennedy's speech to the nation on TV, a week after the accident and well after the event had turned into a media frenzy. Before that speech, no one had any idea that Markham and Gargan had ever been near Dike Bridge that night. They were never named in Kennedy's original statement to Chief Arena on July 19. They were never mentioned at the hearing in Edgartown when Kennedy pled guilty to leaving the scene of an accident and received a suspended sentence and a year's probation. They were never named as participants by any of the other guests at the cookout. Damore describes the "wave of editorial revulsion and reproach" that swept across the nation after Kennedy "acknowledged belatedly" the role of Gargan and Markham at Dike Bridge. "How defensible was the inaction of two men, in full possession of the facts, not in any state of shock, trained in the law and politically astute?"[2] Sherrill writes that their late introduction into the senator's version of events endowed his story with "an element of creepiness."[3]

---

[1] *Death at Chappaquiddick*, pp. 89-90
[2] *Senatorial Privilege*, p. 218
[3] *The Last Kennedy*, p. 118

Many have wondered, why would Kennedy's lawyers have involved these two men at that late date? More important, why would Gargan and Markham consent to it?

Boiler Room Girls

By the early morning of July 19, Gargan had swept Lawrence Cottage completely clean with the help of Ray LaRosa and Mary Ellen Lyons, one of the Boiler Room Girls. All liquor bottles had disappeared, glasses were washed, beds were made, not a speck of dust could be found, and the five girls had been sequestered in their rooms at the Katama Shores Motel. Tretter was deputized by Gargan to get the girls off the island as soon as he could. By late afternoon, the Boiler Room Girls were on a ferry to Woods Hole and off the Vineyard. Not one had ever been questioned by police.

Chief of Police Arena was not even made aware of exactly who was at party until four days after the accident, long after everyone had left the island and could not be questioned. After a week, the girls refused to talk to reporters, even when offered as much as $50,000 by several magazines to open up.[1]

At the inquest the Boiler Room Girls were sequestered together and monitored by the Kennedys at all times. None were allowed to talk to anyone outside the courthouse, and each has kept a tight lip about the incident to this day.

Except for Rosemary Keough, that is. Amid much fanfare, the BBC announced that Rosemary Keough would finally speak out after 25 years of silence. In their documentary *Chappaquiddick* released in 1994, this was the sum total of Keough's thoughts and insights in that film:

1) 1969 was a time of people standing up and taking a stand, a time of political conviction. Today that sounds trite because politics are much more cynical.

2) It is a myth that a bunch of single girls were being served up to married men. It just didn't happen.

3) No one asked me to come into the police station to ask questions. I think people were informed we were there. I think people were informed we were leaving.

4) Not one of us ever wanted to hurt Mary Jo or sully her reputation.

5) Senator Kennedy is the only one who really knows what happened.

6) As far as intentions, I believe whatever happened, happened in an instant.

7) The relationship we all had with Ted Kennedy was based upon mutual loyalty and mutual affection. Period.

8) People have portrayed Mary Jo as a saint. She was not a saint. She was a red-blooded, normal girl.

---

[1] As reported by the New York monthly *Spy* in their edition of November 1987, among many other news reports; *Death at Chappaquiddick*, p. 193, Kennedy's letter of November 6, 1974, to *Time* magazine, etc.

No BBC commentator was observed asking Keough a direct question. Keough never addressed the numerous inconsistencies in her inquest testimony or explained what she and Charles Tretter had been doing, where they had been, or what they might have seen as they were walking between Lawrence Cottage and the Dike Road intersection for two and one-half hours the night Kennedy drove off Dike Bridge.

Phone calls

Although Kennedy testified that he did not report the accident due to his "confused state," the Manchester *Union Leader* reported on August 13, 1969, that 17 calls were made on Kennedy's credit card on July 18 and 19; 5 from Lawrence Cottage on Chappaquiddick and 12 from the Shiretown Inn in Edgartown. Ulasewicz and Damore said that investigative reporter Arthur Egan of the *Union Leader* had obtained the information from a close friend, lawyer/realtor James Gilmartin of 147 East 230 St. in the Bronx, New York, who learned of the record from an accountant at the telephone company.[1] New England Telephone Company officials said they could not confirm or deny the story due to legal constraints. Interestingly, Edward Hanify, one of Kennedy's lawyers, was Director of the New England Telephone Company in 1969.

The 17 calls were confirmed by the *New York Times* in their edition of March 12, 1980. The *Times* wrote, "Records of Senator Edward M. Kennedy's telephone calls in the hours after the accident at Chappaquiddick were withheld by the telephone company from an inquest into the death of Mary Jo Kopechne without the knowledge of the district attorney who asked for them." However, Egan said he talked to Chief Arena at police headquarters about the list of calls, long before the inquest. When Tony Ulasewicz asked Egan what Arena was going to do about it, Egan said, "Nothing. As far as [Arena's] concerned the case is closed." Ulasewicz then wondered how Arena was going to deal with the calls when the inquest was eventually held. "Phone records were going to be subpoenaed and Arena was going to look like a fool for not questioning everyone who attended the Kennedy party about the calls."[2] The complete list of calls had also been described and published in the *New York Graphic* a full three months before the inquest.

Kennedy aide Rick Burke later admitted that the 17 calls reported by the *Union Leader* and the *Times* were indeed made that night on Kennedy's credit card, "several" to Helga Wagner.[3] Helga Wagner, then a 24-year-old "soigné Central European beauty with a marvelous head of leonine streaked-blond hair and sparkling blue eyes," who had an on-again, off-again affair with Kennedy for decades, was interviewed by

---

[1] *The President's Private Eye*, p. 218; *Senatorial Privilege*, p. 272
[2] *The President's Private Eye*, p. 217
[3] *Edward Kennedy*, p. 391

Kennedy's biographer, Burton Hersh. Helga admitted to the calls, at least one made from the Shiretown Inn after Kennedy allegedly swam the Edgartown Channel, but told Hersh, "He did not tell me anything about the accident. I have no idea." Hersh says that the information Kennedy really wanted was the whereabouts of his brother-in-law Stephen Smith, but that Helga was unable to help.[1] But Damore, who also interviewed Wagner, was told, "He just said something *very serious* had happened and I need to have Stephen Smith's number. He knew I had it because I was on my way to Europe to join Stephen Smith and his wife, Jean."[2]

Ralph L. Clifford, Editor/Publisher of the *New York Graphic,* a small newspaper in New York City, detailed 12 of those 17 calls on October 6, 1969.[3] The first call was made from a number registered to Sydney Lawrence, owner of Lawrence Cottage, at 11:57 p.m. on July 18 and the last was made from the Shiretown Inn and ended at 9:12 a.m. on July 19. Clifford noted with interest that none of the calls were made to the police, fire rescue, Coast Guard, or indeed anyone in a position to help or determine the fate of Mary Jo.

One of the calls made on Kennedy's credit card from the Shiretown Inn, described by the *Graphic,* was a 27-minute call to (202) 393-3111, a number registered to Stephen Smith, Kennedy's brother-in-law. That call was logged at 5:54 a.m. If Kennedy called Helga Wagner to tell her that something "very serious" had happened and to get Stephen Smith's number, this is an important detail because many theories postulate that Kennedy was never aware that the Oldsmobile had been involved in an accident, or that Mary Jo had drowned, before being advised of that fact by Gargan and Markham when all three met up at the Shiretown Inn at 8:00 the next morning; or before being told by the ferry operator that a body had been found in his Oldsmobile after 9:15 a.m.

Kennedy testified at the inquest that he walked down to the Shiretown lobby and talked to the receptionist very shortly after 8:00 on the morning of July 19, then made one phone call to Stephen Smith at the public phone booth. However, Damore says that Kennedy made a call from the public phone booth at the Shiretown Inn just before his meeting with Ross Richards and Stan Moore at 7:30 a.m., a time confirmed by Mrs. Stewart, the Shiretown Inn receptionist who had loaned Kennedy a dime to contact the operator.[4] According to the *Graphic,* that call was logged at 7:19 a.m. to (202) 233-9600, the Washington D.C. headquarters of Marshall & Hamilton, the office of

---

[1] *Edward Kennedy*, pp. 365-366

[2] *Senatorial Privilege*, p. 88

[3] The times and duration of several of these calls, as well as the persons called, are inconsistently reported. See, for instance, *Death at Chappaquiddick*, p. 56 and *Senatorial Privilege: The Chappaquiddick Cover-up*, p. 272. I have copied the list of calls, as found here and elsewhere within this book, exactly as described by the *New York Graphic,* the only entity that has ever published the full list of calls.

[4] *Senatorial Privilege*, pp. 87-88

Kennedy's Washington attorney, Burke Marshall, former Assistant Attorney General of the United States. According to the *Graphic*, two other calls were made from the public phone booth at the Shiretown on Kennedy's credit card before Kennedy took the ferry over to Chappaquiddick: a 42-minute call to Theodore Sorensen at (212) 935-8790 beginning at 8:14 a.m.; and another to Stephen Smith at 9:01 a.m. lasting 11 minutes.

Nevertheless, Kennedy testified, under oath, that he made just two calls from the time he ran off the bridge to the moment he reported the accident to the police. In 1980, Kennedy finally confessed to calling Wagner, having consistently denied it for more than a decade.[1]

Familiarity with Chappaquiddick

Although Kennedy said that he was unfamiliar with the roads on Chappaquiddick and stated under oath at the inquest that he had never been to Chappaquiddick "before 1:30 on the day of July 18," the *Post Standard* of August 13, 1969, said that Pulitzer Prize winner Jack Anderson's sources had confided that Kennedy was very familiar with Dike Road and East Beach. The *Standard* wrote, "He and his late brother, President Kennedy, often used this particular beach to escape prying eyes." On January 20, 1980, the *New York Post* published statements given by five different individuals who had seen Ted Kennedy on Chappaquiddick "several times" and "at least half a dozen times." Dodie Silva, wife of Foster, the caretaker of Lawrence Cottage, said that her son once had lunch with Ted Kennedy at the Chappaquiddick Beach Club.[2] After interviewing Kennedy insiders, including close friends of Kennedy's wife, Joan, Hastings writes that it was common knowledge to the Kennedy family that East Beach was well known to Ted. "It was a standing joke among all the Kennedys that this secluded beach was a perfect place to take a pretty girl." Hastings was told that Ted's wife "fully realized his intended rendezvous as soon as she heard about the accident."[3]

At the inquest it was determined that on the day of the incident, Kennedy had driven over Chappaquiddick Road three times and Kopechne five times. Kennedy also admitted that he and the rest of his guests had crossed over the bridge to swim at East Beach on the morning of the incident, but Mrs. Malm, renter of Dyke House, told *Life* magazine she had seen the Oldsmobile driving back and forth past their cottage and over Dike Bridge multiple times that day at high speed.

---

[1] *Senatorial Privilege*, p. 358
[2] *The President's Private Eye*, p. 204
[3] *The Ted Kennedy Episode*, pp. 58-59

Mary Jo was set up to take the fall

According to an interview Gargan had with Damore, Kennedy had told him, just before he jumped into the Edgartown Channel that night, he was planning to say that Mary Jo, unbeknownst to himself, was driving the car when it went over the bridge. When Gargan met up with Kennedy at the Shiretown Inn at 8:00 on the morning of July 19, Gargan warned him, "There's no way you can say that! You can be placed at the scene!"[1]

Yet Kennedy claimed that he never saw Huck Look or anyone else at 12:40 a.m. Gargan has always steadfastly maintained that Kennedy drove off the bridge with Kopechne a few minutes after 11:15 p.m., and that Huck Look must have been mistaken or lying about seeing the Oldsmobile at 12:40 a.m.

So the question is, if Kennedy and Gargan sincerely believed that Huck Look had lied or been mistaken about seeing Kennedy's Oldsmobile, how could Kennedy be placed at the scene? Are we supposed to believe that Markham or Gargan would have ratted on Kennedy themselves?

Record of reckless driving

Kennedy was driving without a license on the night of July 18. Although a license was mysteriously found for Kennedy later, it has been determined that Kennedy's license had expired before the incident and had not been renewed.[2]

Although Kennedy's lawyer testified at the inquest that Kennedy's driving record was unblemished, Hastings, Damore, and the Tedrows detail Kennedy's driving record before the incident: March 1957, convicted of speeding. March 14, 1958, a vehicle belonging to Ted Kennedy ran a red light, sped off, and then cut its taillights to elude pursuit. The maneuver was successful. Incredibly, a week later the same vehicle ran a red light, sped off, then cut its tail lights to avoid pursuit. Deputy Sheriff Thomas Witten gave chase and found the vehicle parked in a driveway with Ted Kennedy stretched out on the front seat to avoid detection. Kennedy was subsequently convicted of reckless driving, racing with a police officer to avoid arrest, and operating a vehicle without a license. April 1958, cited for speeding and operating a vehicle without a license; June 4, 1958, cited for speeding and charged with operating a vehicle without a license; June 15, 1958, convicted of reckless driving; December 1959, fined for running a red light.

The Tedrows recount another incident when Kennedy hit a child with his car while at law school at the University of Virginia. Kennedy panicked and tried to flee, hands

---

[1] *Senatorial Privilege*, p. 81; p. 90
[2] *Senatorial Privilege*, pp. 420-421

frozen to the wheel. It took several blocks before his friends could prevail upon him to stop and report the incident. No charges were filed.[1]

One of Kennedy's friends was reported to have said, "Ted is a very erratic driver and I refuse to drive with him. He said many times he drives like he doesn't give a damn."[2] In 1986, almost 20 years after the Chappaquiddick incident, Kennedy was again fined for speeding without a license in Duxbury, Massachusetts.[3]

Speed of the car

Contrary to Kennedy's stated speed of about 20 mph before he slammed on his brakes at the bridge approach, Richard and Thomas Tedrow confirmed through a witness that the Registry of Motor Vehicles of Massachusetts offered evidence at the inquest to show that the car was going 35 to 40 mph before the brakes were applied, but Judge Boyle would not accept it. Not only did he not accept it, Boyle had the references physically expunged from the record. The Registry had arrived at its 35 to 40 mph speed after an exhaustive study of all physical aspects and measurements, skid marks, heights, depths, distances, weight, trajectories, influence of the rub rail, etc.[4]

Nevertheless, in spite of what nearly everyone has reported, Huck Look did not say that the Oldsmobile sped off at an excessive rate of speed after he observed it between 12:40 and 12:45 a.m. At the exhumation hearing, when questioned about the speed, Look said it left "at about 25 to 30 mph." But at the inquest, Look admitted, "I would say it hurried moderately."

The posted speed limit today at Dike Road is 20 mph. However, the speed that seems right over the washboard surface of Dike Road these days, with no potholes, is 15 mph, or slightly less. Observing over 50 cars drive down Dike Road one day, I saw only 2 actually approach 20 mph while all the rest stayed well below that. In 1969, Dike Road was much narrower than today and littered with potholes. Yet we are supposed to believe that someone consciously approached Dike Bridge at close to 40 mph? That speed is even too high for the paved road on Chappaquiddick. If someone had driven a heavy car at that speed over even a portion of Dike Road in 1969 it very likely would have resulted in a broken spring or damage to the undercarriage. Even blind drunk, the potholes and washboard surface should have been noted. As so many have observed, it just does not make sense.

[1] *Death at Chappaquiddick*, p. 76
[2] *The Ted Kennedy Episode*, p. 48
[3] *Chappaquiddick Revealed*, p. 10
[4] *Death at Chappaquiddick*, pp. 209-210

Lights

Although neither Kennedy, Gargan, nor Markham admitted to seeing any lights burning on any cottage, Mrs. Malm testified she had left a light on clearly visible from the bridge only 450 feet away. A light was also on all night in the bedroom of Tom, a four-year-old child, on the other side of the road occupied by Rev. and Mrs. David Smith. At the inquest, Arena testified that the light in the Smith cottage was located on the Dike Road side of the house. While walking back to Lawrence Cottage, Kennedy would have passed the Chappaquiddick firehouse with a red light glowing above an emergency telephone. Foster Silva, Captain of the volunteer fire company who lived just down the road from Lawrence Cottage, said that if anyone had pulled the alarm inside the unlocked firehouse, he would have been on the bridge immediately. "I would have been there in 3 minutes and my volunteers and half the people on the island could have showed up within 15 minutes."[1]

Ray LaRosa

It was later determined that Ray LaRosa, who Kennedy first contacted after stumbling back to Lawrence Cottage after the accident, was a trained and accomplished SCUBA diver who never drank alcohol. Nevertheless, Kennedy made no effort to have LaRosa included in the group which drove back to Dike Bridge to rescue Mary Jo, even though he had known LaRosa well for at least eight years.

Q: How long had you known Mr. LaRosa prior to this evening?
Kennedy: Eight years, ten years, eight or ten years.
Q: Did you have any knowledge that Mr. LaRosa had some experience in skin-diving?
Kennedy: No, I never did.

Tides

In February 1980, the *Reader's Digest* commissioned Bernard LeMehaute, an internationally recognized oceanographic engineer, to ascertain the tide conditions at Chappaquiddick on the night and morning of the incident.

LeMehaute determined that at 11:30 p.m., about 10 minutes after Kennedy stated that the accident occurred at Dike Bridge and when the tide had swept him about 30 to 40 feet down into Poucha Pond making the rescue attempt impossible, the tide at the bridge was near slack water and was flowing at about one knot into the pond in the

---

[1] *Teddy Bare*, p. 65

area where the car sank, "not a difficult obstacle for an experienced swimmer."[1] At 1:30 a.m., when Kennedy said he was at the ferry landing talking to Markham and Gargan, LeMehaute said the current in the Edgartown Channel was "weak to zero." After 1:30 to about 4:00 a.m., which encompasses the time Kennedy said he impulsively dove into the water and nearly drowned as he was swept by the strong currents to the Edgartown lighthouse, the current increased in velocity but away from the lighthouse and toward Katama Bay, opposite to the direction Kennedy said he was swept.

The tide tables, which Kennedy's lawyers had probably consulted before inventing this story, were almost certainly based on erroneous data. The beach between Chappaquiddick and Edgartown in upper Katama Bay at Norton Point opens and closes to the sea on a cycle that can span decades, with a corresponding change in the tide flow through Edgartown Channel. From 1953, Katama Bay had been open to the sea; however, in 1969 it had all but closed and in fact closed completely in the winter of 1969-1970. What the Kennedy team thought was the flow in July of 1969, and which the tide tables in books printed before 1969 reflected, was not the actual tide on that morning.

The change in tide is so dramatic, especially when the rupture occurs suddenly, that after the next breach 37 years later on April 17, 2007, the Edgartown harbormaster printed this notice:

"The current has increased in the harbor! With the new cut at Norton Point the tide *has switched* and is ebbing and flooding to the Atlantic. Tide tables for Edgartown are not accurate. Where there was one knot we now have three. Please plan your approach to moorings and docks accordingly. The ferry running between Memorial Wharf and Chappy Point is taking longer to make their passage, and we urge vessels to be aware of this crossing and use caution."

The *Washington Star* reported on January 16, 1980, "New evidence, found by a team of *Washington Star* staff reporters during the past seven weeks, relates to the tides, currents, and topography of the Chappaquiddick area. The newspaper study shows the currents were running into the mouth of Edgartown Harbor, not out of it, at the presumed time of the swim and for a considerable period before and after. The change in the direction of the current occurred as a result of changes in the topography of the island.

"Kennedy's claim that the strong currents swept him far off course and almost drowned him is consistent with the official tidal current tables of 1969 at Edgartown.

---

[1] Slack water at Dike Bridge on July 18 occurred at 11:05 p.m. Calculations from data supplied to the author by NOAA indicate that the tide would actually have been flowing into the pond at less than half a knot at 11:30 p.m.

But the tables, published by the National Oceanic Survey, are based on the topography of Martha's Vineyard and Chappaquiddick as it existed in 1964. In brief, a wide opening that had existed in 1964 at the south end of Katama Bay, which then separated Chappaquiddick and Martha's Vineyard, had almost closed by July 1969. The result was that the rising tide no longer flowed outward through the harbor mouth, from the south, but inward, from the northeast. The direction of the tidal currents in the narrow channel between Edgartown and Chappaquiddick, which Kennedy says he swam, was thus essentially the reverse of what was shown on the official tables and essentially the reverse of what Kennedy has described. Among those who confirm that the government's current tables for Edgartown are wrong is Jared Grant, the owner of the Chappaquiddick ferry, who captained the ferry the day and evening of Kennedy's accident."

As I am writing this, the opening at Norton Point is on the verge of closing once more. Soon the tide tables for Edgartown Channel will need to be revised yet again.[1]

Alcohol

The Tedrows recount incidents of reporters observing heavy drinking by Kennedy and drunken revelry on planes and elsewhere. Damore recounts alarmed reports from Kennedy's staff reacting to the senator's heavy drinking, especially after the death of his brother Bobby. *Newsweek*, in their edition of July 28, 1969, wrote, "The senator's closest associates are known to have been powerfully concerned over his indulgent drinking habits, his daredevil driving, and his ever-ready eye for a pretty face."

Nevertheless, Kennedy testified under oath at the inquest that both he and Mary Jo were completely sober when they drove down toward Dike Bridge.

Judge Boyle: Was there a sustained amount of drinking by the group?
Kennedy: No, there wasn't.
Judge Boyle: By any particular person?
Kennedy: Not that I noticed. There wasn't prior to the time I left.
Judge Boyle: Were you at any time that evening under the influence of alcohol?
Kennedy: Absolutely not.
Judge Boyle: Did you imbibe any narcotic drugs that evening?
Kennedy: Absolutely not.
Judge Boyle: Did anyone at the party to your knowledge?
Kennedy: No, absolutely not.
Judge Boyle: In your opinion, were you sober at the time that you operated the motor vehicle to the Dike Bridge?
Kennedy: Absolutely sober.

---

[1] The opening closed during the night of April 1, 2015.

Many witnesses who testified at the inquest or who were interviewed by police or the press reported seeing Kennedy with a drink in his hand – usually rum and coke – almost continuously before the yacht race and after. Leslie Leland, pharmacist and foreman of the grand jury which attempted to investigate the accident at Chappaquiddick, made a meticulous count of the drinks mentioned by eyewitnesses and found that Kennedy was known to have consumed over a dozen ounces of alcohol on July 18. He suggests that if Kennedy was known to have consumed over a dozen ounces, it is a good bet that he consumed far more. Leland points out that a body cannot absorb more than half an ounce of alcohol each hour.

A sample of Mary Jo's blood, analyzed by Dr. McHugh, Director of the Massachusetts State Police Crime Lab, showed a content of 0.09 percent, equivalent to 3.5 to 5 ounces of liquor consumed in an hour, or considerably more if consumed over a longer time. If the witnesses at the party were actually telling the truth when each of them testified they consumed just one or two drinks throughout the evening, or no alcohol at all, this makes Kopechne the heaviest drinker at the party, even though the witnesses also said that she, of all of them, drank the least.[1]

Detective Killen discovered a package store in South Boston where Jack Crimmins purchased three half gallons of vodka, four-fifths of scotch, two bottles of rum, and two cases of beer for the party at Chappaquiddick. This parcels out to a quart of liquor and a six pack of beer for each of the twelve persons.

The Tedrows sum it up this way: "By cleanup time Saturday morning about 14 to 16 ounces of liquor per person were gone, although by their sworn testimony the partygoers had only two drinks each. This leaves us with the known scientific fact that alcohol evaporates when opened and exposed to the air, but disappears even more quickly when exposed to people."[2]

Carbon monoxide

On the day of the accident, Dr. Mills asked Eugene Frieh, the undertaker, to withdraw a sample of Mary Jo's blood and send it to the state police lab for testing. At the exhumation hearing three months later, Mills was asked to interpret the lab's carbon monoxide findings. Mills replied, "That she had been smoking that day, or that she had inhaled a little [carbon] monoxide from a car exhaust."

At the inquest the following January, when the prosecution asked what his crime lab had found in Mary Jo's blood, Dr. McHugh mentioned just two things: an alcohol level of 0.09 percent; and a carbon monoxide level of "under 5 percent." Some have interpreted the carbon monoxide percent as a negative finding and wondered why

---

[1] Not counting Ray LaRosa who never drank.
[2] *Death at Chappaquiddick*, p. 21

McHugh had even bothered to bring it to the attention of the inquest court. However, Dr. Mills's exhumation testimony three months before indicates that Dr. McHugh was referring to a carbon monoxide level of "just under 5 percent" or "a little under 5 percent," which indeed would be a discovery worth mentioning.

The normal level of carbon monoxide in the blood of a nonsmoker is less than 2.3 percent and in an adult smoker between 2.1 and 4.2 percent. A level of nearly 5 percent would suggest that Mary Jo was a heavy smoker; however, Mary Jo did *not* smoke. Somehow, Mary Jo appears to have inhaled carbon monoxide gas from a car exhaust prior to her death.

Arrival at the Shiretown Inn

Gargan testified at the inquest that on the morning of July 19 "in the vicinity of 8:00," he and Markham, accompanied by Charles Tretter, Rosemary Keough, and Susan Tannenbaum, took the ferry over to Edgartown to meet with Kennedy at the Shiretown Inn. This was confirmed by Ross Richards, who testified that Gargan and Markham arrived at the Shiretown "just as the 8:00 a.m. bell sounded." However, no ferry operator or deckhand could remember any of them crossing over to Edgartown at 8:00 that morning, or earlier.[1]

Behavior of Gargan and Kennedy at the Shiretown Inn

Mrs. Richards told Detective Dunn that when Gargan and Markham met Kennedy on the Shiretown Inn porch at 8:00 on the morning of July 19, she was surprised at the coarse manner in which Gargan announced his presence, "demanding to speak to Ted Kennedy at once." He was "very definite about wanting to see him... aggressive... sense of urgency... more or less ordered him into the room."[2] Ross Richards stated to Detective Dunn that Gargan grabbed Kennedy's arm and physically dragged him inside. He said that when all three eventually left the Shiretown Inn, Kennedy was "not the same man" and clearly "upset and excited." He rushed right by them without even acknowledging their presences or saying good-bye, which they found strange.[3] Richards also said he heard an argument going on between Gargan and Kennedy in Kennedy's room before the three men left.[4]

Nevertheless, when Kennedy, Gargan, and Markham rode the ferry to the Chappaquiddick side just a minute or two later, the ferry deckhand described Kennedy's behavior as "jovial."[5] "Kennedy still looked good," Steve Ewing said.

[1] *Death at Chappaquiddick*, p. 59
[2] *Senatorial Privilege*, p. 88
[3] BBC documentary *Chappaquiddick*, 1994; *Senatorial Privilege*, p. 90
[4] *Senatorial Privilege*, p. 255
[5] *The Bridge at Chappaquiddick*, p. 127

"When I saw Kennedy Saturday morning he wore no neck collar and he moved about as though he had suffered no neck injuries. His movements, and I watched him closely, were completely normal."[1] Ewing said that when he went to collect three 15-cent fares from Kennedy, "The senator greeted [me] with a cheerful 'Hi!' "[2]

Appearance of Joe Gargan and Paul Markham at the Shiretown Inn

Ross Richards told Detective Dunn that when Gargan and Markham showed up at the Shiretown Inn porch at 8:00 a.m. on July 19, both men were "soaking wet." Mrs. Richards said she was surprised at Gargan's appearance. "Joe looked awful. His clothes were all wrinkled and his hair was sticking out."[3]

At the inquest five months later, Richards had changed his story. He claimed that they looked "damp," perhaps "wet from the night's dew or fog or something." When Assistant District Attorney Fernandes asked if he recalled telling Lieutenant Dunn that they were both soaking wet, Richards insisted, "I don't remember." In a personal interview, Gargan told Damore, "I was soaking wet because it was a hot, muggy morning and I was very agitated and eager to find out what the hell was going on."[4]

However, Robert Cutler interviewed Ross Richards in September 1971, two years after the inquest. Richards admitted to Cutler that "Gargan and Markham arrived on the porch soaking wet, meaning closer to 1½ hours dry than 5½ hours dry."[5] BBC investigators questioned Marilyn Richards in 1994, after the death of her husband, Ross. Mrs. Richards confirmed that both Gargan and Markham were, indeed, *wet* when they confronted Kennedy that morning.

Report of the accident to police

Kennedy was up by 7:15 a.m. making a phone call to the Washington D.C. headquarters of Washington & Hamilton at the public telephone at the Shiretown Inn on the morning of July 19. He then spent a half hour in innocuous conversation with Ross Richards, Marilyn Richards, and Stan Moore, then spent more than an hour with Joe Gargan, Paul Markham, and Charles Tretter at the Shiretown Inn from 8:00 a.m. Phone records show that someone using Kennedy's credit card was on the Shiretown public phone continuously from 8:14 to 9:12 a.m. Kennedy then proceeded to the ferry landing with Gargan and Markham, arriving at the Edgartown dock at 9:15 a.m. The

---

[1] *The Last Kennedy*, p. 61

[2] *Senatorial Privilege*, p. 11

[3] *The Last Kennedy*, p. 60

[4] *Senatorial Privilege*, p. 88

[5] *You, the Jury*, p. 389

ferry operator testified that Kennedy appeared cheerful and full of energy when he crossed to Chappaquiddick.[1]

The group then milled around the public telephone booth on the Chappaquiddick side of the landing until seeing a hearse leave for Dike Bridge and being advised soon after 9:20 a.m. by Tony Bettencourt that Ted Kennedy's car had been found at Poucha Pond with a dead girl in it. It was only after the ferry had made several more round trips, and only after being advised again by Steve Ewing, the ferry's 16-year-old deckhand, that Kennedy's car had been found, that Kennedy and Markham finally took the ferry back to Edgartown to report the accident, arriving on the Edgartown side at 9:45 a.m.

Although Kennedy testified that he reported the incident "immediately when he fully realized what happened," more than two and one-half hours had elapsed between the time he appeared in the lobby of the Shiretown Inn and when he reported the accident to the police. During that period, Kennedy aides had been informed of the accident, and one of those aides had already landed at the Martha's Vineyard airport to remove the body of Mary Jo from the island.

[1] *Senatorial Privilege*, p. 90. Several books state that the three arrived at the Chappaquiddick ferry at 8:30 a.m. However, Olsen says that the time was "a few minutes after 9:00" [*The Bridge at Chappaquiddick*, p. 126]. Dick Hewitt, the ferry operator, testified at the inquest that Kennedy and the others arrived "approximately in the vicinity of 9:00," but earlier had told reporters it was "about 9:10 a.m." [*The Ted Kennedy Episode*, p. 28]. The last call from the Shiretown Inn on Kennedy's credit card ended at 9:12 a.m., and the walk from the Shiretown Inn to the ferry takes a minute and a half.

Ted Kennedy leaves the Edgartown Courthouse on July 5, 1969, after receiving a two-month suspended sentence and a year's probation.

4

Uncertain Cause of Death

John Farrar, Captain of the Search and Rescue Division of the Edgartown Volunteer Fire Department who retrieved the body, has always maintained that Mary Jo Kopechne died of suffocation rather than by drowning.

$\mathfrak{M}$ary Jo's body was found by Farrar in the throes of rigor mortis, positioned upright and facing backwards in the upside-down rear seat of the submerged car. Farrar says he observed her hands gripping the bottom of the seat. Mary Jo's head was craned "in a conscious position" into the highest part of the footwell of the car and both her legs were pressed together and perfectly aligned with the back of the rear seat. The car was in an inclined position, with the front on the sand and the rear elevated off it. When the car was rolled over, Farrar says he observed bubbles of air boiling to the surface.

Farrar was able to get the body out of the car by maneuvering it carefully through the blown-out rear passenger-side window. When Mary Jo was brought to the surface, her body floated. Farrar says this would indicate that she could not have drowned. He says that Mary Jo was slim and if her lungs had filled with water, she would have sunk.

Before the inquest, Farrar made a sketch of the car showing Mary Jo's position within the vehicle when he found her. The sketch was admitted into evidence as Exhibit No. 14. In *You, the Jury*, Robert Cutler, after consultations with Farrar, later added dotted lines to the sketch showing three levels of water: the level of water within the vehicle that would be expected to have existed immediately after the accident occurred (water level A); the water level within the vehicle at the time Farrar recovered the body (water level B); and the level of the water in the pond when Farrar arrived on the scene (pond level).[1]

When the car plunged into the water on its roof, air would have been trapped inside just as air is trapped in an overturned glass that is placed in a tub of water. By the time Farrar was called to the scene, he believes all of the air in the interior of the car had escaped through the overturned trunk. But when the car was pulled from the pond, Farrar says the trunk itself was mostly dry. Farrar believes it was this air that had helped elevate the lighter rear of the car off the bottom and it may have been some of this air that boiled to the surface when the vehicle was righted. Farrar believes this would indicate that the initial volume of air at the time of the accident in the interior of the car had leaked out slowly in the hours of the night through small holes in the

---

[1] *You, the Jury*, p. 376, Fig 8

undercarriage at the rear of the trunk. By calculating the volume of air which he believes existed for a good deal of time in the interior of the Oldsmobile, and after research into the effects of carbon dioxide poisoning, Farrar estimates that Mary Jo must have been alive "at least an hour" before succumbing. Farrar has always maintained that Mary Jo could have been saved had Kennedy made an emergency telephone call after driving off the bridge.

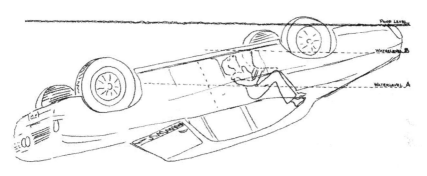

E X H I B I T   No. 14

Nevertheless, contrary to what is generally reported,[1] Farrar brought little of this to the attention of the court at the exhumation hearing in October or at the inquest the following January. At the exhumation hearing, these were the only words addressing his theories: "I observed the victim inside the car. Her head was cocked back and her face pressed into the footwell, hands holding on the front edge of the back seat." Likewise, at the inquest, Farrar said just this: "On entering the open right window and

---

[1] *Wikipedia* (2017) says Farrar told the inquest court, "It looked as if she were holding herself up to get a last breath of air. It was a consciously assumed position. She didn't drown. She died of suffocation in her own air void. It took her at least three or four hours to die. I could have had her out of that car twenty-five minutes after I got the call. But he [Ted Kennedy] didn't call." *Wikipedia* continues, "Farrar testified later at the inquest that Kopechne's body was pressed up in the car in the spot where an air bubble would have formed. He interpreted this to mean that Kopechne had survived in the air bubble after the accident, and concluded that, 'Had I received a call within five to ten minutes of the accident occurring, and was able, as I was the following morning, to be at the victim's side within twenty-five minutes of receiving the call, in such event there is a strong possibility that she would have been alive on removal from the submerged car.' " None of this supposed dialogue is found in the inquest testimony, or in Farrar's exhumation testimony, either.

looking up, I found the victim's head cocked back, face pressed into the footwell, hands holding onto the front edge of the back seat. By holding herself in a position such as she could avail herself of the last remaining air in the car." And later, "I observed large air bubbles at the time it was being towed out emanating from the vehicle."

Professional opinions

Dr. Mills, who examined the body at the scene, mentioned the odd position of her arms extended in front of her body in rigor mortis as she lay on her back. At the exhumation hearing he said her hands were "in a semi-claw." He said that the awkward position of her arms would have made it impossible to remove her blouse unless it was cut away. At the inquest three months later, Mills said, "Her arms were raised. Her hands were in a sort of semi-claw position. Her head was tipped back a little to one side."

Dr. Mills pronounced death by drowning based on a cursory examination of "probably 10 minutes." Mills said he observed a light pinkish froth exuding from her nose and copious amounts of water welling from her chest when depressed as she lay on her back on a stretcher.

However, this was refuted by the undertaker, Eugene Frieh, who observed Mills's examination closely. Frieh did not see any great outpouring of water, and the water that he did see appeared to come from her stomach. Farrar says he did not see much water either, although he did see foam emanating from her nose and mouth.

In an interview reported by the *Boston Herald Traveler* on July, 17, 1970, Frieh stated that it was "conceivable that she could have died from breathing her own carbon dioxide" and when he was traveling to Wilkes-Barre, Pennsylvania, for the exhumation hearing he suggested to Mills that he change his finding from "drowning" to "asphyxia." He said they were able to extract "no more than a cup" of water from her body. At the hearing to determine whether the body of Mary Jo would be exhumed, Frieh stated that when he embalmed the body he observed "a very little bit of moisture" and "a slight pinkish frothy exudate from the nostrils" but no blood from the throat. "I did raise an eyebrow, sir, in the sense that I was expecting much more moisture." At the inquest, Frieh said, "It produced some water flow, water and foam, mostly foam."

Interviewed by the BBC for their documentary of 1994, Arena remembered observing a discharge of foam from the mouth and nose as he held her body while sitting on top of the Oldsmobile.

Dr. Werner Spitz, Deputy Chief Medical Examiner for the State of Maryland brought in by the Kopechnes to testify on their behalf against the petition to exhume the body, said that drowning was one of the most difficult diagnoses to make in forensic pathology because it so frequently resembled other causes of death. However,

Spitz said that it was all but certain her death was caused by drowning. He said, "There is no question in my mind that at this point she also inhaled water. It is also apparent to me from the record that she lived for a certain time under the water. Otherwise, why should the froth have developed? You're talking about pink foam."

Dinis: Isn't it a fact, Doctor, that the foam is present and blood foam is present in other forms of death?

Spitz: Yes, it is true; however, the foam that you see in other modes of death it's in all likelihood white. You're talking about pink foam, and let me remind you of another thing, that foam is the combination of water and protein that is being shaken, and the shaking action is the breathing action. So she breathed, that girl, she breathed. You're not going to find a cause for instantaneous death whether you exhume her or you don't. So she inhaled water.

True Forensics says this about drowning (mechanical asphyxia): "Classically, there will be a plume of froth at the mouth and nostrils in a drowning which may sometimes be tinged with blood. This froth fills the air passages and exudes onto the face. It is composed of water containing plasma protein and surfactant that has been whipped into a froth by the violent terminal respiratory actions... If a dead body is thrown into water, water can enter the lungs due to hydrostatic pressure; however, frothy fluid in the lungs is diagnostic of drowning."[1]

Dr. George Katsas, who would have carried out the autopsy on Mary Jo if exhumation had been allowed, told BBC investigators in 1994, "Certainly the findings discovered by Dr. Mills are more consistent with drowning than suffocation, although pulmonary edema can be very severe in cases of suffocation." The BBC commentator explained that pulmonary edema is a swelling of the tissues of the lungs which can cause internal bleeding.

---

[1] http://writeworld.tumblr.com/post/50340132890/true-forensics-drowning-mechanical-asphyxia

PART 2: NEW WITNESS

5
Carol Jones — Her Eyewitness Account

*S*n July of 1969 I was 17 years old. Scott Donahue, my boyfriend at the time, and Chris Casey, a friend of his, had decided to bicycle across the country starting from Mountain Lakes, New Jersey. Chris' family was vacationing on Chappaquiddick that summer and had rented a small cottage, called the Martin House, on the island. The Martin House is located on Chappaquiddick Road between the ferry landing and the sharp right-angle curve leading to School House Road, and only 950 feet from the Dike Road intersection.

Chris had told his parents that he would call them at the Martin House at 11:15 p.m. on the night of July 18 to say good-bye. I would be there as well to say good-bye to Scott. It would be a long time before I would have an opportunity to speak with Scott again so this call was very important to me.

I was living at our home at Wasque Farm on Chappaquiddick as I had done every summer since I was three weeks old. In 1969, the farm, of about 120 acres, was known as the Turnbull place. Dorothy Turnbull, my grandmother, owned the property which she purchased back in the 1940s after her husband had passed away. My grandmother's permanent home was in Summit, New Jersey, where she employed a woman, Lula Tolliver, to cook and care for her, and Lula and her young son, Clarence, had traveled with my grandmother to Chappaquiddick for the summer. A few of my five siblings were staying at the farm, too.

My parents were away on a sailing trip and had left their VW bus at the farm for me to use until they returned. On the night of July 18 I watched the clock with anticipation as it crawled ever closer to the time I'd be able to speak to my boyfriend. A little before 11:00 p.m., I drove the VW bus to the Martin House so that I would be on time when the call came in. Back in those days long-distance phone calls were expensive and so the conversations were short. If I wasn't on time, I'd miss my opportunity to speak with Scott.

The call arrived on the dot of 11:15 p.m., but my few minutes of conversation with Scott were stiff and quite formal because Chris's parents and siblings were milling around in the kitchen where the phone was located. With Chris's family listening to every word I wasn't able to pour my heart out to Scott and tell him my true feelings because that would be revealing too much.

Carol Jones standing on the side of Chappaquiddick Road where Kennedy's Valiant passed her VW bus.

Feeling really sad about the missed opportunity of telling Scott how I felt, I stayed only a short time after the call, and at precisely 11:30 p.m. I said that I had to get back home. As I climbed into the VW bus I thought maybe I'd go down to East Beach on the other side of Dike Bridge to walk around for a bit, think about how much I missed Scott, and have a girlish cry. It just seemed at the time like the comforting thing to do.

I pulled out of the driveway, looking to my left and right, and saw nothing coming. Of course, I did not expect any traffic – there just weren't that many cars on Chappy in 1969. I had driven about 25 feet down the road when to my great surprise a white compact car flew up behind me and immediately began to pass me on the left. I was shocked because the road at that point was all blind curves with a snake right and a snake left before it swung into the blind right-angle turn to School House Road. Just in front of Liz Stephens's house, 350 feet from the Dike Road intersection, the car swerved back into the right lane in front of me, narrowly missing my bus, and my headlights illuminated the rear passenger seat through a large, squared-off rear window. Through that window I clearly saw three people in the back seat of the car:

two rather large men in white shirts, and squished in between them a very short woman with short hair.

As the car drove on I was literally shaking. I was thinking, "What idiots, they'll never make that sharp right turn at that speed. There's going to be a terrible accident!" Instead, to my amazement the car rocketed straight down Dike Road and didn't stop or even slow much. I would have seen the brake lights if it had.

I abandoned all thought of a good cry at East Beach and drove slowly on home, wondering who those people could have been in that car and why they were driving so fast. The car had come up behind me at a speed I estimated to be between 45 to 50 mph – much too fast for Chappaquiddick – then actually passed me! On a blind curve! This was absolutely unheard of on Chappy, even in the daytime. No one passes another car on Chappaquiddick, ever, unless the other car comes to a complete stop. The roads on the island are narrow and lined with tall trees and there are so few places where it is possible to see oncoming cars from any great distance ahead. Pedestrians and bicyclists, who usually make little effort to keep to the edge of the road, have the right of way by default. It's not legal to pass another moving car anywhere on Chappaquiddick. In 1969, the centerline on the only paved road was a solid white from the ferry landing to where it ends near Wasque. Today, it is a double solid yellow, and the posted speed is just 25 mph near the ferry and 20 mph elsewhere. Excepting, perhaps, an emergency vehicle or two, I believe this may have been the first time any car had ever passed another at high speed on Chappaquiddick.

I didn't recognize the car, which was also strange because in those days the population of Chappaquiddick was very small and I was familiar with pretty much every car on the island. As teenagers we just hitchhiked whenever we felt like it. Cars always stopped for us and we didn't even have to stick a thumb out. Everyone knew everyone else in those days and many of the residents were my cousins anyway. This car was really different than anything I was accustomed to on Chappy. It was new and powerful, not like most cars here at that time. I thought that it was nothing less than criminal to shoot through the intersection the way it did. If a bicycle was coming toward them on the way to the Chappy ferry, hugging the right lane, it would have been center-pinned as it crossed Dike Road. Just about everyone rode bikes on Chappaquiddick in those days, even late at night. I often did, too, and if I hadn't had the use of my parents' VW, I probably would have been on one that evening.

But what really confused me was why those people would be driving down Dike Road. There was nothing there at that time of night. It was all a big mystery to me and I couldn't stop thinking about it.

My parents returned from their sailing trip the next morning, and as they were crossing over on the Chappaquiddick ferry they heard from the captain that a car had gone over Dike Bridge with a young girl inside. Worried that I might have been that girl, my father drove straight to the bridge to make sure it wasn't me, then reassured that I was OK, drove to the farm to tell us all about it.

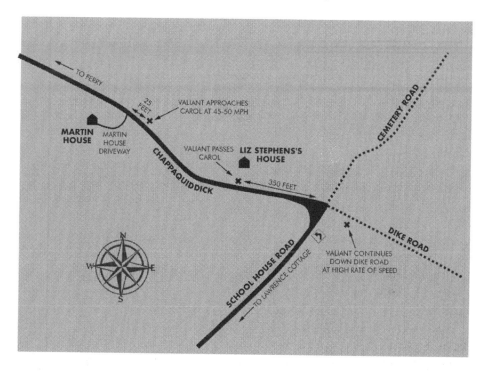

Carol's encounter

As soon as I heard what had happened, I was thinking, "Oh my God, it must have been that car I saw that passed me." I wondered if the driver of the car had continued straight ahead onto Dike Road instead of making the right turn onto School House Road because at the exact moment he passed me he had no other choice. I told Lula what I had seen the night before, then hopped in the VW to see the accident for myself

When I got to Dike Bridge the car was already pulled out and there were about 15 to 20 people milling about – a big crowd for Chappy. It was scary and very mysterious because car accidents almost never happened here where slow and then slower is the rule. But the car they had pulled from the channel was big and black whereas the one I had seen the night before was white and much smaller. I was relieved, but at the same time I didn't know what to make of it. I also wondered what might have happened if I had left the Martin House just a little sooner or stayed just a few minutes longer. I would have driven down Dike Road and seen everything.

A few days later, Lula pulled me aside and begged me not to ever tell a soul what I had seen. I have never seen anyone look so terrified. She said she had a cousin who worked for the Kennedys in Hyannis Port, either as a cook or as a housekeeper, I cannot be certain now. Lula said that her cousin had told her that the Kennedys didn't mess around and would have me killed if I told anyone what I had witnessed. I listened to Lula, and I believed her. The Kennedys were God in those days, and reporters were crawling all over the island. I never went public with what I observed.

Still, over the years I've told close friends and family my story. In fact, I often reenacted the events of that night from my perspective, for folks I trusted, and let them draw their own conclusions. I would start out from the Martin House at 11:30 p.m., show them where the car passed me, and then drive all the way down to the bridge. I even tried to bring it to the attention of John John Kennedy, President Kennedy's son, in Aspen, Colorado, when I was house sitting for his girlfriend's mother, Joyce Hatton, in 1980. But John John wasn't interested at all. He said he didn't care about any of that. It didn't have anything to do with him and he was tired of people bringing the subject up.

After Jack Olsen's book was published in early 1970 I realized that the car I saw must have been the white Valiant rented by Kennedy that weekend, but I couldn't understand how it could fit in because I was sure I had seen Mary Jo in that car, but Huck Look thought he had seen Mary Jo in the Oldsmobile at a quarter to one. I just couldn't figure it out, but I knew what I had seen was important.

Word had gotten around that Huck Look was writing a book about Chappaquiddick, so when I happened to run into him near the Edgartown Yacht Club one afternoon in 1998, I decided that this was my chance. Maybe together we could make some sense of it all.

Huck Look

Carol could not reconcile what she had seen with Look's testimony. It just didn't make sense. She was sure she had seen Kennedy's rented vehicle pass down Dike Road at a high rate of speed with a woman passenger at 11:35 p.m., but Look claimed he had seen Kennedy's Oldsmobile head down Dike Road with a woman passenger between 12:40 and 12:45 a.m., more than an hour later. Surely both female passengers could only be Mary Jo, found dead in the Oldsmobile afterward. Since Carol was absolutely sure of what she saw, this just didn't make sense.

Carol was right, at least about the white compact car. There were so few people and so very few cars on Chappaquiddick in those days that the Edgartown ferry operators knew them all. Steve Ewing, the ferryboat deckhand during the summer of 1969, says that there was no white or light-colored Valiant-like car owned by anyone on the island of Chappaquiddick that summer.

Ewing was not just making this up. When I talked to Ewing in 2013 I found him covered in oil as he was overhauling his tugboat engine. I had brought with me a long list of questions on such subjects as times, conversations, who was where, etc. and as I started down that list, each was answered with, "Sorry, I just can't remember." His shoulders began slumping, and they continued to slump until I reached the question about the Valiant. His countenance brightened, a smile lighted his face, and Ewing gave me a rapid-fire account of every car on the island of Chappaquiddick in 1969 and who it belonged to. Cars were Ewing's life in those days, and still are. He says he is positive he would have remembered a white or light-colored Valiant-type car if there was one on the island, and he would have remembered if a car like that drove off the island sometime later that summer. Doug Batten, Jon Ahlbum's assistant who worked at the Depot gas station in Edgartown where Kennedy's Oldsmobile was first towed, joined us later. Batten, who is an expert on anything related to automobiles, also affirms there was nothing like that car on Chappaquiddick during the summer of 1969. Questioned as to how certain they were, both replied, "Absolutely one hundred percent dead certain."

So Carol went up to Huck and asked if they could talk. Look said, "Sure." Carol told her story, hopeful that Look would be intrigued.

But Carol appears to have run up against a problem. Look had been hounded by Kennedy operatives from day one. His life, and the life of his family, had been threatened. He had been accused of being an outright liar. Beleaguered and frustrated, he had resorted to repeating the same mantra: "You can believe him, or you can believe me. But I know what I saw."

Carol's story might have seemed like one more attempt to discredit his own. And just like Carol, Huck probably could make no sense of any of it. It was a story so like his but with an hour difference to account for. And then there was the strange anomaly of Carol observing the Valiant traveling from the ferry landing toward Dike Bridge. What was up with that? And with a whole group of people in the car including, it seemed to be, Mary Jo Kopechne herself. How could that work? He had seen what appeared to be Mary Jo in Kennedy's Oldsmobile traveling in the opposite direction, from Lawrence Cottage toward Dike Bridge. It probably didn't make any sense at all to him.

Huck Look listened politely but without showing much interest and without saying much. Carol got the feeling that he just didn't believe it. He knew what he saw. Two persons, equally convinced of what they had seen, could not imagine how the other's observation could fit with their own.

Huck thanked Carol for her time and Carol left, feeling let down and very confused. And thus a rare chance to solve one of the most perplexing mysteries of our time slipped away.

Color and length of hair

When I mentioned to John Farrar that a new witness had seen a woman near the scene, one of the first questions he asked was, "What color was her hair?" And the strange thing is, no one had ever asked. It just never occurred to me, or to Carol, that this might be important. No one appears to have asked Huck Look if he had noticed the color of the hair of the passenger in the Oldsmobile, either. But, of course, this is vitally important because Mary Jo's hair was shoulder length at the time of the accident and distinctively blond. So I asked Carol, whose own hair is a natural towheaded blond, if she could remember. Her immediate and emphatic response: "Not blond!"

Number of passengers

Carol saw two men and one woman in the back seat. She remembers that the three people in the back seat were "squished together" which suggests another person sitting in the front seat with the driver. The car probably held four males and one female.

Clarence Tolliver

Clarence Tolliver, Lula's son, was asked what he remembered from that time and sent this message to Carol.

"A few days after Kennedy's accident I was playing tennis at Pimpneymouse Farm [between Lawrence Cottage and Dike Bridge] and a friend told me he saw two people cut behind the house late that night from Dike Road to School House Road but didn't know who they were. My mother and a close friend Gertrude Stephenson, the cook at Pimpneymouse Farm, decided that I must know something, too. I was told in no uncertain terms to keep my mouth shut. To make their point, I was given a good beating and told to say nothing or we were all going to wind up dead.

"I got the impression that Gertrude and my mother knew something others didn't but for some reason were too scared to reveal it. I thought she and my mother might have decided I had overheard them talking about what they had seen or heard and were scared that I'd repeat it. After my beating, my mother never talked much about what might have happened that night at Dike Bridge. For the rest of her life the subject was studiously avoided."

The Plymouth Valiant V100 rented by Kennedy on the weekend of July 18, waiting in the Chappaquiddick ferry line to cross over to Edgartown. Carol would have observed the Valiant from this angle as it passed her on Chappaquiddick Road. Coincidently, Carol's VW bus may also be waiting in line three vehicles ahead. Photo Jack Hubbard

6

Affidavits

Affidavit from David Maddox, present US and International Olympic official, and US Olympic coach and manager of luge from 1984-86.

I swear that:

In July of 1969, Carol Jones told me that she had seen a white car pass her near the Martin House on Chappaquiddick Road and witnessed it proceed down Dike Road at a high rate of speed at around 11:30 p.m. on the evening of July 18, 1969;

In the back seat of the car were two men and a short woman squeezed in between them;

I had arrived on Chappaquiddick from New Jersey on July 18, 1969, and saw Carol that day on her family place on Chappaquiddick;

Lula Tolliver, Carol's Grandmother's help, had told Carol not to say anything to the authorities as she feared that the Kennedy's would have Carol killed if she did;

I was also with Carol when she met with Huck Look in 1998 to tell him what she had seen. In fact, I was instrumental in encouraging Carol to speak to Huck regarding what she had witnessed.

I confirm that Carol Jones is an honest person and is not the type of person to make up stories;

I am confident that Carol witnessed the event as she has described.

Signed: David C. Maddox, Feb. 19, 2014

I swear that:

- In July of 1969, Carol Jones told me that she had seen a white car pass her near the Martin House on Chappaquiddick Road and witnessed it proceed down Dike Road at a high rate of speed at around 11:30 pm on the evening of July 18, 1969;

- In the backseat of the car were two men and a short woman squeezed in between them;

- I had arrived on Chappaquiddick from New Jersey on July 18, 1969 and saw Carol that day at her family place on Chappaquiddick;

- Lula Tolliver, Carol's Grandmother's help, had told Carol not to say anything to the authorities as she feared that the Kennedy's would have Carol killed if she did;

- I was also with Carol when she met with Huck Look in 1998 to tell him what she had seen. In fact, I was instrumental in encouraging Carol to speak to Huck regarding what she had witnessed.

- I confirm that Carol Jones is an honest person and is not the type of person to make up stories;

- I am confident that Carol witnessed the event as she has described.

Signed: _David C. Maddox_

Printed Name: _David C. Maddox_

Date: _Feb 19th 2014_

Affidavit from Gerald S. Jones, private management consultant and former Executive Vice President of the Forum Corporation.

I swear that:

Sometime soon after 1969, Carol Jones told me that a car had passed her on Chappaquiddick Road on the late evening of July 18, 1969, as she was heading home to Wasque Farm. She told me she had witnessed it proceed down Dike Road at a high rate of speed and that the car never stopped or slowed. She related other details at the time, but I honestly cannot remember what those details were after so many years.

I can and do confirm that Carol Jones is an honest person and is not the type of person to make up stories or tell lies;

I am completely confident that Carol witnessed the event as she has described.

Although my last name is also "Jones," I have no family relationship to Carol.

Signed: Gerald S. Jones, 18 July 2014.

I swear that:

- Sometime soon after 1969, Carol Jones told me that a car had passed her on Chappaquiddick Road on the late evening of July 18, 1969 as she was heading home to Wasque Farm. She told me she had witnessed it proceed down Dike Road at a high rate of speed and that the car never stopped or slowed. She related other details at the time but I honestly cannot remember what those details were after so many years.

- I can and do confirm that Carol Jones is an honest person and is not the type of person to make up stories or tell lies;

- I am completely confident that Carol witnessed the event as she has described.

- Although my last name is also "Jones," I have no family relationship to Carol.

Signed: _Garld S.Jn_

Printed Name: _Garld S. Jones_

Date: _18 JPLY 2014_

Affidavit from Linda Constantino, MA, MFA, Professor of Illustration at Savannah College of Art and Design.

I swear that:

Carol Jones and I spent two weeks in May of 1974 at Carol's family home on Chappaquiddick. The film JAWS was being shot on location on Martha's Vineyard and Chappaquiddick at that time;

During my visit, Carol told me that she had seen a white compact car matching the description of Kennedy's white rented Valiant pass her at an extreme rate of speed near the Martin house on Chappaquiddick Road, and witnessed it proceed down Dike Road at around 11:30 p.m. on the evening of July 18, 1969;

In the back seat of the car were two men and a short woman with short hair squeezed in between them;

Carol and I spent countless hours going over what Senator Kennedy had said had occurred that night, and what Sheriff Huck Look said he had seen, to see how Carol's observation could "fit" with both those accounts; however, we could make no sense of any of it;

Carol related to me that Lula Tolliver, her Grandmother's help, had warned her not to say anything to the authorities as she feared that the Kennedy's would have Carol killed if she did;

We were both afraid to go to the authorities because Kennedy was a senator and still a possible candidate for President at that time;

I confirm that Carol Jones is an honest person and neither she nor anyone else in her family is the type of person to make up stories;

I am absolutely certain that Carol witnessed the event as she has described.

Signed, Linda Warner Constantino, October 12, 2014

I swear that:

* Carol Jones and I spent two weeks in May of 1974 at Carol's family home on Chappaquiddick. The film "JAWS" was being shot on location on Martha's Vineyard and Chappaquiddick at that time;

* During my visit, Carol told me that she had seen a white compact car matching the description of Kennedy's white rented Valiant pass her at an extreme rate of speed near the Martin House on Chappaquiddick Road, and witnessed it proceed down Dike Road at around 11:30 P.M. on the evening of July 18, 1969;

* In the backseat of the car were two men and a short woman with short hair squeezed in between them;

* Carol and I spent countless hours going over what Senator Kennedy had said had occurred that night, and what Sheriff Huck Look said he had seen, to see how Carol's observation could "fit" with both those accounts; however, we could make no sense of any of it;

* Carol related to me that Lula Tolliver, her Grandmother's help, had warned her not to say anything to the authorities as she feared that the Kennedy's would have Carol killed if she did;

* We were both afraid to go to the authorities because Kennedy was a Senator and still a possible candidate for President at that time;

* I confirm that Carol Jones is an honest person and neither she nor anyone else in her family is the type of person to make up stories;

* I am absolutely certain that Carol witnessed the event as she has described.

Signed: _Linda Warner Constantino_

Printed Name: _Linda Warner Constantino_
Linda Warner Constantino

Date: _10/12/14_

7

Intimidation and Death Threats

Carol's fear for her life if she went public with her story was not unfounded.

It was reported that Huck Look was investigated by private investigator J. E. Gautreau of Confidential Services Ltd. of Arlington, Massachusetts, hired by the Kennedy team to find out whether Look could be discredited by showing he was a drunk or philanderer.[1]

I have talked to close friends of Look who have revealed to me that Look had received death threats. These friends told me that Look, as an Edgartown deputy sheriff and, later, Sheriff of Dukes County, took these threats so seriously that he had advised Kennedy insiders that he knew more than what he had publicly revealed and that this information was in the hands of a lawyer. If Look died in mysterious circumstances, the lawyer would send that information to the press. Perhaps what was in the hands of his lawyer included Carol's eyewitness account. Maybe Look believed more of it than he let on. According to Look's son, these papers were willed to Dukes County Sheriff Mike McCormack on Huck's death.[2]

Chris Look, Huck's son, said that his father would not talk about it much, but he had begun receiving heavy-handed threats immediately after the incident. Huck's taxes were audited almost every year from 1969 through 1980. For 10 years, he was continuously harassed with one government snafu after another. Although it was nothing he could prove, the persistence and sheer number of these problems had convinced him it was related to his testimony, and his refusal to recant.

Leslie Leland, foreman of the grand jury charged with investigating Kennedy, recollects in his book, *Left to Die*, an incident of intimidation orchestrated by Edgartown Chief of Police Arena and Walter Steele, the county prosecutor. And these were supposed to be the very individuals who were *prosecuting* Kennedy.

---

[1] *Senatorial Privilege*, p. 315
[2] An e-mail sent to Mike McCormack in late August 2014 concerning these papers was never answered.

Leslie Leland, foreman of the grand jury, at the rebuilt Dike Bridge in 2009.

Leland writes that a few days after the incident he was told to meet Chief Arena at the intersection of Vineyard Haven/Edgartown Road and Barnes Road, in those days a remote location in the middle of Martha's Vineyard Island. Leland was asked to get in the back of Arena's car. In the front seat, next to Arena, sat Walter Steele, the Dukes County prosecutor. While driving around the back roads of the island, Arena and Steele explained to each other why there was no need for further investigation or trial. It was simply an unfortunate accident, worthy, at best, of a minor traffic violation. It was so hard on the senator. Arena lamented to Steele, "If we could only get rid of the press, but they're determined to create something just to keep people reading their newspapers or listening to their reports. If it wasn't for them, this whole thing could be forgotten."

Neither man spoke to Leland directly, asked him a question, or even acknowledged his presence. At the end of a long ride, Leland was dropped off at his car without a word of explanation. Leland's reaction to the bizarre episode: "It shook me up. Intimidated me."[1]

---

[1] *Left to Die*, pp. 32-33

Interestingly, when Leland spoke to reporters about his experience of being intimidated by Arena and Steele, Arena called Leland a liar. Arena said he had never had any meeting with Leland and that Leland's story was a fabrication. But when Leland said he would take a lie detector test to prove it, Arena backed down and shut up. As for Steele, he couldn't be found and was unavailable for comment.

Leland also recounts telephone death threats to his wife and children from two different individuals, the second individual ominously referencing the call of the first, which necessitated around-the-clock police protection for his family in 1970. His pharmaceutical license renewal notice did not arrive automatically at the end of 1969, as it usually did, and it was only by virtue of a kind employee at the state pharmacy board, who begged Leland not to tell anyone or she would lose her job, that Leland heard that the police had orders to close and padlock his pharmacy doors the next day. Somehow, Leland managed to find a last-minute flight to Boston to renew the license, just minutes before the government doors closed at 3:00 p.m. on New Year's Eve.

Farrar was told to "keep quiet or there could be trouble" and received death threats, too. Soon after the incident at Chappaquiddick a gun-wielding assailant assaulted Farrar in a hotel room after he was interviewed about his theories on a Boston radio station. In a radio interview in 1994, Farrar relates instances of intimidation and said that his taxes were audited three times immediately after the incident, all in the same year.

In a personal interview in 2013, Leland told Carol she had been very smart not to reveal what she saw. "These people played hardball. I got away with standing up to them, and Look did, too, but we were public figures. You could very well have ended up dead. These people would have had no problem making it happen." Leland himself was advised by his father, a selectman for many years, to leave things alone if he valued his life. "You better leave this alone and walk away. You are dealing with the biggest, most powerful political machine in the country. The Kennedys will destroy you if you continue." Leland found it hard to put into words how difficult it was for his family to live with continuous death threats. "I don't think you can really understand the feeling unless you personally experience it."

Carol was not aware of any of this in 1969. However, a reporter from the *Herald News* of Passaic, New Jersey, stayed at Carol's home for much of the time he was reporting the incident. Carol was driving a distinctive VW bus when the vehicle passed by her and there were so few cars on the island in 1969 it would have been a simple matter to determine who it belonged to. Any ferry operator could have made the identification. Carol was afraid the reporter might be a Kennedy plant, sent to her home to find out how much the family knew or whether anyone intended speaking up. To be on the safe side, Carol was careful to look cute, but say nothing.

8

Huck Look

Three affidavits confirm that Carol has not lied about what she saw on the night of July 18, 1969. Carol knows what she saw and nothing whatsoever will convince her otherwise. Huck Look never solicited any affidavits from anyone, but he never had to. Look's character speaks for itself.

Huck Look, whose ancestors lived on the Vineyard for more than 300 years, was always known to be a man who took great care when it came to the truth. Carol's father, Curry, describes Look as one of the most honest men he's ever known. Look was a Kennedy man, at least before the accident, and there is no reason he would have lied about any of the details. Nor could he have been mistaken.

That Look took his job seriously as a deputy sheriff is an understatement. Look quit his job as a lieutenant in the Edgartown fire department after his company began selling oil to the department because he was concerned he might be accused of a conflict of interest. He was scrupulous about his uniform and was never known to take a drink while on duty. Olsen recounts a time when Huck Look, relaxing at home, was called to help the sheriff process several dozen narcotic suspects. Huck refused to assist, explaining that he just had two beers and couldn't put his uniform on. When the sheriff insisted, Look compromised by refusing to wear his star at the station.[1]

At only age 20, Look earned local hero status by diving into the water off Memorial Wharf in Edgartown to save a 7-year-old child from drowning. He was a sergeant first class in the Korean War and became an Edgartown deputy sheriff in 1953. Look was very active at St. Andrew's Church in Edgartown. St. Andrew's was always our family church from the time it was an Episcopal mission in 1895. Several of our family were married there, including the author. Many of us knew Huck Look well through his involvement with St. Andrew's, including my grandfather and Carol's father.

In the aftermath of the incident, Look was offered several hundred thousand dollars to appear on a TV talk show just to relate what he had seen. He turned it down because "he did not feel it was right to make money off a tragedy." Over the next 10 years, at every anniversary of the accident, he was continuously offered money to appear on TV, and continuously turned it down. At the end of it all, Look had walked away from at least a million dollars. Look considered writing a book but eventually decided against it for the same reason: it wouldn't be "right."

---

[1] *The Bridge at Chappaquiddick*, p. 94

Look got into the habit early of memorizing license numbers just in case. If a car looked at all suspicious, he would memorize or mark down the number because one never knew whether it would become important later. His oil truck was littered with license plate numbers of vehicles he had seen. He was the type of officer no criminal ever wants to run into: intelligent, hard working, diligent, persistent, incorruptible, careful, honest, and *observant*. Look's character and talents were recognized by the people on the island and Look was elected Sheriff of Dukes County in 1972, a position he held until retirement in 1998. Look died in 2011 at age 82, beloved and respected by everyone who knew him. His portrait hangs proudly in the Edgartown courthouse today.

Neither Carol Jones nor Huck Look lied about what they observed that night. An assessment of what may have occurred must take into account the testimony of each of them. The question is, what might that assessment be?

9
Dike Bridge Theories

Mary Jo drove off the bridge alone

𝒥ack Olsen's *The Bridge at Chappaquiddick*, published five months after the incident, supports a theory favorable to Kennedy. Concerned for his reputation and worried that he might be followed, Kennedy got out of the Oldsmobile after observing Look's uniform and badge around 12:40 a.m. Kennedy instructed Mary Jo to drive herself to East Beach, explaining that after making sure that everything was OK, he'd follow along on foot.

Driving an unfamiliar car and probably a little drunk, Mary Jo drove off Dike Bridge herself and was unable to escape the vehicle. Olsen suggests that after confirming that Look was not following the Oldsmobile, Kennedy might have walked back to Lawrence Cottage for the help of his friends. These probably drove over Dike Bridge to East Beach, but unable to see the car submerged in the water because of the darkness, reasoned that Mary Jo had somehow found a different route back to the cottage. The first time Kennedy heard about the accident was after 9:20 a.m. when he was advised by ferry operatives that his car had been found in Poucha Pond.

The Inspector's Opinion, a romantic novel by Malcolm Reybold of dubious literary merit, is Olsen's story with a twist. Kennedy got out of the Oldsmobile after confusing the headlights of the rented white Valiant, driven by Gargan and Markham, for Look's automobile.

Chappaquiddick Decision, an unabashed tribute to Kennedy by Larryann Willis, is Olsen's story with twist number two. Suddenly realizing that Mary Jo had forgotten her purse and hotel room key, Kennedy decided to turn around at the Dike Road intersection to return for it at the exact time Huck Look's station wagon was blocking his way. Suspecting that Look was a Mafia assassin, Kennedy took off down Dike Road, then bailed out of the vehicle to escape the hit. A terrified Mary Jo inadvertently drove off the bridge alone. Kennedy never knew about Mary Jo's death until advised by ferry operators late the next morning. Willis finds Kennedy not only blameless for his actions but a true American hero for assuming responsibility for something he did not do, and argues that Gargan, Markham, and all government figures who were involved in the immediate aftermath have been cruelly maligned by Republicans using underhanded Gestapo tactics.

A documentary released by the BBC in 1994, called *Chappaquiddick*, is Olsen's story with a tweak to the timeline. Kennedy first heard about the accident when he met up with Gargan and Markham at the Shiretown Inn at 8:00 a.m.

On publication of *Senatorial Privilege: The Chappaquiddick Cover-up* in 1988, Leo Damore revealed that Olsen, the original inventor of the Kennedy-was-not-the-driver hypothesis (and by extension, every one of the variants that had spun off from it), had been fed his theory by Bernie Flynn, a state police detective, who had worked behind the scenes as a spy for Kennedy's lawyers throughout the period leading up to the Kopechne exhumation and inquest proceedings.

Kennedy's story is true

Like Olsen, Reybold, Willis, and the BBC, the authors of *Chappaquiddick: The Real Story* insist that Kennedy was given a bum rap. Kennedy did drive off the bridge with Mary Jo after being observed by Look but claimed it was soon after 11:15 p.m. because he was confused, in shock, and suffering from traumatic amnesia. The memory loss also caused him to forget about Look's sighting. Lange and DeWitt suggest that between 11:15 p.m. and 12:45 a.m., Kennedy might have been holding Mary Jo's head as she was puking on East Beach from excessive binge drinking. They also argue that Markham and Gargan testified to the veracity of Kennedy's timeline so that he could not later be accused of mental instability.

Far-out conspiracy theory

In *The Gemstone File*, Bruce Roberts imagines that Mary Jo, fed up with Ted Kennedy's constant use of paid assassins to murder political enemies, told him she would spill the beans to consumer advocate Ralph Nader. Nevertheless, she agreed to Kennedy's offer of a ride to the ferry landing and climbed into the back seat of the Oldsmobile. Arriving at the Dike intersection, Kennedy took off down Dike Road to avoid Huck Look. Distracted by Mary Jo as the vehicle approached the bridge, Kennedy backhanded her across the face, then threw himself out of the car before it went over. Mary Jo survived for several hours within the Oldsmobile, bleeding profusely all over the back of her blouse from a broken nose, eventually suffocating as the nose swelled shut. Kennedy was able to cover up Mary Jo's injury and other facts by enlisting the eager help of the Massachusetts highway patrol, the Massachusetts legislature, Dr. Mills, Chief Arena, Cardinal Cushing, the Pennsylvania mortuary, East and West Coast phone companies, the entire US Senate, Judge Boyle, and James Reston of the *Vineyard Gazette*. Bruce Robert's theory is justly considered the mother of all conspiracy theories, and if you subscribe to it, this book is probably not for you.

Kennedy jumped out of the vehicle

Teddy Bare: The Last of the Kennedy Clan is a far-right condemnation of the country's liberals. Nevertheless, the book is very factual and informative. Although

Rust never advances any concrete theory, he does suggest that Kennedy may have jumped out of the car before it plunged into the water.

Second passenger

A rumor circulated very soon after the accident suggests that Mary Jo, unbeknownst to Kennedy, was asleep in the back seat when the vehicle went off the bridge, and that no attempt was ever made to save her because neither Kennedy nor his *real* companion knew she was there. This theory proposes that the person seen by Look in the back seat of the Oldsmobile was a sleeping Mary Jo, and that Kennedy's real companion that night was Rosemary Keough, whose bag was found in the car the next morning. The theory was proposed by Ladislas Forago in *Worse than a Crime*, a book that was never published,[1] and discussed (and dismissed) in *The Ted Kennedy Episode*, *Death at Chappaquiddick*, *The Last Kennedy*, *Chappaquiddick Decision*, and *Chappaquiddick: The Real Story*. Donald Nelson has finally given the theory a permanent home in *Chappaquiddick Tragedy: Kennedy's Second Passenger Revealed*, published in 2016.

Joseph Kennedy

Another theory, accepted by some, purports that Kennedy took the blame to cover up for his nephew Joseph Kennedy, who was also sailing in the Edgartown Regatta that weekend.

Conventional theory

However, the *reasonable, conventional* version of what happened that night, as summed up so eloquently by Richard and Thomas Tedrow in *Death at Chappaquiddick*, goes like this:

Kennedy left the cottage at about 12:40 a.m. with Mary Jo Kopechne to drive down to Dike Bridge for a sexual tryst. Kennedy cooked up the story of leaving at 11:15 p.m., when the ferry was still operating, because had he admitted to 12:40 a.m., he could not have explained why he was driving with Mary Jo to the ferry at that hour.

More than a bit inebriated, Kennedy mistakenly went straight into Cemetery Road, meeting Huck Look who was driving around the corner at the same time. Backing up, and recognizing a police officer, Kennedy sped down Dike Road in panic, forgot all about the bridge, hurtled over the side, but managed to free himself at the expense of his passenger.

---

[1] *Chappaquiddick: The Real Story*, p. 77

Kennedy did not attempt to free Mary Jo. Instead, concerned for his career and reputation, Kennedy returned on foot to Lawrence Cottage for the help of his trusted companions Gargan and Markham, ignoring the lighted cottages along the way. These two might have taken a quick look at the bridge and the submerged car but also attempted no rescue. If they had, these strong and fit men would have been able to extricate Mary Jo from the Oldsmobile. Instead, they drove Kennedy to the ferry landing in the rented Valiant, then borrowed a boat to take him back to Edgartown.

Hoping to solve the problem in some fashion the following day, they were thwarted when the car was discovered by two persons fishing the next morning.

Inconsistencies

Unfortunately, the reasonable, conventional version does not account for the testimony of Mrs. Malm's daughter, Sylvia, who claimed she clearly remembered hearing a car go very fast down Dike Road in the direction of the bridge between 11:15 and 11:45 p.m. Nor does it square with the eyewitness account of an American-type car seen driving unusually fast to the ferry landing at about 12:30 a.m., when the ferry was no longer operating, just before Huck Look saw Kennedy's Oldsmobile drive down Dike Road about 12:40 a.m. Nor does it account for a series of telephone calls from Lawrence Cottage charged to Kennedy's credit card beginning at 11:57 p.m. Finally, it does not take into account the testimony of most of the witnesses at the party who said that Kennedy left the cottage with Mary Jo at 11:15 p.m.

Faced with these contradictions and with the impeccable reputation of Huck Look, a deputy sheriff, most versions have tended to side with Look as to the time of the accident and ignore all evidence to the contrary.

However, Carol's eyewitness account not only challenges the conventional version, it calls into question most other theories, too. Carol observed, through a large, squared-off rear window of an unfamiliar white compact car, two men in white shirts and a short, non-blond woman with short hair in the back seat, and a driver and probably a passenger in the front, race by her at 11:35 p.m. at an extreme rate of speed, then hurtle toward Dike Bridge *on purpose*. The only white compact car that could really have been going down to Dike Bridge at that hour and at that speed was Kennedy's white rented Valiant V100, which did indeed have a large, squared-off rear window. Moreover, *this was at the exact time Kennedy said he was diving in the water to save Mary Jo.*

Carol's account supports the Malms' testimony, earlier phone calls, Kennedy's timeline, and the others at the party. It suggests that much more was going on that night than most have suspected.

10
Author's Involvement

I have known my cousin Carol all her life. She and her brothers and sisters were very close to my sister and me, and two of her brothers, Barton and Peter, were my best friends when they were living on Chappaquiddick in the summer. Sailing was the principal activity in those days, and that's what we did. Carol's mother, Peggy, was my father's best friend when he was a young boy growing up on Chappaquiddick and the friendship continued throughout their lives.

I was one of the personal friends who was told of Carol's secret at an early time. But I was just not that interested. Sure, it was a mystery, but there were better things to waste my time on. Like sailing!

In the summer of 2013, my Brazilian wife, Raquel, only recently introduced to Chappaquiddick, became interested in the story of Ted Kennedy and Dike Bridge. She had heard about it while growing up in Brazil, but it wasn't something that really grabbed her attention. It wasn't real and immediate. But now it was.

So the questions began: "What were you doing that day?" "How could he have gone down that road by accident?" "Look at that current – do you think he really swam across to Edgartown?" "What do you think really happened that night?"

And inevitably, I became curious, too. So I decided to purchase every book that had been written about the incident. First stop: *Amazon.com*. I found most were out of print but eventually managed to find each book mentioned in the preface. The exhumation and inquest testimonies were out of print, too, and finding those proved more difficult to overcome. Several books had reprinted Kennedy's testimony, but I wanted to know what the others had said. A transcript of the exhumation testimony required a personal visit to the Luzerne County courthouse in Wilkes-Barre, Pennsylvania, and I finally managed to find a forgotten copy of the inquest testimony that was collecting dust in the clerk's office safe at the Edgartown courthouse.

And then I began reading.

And after I had read everything, had scoured the internet, and watched the 1994 BBC documentary called *Chappaquiddick* several times, I remembered my cousin Carol. So we all got together at a local bar in a restaurant called l'étoile in Edgartown where my nephew Andrew was a chef and Carol's daughter, Nika, had a part-time summer job as the bar waiter. Over a lot of laughs, I heard Carol's story all over again.

But this time I was prearmed with knowledge. I was convinced Carol was telling the truth if for no other reason than because her story was so utterly bizarre. No one would dream up a story so out of synch with what everyone else had assumed had happened that night.

But the drinks helped, and I remembered one book…

11
Kenneth Kappel

I n *Chappaquiddick Revealed: What Really Happened*, Kenneth Kappel, a former Associate Merchandising Director of *Life* magazine, analyzes the long, deep, vertical dents in both passenger-side doors of Kennedy's Oldsmobile as it was pulled from the water, the deep dents in the roof and the shattered windshield, and most importantly, the open driver-side window and detached mirror hanging by just one fastener from the otherwise undamaged and scratch-free driver side. John Davis, author of *The Kennedys: Dynasty & Disaster*, writes in the forward that Kappel's analysis was "confirmed by a national expert in the field of automobile accidents."[1]

Kappel argues that much of this damage could not have been caused by impact with water. Specifically, the dents in the passenger-side doors were deep and localized. Had the car landed partially on its side and partially on its roof, as has been generally believed, the dents in those doors should instead have been far shallower pancake-type dents spread out over a much larger area, just like the rest of the dents on the passenger side of the vehicle.

And what could have caused the mirror on the driver side to have been all but ripped off? The photos of the Oldsmobile do not show other damage to the driver side of the car at all – not even so much as a scratch. The chain pulling the vehicle from the water was attached to the left rear chassis, rolling the car over onto the passenger side before pulling it to an upright position. It seemed unlikely the mirror would have been broken off during the recovery process.

Finally, Kappel argues that no definitive skid marks appear to have been observed on the bridge itself. As Olsen wrote in *The Bridge at Chappaquiddick*, "Light scuff marks showed where the car had continued steady on course and off the right side of the bridge, but the wood had been damp and easily scored. No rubber residue had been left on the planks, and no deep braking gouges were visible in the sandy approach." The Oldsmobile had somehow managed "to go off in a straight line, plunging up and over the side of the angled bridge, almost as though the car were on a track, as though the steering wheel had been frozen into position."[2]

Unfortunately, the Oldsmobile is no longer with us today. The Oldsmobile belonged to the insurance company after it had paid out for a total loss. Edward Hanify, one of Kennedy's attorneys, purchased the automobile back from the insurance company at the first available opportunity. Jimmy Smith, Chairman of the Woods Hole, Martha's Vineyard, and Nantucket Steamship Authority and a Kennedy

---

[1] *Chappaquiddick Revealed*, p. vi
[2] *The Bridge at Chappaquiddick*, p. 257

campaign coordinator, arranged transportation for the Oldsmobile by ferry to Woods Hole. A wrecker brought the automobile to Plymouth to be gutted for parts, then crushed into scrap.[1]

Nevertheless, the photos tell the story, and Kappel hypothesized the following:

Kennedy left the cottage with Mary Jo around 11:15 p.m., as he and most of the witnesses at the party consistently maintained. Soon after, somewhere on the island but presumably to the south of the cottage toward the area known as Wasque (i.e., away from the ferry landing), Kennedy's car skidded to the right and slammed into some trees on the passenger side, turning over onto its roof. The accident caused the vertical dents to the passenger-side doors and damage to the roof of the Oldsmobile. Kennedy, gripping the steering wheel, was uninjured, but Mary Jo, sitting on the passenger side, sustained a blow to the back of her head leaving her bleeding and comatose.

By midnight, Kennedy had returned to the cottage on foot. He retrieved Gargan and Markham, and possibly a third individual. These drove the rented white Valiant back to Kopechne and the overturned car. Unable to find a pulse on the woman, with no medical training, and undoubtedly befuddled from the alcohol they had consumed, they came to the conclusion that Mary Jo was dead. But Kennedy was drunk and he'd just killed a woman. If they went to the police, he'd be thrown in prison. His presidential aspirations would be over. A scheme was hatched to preserve the reputation and career of Ted Kennedy: they would make it appear as if Mary Jo drove off Dike Bridge alone and drowned.

By 12:40 a.m., the Oldsmobile had been successfully righted somehow and the two cars were driving back past the cottage toward Dike Road, with the Valiant scouting the way. The Valiant got through unseen, but the Oldsmobile, with one of the men and the "dead" Mary Jo propped up on the front seat, was seen by Look near the intersection to the bridge. Spotting Look's uniform, the driver accelerated the vehicle down Dike Road to get away.

The Oldsmobile was rigged for a self-destruct by lining up the car with the bridge and tying off the steering wheel to the side mirror through the open driver-side window, a trick towtruck operators use all the time to keep the front wheels straight before pulling cars onto a flatbed. Mary Jo's body was placed on the front seat behind the wheel, and the Oldsmobile was accelerated over the side by wedging the gas pedal to the floor. Alternatively, the Oldsmobile may have been pushed off the side by another car, possibly Ray LaRosa's Mercury.[2] In the words of Olsen once more, the Oldsmobile took off "in a straight line, plunging up and over the side of the angled bridge, almost as though the car were on a track, *as though the steering wheel had been*

---

[1] *Senatorial Privilege*, p. 397

[2] According to inquest testimony, the Mercury was parked in Edgartown on the night of July 18.

frozen into position." The rearview driver-side mirror was a casualty of the 4-inch high, 10-inch-wide rub rail which caused the front wheels to wrench to the left when the car went over. Afterwards, one of the men waded in to retrieve the rope and anything they might have used to depress the accelerator pedal.

With a police officer a known witness, the original plan was changed. Kennedy, who was responsible for the accident, would have to claim he was driving the car when it went off the bridge.

Nevertheless, Kennedy procrastinated reporting the incident hoping, perhaps, that Gargan, his cousin, would take the fall for him, or perhaps hoping everything could be fixed by powerful friends the next day. But the car was discovered early the next morning and the rest is history.

Robert B. Cutler

Robert Cutler, in collaboration with Joachim Joesten, also arrived at the conclusion that the accident was staged using many of same arguments put forth by Kappel such as the deep door dents, detached mirror, etc. Kappel says that he arrived spontaneously at the conclusion that the accident must have been engineered after viewing the photographs of the Oldsmobile damage at Cutler's office in Manchester, Massachusetts, in 1982. After asking Cutler what he thought of his theory, Kappel was told that Cutler had already suggested the very same thing in *You, the Jury,* self-published in 1973.

However, whereas Kappel suggests the simpler explanation, Cutler arrives at a far more complicated scenario. Notice how Cutler describes some of the action that night:

"About 0020, the third man of C-squad, a reasonable double for Kennedy, orders LaRosa to fetch Gargan, gets into the back of the Valiant, and kidnaps Gargan and Markham at gunpoint; they are told Kopechne is being held for ransom and are shown Kennedy's wallet as an indication of K-2's intentions. About 0035, B-squad starts driving the Oldsmobile, with Kopechne 'out' in the back seat, towards the bridge. En route, they miss the right turn onto Dike Road, and Look almost becomes a casualty while trying to be helpful. Fleeing Look, B-squad hurries to the bridge and engineers the 'accident' about 0100. Meanwhile, K-2 has had Markham write a note to Kennedy for delivery by K-2 instructing him, Kennedy, to do nothing until Markham arrives on the first ferry about 0730. Gargan and Markham are released by K-2 with orders to have Kennedy at the public telephone at the ferry crossing by 0900 to talk about Kopechne's ransom."[1]

And so on. Whereas Kappel suggests that the dents to the passenger-side doors were caused by a crash into trees, Cutler imagines they were bashed in by a team of operatives with sledgehammers for no reason that is ever explained. Whereas Kappel

---

[1] *You, the Jury,* p. 404

suggests that the elevated alcohol in Mary Jo's blood was a result of drinking a few too many, Cutler imagines that Mary Jo was injected with alcohol and then deliberately murdered by B-squad at Dike Bridge. Whereas all evidence suggests that Kennedy spent much of the night by himself at the Shiretown Inn, Cutler believes Kennedy was drugged and the person who spoke to the innkeeper at the Shiretown Inn was a Kennedy double. Cutler suggests that all this was an elaborate scheme orchestrated by Republicans to prevent Kennedy from reaching the White House, and he imagines that it could have taken place on a sparsely populated, very private island and in the village of Edgartown at a time when even one or two strangers was an anomaly and worthy of gossip.[1]

Kappel uses Occam's razor to come up with the plausible explanation whereas Cutler drifts off into fantasy. Kappel writes, "With respect for Cutler's prodigious research efforts, this author feels that Cutler has veered into uncharted waters in terms of the final analysis of the mystery of Chappaquiddick. Cutler and this author have agreed to disagree."[2] Amen.

---

[1] Cutler's far-out conspiracy theory and many modifications of it, all with a political leaning, take up an inordinate amount of space on the internet. Many of these theories postulate such things as a mythical land bridge between Martha's Vineyard and Chappaquiddick to suggest how all this could have been accomplished.

[2] *Chappaquiddick Revealed*, p. 295. Cutler did, indeed, do a prodigious amount of research. It might have been far better had he left it at that.

12
Our Theory

*C*arol believed the woman she saw in the car passing her with, probably, four men at 11:35 p.m., was Mary Jo. Who else could she be? The car she had seen matched the description of the white Valiant rented by Kennedy, and Mary Jo was the one found in Kennedy's Oldsmobile the next morning. Carol had been warned that had she revealed what she saw she could be killed. Faced with that threat, and not realizing the significance of the hair color or its length, Carol assumed the woman she saw in that car – Mary Jo – had been assassinated by these four men and for the past 45 years she has lived with that belief, and with the fear.

However, Look saw Kennedy's Oldsmobile with a male driver and a woman sitting next to him in the front seat between 12:40 and 12:45 a.m., more than an hour later. Either Mary Jo was seen two different times; these were two different women; neither woman seen by the two eyewitnesses was Mary Jo; or one or both are lying.

Assuming Carol was correct – that Mary Jo was indeed assassinated – and assuming with confidence that both Carol and Look were telling the truth, is there some way to imagine how the pieces of the puzzle could fit together?

Mary Jo was a member of Robert Kennedy's staff. After his assassination she was tasked with organizing and cataloging his files. An hypothesis has been made that Mary Jo may have discovered something sensitive. After all, Robert Kennedy was Attorney General of the United States, charged with prosecuting organized crime. Ted Kennedy was given this sensitive information in confidence, but the Kopechne discovery was so explosive that Mary Jo was marked for death.[1]

It isn't too difficult to imagine what that information might have been. President John Kennedy was also assassinated, and many have suspected that there was more going on that day in Dallas than has ever come to light. Perhaps the remote island of Chappaquiddick was chosen for the party, rather than a more likely location on Katama Shores at South Beach on the Vineyard "the way Gargan wanted,"[2] to effect the plan.

Others have suggested that Mary Jo might have learned something incriminating from Nancy Tyler, one of her roommates in Washington, D.C., who was Bobby Baker's personal secretary. Baker was investigated in 1963 for allegations of congressional bribery using cash and arranged sexual favors in exchange for government contracts. According to rumor, Attorney General Robert Kennedy was able to persuade FBI Director J. Edgar Hoover to limit Senate investigation of Baker

---

[1] *Left to Die*, p. 20; see also *The Gemstone File*, p. 77.
[2] *Senatorial Privilege*, p. 96

by promising Hoover job security and allowing him free rein to proceed with wiretaps on Martin Luther King.

Tyler died in a private plane crash in 1965 which some have labeled suspicious. As early as July 31, 1969, Penn Jones Jr. wrote in the *Midlothian Mirror* of Midlothian, Texas, "Now both Miss Tyler and Miss Kopechne have died strangely. We think it quite possible that Senator Kennedy knows no more of what happened in his 'accident' than did Miss Tyler and her pilot who dived so mysteriously into the Atlantic Ocean."

Perhaps the persons in the car seen by Carol were the advance hit squad charged with carrying out an assassination. The woman with them was one of these. With his people in place near the bridge, Kennedy went back to the cottage, picked up Mary Jo in his Oldsmobile with some excuse at about 12:40 a.m., and delivered her to her executioners. The car was then deliberately driven off the bridge with Mary Jo inside.

Conversely, the woman in the car seen by Carol was Mary Jo, she was deliberately drowned a few minutes later, and the woman seen in the car by Look was a member of a cleanup squad sent to sanitize the area by staging an accident. In this scenario, Carol must have been mistaken about the hair color and its length. Until that night at l'étoile, Carol herself thought something like this might have happened.

I do not believe either of these scenarios can be taken seriously. No hit squad with any sense would hurtle past another car and scream down a dirt road, advertising their presence so blatantly. Seeing a car ahead they would be expected to slow down, douse their lights, and wait for the lead car to make the turn and head away. Even if they had come upon Carol suddenly with no warning, why would they be driving so quickly? Forty-five to fifty mph is unbelievably fast for Chappaquiddick. And why would they continue to drive so quickly toward the bridge after they passed?

Instead, the extreme haste and disregard for caution makes it appear far more likely these people were on their way to attempt a rescue. Carol's observation suggests panic.

Moreover, a premeditated assassination would almost certainly never have been handled the way it was. It should be fairly obvious to anyone who has considered the evidence that the incident at Chappaquiddick was botched and bungled from the beginning. These individuals were flying by the seat of their pants and entirely preoccupied with major damage control in the aftermath.

The hypothesis

Let's assume Mary Jo was injured in a car accident while with Ted Kennedy, as Kappel suggests, but injured somewhere on Dike Road around 11:15 p.m. Placing a bleeding Kopechne faceup on the rear seat of the car, Kennedy walked and jogged back to the cottage to get the help of Markham and Gargan. These three then headed toward the ferry landing in the Valiant to pick up two more of their friends who were attending the party – a man and a women – who Markham and Gargan knew were walking that way. It was these five who passed Carol at 11:35 p.m. at high speed, heading back from the direction of the ferry landing to Dike Bridge.

The woman seen by Carol in the Valiant at 11:35 p.m. was one of the Boiler Room Girls.

Arriving at the scene of the accident, the group came to the reluctant conclusion that Mary Jo was dead. Mary Jo was left on the rear seat of the Oldsmobile, or perhaps inserted into the trunk, and driven back to Lawrence Cottage. At around 12:40 a.m., the Oldsmobile was driven toward Dike Bridge, encountering Huck Look at the Dike Road intersection. An "accident" was then staged at the bridge by angling the car to the right, placing a rock on the accelerator pedal, tying off the steering wheel to the driver-side mirror, and then accelerating the vehicle over the side.

Science

This, of course, is just an hypothesis. Maybe the persons in the Valiant observed by Carol were on a joyride, speeding down Dike Road for fun. Maybe the car Carol saw was not Kennedy's rental at all. There are a whole lot of maybes when it comes to Carol's sighting.

But what is remarkable about the staged-accident theory is that it is subject to proof, or disproof, by the forensic evidence. This makes it very different from all other theories which mostly depend on inquest testimony to make their case. Carol's observation gives us a motive for investigating Kappel's theory. But the forensic evidence should speak for itself.

This will involve a detour into science. Science is not a favorite subject for the average reader. But it is necessary in this particular instance, and it is the only way the mystery of Chappaquiddick can ever be solved.

Throughout Part 3, the author will do everything possible to keep things simple. But the reader will be asked to do her part by at least attempting to understand the evidence and what that evidence implies, all the way to Dr. Cross's three chapters near the end, and then to my final chapter in Part 3 entitled, "From Speculation to Certainty."

Along the way, the reader will find that many of the author's conclusions are disputed by John Farrar, the SCUBA diver, who asked that I include his strong objections to just about everything.

The author at Dike Bridge in the summer of 2017. Many enjoyable hours have been spent here timing the tides and currents and surveying the channel depths and bottom for this book.

PART 3:
FORENSIC EVIDENCE

13
Dike Bridge Channel

Tides

ℰ dgartown has a semidiurnal tide pattern, which means on average there are two high and two low tides each 24 hours, 50 minutes, 28 seconds. One complete tide cycle will occur about every 12 hours, 25 minutes, and the average time between a high and low tide is about 6 hours, 12½ minutes.[1]

It is important to remember that these times represent the average and in no case should be thought of as a rule. When asked at the inquest whether he knew how often the tide changed at Dike Bridge, Farrar said, "Well, of course, every 6 hours is the oscillation of the tide." But 6 hours (or more accurately, 6 hours, 12½ minutes) seldom occurs in nature. For instance, in 1969 there was a difference of about 6 hours, 50 minutes between low tide on the evening on July 18, around the time the Oldsmobile went off the bridge, and the next high early the following morning on the nineteenth; but just 5 hours, 35 minutes between that high and the low later in the morning when the Oldsmobile was hauled from the channel.

Tidal currents

Tidal currents are a whole different kettle of fish. A so-called slack tide, or more correctly, slack water, occurs when there is no tidal current in a channel; in other words, the brief interval between the moment a tidal current flows in one direction in the channel and reverses to the other.

It is a common misconception that slack water always occurs when the tide is at its highest or lowest. And most assume that when the current is running into a pond, the tide in the pond is on the rise, and when it is running out, it is on the ebb. But none of these assumptions are correct for inland bodies of water.

---

[1] In many places on the earth there is only one tide each day, and in a few specific places, such as parts of the Caribbean and French Polynesia, there is only a very weak tide of a few inches corresponding to the movement of the sun.

Where an inlet lies a fair distance from the ocean, slack water will lag behind the tide itself for a certain number of minutes or hours. In other words, there will usually be a significant tidal flow running into an inland body of water after the tide has peaked and started to fall, and a significant current that is still flowing out of it after the tide has bottomed and has begun to rise. In many places, the lag time is such that the very strongest currents run into and out of a channel at the extremes of high and low water and slack water occurs at the midpoint of the tide. This runs counter to common sense, but nevertheless, it is the way the world works.

Because the relationship between tides and tidal currents is unique to each location and depends on the shape of the shore and bottom it cannot be determined by any rule of thumb. Someone must spend the time to make the observation. Fortunately, in most places where the current and tide are both semidiurnal, such as occurs in Dike Channel, there is a distinct relationship between the times of slack water and the times of high and low water. When the basic relationship between the tide and current in these types of channels is established it will generally hold true throughout time, and the value can often be found inscribed on nautical charts.

Speed of tidal currents

For practical purposes, the speed of a tidal flow can be assumed to be inversely proportional to the midpoint between slack water. This means that a tidal current will usually run at its maximum rate midway between slack water and at roughly half its maximum when it is a quarter and three quarters of the way through its run. And so on throughout the curve. However, again what must be remembered is that because tidal currents in inland ponds or bays are rarely in synch with the tides, the relative speed of the tidal current will often have little to do with the state of the tide itself.

Tides and currents at Dike Bridge

I have spent long hours analyzing the tides and current at Dike Bridge for this book and have found that slack water in Dike Channel lags behind the high and low tide by 23 minutes. Slack water at the bridge occurred at about 11:30 a.m. on the morning of July 19, 1969. When Farrar testified at the inquest that the "tide turned" at 11:30 a.m. he was actually referring to the tidal stream, not the tidal height. At 11:30 a.m., when there was no current at all in the channel, the tide had already been rising in Poucha Pond and in the channel itself for the previous 23 minutes.

The tides at Dike Bridge lagged behind the tides in Edgartown Harbor by about 100 minutes in July 1969.[1] Comparing the tides at Dike Bridge with those of Edgartown Harbor on July 18 and 19, courtesy of NOAA (the National Oceanographic and Atmospheric Administration), the following is an accurate assessment of the relevant tidal and current conditions at Dike Bridge on the evening of July 18 and the morning of July 19, 1969.[2] The times have been rounded up or down to the nearest five minutes. I will refer to these values several times throughout this book.

	Max. Current	Tide Break	Slack Water
July 18		10:40 p.m. (low)	11:05 p.m.
July 19	2:30 a.m.	5:30 a.m. (high)	5:55 a.m.
	8:40 a.m.	11:05 a.m. (low)	11:30 a.m.

Consequences

The common misconception that slack water always occurs at the tidal lows and highs was on full display by the witnesses with local knowledge who were on the scene at Dike Bridge on the morning of July 19. When these persons were consulted as to the probable time of low tide on the previous evening of July 18, they placed it at "between 11:00 and 11:30 p.m., when the water was at its shallowest and calmest."[3] That timeline has led to egregious errors by numerous authors who have accepted it.[4]

Presumably, these local individuals arrived at their estimation of 11:00 to 11:30 p.m. by deducting 12 to 12½ hours from 11:30 a.m., the time of slack water on the morning of July 19. However, slack water at Dike Bridge, while certainly being at its calmest, could never have been at its shallowest. As a consequence, their estimation of the time of low tide on the evening of July 18 was off by 20 to 50 minutes.

Citing the times of high tide for Edgartown printed in the *Vineyard Gazette* for July 18 and 19, 1969 (the *Gazette* had not published the lows), Cutler estimated that low tide at Dike Bridge on July 18 was at 10:44 p.m., which is off by just three minutes; however, Cutler estimated the current flowed at its maximum rate on July 19 at 1:54

---

[1] The lag time between the tides at Edgartown Harbor and Dike Bridge varies by as little as 45 minutes and as long as 2 hours. In the summer of 2014, it was about 50 minutes.

[2] In 1969, lows in Edgartown on July 18 occurred at 0849 and 2102; and on July 19 at 0928 and 2146. Highs on July 18 occurred at 0310 and 1543; and on July 19 at 0350 and 1621 (NOAA). The times of high water in Edgartown, as found in the *Vineyard Gazette* in the summer of 1969, are 0313 and 1543 on July 18; and 0349 and 1619 on July 19, which agree with NOAA exactly or to within a difference of no more than 3 minutes. The *Gazette* did not publish the times of low tide.

[3] *The Bridge at Chappaquiddick*, p. 261; *Death at Chappaquiddick*, p. 50

[4] See, for instance, *Death at Chappaquiddick*, pp. 210-211; *Chappaquiddick Decision*, pp. 60-61; *Chappaquiddick: The Real Story*, p. 35; p. 45; p. 71; pp. 113-114, etc.

and 8:17 a.m., and that low tide at the bridge occurred at 11:30 a.m., illustrating once more that the relationship between tides and currents is poorly understood. The problem was compounded by Cutler's assumption that tides always turn midway between the extremes of high and the extremes of low – in other words, the common misconception that the tides always turn every 6 hours, 12½ minutes – however, on July 18 and 19 they decidedly did not. As a result, Cutler's tide and current tables for Dike Channel, painstakingly drawn with artistic curves and calligraphy, are hopelessly in error.[1]

At the exhumation hearing, Farrar testified that he arrived on the scene at 8:45 a.m. when the tide was "approximately one hour to one hour and a half before dead low." This would put low tide at no later than 10:15 a.m. As low tide occurred at the bridge at 11:05 a.m., and slack water at 11:30, it is no wonder that writers have been unable to get a reliable handle on the actual tidal and current conditions at Dike Bridge the night the accident occurred.

Channel bottom

Dike Channel runs for one and one-half miles in a north/south direction from Cape Poge Pond to Dike Bridge. I have dragged our family catboat through Dike Channel many times and have found that the bottom all along the channel before the bridge consists mostly of hard-packed sand intermixed with crushed shell.

The channel under Dike Bridge was dredged about a year before Kennedy's accident but has not been dredged since. When channels are dredged, particular care is spent making sure there are no large rocks at the bottom of the channel. This is because boats always try to keep to the middle of a channel and boat hulls of all sorts sustain damage when they hit rocks.

In a conversation with John Farrar in 2014, Farrar told me that there were no rocks in the channel where the vehicle was resting. At the exhumation hearing, Farrar said, "Well, as far as the bottom is concerned, it had just been dredged, it was hard-packed sand, sand, a combination of sand and mud, fairly hard packed, and the car was in a position against the far side of the channel, just where the channel begins to rise toward the surface." At the inquest he said, "The bottom of [the channel] where it was resting had some small rocks in it. However, it is ostensibly flat due to the fact that it has been just recently dredged, and the car was resting near the right-hand bank of the stream where the dredge had cut away."

I have dived on the channel and found that today, the dredged portion, from its western edge to the far east bank where the vehicle came to rest, is hard-packed sand intermixed with small flat rocks no more than an inch high. However, between the

---

[1] *You, the Jury*, pp. 364-365; pp. 392-395; and Fig. 2

western edge of the dredged channel and the far western shore, where the vehicle was extracted, the bottom is littered with boulders up to a foot and a half in height. This appears to be because the engineers who dredged the channel tossed any rocks they found onto the shallower, gently sloping western side. Once well past the bridge and into Poucha Pond, the bottom turns once again to hard-packed sand and crushed shell.

Depth of Dike Channel

Many books about Chappaquiddick and Ted Kennedy have wildly overestimated the depth of the water under Dike Bridge in 1969. Don Hastings, for instance, says the depth was 10 feet.[1] Zad Rust says it was 12 feet.[2] Lange and DeWitt claim it was 11 feet at high tide or 9 feet at low.[3] J. B. Shaffer says that less than a year before the accident, the Army Core of Engineers had dredged the channel beneath Dike Bridge from a depth of 3 feet to 15 feet. In *Left to Die*, Shaffer writes, "Of course, without the dredging the accident undoubtedly would not have caused the death of Mary Jo."[4]

I am here to report that it just wasn't so, at least as regards the depth. The depth today at mean low water in the middle of the channel is 8 feet. However, the vehicle did not come to rest in the middle of the channel. It came to rest on its far eastern edge where the channel slopes upward before encountering a near-vertical bank.

So what was the actual depth on July 18 and 19, 1969, where the vehicle came to rest? Inspector George Kennedy said he measured a water depth of 6 feet with his tape measure when he arrived at the scene. This depth is shown on Arena's accident diagram included with the exhumation testimony. Kennedy made his measurement at about 10:30 a.m., a half hour before low tide. Is that depth correct?

According to data sent to me by NOAA, the tidal range in Edgartown on the morning of July 19 was 1 foot 11 inches. When Arena first observed the overturned Oldsmobile at about 8:30 a.m. he said that the tires on the Oldsmobile were just beginning to break the surface. At 8:30 a.m., the tide would have been about 2½ hours away and about 10 inches from a low tide, and falling.

---

[1] *The Ted Kennedy Episode*, p. 4

[2] *Teddy Bare*, p. 255

[3] *Chappaquiddick: The Real Story*, p. 37. The authors also claim that the bridge was rebuilt "as a concrete-and-steel span with guard rails" (p. 168). In 1993, when that was written, the bridge was a partially torn-down wreck. The new bridge, built in 1994, is still wood, and there are no concrete or steel spans.

[4] *Left to Die*, p. 5

Detail of a photo shot shortly before the extraction chain was attached to the vehicle. The left rear tire protrudes into the air about 9 inches and the right tire 2 inches. Although the tide still has about another inch to fall, the level of the water in this photo would have been about the level of low tide the previous evening because low tide on the evening of July 18 was just over an inch higher than low tide on the morning of July 19. Photo Jack Hubbard

Now examine the photo above, shot shortly before car was towed from the water. The 1967 Oldsmobile Delmont 88 was fitted with an 8.55 x 14 tire, a specification no longer used today. Jim Crandall, a Massachusetts repair specialist and owner of a Delmont 88, had that tire and found that the sidewall height, from rim to tread, was 6 inches. Since about 3 inches of wheel rim on the left rear wheel is visible in the photo, that wheel protrudes into the air about 9 inches and the right one about 2 inches.

Assuming the tide had about another 10 inches to fall when the left tire was just beginning to break the surface, this photograph was taken when the tide was about an inch from a dead low. Nevertheless, the level of the water in the photo would have been about the level of low tide the evening before because according to NOAA, low tide on the evening of July 18 was just over an inch higher than low tide on the morning of July 19.

John Farrar's sketch shows the Oldsmobile resting on the bottom at a pitch of 13 degrees. Using basic trigonometry we can see that he got it just right. In the photograph, the right rear wheel is shown protruding into the air about 2 inches while the rear bumper behind it is just beginning to break the surface. With a distance of 47 inches from the rear axle to the rear bumper, and a 27-inch diameter wheel, the angle of the Oldsmobile at rest on the bottom was about 13 degrees, give or take a degree.

The left rear wheel protruded into the air about 19 inches higher than it would have had the vehicle been lying on its roof at a level position on the bottom.[1]

So what was the height of the Oldsmobile? The Oldsmobile Kennedy was driving was a Delmont 88; specifically, the four-door Town Sedan model with "B" pillar posts and window frames. The height of that car, from the top of the roof to the bottom of the tires, was 55½ inches, or 4 feet 7½ inches. So take off 9 inches to account for the rear tire that was seen protruding from the water in the photograph, but then add 19 inches to account for the raised rear end of the vehicle, and we arrive at an actual low tide depth of 5 feet 5½ inches on the easternmost side of the car where the Oldsmobile was resting. On the westernmost side the depth was 7 inches more, or 6 feet ½ inch. Inspector Kennedy's measured depth of 6 feet is basically correct.

This means that soon after 11:15 p.m. on July 18, when a 6-foot 2-inch Kennedy testified he dove repeatedly in the "deep" channel in attempts to rescue Mary Jo, the water immediately around the Oldsmobile would not have covered the top of his head. There could have been no more than 40 inches from the surface of the water to the top of the open rear passenger-side window, and if Kennedy had actually pushed his hand through that window, without ducking his head underwater by more than a foot, he would have touched Mary Jo's legs or buttocks. Nor would the "strong" current he said he experienced have existed, either. If Kennedy drove off the bridge around 11:20 p.m., as he testified, he would have landed in the pond just 15 minutes past slack water.

Final position of the Oldsmobile

There has been a general misunderstanding as to how the vehicle was positioned in respect to the bridge. Chief Arena, who was the first official on the scene and who sat on the rear of the car looking back at the bridge while waiting for Farrar and others to arrive, and then continued to sit on the vehicle during the recovery of the body, produced a diagram of the accident which was entered into the exhumation hearing record. Arena's drawing shows the vehicle angled at about 45 degrees in respect to the bridge, with its front end toward it, and when Gargan was asked at the inquest if "the illustration" of the position of the vehicle in respect to the bridge was correct, he said, "That is pretty close to correct. I would have the car even straighter than that, but it is pretty close to correct." When it was his turn to testify as to the accuracy of "the diagram," Markham told the court, "I think it was a little bit more of an angle, [but] that is a fair representation of it." Olsen says that the car had "rolled completely over, and the front end had turned through 180 degrees, so that it was facing almost exactly opposite to its initial path of travel."[2]

---

[1] The distance from the front of the roof to the rear axle in a Delmont 88 is 83 inches. Tilted 13 degrees, the rear axle rises 19 inches.

[2] *The Bridge at Chappaquiddick*, p. 125

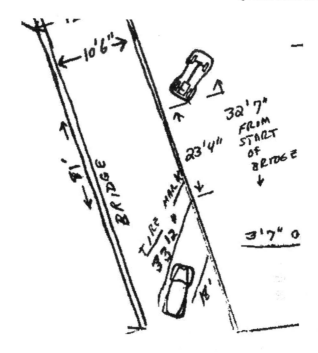

Detail of Arena's accident drawing entered into the exhumation hearing record. The upside-down Oldsmobile is shown with its front end facing the bridge, angled about 45 degrees against the incoming flood current.

Olsen's description and Arena's accident diagram have led every author who has mentioned the position of the vehicle to assume that the car must have somersaulted forward through the water before landing on the bottom. However, that assumption is incorrect.

At the exhumation hearing, Farrar told the court – three times – that he found the vehicle positioned "perpendicular to the bridge." And at that same hearing, Arena's testimony implies that the vehicle came to rest at much less of an angle than indicated on his accident drawing. "[It was] a bit of an angle, the nose of the car pointing towards the bridge, it was a very slight angle."

Farrar's description of the vehicle lying perpendicular to the bridge is the correct one. A characteristic of Dike Channel is that the incoming flood current runs perfectly perpendicular to the bridge, from one side of the channel to the other, and from under the bridge to far out toward the middle of the Poucha Pond. However, on the eastern edge of the channel, where the vehicle came to rest, the ebb current flows out of Poucha Pond in a south-southeast/north-northwest direction at an angle of about 20 degrees, as depicted in the photo below. This can be seen clearly from the bridge today.

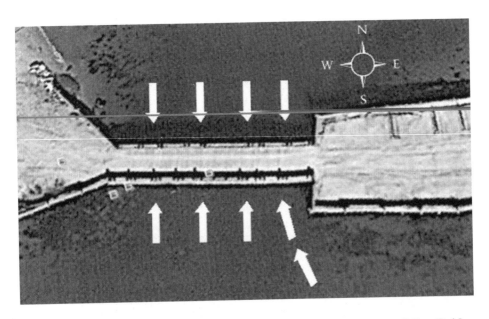

The incoming flood current (top row of arrows) flows under Dike Bridge perpendicular to it, from one side to the other and from well before the bridge to far out in Poucha Pond. The outgoing ebb current (bottom row of arrows) flows out of the pond perpendicular to the bridge from the middle of it to its western side, but at an angle of about 20 degrees in respect to the bridge at its far eastern edge where the vehicle came to rest.

Notice the photo at the top of the opposite page. The outgoing ebb current is approaching and running over the vehicle at about 20 degrees from the south-southeast, as it would if the vehicle was positioned perpendicular to the bridge at the eastern edge of the channel.

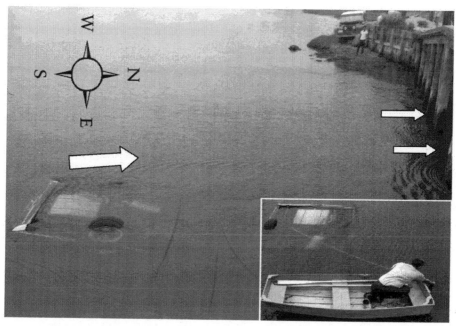

This photo, shot before the extraction chain had been attached to the left rear chassis (see insert), shows the direction of the outgoing current and the correct orientation of the vehicle in respect to the bridge. The current at the rear bumper of the car is flowing over the vehicle from the south-southeast as it does on an ebb tide at this location in the channel (large white arrow). Notice also that the vehicle is at the far eastern edge of the channel, well past the center span demarking the deepest depth of the channel (two thin white arrows). Photos Jack Hubbard.

Although the ebb current flows out of the pond at an angle to the bridge where the vehicle came to rest, the flood current flows into the pond perpendicular to it (large white arrow). Two thin white arrows demark the center span.

So why would Chief Arena assume the vehicle came to rest at an angle in respect to the bridge? The photo below is included in Arena's personal photo collection. Does it appear to the reader that the water is flowing over the vehicle from the left, or from the right? Many will find it confusing.

This photo shows Arena sitting on the rear of the vehicle as Farrar approaches him (bottom right of photo). The direction of the flow over the vehicle is confusing. Photo Dominick Arena collection

Arena may have been influenced by this photo before he drew his accident diagram. To a layman, the current might seem to be approaching the vehicle from the right rather than the left, an assumption reinforced by the deceptive angle of the car in respect to the perspective of the photographer. If one simply assumed that the outgoing ebb current ran perpendicular to the bridge at this location in the channel (and why not?), this would imply that the rear of the car was pointing substantially toward the east, as depicted in Arena's accident diagram.

Here is another photograph that is ambiguous. At first glance, the photo below would seem to confirm the orientation of the car as shown in Arena's accident drawing. However, once again the perspective is deceiving. Notice that the ebb current is flowing over the vehicle from left to right. If the rear of the vehicle was actually pointed toward the east, the way it seems to appear in this photo, the current would be running over the undercarriage in the other direction. In fact, if one simply assumed the current flowed out of the pond perpendicular to the bridge from one side to the other, which is the natural assumption, the direction of the flow would suggest that the rear of the car was pointing toward the west, *opposite* to the way Arena drew it.

Jon Ahlbum approaching the vehicle prior to attaching a chain to the left rear chassis. The vehicle is positioned perpendicular to the bridge, and the current is running over the undercarriage from the south-southeast at an angle of about 20 degrees as it does at this location in the channel. Although the tide has only about another inch to fall, it is still running out of the pond strongly because slack tide at the bridge lags behind the high and low tides by 23 minutes. Photo Jack Hubbard.

The fact that the vehicle came to rest perpendicular to the bridge, and parallel to the incoming flood current, does not mean that it landed in the water that way. When a sedan lands in deep water it quickly inverts to a near-vertical position due to the weight of its engine and air in the trunk. If the water is shallow, the front end will anchor itself to the bottom and the rear end will rise as far as it can.

Including the trunk, Kennedy's upside-down vehicle would still have about two-thirds of the air in it for at least 10 minutes or so, even with three windows blown in, and it had an exceptionally large trunk and heavier-than-usual engine. After landing on the water and striking the sand, the rear end would have risen toward the surface. Assuming the vehicle came to rest on the bottom at an initial pitch of about 20 degrees, and assuming the incoming current was running at just 2.3 knots at the time of the accident,[1] it would have pushed against the car with an initial torque of just over 6,000 foot-pounds, pivoting the car on its nose like a wind vane until it eventually ended up parallel to the direction of the flow.[2] When the outgoing ebb current began pushing against the rear of the car in the opposite direction, beginning at 5:55 a.m. and increasing to its maximum rate at 8:40 a.m., the vehicle would have been protected from much of its force by the near-vertical east bank of the channel. Most of the easterly component of the flow would have passed over the vehicle rather than pushing directly against it.

Relevance

The relatively shallow, 6½-foot predicted channel depth at the time of the accident compared to the oversize, 18-foot length of the car; and the absence of large rocks where the vehicle came to rest; expands and limits respectively the physical forces that could have caused impact damage to the vehicle.

An understanding of the correct orientation of the Oldsmobile at rest is equally important since it significantly alters the calculated launch speed off the bridge. A straight-on landing followed by a counterclockwise rotation due to the current would require a far lower launch speed to reach its final position than a forward somersault. A straight-on landing also leads to different assumptions as to where impact damage should expect to be found on the vehicle.

Temperature of water

There is one final error that should be addressed. Lange and DeWitt in *Chappaquiddick: The Real Story* base much of their conclusions regarding the timeline of Mary Jo's death on the belief that the water in Dike Channel is icy cold in the

---

[1] This calculation will be found in a later chapter.

[2] The calculation can be found in the Appendix, Note 1

summer, "bathed by the Labrador Current." However, the Labrador Current flows south along the Massachusetts coast, then is turned back at Cape Cod by the warm waters of the Gulf Stream sweeping up from the south. Martha's Vineyard and Chappaquiddick lie south of the Cape and are influenced primarily by the Gulf Stream The average water temperature off the Vineyard in July is 71 degrees Fahrenheit; however, the water in Dike Channel is even warmer than this because it flows into and out of a large but shallow and warm inland bay called Cape Poge Pond.

14

Burst Bubbles

John Farrar has always argued that a significant amount of air was trapped in the overturned Oldsmobile for a substantial period of time. This has become known as the "bubble theory." Unfortunately, the bubble theory does not hold up under scrutiny.

𝒥 he water level marked "A" on Farrar's sketch shows his estimation of the level of water within the Oldsmobile as it settled onto the bottom. Water level "A" is just above the smashed in passenger-side windows, and it is a good bet that line A is fairly accurate in this respect. The water would initially have been at that level, give or take an inch or two, as the car impacted the sand.

E X H I B I T No. 14

If the Oldsmobile touched the bottom soon after Look saw it, about two hours after dead low tide, the level of the water outside the vehicle would have been about at the level on Farrar's drawing marked as the "pond level" (the level of the channel when Farrar arrived on the scene). If the accident was rigged and took place later, the water would be higher. Either way, the water outside the vehicle would have been well over the level of the footwell when it plunged into the pond and therefore well over the head of Mary Jo, and rising rapidly with the incoming flood tide. The difference between the water levels within the car and outside it would have resulted in considerable pressure within the vehicle, forcing the air out through the major leaks between all three edges of all four doors and through the trunk. Although car doors and trunks are built to shed water, they are not designed to be watertight.

In the 1994 BBC documentary *Chappaquiddick* there is a very good film clip of a test sedan, similar to Kennedy's Oldsmobile, driven off a ramp into deep water. All the windows are tightly closed. The vehicle quickly inverts to a near-vertical position, nose down, and begins sinking at the rate of about an inch every three seconds. The air is escaping through those doors and the trunk at the rate of about 25 cubic feet a minute. But with Kennedy's Oldsmobile the air would have escaped far faster than this. The two passenger-side doors were badly smashed inward, creating much larger gaps at two vertical edges.

If you look at Farrar's sketch of the Oldsmobile in the water, you will see that the rear seat bottom extends forward of the trailing edge of the rear doors. This is made even clearer in the following drawing, traced from a photo of a Delmont 88 interior. The trailing edge of the rear door is about parallel with the seat back. The bottom portion of the rear seat extends forward of the trailing edge of the rear door 18 inches and rises above the rocker panel 8½ inches.

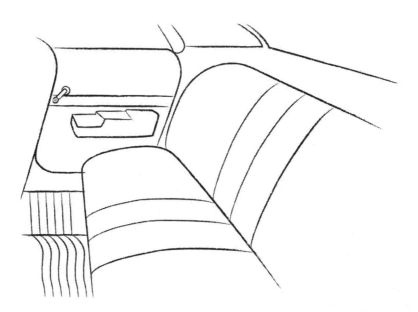

Trace of a Delmont 88 rear interior.

Now look at the trailing edges of both passenger-side doors in the photo of the Oldsmobile after it was pulled out of the pond. Those doors have been badly crushed inward and pulled back from the door frames several inches. Especially, a significant gap exists in the rear door from the bottom of the window all the way down to the rocker panel. This means that large quantities of air would have escaped very quickly through the entire length of that crack. The pressure from the weight of water outside the vehicle through the three open windows would have caused the water within the vehicle to rise quite rapidly until it covered that crack completely.

Detail of Kennedy's Oldsmobile a few minutes after it had been pulled from the water showing the deep, vertical dents to both passenger-side doors and large gaps between the doors and frame. The gap in the rear door extends from the bottom of the window down to the rocker panel. Photo Jack Hubbard

How rapidly? Assuming modest gaps two feet in length and one-half inch in width at the aft edges of both passenger-side doors, and an equally modest three-foot water column between the surface of the channel and upper window frames, the air would have escaped through those gaps at an initial rate of 118 cubic feet per minute, tapering off to zero as the water approached the top of the aft crack.[1] This does not include the loss of air from the lesser gaps in the other ten edges of all four doors or the drain holes in the trunk. Considering that there could be no more than 80 cubic feet of air in the inclined interior of the car after it overturned,[2] that's not a lot of time.

As has been noted, the vehicle came to rest at an incline of about 13 degrees. By the time the water approached the level of the rocker panel, most of the air would have

---

[1] The calculations can be found in the Appendix, Note 2.

[2] The interior volume of an Oldsmobile Delmont 88, from the bottom of the floor pan to the bottom of the windows, is about 103 cubic feet. Inclined at 13 degrees, the volume drops to about 80 cubic feet. The volume would be further reduced by the space taken up by the front seat.

escaped from the interior. But not all of it. The footwell in a Delmont 88 is four inches lower than the rocker panel, separated into two sections by a driveshaft tunnel averaging six inches in width. From accurate measurements, I have calculated that no more than 2,600 cubic inches of air could still have been trapped in the inclined rear footwell if it were airtight. That translates to 1½ cubic feet.

The inverted sketch below of the Oldsmobile's interior, tilted 13 degrees, shows the real state of affairs as it would have been experienced by someone attempting to cling to life that night inside the car. The only air that could have remained within the vehicle after about a minute or so would have been located in the rear footwell, or in the trunk. Of these places, only the air in the footwell forward of the bottom edge of the rear seat would be accessible to a person trapped in the interior.

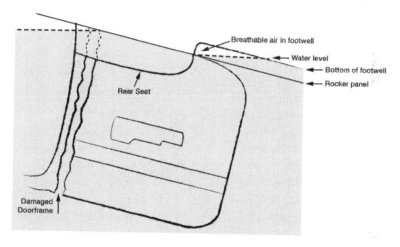

Sketch of trapped air in an inverted Delmont 88 rear interior drawn to scale, tilted 13 degrees. Once the water had risen to within a few inches of the bottom of the damaged door frame on the trailing edge of the rear passenger-side door, there would have been a limited amount of breathable air in the shallow four-inch-deep footwell forward of the bottom edge of the rear seat, separated into two small volumes by the driveshaft tunnel. The rear seat itself could not act as a barrier to air due to the large gaps between the seat and doors.

According to *Wikipedia*, the average person in a relaxed state breathes about one quarter of a cubic foot of air each minute. Putting aside the fact that anyone inside that car could hardly have been relaxed, it means that once the water had risen to within a few inches of the top of the crack in the damaged passenger-side rear door, Mary Jo could have remained alive for no more than six minutes before depleting 100 percent of the oxygen available to her.

Of course, all this assumes the footwell was airtight. That appears improbable as Farrar has said there was no air at all within the interior of the Oldsmobile when he arrived on the scene.

A Delmont 88 has two 2½-inch by 3½-inch drain holes in the passenger footwell normally covered by plates factory-sealed with liquid silicone. If those plates had been removed and then refastened in the two years the car was owned by Kennedy, perhaps to allow water to drain after a cleaning; or if the silicone seal was not strong enough to withstand the pressure of a three-foot water column; any air trapped in the footwell would not have remained there for long.

Farrar has a different theory. He believes the air in the footwell had leaked into the trunk over a period of many hours, and as evidence he says he observed air bubbles emanating from the vehicle when the car was righted and a mostly dry trunk when it was opened by officials on the side of the channel. As Larryann Willis explains, "Since the trunk was the highest part of the car, any trapped air [in the footwell] would have ended up there, which is precisely what happened."[1]

But even if there had been a large quantity of air in the trunk after more than 10 minutes or so, which seems most doubtful,[2] that could not be used as evidence that there had been air in the footwell for a significant period of time. Any air still trapped in a leaky footwell would have escaped directly into the channel, *not into the trunk*.

Compare the previous drawing of the inverted Oldsmobile interior with the two illustrations and one photo on the opposite page. As depicted on pages 2-30 and 3-20 of the 1968 Delmont chassis service manual, the so-called beam perimeter frame in a Delmont 88 rises *up and over* the rear axle and differential whereas the floor pan is positioned *below* and *within* that frame and ends at the forward edge of the rear seat.

And even if the rear footwell did retain its air for at least six minutes, to actually breathe all of it, at some point Mary Jo would have had to consciously duck underwater to clear the driveshaft tunnel separating the two sections – an all-but-impossible maneuver for a confused victim struggling against panic in a water-filled, pitch-black coffin.

Crash analyst Bill Fischer, after observing those damaged doors, came to the same conclusion in the 1994 BBC documentary. Fischer said, "The side doors were ruptured all the way down to the rocker panel. There is absolutely no reason to believe that an air pocket could have existed in the car for any period of time." The BBC concluded, "Bill Fischer's investigation has finally lain to rest the ghost of the air-bubble theory."

---

[1] *Chappaquiddick Decision*, p. 128

[2] There are two open 1-inch diameter drain holes in the trunk of a Delmont 88 and two other 2½-inch x 3½-inch drain holes covered by plates sealed with silicone. It would be most improbable that both of the 1-inch drain holes would be blocked at the same time in a two-year-old vehicle. It seems more likely that the trunk was mostly dry when opened on the bank because once the car had been rolled over onto its wheels, much of the water in the trunk had drained out of it in the meantime.

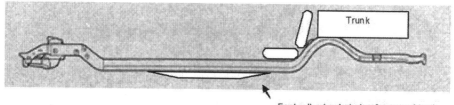

Footwell extends *below* frame and trunk.

Side view of a typical beam perimeter frame from front to rear, standard in most full-size GM cars from 1965. The design allows for a lower floor pan than the so-called x-frame.

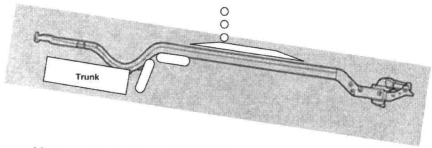

Inverted beam perimeter frame, tilted 13 degrees.

Rear footwell of an Oldsmobile 1987 Delta 88, similar to a 1967 Delmont 88, separated into two sections by the driveshaft tunnel. The floor pan is positioned within and below the frame and rocker panel and extends just to the front of the rear seat. Any air that found its way out of the overturned footwell would have leaked directly into Dike Channel.

15

Death of Mary Jo

The smashed in passenger-side doors of the Oldsmobile forever lay to rest the suffocation theory, at least as it was imagined by Farrar. There would have been no air in the vehicle for Mary Jo to breathe for more than a few minutes.

*A*t the exhumation hearing, Frieh said that when he embalmed the body he observed "a slight pinkish frothy exudate from the nostrils." At the inquest, Frieh said, "It produced water and foam, mostly foam." Mills said he observed a light pinkish froth exuding from her nose at the scene, and both Arena and Farrar said they observed foam at her mouth and nose. Foam, sometimes tinged with blood, is the classic indicator of a drowning.

Dr. Mills said he observed a good deal of water flowing from Mary Jo's lungs when he pressed on her chest as she lay on the stretcher. Farrar and Frieh, on the other hand, said they observed very little water flow, with Frieh arguing that the water Mills thought was coming from her lungs was actually coming from the stomach. A good deal of time was wasted at the exhumation and inquest hearings attempting to resolve this very point. The argument is irrelevant. In a significant percentage of drownings – *Web*MD, the online medical authority, puts the figure between 10 and 20 percent – a reflex action restricts the larynx and prevents much water from entering the lungs. *Wikipedia* explains it this way:

"If water enters the airways of a conscious victim, the victim will try to cough up the water or swallow it, thus inhaling more water involuntarily. Upon water entering the airways, both conscious and unconscious victims experience laryngospasm; that is, the larynx or the vocal cords in the throat constrict and seal the air tube. This prevents water from entering the lungs. Because of this laryngospasm, water enters the stomach in the initial phase of drowning and *only a very little water enters the lungs*. In most victims the laryngospasm relaxes some time after unconsciousness and water can enter the lungs causing a 'wet drowning.' However, about 7 to 10 percent of victims maintain this seal until cardiac arrest. This is called a 'dry drowning,' as no water enters the lungs. In forensic pathology, water in the lungs indicates that the victim was still alive at the point of submersion. Absence of water in the lungs may be either a dry drowning or indicates a death before submersion."

Moreover, bloody froth is typically found in the airways of a dry drowning just as it is in a wet one because the lack of oxygen triggers a pulmonary edema. As *Wikipedia* explains it, "In the case of a dry drowning there is no oxygen available in the lungs; there is only a partial vacuum. This partial vacuum draws some of the fluid from the vasculature into the air spaces of the lungs, creating a pulmonary edema, and the patient is now drowning in their own fluids. At the same time, the sympathetic nervous system responds to the emergency of the closed larynx. Among other things, it constricts much of the body's vasculature. This vasoconstriction increases the blood pressure against which the left ventricle must pump and may cause enough backpressure to ripple back through the left ventricle, into the left atrium, and into the pulmonary vasculature. This additional pressure on the blood in the lungs' blood vessels exacerbates the pulmonary edema described above."

Dry drowning

Frieh told the *Boston Record-American* in July 1970 that they were able to extract "no more than a cup" of water from Mary Jo's body. He said it was "conceivable that she could have died from breathing her own carbon dioxide," and when he was traveling to Wilkes-Barre, Pennsylvania, for the exhumation hearing he suggested to Mills that he change his finding from drowning to asphyxia. At the exhumation hearing, Frieh testified that he observed "a very little bit of moisture. I did raise an eyebrow, sir, in the sense that I was expecting much more moisture." Frieh appears to have been unaware that a limited amount of water in the lungs would be consistent with a dry drowning.

Likewise, Farrar told *Esquire* writer Ross Rosenbaum in their edition of February 1972 that water in a drowned person is measured in "gallons, not half a teacup." Quoting Eugene Frieh, Farrar said that a drowned person should be "full of water, from their assholes to their appetites." But, as we have seen, this is not always so. Some drowning victims are found with significant quantities of water in the lungs, some with very little, and some with none at all.

In most cases, just a small amount of water will enter the lungs in the initial phase of drowning before the laryngospasm kicks in. Although the laryngospasm usually relaxes after unconsciousness and the victim may subsequently breathe in a large volume of water involuntarily, in a dry drowning the laryngospasm is maintained until death. This prevents more water from entering the lungs. David Guay, Frieh's assistant who was responsible for much of the preparing and embalming of the body, was interviewed by the Tedrows in October and November 1975. Guay said they found "8 to 10 ounces of water in her body," or about 1 to 1¼ cups. To the consternation of the Tedrows who had accepted Farrar's conclusion that Mary Jo died of asphyxia, Guay told them that 8 to 10 ounces was "consistent with drowning"[1] – an opinion he reiterated to BBC investigators in their documentary of 1994.

---

[1] *Death at Chappaquiddick*, p. 216

Positive/negative debate

Farrar says Mary Jo had positive buoyancy when she was removed from the car. Because Mary Jo was slim, he believes this would prove she died by suffocation rather than by drowning. Farrar's conviction has been shared by virtually every author who has written about the Chappaquiddick incident. The Tedrows, for instance, write, "To reach [the conclusion of] drowning you must ignore the fact that the 'drowned' body didn't sink. If it didn't sink, it didn't drown."[1] However, while that statement might be correct if Mary Jo had been found in a lake or river, it is not necessarily true for bodies found in harbors, bays, or saltwater channels.

The specific gravity of a human body is very close to seawater. This means that a corpse will float in saltwater if the lungs are mostly full of air at the time of death. This will be the case in a dry drowning. Furthermore, the victims most likely to remain afloat in the immediate aftermath of a saltwater drowning are women, who generally have more subcutaneous fat, less muscle, and lighter bones than men. Considering that Mary Jo would have had a predicted aspirated lung capacity of about 15 cups of air,[2] but little more than a cup of water was found in her body, it should be expected that she would have positive buoyancy if she drowned. The corpse would have behaved in much the same way as any non-drowned body that finds its way into the ocean.

The same thing holds true for the extremities. All diving instructors know that whereas men's heavily muscled and big-boned limbs often sink in saltwater, women's lighter limbs typically float. This often can make it difficult for women to dive underwater without weights. It would not have been unusual for Mary Jo's arms to float up and assume a cocked position in front of her before rigor mortis froze them into that position. Likewise, the hand at rest, or in death, naturally assumes a cupped position. It takes continuous contraction of muscles in the wrist or a surface to keep a hand flat.

For the skeptical, try it yourself. The next time you find yourself in a pool of seawater, relax and exhale. Most will find there will still be more than enough air in the lungs to keep the body from sinking completely. If the body is oriented in a vertical position, the arms will float up to the shoulders, perpendicular to the torso. The hands will assume a cupped position – or, as Dr. Mills phrased it, "a semi-claw."

---

[1] *Death at Chappaquiddick*, p. 218
[2] A woman of Mary Jo's height, age, and weight, in good health, would have a predicted forced vital lung capacity (FVC) of 3.55 liters. See
http://www.dynamicmt.com/dataform3.html

Rear seat

At the inquest, Farrar testified that he observed Mary Jo's hands "holding onto the front edge of the rear seat. By holding herself in a position such as she could avail herself of the last remaining air in the car." However, the only air available to Mary Jo after a minute or so would have been located between the floor of the footwell and the rocker panel. Now look once more at the sketch of the tilted Oldsmobile interior in the previous chapter. Mary Jo would have needed to pull herself up into the footwell to reach that air, but there would have been nothing her hands could have gripped on the upside-down rear seat which would have helped her accomplish this. If actually true that Mary Jo was holding the front edge of the rear seat, she would have been pushing herself *away* from any air trapped in the footwell.

Farrar found Mary Jo's head pressed into the top of the footwell because her body was buoyant. If she had negative buoyancy, she would have sunk to the overturned roof of the car before rigor mortis set in. But this could not constitute proof, or even persuasive evidence, that she died by suffocation rather than by drowning.

Ironically, if Farrar is actually correct that Mary Jo did not drown, it would be a powerful argument for the staged-accident theory – a theory Farrar categorically rejects. Since Mary Jo could not realistically have suffocated within the vehicle, and there were no bruises or fractures to her head or body, it would strongly suggest she was dead before the vehicle was driven off the bridge.

16
Blood Trail

At the exhumation hearing, District Attorney Dinis insisted that the blood evidence discovered by Dr. McHugh forced the whole episode into a different position where suspicion of foul play might be reasonably entertained.

*N*evertheless, the blood found on the back seat of the Oldsmobile and on the back of Mary Jo's blouse – both discovered by the Benzidine test and ultraviolet light – does not fit with most theories, and therefore the natural response has been to ignore it or explain it away. The blood has been a thorn in the side of just about everyone who has tried to imagine what might have happened that night.

Blouse

In a radio interview in 1994, John Farrar said he thought the blood on her blouse might have come from the blood-tinged froth from her nose observed by Mills and Frieh, the undertaker. If there was air in the interior of the car for some time, and if her head was tilted back, the frothy blood might have flowed onto the back of her blouse and then have been washed away by the water as it slowly rose over her.

Farrar also suggested that the frothy blood might simply have contaminated the blouse as bloody water swirled around her after it rose over her shoulders. Dr. Mills suggested this, too. At the inquest, Mills was asked, "Expert evidence already introduced has indicated that the white blouse was subjected to chemical analysis and shows evidence of blood. Are you able to express a medical opinion [as to the origin of the blood]?" Mills replied, "Yes. [After a drowning] blood may be evidenced in the mouth and nose. Such blood might, in the physical efforts to avoid drowning, spread almost anywhere to the person's clothing."

Richard and Thomas Tedrow in *Death at Chappaquiddick* dismiss the blood on the back of Mary Jo's blouse as grass stains, acquired by Mary Jo as she lay on her back for the obvious reason, which also can be detected by the Benzidine test but take much more time to react.

In a later interview with the author in 2013, Farrar argued that the blood must have come from ripped fingernails he says he observed at the scene. If her arms were above her as she was gripping the seat or clawing the carpet in the dry footwell for an hour or more, the blood from broken fingernails might have flowed back down over her sleeves and onto the back of her blouse.

Joseph Flanagan, the Kopechnes' lawyer, suggested that the blood may have come from a wound sustained from a blow to the back of Mary Jo's head or from slivers of shattered glass as the car hit the water.[1]

Lange and DeWitt note that Mary Jo was laid on her back on a stretcher after she was removed from the water. They suggest that the stains on her blouse could have occurred after blood from her nose and mouth had saturated the stretcher. Willis thought so, too. "It is obvious from the location of the bloodstains on the blouse that the bloody water and foam which was expelled when Dr. Mills pressed on her chest ran out of her mouth and nose, down her neck, and onto the back of the blouse and sleeve, the only logical place for it to go."[2]

Kennedy's lawyers appear to have attempted to introduce blood into the car by claiming that Gargan had injured his arms as he was trying to extricate himself from the Oldsmobile after swimming into it. Like Farrar and Mills, they also suggested that the blood might have come from the blood-tinged froth observed exuding from Mary Jo's nose as the water in the car swirled around her.

Let's first dispense with the grass stains.

The grass stains can be ruled out. Attorney Joseph Flanagan, representing the Kopechne family at the exhumation hearing, had no success at all in impeaching Dr. McHugh's credibility as to the technique used to determine that these were, irrefutably, bloodstains rather than citrus stains. In fact, the Benzidine test can be used to determine the presence of many other substances: certain chemicals, oxidants, paints, etc. Investigators are trained to know the difference. McHugh also testified at the inquest two months later that the stains were reddish-brown under ultraviolet light whereas the stains would appear as greenish-brown if they were due to a chlorophyll-based substance. By that time, Kennedy's lawyers had abandoned all thought of questioning his judgment.

Dr. McHugh was not just anyone – he was the Director of the Massachusetts State Police Crime Lab with many hundreds of hours performing the Benzidine test in connection with the most serious crimes in Massachusetts, and a lawyer, too. At the time of his death in 2008 at age 89, McHugh had spent 41 years with the crime lab and 22 as Director and was the senior chemist for a lab that developed techniques to detect the presence of performance-altering drugs. He had examined evidence in many high-profile cases including the Boston Strangler and countless felonies related to organized crime. Kennedy's accident qualified as one of the most delicate of his career. The testimony at the exhumation hearing describing the time and methods used to examine the clothing were precise, correct, and irrefutable.

---

[1] *Senatorial Privilege*, p. 306
[2] *Chappaquiddick Decision*, pp. 148-149

Moreover, one must remember that there were very few lawns, as such, on Chappaquiddick in 1969. The ground on Chappaquiddick was and still is generally covered with poison ivy and infested with voracious mosquitoes and ticks. Esther Newberg, one of the Boiler Room Girls, testified at the inquest that the party had moved inside at an early hour because of the bugs. It would make absolutely no sense for Mary Jo to have voluntarily laid on her back on Chappaquiddick vegetation for any reason, and if a romantic interlude was on her mind, there were far better places to do it, such as in a car or on a beach.

The blood-tinged froth seen exuding from her nose, (alleged) broken fingernails, or a blow or cut to the head when the vehicle hit the water can be ruled out, too.

Dr. McHugh said he found bloodstains on the back of her blouse extending from the collar all the way down the back of the blouse and back of both sleeves. For blood to have flowed and then settled onto these areas long enough to have created stains, Mary Jo would have to be sitting upright in the Oldsmobile within an extensive air pocket for a significant period of time. But as we have seen in a previous chapter, that could not happen.

Dr. McHugh also testified that unusually strong Benzidine reactions were obtained on the outside rear collar area of the shirt. McHugh said that the bloodstains on the inside of the collar were far less pronounced. This would certainly rule out froth from her nose and broken fingernails. Even if Farrar was correct about his bubble theory, blood from these areas would have trickled down her neck or arms and first saturated the inside of the collar, if they reached the collar at all.

McHugh: The maximum amount or the maximum reaction to Benzidine is in this collar area here.
Q: Are you pointing to the outside of that collar?
McHugh: Yes, the outside as it fits on; as it would fit in the normal position.
Q: As it is worn?
McHugh: That's right.

Nor is it likely that blood-tinged froth – the theory accepted by most – could have accounted for the sheer quantity of blood necessary to stain the collar, entire back of the blouse, and both sleeves. At the exhumation hearing, Dr. McHugh said, "On the back part of the blouse you pick up positive Benzidine tests *all over* the back part, including the back of both sleeves." But when it was his turn to testify, Dr. Mills said, "I did not see any blood, not in the sense that you call 'blood.' There was a little cobweb of blood in the foam *which was barely visible; it was so very fine*, and it went directly to a little capillary area just on the left-hand edge of the nostril." Frieh said, "There was a *slight* bit of moisture, but *very slight*, and a slight bit of froth around the nasal area, and it was of a *pinkish hue*."

Willis, Lange, and DeWitt argued that the blood stains must have occurred as Dr. Mills pressed on her chest and water poured out of her mouth as Mary Jo lay on her back on the stretcher. In a 1995 article for the Midwest Association of Technical Accident Investigators (MATAI), accident specialist Bill Fischer, who had appeared in the 1994 BBC documentary *Chappaquiddick*, came to the same conclusion. It's a reasonable theory on the face of it, but if the exhumation testimony had been examined closely, they would have seen that this possibility had already been painstakingly explored by Joseph Flanagan, attorney for the Kopechnes. The theory was discredited so thoroughly that Kennedy's lawyers never introduced it at the inquest three months later.

At the exhumation hearing, Mills said that Mary Jo's arms were "rigidly extended" out in front of her making it "difficult to turn her completely over." He said, "Her body was as solid as stone. She was in 'this position.' " The court explained, "The doctor has raised his hands above his shoulders." So, if the arms were raised and extended out in front of her while Mary Jo was lying on her back on the stretcher, how could the back of both sleeves be stained with blood all the way up to the cuffs?

So Flanagan asked Mills if he had rolled her over onto her sides. Mills said he had rolled her body very briefly to "one side" to examine her back. "I did not roll it over on its stomach," explained Mills. Flanagan wondered if Mills might have forgotten that he had rolled the body onto both sides, but Mills said no, it was just one side. Flanagan continued to wonder if Mills might have forgotten that he had rolled the body onto both sides, but Mills continued to insist it was one side. When an exasperated Flanagan finally asked what side he had tilted it to, Mills replied, "I tipped it over on its left side." But Dr. McHugh then testified that bloodstains were found on both sleeves, and, moreover, that it was the *back* of those sleeves and the *back* of the blouse that were stained. The sides of the blouse and sleeves had no stains at all. This was particularly emphasized by Dr. Melvin Topjian, assistant to Dr. McHugh.

This testimony proves that if the stains on both sleeves had occurred as Mary Jo was lying on her back, they must have occurred before rigor mortis, and while both arms were lying at her side.

At the inquest three months later, perhaps out of desperation, Dr. Mills and Kennedy's lawyers argued that the stains must have occurred as Mary Jo lay submerged in swirling water contaminated by blood. Farrar has suggested this, too. But it should have been fairly obvious to these learned individuals that any blood that contaminated the water inside the vehicle, for whatever reason, would have contaminated all areas of the blouse covered by the water, not just the back. Or at least it should have been obvious to anyone who was not trying to find a reason to explain the blood evidence away. Blood contamination in the water would also have permeated the slacks and other articles of her clothing. Even in the unlikely event that blood had remained on the surface of the water at level "A" in Farrar's sketch for a period of time, with Mary Jo lying back on that surface in some fashion, traces of blood should also have been found on the back of her slacks at her seat and calves or at the top of her knees. But neither the front nor sides of the blouse nor the slacks nor bra nor sandals had any blood trace at all.

At the exhumation hearing, Dr. Topjian was asked,

Q: Do I understand your testimony, Doctor, that generally speaking, the front of the blouse tested negatively?
Topjian: That's right.
Q: Now, whether or not you submitted the other articles which are numbered, specifically, the dark slacks and the bra and the sandals to the same tests?
Topjian: I did sir.
Q: Would you tell the court what the test or tests were?
Topjian: I examined them under visible and ultraviolet light and nothing of evidential value was detected.

At the inquest, McHugh was asked,

Q: All right. Did you examine any other items?
McHugh: All of the tests on the submitted clothing [other than the back of the blouse and both sleeves] were negative.

Rear seat

Following extraction from the water, the Oldsmobile was towed to the Depot gas station in Edgartown near the head of Main Street. In the four days it remained there, Olsen says that looters stripped the car of the gas cap, the Oldsmobile medallion, door locks and handles, armrests, dashboard knobs, windshield wipers, heater cowling, gas pedal pad, the windshield visor, and some pieces of shattered windshield and chrome trim.[1] Damore adds three ashtrays and the radio.[2] Douglas Batten, who worked at the Depot station in those days, told me that three days after the vehicle was towed to the station they threw a tarp over the Oldsmobile to control the looting, but it did little good. Looters just crawled under it.

After four days the vehicle was towed from the Depot station to the secure compound at the police barracks in Oak Bluffs, where it sat for several months before finally being examined by Dr. John McHugh, Director of the Massachusetts State

---

[1] *The Bridge at Chappaquiddick*, p. 190
[2] *Senatorial Privilege*, p. 242; p. 281

Police Crime Lab. When the Depot tarpaulin covering the Oldsmobile was removed, Dr. McHugh told Damore he discovered fresh blood on the back seat.[1]

But was it really "fresh" blood? Dr. McHugh told Damore that he thought the blood on the back seat might have been left by one of the thieves who stole car items in the four days the Oldsmobile was parked at the Depot station, presumably after cutting himself on the shards of glass that covered the seats and floor when the passenger-side windows of the Oldsmobile were blown or smashed inward. "The trouble is, everyone had been in that car," explained McHugh. "They'd stripped everything off. Somebody had taken the radio, somebody else had cut himself." McHugh could be right because Batten told me he personally knew of a female friend who had cut herself removing souvenirs. But Batten wouldn't tell me the name of this person for personal reasons, even though she is still alive, and had no idea if the bleeding occurred in the back seat. Asked if he could find out, Batten said no.

Dr. McHugh appears to have assumed the blood was fresh simply because no other explanation made sense. When questioned by Damore, McHugh explained, "Obviously there wouldn't be blood after the car was immersed."[2] If Dr. McHugh had found some specific evidence indicating that the blood came from a souvenirs thief – for instance, if some of that blood covered shards of glass as well as the seat – he would have stated it, and Damore would have reported it.

To Dr. McHugh, it was clear that blood could never have settled onto a well-defined area of the seat after the vehicle was immersed in water. Furthermore, if Mary Jo had been injured after driving off the bridge, the back seat would have been on top of her. Obviously, she could not have bled up into the seat. But if Mary Jo was lying and bleeding on the back seat before the car went over the bridge, those arguments no longer apply. Because he could see no point, Dr. McHugh made no effort to determine whether Mary Jo's blood he had tested for alcohol and carbon monoxide matched the blood type found on the rear seat of the Oldsmobile. In 1969, such a test could never have proved with certainty that the blood on the seat came from Mary Jo, but it might have definitively ruled her out.

Gargan's injuries

At the inquest on January 5, four months after it was made known that bloodstains had been found on Mary Jo's blouse, Kennedy took pains to point out that Gargan had suffered deep, bloody scratches on his arms after he had entered the car on one of his dives and was trying to get out again.

---

[1] *Senatorial Privilege*, p. 281
[2] *Senatorial Privilege*, p. 281

Q: Now, how long did Mr. Markham and Mr. Gargan remain there with you on that particular occasion?

Kennedy: I would think about 45 minutes.

Q: And they were unsuccessful in entering the car?

Kennedy: Well, Mr. Gargan got halfway in the car. When he came out he was scraped all the way from his elbow, underneath his arm was all bruised and bloodied, and this is the one time that he was able to gain entrance, I believe, into the car itself.

At the inquest, Gargan testified that his back, chest, and arm had been "badly scraped" when he entered the car. "I reached an opening which I assumed to be one of the windows. I forced myself – I am sure it was a window, quite frankly – I got myself in. I went in sideways like this (indicating), and I got myself in and I began to feel around, feeling around, feeling around."

"Feeling around, feeling around, feeling around" sounds a lot like "mixing around, mixing around, mixing around." It suggests that Gargan's blood was thoroughly mixed in with the seawater in the interior of the car soon after the Oldsmobile plunged off the bridge. To Kappel, that sounded like Kennedy and Gargan were trying to account for the blood found on the blouse and back seat because they were aware of the real reason it got there. Before the inquest, neither man had ever mentioned someone swimming right into the car. Kappel wondered, if actually true that Gargan had even halfway entered the car from a window and was "feeling around, feeling around, feeling around," how could he not have touched or bumped into Mary Jo when she was found to be only 18 inches from the blown-in rear window when Farrar discovered her?

Look at Farrar's sketch of the Oldsmobile. When the car overturned, all the windows were below the seat backs. It would appear to have been nearly impossible for Gargan not to have touched Mary Jo's legs if he had entered the car and was feeling around, no matter which window he entered and even if he only managed to get partway in.

Gargan was wearing a short-sleeved shirt on the morning after the accident. Richard P. Hewitt, the Chappaquiddick ferry operator who transported Kennedy, Gargan, and Markham to and from Chappaquiddick between 9:15 and 9:45 on the morning after the incident, testified that he did not observe any of these men injured in any way:

Q: Do you recall whether or not [Markham, Gargan, or Kennedy] appeared to be injured in any way?

Hewitt: I didn't notice anything that would make me think that they were injured.

Registry of Motor Vehicles Inspector George Kennedy was with Ted Kennedy, Gargan, and Markham at the police station on the morning after the incident and was asked this at the inquest:

Q: Were you in close proximity to Mr. Gargan?

G. Kennedy: I was.

Q: Would you tell us what he was wearing as you remember?

G. Kennedy: He was wearing a chino pair of pants and a short t-shirt, sport shirt.

Q: Did you have occasion to see his arms?

G. Kennedy: I did.

Q: Did you observe any marks?

G. Kennedy: I did not.

James Arena, chief of police, was asked:

Q: In your observation of Mr. Kennedy, did you make note of any injuries for bruises?

Arena: No injuries. He just appeared to be very depressed mentally, but I noticed no physical injuries.

Q: To Mr. Markham?

Arena: No, sir.

Q: To Mr. Gargan?

Arena: No, sir.

Esther Newberg was asked:

Q: During any of the time that you have mentioned, did you observe any injuries that he [Gargan] had received?

Newberg: No.

Q: Was there any mention by anyone that he had received injuries in any manner at that time?

Newberg: No.

Likewise, Nance Lyons was asked:

Q: In your observations of Mr. Markham that morning and Mr. Gargan that morning and on the day that you discovered Mary Jo's death, did you observe any injuries to Mr. Gargan?

N. Lyons: No, sir.

Unfortunately, the Oldsmobile was destroyed by the Kennedys and Mary Jo's clothes were burned at the insistence of Mary Jo's parents. Neither can now be tested for DNA evidence – a test that did not exist in 1969.

Scalp wound

No scalp wound was noted by Dr. Mills when he ran his hand around the back of Mary Jo's neck to determine whether the vertebrae were fractured. When Frieh and his assistant brought Mary Jo's body back to their examining room prior to embalming, Frieh said he examined the scalp when he shampooed saltwater and seaweed from her hair. At the inquest, Frieh testified that he discovered no bruises or marks on the body except for a slight abrasion on a left-hand knuckle. David Guay, assistant undertaker, told the BBC in 1994 that they could find no injuries, not even broken teeth or broken fingernails. The funeral director in Wilkes-Barre found no marks on her body, either.

To the layman, this would seem to rule out any head wound at all. But the layman would be wrong. *Web*MD says this about head wounds: "Even very minor cuts on the head often bleed heavily because the face and scalp have many blood vessels close to the surface of the skin. Although this amount of bleeding may be alarming, many times the injury is not severe." Just a quick reading on the internet gives many examples of the tiniest of cuts on the scalp bleeding heavily. Mills's examination of Mary Jo was perfunctory and rudimentary, and Frieh was no doctor or pathologist. A small wound on the back of Mary Jo's scalp, covered by a tangle of long, wet hair, might easily have been overlooked, especially since no blood was observed on the back of the blouse. Neither would have been specifically looking for a small cut on the back of the head, just above the collar.

From Frieh's testimony at the inquest it is obvious his examination of Mary Jo's scalp had more to do with looking for fractures than looking for cuts. Frieh said, "I personally took charge of cleansing the hair which was impregnated with much saltwater and a little sea-weedage and things of that sort that we usually find on a decedent, and in so doing I thoroughly examined the scalp and manipulated it in my fingers to see if there were any fractures, feeling in my own mind going over a bridge of that sort and crashing there might be some fractures, but I didn't find any fractures."

Directly after embalming, Mary Jo's body was flown off the island by the Kennedys, and buried. The sad fact is, just two persons examined Mary Jo's body in the 27 hours it remained on Martha's Vineyard. One of these, by his own admission at the exhumation hearing, spent no more than 10 minutes dealing with the matter before heading off to attend to cases he considered more important,[1] and the other was not qualified to make a proper examination. Neither had any reason to suspect at the time that bloodstains would later be found on the back of Mary Jo's blouse and on the back seat of the Oldsmobile.

---

[1] Mills testified at the exhumation hearing that he spent "probably 10 minutes" examining the body; however, Mills upped this time to "10 to 15 minutes" at the inquest hearing. Mills had other cases at Martha's Vineyard Hospital in Oak Bluffs he considered far more deserving of his attention, including a woman who was about to go into labor.

17
Crash Analysis

ohn Farrar told me in 2013 that he observed the deep dents in the passenger-side doors, the crushed windshield, and the shattered passenger-side windows while he was extricating Mary Jo from the Oldsmobile. After the vehicle had been hauled onto the shore it was also found to have sustained flattened pancake-type dents from bumper to bumper all along the passenger side, fore and aft of the two doors, and deep dents in the roof extending from the rear window to the brim of the front windshield.

However, it is unknown when those other dents occurred. They might have been caused by the impact with water or with the sand, or they might have occurred when the vehicle was rolled over onto its passenger side and dragged over the bottom until eventually coming to rest on its wheels. Farrar told me that besides the dents in the doors and the shattered windows he had not specifically examined the rest of the passenger side while he was attending to Mary Jo's body underwater, and of course he was unable to observe possible damage to the overturned roof because the rest of the car was lying on top of it.

With the certainty that the passenger-side vertical door dents, shattered front windshield, and blown-in passenger-side windows, at least, could not have resulted from the recovery process, most have assumed that the vehicle must have landed partially on its roof and partially on its passenger side as it impacted the water. The theory, as expounded by the Tedrows,[1] goes like this: when the Oldsmobile plunged off the right side of the bridge its right wheels would have gone over the rub rail before the left ones causing the car to roll to the right. The vehicle collided with the water, partially on its windshield and partially on its passenger side, some 30 feet later. The impact from the speed of the car and the drop of about seven feet caved in the windshield and created deep dents in the passenger-side doors. The massive shock also caused both passenger-side windows to implode inward, spraying the interior with glass. The vehicle's momentum then caused the rear of the vehicle to somersault forward as it settled upside down on the bottom of the channel.

[1] *Death at Chappaquiddick*, p. 41

Passenger-side windows

Right away we can see that there is a problem with this scenario. If the interior was sprayed with glass by the impact, how is it that Mary Jo, Kennedy's passenger, was not sliced to ribbons when the vehicle hit the water?

Robert Dubois, a crash analyst interviewed by the BBC in 1994, said, "The description of the body [of Mary Jo] after it was recovered is remarkable to me; that the clothing wasn't torn; that there were no superficial injuries at all. I would expect at impact the passenger would be making contact with the door. Almost simultaneously to this the window on the right side is going to be fractured by the force of the water. I would expect the passenger on the right side would exhibit considerable evidence of injury."

Dubois explained, "When a tempered glass window breaks, it breaks into little popcorn-size pieces – very sharp shards of glass. When they hit bare skin they cause an effect called 'dicing.' The lack of any evidence to the skin is simply amazing to me. The only conclusion I can reach is that she must have been somewhere else."

Nor were there any glass particles in Mary Jo's hair. In a 1995 article for the MATAI journal, Bill Fischer, who had been introduced by the BBC as "one of America's leading crash experts," wrote, "In fact, in a 1994 interview, Frieh could not recall any glass particles in the hair which might have been expected from the small particles of glass imploding through the passenger window as the car struck the water."

If Mary Jo's uninjured body was an enigma, the absence of any obvious injuries to Kennedy was, too. On the morning of July 19, Chief Arena observed that Kennedy was fully mobile, bursting with energy, with no evident soreness and scratch-free. He found it very difficult to reconcile Kennedy's appearance with the accident scene he had just witnessed. Arena had investigated many accidents in his career. He wasn't a novice. And yet Kennedy had no visible bruises or cuts, was not banged up or limping – nothing. It did not add up. Kennedy had strode so rapidly from the ferry landing to the police station, even with a back brace, that Markham who was following couldn't keep up, and Steve Ewing's father, who snapped a picture of Kennedy, was not able to get much more than a blur. Kennedy was fit enough to (allegedly) dive repeatedly into the pond and to swim the Edgartown Channel. This never made sense to anyone.

Crash specialist Robert Dubois, referencing controlled experiments of cars being driven into water, spent much of his time in the BBC documentary explaining why it would be almost impossible for anyone to escape the overturned Oldsmobile without immediate outside assistance: the vehicle overturned, it was a pitch-black night, the vehicle was completely submerged, there was considerable current, the impact would have been tremendous, there were no seat restraints. Having "considerable expertise" in interviewing crash survivors, Dubois said Kennedy did not fit the psychological profile that has been built of other survivors of the same kind of trauma. For instance,

Dubois said that it would be very unusual for Kennedy to remember that he tried to find a door handle but then not remember how he exited the vehicle.

There is also the question of how Kennedy would even be able to find a way out of the vehicle in the best of circumstances. The driver-side door was closed and locked when first observed by Farrar. If Kennedy had actually managed to open and escape through that door, he obviously would not have closed it completely and then locked it behind him afterwards. Therefore, most have argued that Kennedy would have had to exit through the driver-side window – a difficult if not impossible maneuver for a person of Kennedy's weight and build.

To account for Kennedy's survival, the absence of visible injuries, and for his unconcerned demeanor after such an ordeal, the BBC had come to the conclusion that Kennedy must have stepped out of the car after observing Huck Look at about 12:40 a.m., and Mary Jo had afterwards driven the car off the bridge alone. Addressing that theory, Dubois said, "If [Mary Jo] was the driver, it is conceivable she could have escaped the type of injury I described, but if she was in the front seat [on the passenger side], it just doesn't make any sense to me at all."

Passenger-side doors

However, this raises its own problem. Crash analyst Bill Fischer told the BBC that when he first looked at the photographs of the Oldsmobile, the extent of the damage on the passenger-side doors "seemed to indicate that the car had been in a previous accident with a solid object." He said he was "puzzled by this and couldn't figure out what was going on." Why were vertical dents that deep found on the doors but nowhere else on the passenger side? However, Fischer said he sent away for the specs of the Oldsmobile and then analyzed the dents in respect to the vehicle's center of gravity. Fischer concluded that if the vehicle "hit the water dead flat, 'hydraulic shock' could have caused the collapse of the [passenger] side of the car."

Fischer explained that water does not compress. If the car hit the water absolutely flat on the passenger side, it could have caused the deep dents to both passenger-side doors but left the rest of that side relatively unscathed. In a computer simulation, Fischer shows the Oldsmobile rolling to the right as it left the bridge, then landing dead flat on its passenger side before sinking.

But if true that the vehicle landed dead flat on its passenger side with enough force to create deep dents in the doors and blow in the windows, the impact would have thrown Mary Jo violently into the passenger-side door wherever she was sitting. The two and one-half feet separating the driver and passenger positions on the front seat could hardly have made much difference in a car decelerating to near zero almost instantaneously, especially if no other person was sitting between Mary Jo and the door to resist her momentum or protect her from the deadly glass projectiles.

Huck Look

Of course, Huck Look would have observed the passenger side obliquely as the Oldsmobile drove away from him down Dike Road. Yet Look reported no damage to passenger side. Granted, it was a dark night, but Look's eyesight was excellent, he was standing only 25 to 30 feet away, and he was exceptionally observant.

But Kappel says he pointed out the passenger-side vertical door dents to Huck Look on November 23, 1988. According to Kappel, Look said, "I find it astonishing that dents of this depth were overlooked at the time of the accident."[1] If Look, who had observed the Oldsmobile before it drove off the bridge, was skeptical of Kappel's theory, it wasn't noted.

Look had testified that he observed at least two persons in the car when the Oldsmobile passed in front of his headlights into Cemetery Road, and this would mean his lights initially lit up the undamaged driver side. The Oldsmobile began backing up before Look had come to a complete stop. By the time Look approached the vehicle on foot its backup lights would have illuminated Look and perhaps diminished his night vision before the car turned enough for Look to observe the passenger side obliquely. Look's vehicle was facing the other way so its own headlights would not have helped. On July 18, 1969, there was just a sliver of a moon, four nights past a new moon, and it had set at 10:22 p.m. Carol says it was "scary dark" by 11:35 p.m. on July 18, and of course the Oldsmobile was black.

Massachusetts State Department of Public Safety Laboratory

Perhaps the police, who had much more to work with than a few photos, might have viewed the passenger-side doors with suspicion, too. The *Boston Herald Traveler* reported on January 7, 1970, that Dr. McHugh of the Massachusetts State Department of Public Safety Laboratory had brought two doors from the Oldsmobile to the inquest. "A state police station wagon became the center of interest for many of the 200 reporters on the island. In the back section were two car doors from Kennedy's car that went off Dike Bridge. The doors were partly covered with burlap bags." According to the *New York Times* in their March 12, 1980, series on Chappaquiddick, Assistant District Attorney Fernandes attempted to introduce the doors into the inquest record but was overruled by Judge Boyle.

Now, the reasonable question to ask is, why in the world would Dr. McHugh bring two doors from the Oldsmobile to the inquest? Zad Rust in *Teddy Bare: The Last of the Kennedy Clan*, suggests that one of the doors "could not have been anything else than the left front door of the Kennedy Oldsmobile, brought there presumably as an important exhibit... to answer the nagging question: could the senator, given his

[1] *Chappaquiddick Revealed*, p. 221

corpulence and the circumstances, have gotten out of the submerged car by the only exit available to him, this door's window?"[1] OK, perhaps. But that theory does not account for the second door. *Why bring two doors to the inquest?*

In fact, it is obvious from the inquest testimony that the doors Fernandes planned to introduce into evidence were the passenger-side doors, and that it was all about the dents. Fernandes asked Farrar, "Could you tell us again with respect to particularly the windows and doors, did you make any observations?" After Farrar related his observations, Fernandes said, "Tell us about the right doors: the front seat passenger's and the back seat passenger's side." After Farrar's answer, Fernandes again asked Farrar to relate his observations about the vehicle damage: "damage to the doors *particularly*." It was probably after Farrar's testimony that Fernandes attempted to introduce the passenger-side doors into evidence but was overruled by a judge with a different agenda.

Center of gravity

Bill Fischer said he arrived at the conclusion that the crushed doors could have been caused by impact on water after analyzing the dents in respect to the vehicle's "center of gravity." However, the Oldsmobile's center of gravity would have absolutely no influence on the outcome. The drag force equations determining the impact force on an object landing on a fluid make no reference to an object's balance point, or even its weight.[2] Instead, it is the entire surface making contact with the fluid at a particular angle and at a particular velocity that determines what that force will be. Of course, to hit the water dead flat, the vehicle would have been rotating forward around its lateral axis very slowly as it made impact because the bridge sloped upward at five degrees. But the forward rotation would have been around its center of mass (i.e., gravity), which was located very close to the two doors. This means that the passenger side of the car toward the front would have impacted the water with slightly greater force since the impact velocity was a bit higher there, and the rear with slightly less, but the net effect of rotation on the doors themselves would have been exactly zero.

Could the impact on water have been sufficient to cause the damage to the passenger-side doors and windows, even if the car hit the water dead flat? That is a physics question that will wait for a further chapter.

---

[1] *Teddy Bare*, p. 156; p. 218.

[2] The total force on an object descending through a fluid is equal to the drag force against the object plus the buoyant force pushing up less the gravitational force pulling down. However, the initial impact force is equal to just the drag force, which is independent of the object's mass.

Dented roof

Dr. Cross, a physicist and accident specialist who will be introduced later, spent almost two years analyzing the skid marks and accident damage at the author's request. Cross has concluded that the 18-foot vehicle knifed front first into the water at an angle of about 10 to 20 degrees while rolling onto its back. Water resistance, pushing up on the front end, exerted a torque on the vehicle about its center of mass, slamming the vehicle's roof against the sand six and one-half feet below.

The force required to create the roof dents in Kennedy's Oldsmobile was determined by mechanical engineer Raul Ochoa and can be found in the Appendix, Note 8. Ochoa found that it would require an impact force of between 16,200 and 21,000 pounds to create a three-inch dent in the Oldsmobile's roof, depending on where the force was applied – in other words, between four and five times the weight of the car on land. The windshield would shatter with a vertical force on its brim of just 5,780 pounds, which means that it was a victim of the roof impact. Ochoa's conclusion: "In my opinion, this high of a force was the result of an impact with solid ground/dirt/sand from a crash event. This damage was not a result of extracting the car from the water."

The paint scratches at the very front of the roof (left photo) probably occurred during the extraction process or when the current rotated the car on the brim of its windshield soon after impact. There is no damage to the front end (right photo). This indicates that the vehicle landed on the bottom of the channel flat on its roof rather than spearing nose first into the sand. Notice that the front bumper appears to have been pushed inward, but this is the bumper design of a Delmont 88. Photos Jack Hubbard

The roof is deeply dented from front to rear and the windshield is crushed. Dr. Cross and Raul Ochoa have determined that this damage could not have occurred on impact with the water or during extraction. The damage to the roof occurred when the vehicle impacted the sand on the bottom of the channel. The glass was stressed when the frame at the brim of the windshield buckled inward, causing the windshield to shatter uniformly from one side to the other.

Of secondary interest, notice the start of a scuff mark on the rub rail at the bottom of the photo, 18 feet from the start of the bridge. The scuff mark was caused by the vehicle's differential or gas tank. The two parallel scratches in the rub rail that precede the scuff were caused by the tailpipe, which in a Delmont 88 is slash-cut at a 45-degree angle at the bottom and exits angled downwards at the rear bumper just to the right of the gas tank. Photo Dominick Arena collection

But if the vehicle, weighing 3,970 pounds, struck the sand on its roof with a force of at least 16,200 pounds, it could never have landed dead flat on its side. With a dead-flat side landing the heavier front of the vehicle would have sunk to the bottom of the channel first. The subsequent impact on the roof could have been no more than the total weight of the car itself as the rear end settled at a slower rate onto the sand. Moreover, the final weight of the vehicle in water would no longer be the same as it was on land. The Oldsmobile would be buoyed up by a force equal to the weight of the water it displaced.

Fischer was aware of this problem. In a 1995 article for the MATAI journal, Fischer wrote, "All the damage could not have been caused simultaneously from a single impact as a result of falling from the bridge. A rational explanation has to be found to explain why the car was damaged both on the passenger side and the roof." However, not being able to imagine a rational explanation, Fischer elected to ignore the problem altogether.

Passenger-side windows

Crash analyst Bill Fischer argued that the deep, vertical dents in the passenger-side doors could have been the result of impact on water *if* the Oldsmobile landed dead flat on the passenger side. However, the absence of any dicing wounds to Mary Jo's body or clothing, the lack of glass particles in her hair, and the deep dents in the roof and crushed windshield rule this out.

If you look at both passenger-side doors, you will notice that the door dents are perfectly aligned with the side windows. So, if those dents could not have been caused by impact with water, then the side windows were smashed in from a previous accident.

The vertical dents in the doors are aligned with the side windows.

When side windows are broken from impacting an object on land they will not necessarily explode inward with the same force as they would if they were subjected to considerable pressure on every square inch of their surface, such as would occur on impact with water. In fact, a relatively mild blow can cause a tempered glass window to fracture on land. A sharp rap with a hammer or rock will break a vehicle's side window easily.

It is entirely plausible that the passenger-side windows blew inward from impact with solid objects while on land causing no damage to Mary Jo's skin or clothing except, perhaps, for one small sliver of glass that flew into the nape of her neck, right around the hairline.

Detached mirror

At the exhumation hearing, Farrar said the Oldsmobile was lying very near an eastern slope making it difficult for him to observe Mary Jo from the driver side of the vehicle. At the inquest he said, "The car was resting very close to the right-hand bank – the right-hand bank of the stream where the dredge had cut away, because I found it was difficult for me actually to look into the left front window." Farrar is skeptical that anything could be inferred from the detached driver-side mirror, pointing out to me that the driver's side was nestled up against the sloping bank when he first observed the vehicle, and noting that the vehicle was dragged across the bottom on its roof for a short distance before being flipped over onto its passenger side with the help of the tide.

However, a careful look at the photos proves that the mirror could not have been broken off by rocks or have become detached when the car was pulled for a ways on its roof across the channel. In fact, if accident investigators in 1969 needed just one smoking gun to point them toward the staged-accident theory, the mirror would be it. In hindsight, it seems amazing that no one has recognized this before.

Notice the immaculate appearance of the driver side of the Oldsmobile. There is not so much as a hint of a dent or scratch on this side. Other than the mirror, the driver side sustained no damage at all. Notice, too, that there is not a dent or scratch on the rear, rear windshield, or trunk. Photo Jack Hubbard

First, look at the photo of the Oldsmobile above. The driver side is unblemished. From this perspective, if you hadn't been told otherwise, you would assume the vehicle in the picture had never been in an accident. If the driver-side mirror had been broken off by a rock, this would mean that the Oldsmobile must have landed or been towed, over at least half its length, to within one to five inches of rocks on the driver side – not more, not less. Possible, but most improbable.

Now look at the mirror itself. The mirror has been pulled toward the rear, snapping the *forward* fastener. This would be expected if the mirror had been tied off to the steering wheel, but totally unexpected if the mirror broke off while the Oldsmobile was pulled backward out of the pond on its roof.

In fact, it seems impossible that the forward mirror fastener could have snapped during the recovery process. Therefore, either the steering wheel was tied off to the mirror, or the Oldsmobile settled upside down on the sand with the mirror pressed up against a rock.

Detail of the Oldsmobile's driver side showing the semi-detached driver-side mirror. There is not a hint of a scratch or dent on the mirror frame or on the door below, to the right, or to the left of the mirror. The mirror has been pulled backward, snapping the forward fastener. Photo Jack Hubbard

But notice, too, that the mirror frame has no dents or scratches on its upper surface. In the original photo, this is made far clearer than what the reader will see in print. This would not be the case if the mirror had been broken off by a rock. A mirror frame is not especially robust. It dents easily. The mirror appears to have been attached to the car by an exceptionally strong bolt – perhaps 5/16 inch in diameter. It seems impossible that a rock could have snapped such a strong fastener without leaving any noticeable damage to the mirror frame, or breaking the glass.

And not only is the mirror undamaged, but it has not even been pushed down. In 1967, vehicle side mirrors were adjustable by hand. They could be swiveled up, down, forward, and back to conform to the height and leg length of the driver. So, if a rock broke off the mirror from the top, why then is the mirror angled slightly up? Likewise, if the mirror had been broken off while the car was being pulled backward out of pond, why has the mirror not swiveled forward, and why is the glass still intact?

There is really no way to imagine how that mirror might have become detached by rocks, either when the vehicle settled onto the bottom or when it was pulled from the pond. Nor could it have broken off when the car landed in the channel. Even if the Oldsmobile landed precisely on its windshield or on its roof, the force of any water that might have reached the mirror would have twisted the mirror toward the rear and down, not up. Additionally, if the impact on water was sufficient to snap the bolt, it would have distorted the mirror frame and shattered the mirror glass, too.

In *Chappaquiddick: The Real Story*, Lange and DeWitt attempt to debunk Kappel's theory by suggesting that Kennedy could have kicked the mirror and dislodged it as he was attempting to rescue Mary Jo. But if the mirror was kicked from in front with enough force to break the fastener, why wouldn't the mirror frame be distorted? Why is the glass still intact? Moreover, the driver-side mirror in a Delmont 88 can swivel 360 degrees in its socket. If the mirror was detached by a kick, it would be quite a coincidence for the mirror to be found afterward in an almost, but not quite, normally aligned position.

Especially this would be true if someone had kicked the mirror from underneath or if someone had dislodged the mirror by standing on top of it, a far more likely way to break off a mirror than a kick from the front. The person's foot would have contacted the edge of the mirror frame before it was able to apply any pressure to the mirror post. The mirror should then have swiveled much further counterclockwise than what is shown in the photograph. Or, if the mirror was unable to swivel further because the foot had exerted pressure evenly over the mirror frame and its base, the force should have distorted the frame and cracked the glass long before the fastener gave way, just as a rock would.

In fact, let's take a look at that fastener. A side mirror's base is designed to change a leveraged vector of force on its fasteners from sideways (shearing) to vertical (tensile). Any force applied to the mirror itself or to the mirror post would have stressed the fastener along its strongest longitudinal axis. A common (cheap) 5/16 inch coarse-threaded (low) Grade 2 zinc-plated steel machine screw has a tensile strength of 3,900 pounds, or about two tons. The most powerful foot kick recorded in a lab by a fighter is reported to be a taekwondo spinning back kick which delivered slightly more than 1,500 pounds of impact force, or just three-quarters tons. And that was a kick through air, not water. It would take a significant force to have snapped off that bolt, far more than any normal kick or a person's weight could have accomplished even with a three-to-one leverage advantage, and certainly far more than the mirror frame, or the socket pin, could have supported.

But now imagine a vehicle rigged with a rope tied tightly between the steering wheel and mirror post. When the heavy car's front tires jerked hard to the left after contacting the rub rail obliquely it would have yanked the mirror post backward with tremendous force. The sudden shock could have *sheared* off the forward fastener without damaging the mirror frame, the mirror glass, or paint on the door (the computed force to shear a 5/16 inch low-grade steel machine screw is about 2,400 lbs, or 62 percent of its tensile strength). If the mirror moved at all in its socket, it would have swiveled upward. This is *exactly* what the photo shows us.

Update: In *Chappaquiddick Tragedy: Kennedy's Second Passenger Revealed* published in 2016, Donald Nelson says Farrar told him the vehicle hit a bridge piling as it was towed backwards out of the channel on its wheels, tearing off the mirror and inspiring "wild speculation in one book."[1] However, Farrar is hostile to the staged-accident theory, for reasons that are not clear, and never mentioned the vehicle hitting a piling when I questioned him specifically about the mirror and Kappel's theory in the summer of 2013, probably not very long before Farrar talked to Nelson. Nor can I find a report of the vehicle scraping against a piling in any book or magazine article, or in any of Farrar's numerous interviews.

Farrar's recollection is inconsistent with the evidence. If the mirror was torn off by a piling as it was dragged backward out of the pond on its wheels, the mirror's rear fastener would have given way before the front one and the mirror glass or the mirror frame could never have survived such a blow without showing some visible damage. The driver's side should show some barnacle scratches, too. But more important, the photos disprove it. Hubbard's collection of photos includes 12 shots of the vehicle as it was pulled from the pond. Three of those photos are shown on the following page. The driver-side mirror never had a chance to collide with a bridge piling, or even get close to one.

---

[1] *Chappaquiddick Tragedy*, p. 63

In the first frame, the Oldsmobile is dragged over the sand on its passenger side through the middle of the channel. The second frame shows the Oldsmobile at the moment it rotates to its wheels, close to the western shore where large rocks are found. These rocks appear to have been deposited on the far western side of the channel during dredging operations and can be seen from the bridge at low tide today. To this point, the vehicle has been oriented nearly perpendicular to the bridge, with its front end toward it. The vehicle then tracks directly back on its wheels over the short distance to shore, exiting the water about 15 feet from the bridge. At no time does the driver side, or the mirror, touch a bridge piling. Photos Jack Hubbard

Absence of injuries to Mary Jo's head

The accident does appear to have been staged. The vertical dents in the two passenger-side doors appear to have been the result of the vehicle sliding into vertical objects on land. But if the front windshield was crushed in by the impact with the sand, it raises another question: if a comatose Mary Jo was inserted into the front seat of the Oldsmobile before the car was driven off the bridge, how is it that Mary Jo sustained no obvious injuries to her head or to any other part of her body?

According to Dr. Cross, after landing on the channel's surface upside down, the vehicle would have decelerated from 18.8 mph to about 10 mph in the first few feet of water as it headed to the bottom. However, whereas the vehicle would have slowed substantially during its descent to the bottom, Mary Jo wouldn't. With no seatbelt to restrain her she would continue to move forward within the car at 18.8 mph. It would be expected that Mary Jo would have been pinned hard against the windshield, head first, when the car decelerated abruptly to zero as it impacted the sand on the brim of its roof and the windshield shattered.

This would be the expected position of Mary Jo at the moment of impact on the bottom of the channel.

When an unrestrained head is driven into a shattered windshield at even a moderate speed, accident studies show that there will always be cuts that bleed profusely. Tiny slivers of glass are driven into the forehead and other areas of the face or skull even though the safety glass itself hangs together on both sides of its interior plastic sheet. I can attest to this because that happened to me as the driver in a car crash in Miami in 2000, back in the days when I rarely wore a seatbelt. My forehead looked like a warzone, and although doctors removed most of the larger shards of glass from my head at the hospital, I was removing miniature slivers for the following year with tweezers as they eventually surfaced and poked through the skin. Even today there are a few that have remained behind. Chief Arena, who had investigated many accidents in his early career while stationed in Boston, must have realized this, too. Arena told Damore, "The windshield on the driver's side was badly smashed in. I found it hard to believe the senator had been in a major automobile accident. His face bore no traces of any marks."

Moreover, the impact will usually create a unique fracture pattern on the windshield. But as Bill Fischer wrote in a 1995 article for the MATAI journal, "The windshield does not show the 'spider web' fracture pattern typical of interior impacts from unrestrained passengers."

But what if, as the crash experts consulted by the BBC surmised with Kennedy, Mary Jo was never in the car when it went over? What if she had been inserted into the Oldsmobile after the vehicle was in the pond? Notice crash specialist Dubois's comment again: "The only conclusion I can reach is that she must have been *somewhere else.*"

Deceleration of the vehicle

Although an analysis of the accident at Dike Bridge is critical to an understanding of what must have occurred that night, not one book has devoted so much as a line of copy to it. Every author appears to have based his assumption on how severe the accident must have been according to what his theory requires rather than what the math tells us. Crash analysis is *science*, and most writers may be more familiar with dangling participles and run-on sentences than they are with right-brain mysteries like physics and math. Even the BBC documentary *Chappaquiddick*, which devotes more time to an analysis of the accident than any book ever did, ignores the physics of the crash itself. And while most authors have assumed that a car crash into water upside down and front-first could be survived quite easily, for passengers who have neglected to buckle up the truth is actually much different.

Dr. Cross has determined that the vehicle impacted the bottom of the channel on its roof at a vertical speed of at least four mph. Unrestrained by seatbelts, passengers within the vehicle would hit a solid wall of glass or steel, and the relevant compression distance to impact in their case would be the thickness of the soft skin and tissue covering their bodies and the compression of the solid bone beneath it.

Kennedy is said to have weighed about "220 pounds of muscle and fat" at the time of the crash.[1] At the exhumation hearing, Dr. McHugh estimated that Mary Jo weighed about 110 pounds. It takes about one-third tons of impact force to crack a rib 25 percent of the time and about one-half tons to crack a femur.[2] Human bones are protected by fat and muscle that may be as much as two inches thick, but flesh will compress to at least half its thickness before it starts becoming stiff.

Assuming both bodies decelerated from just four mph to zero over one inch of compressed flesh, Kennedy's body would have experienced a peak impact force of about 1.4 tons and Kopechne's body a peak impact force of about 0.7 tons.[3] Kennedy would have exceeded the force required to snap a femur by about three times and Kopechne by about one and one-half times. Both passengers, driven into the Oldsmobile by the weight of their bodies, should have exhibited clear evidence of trauma.

Now let's look at the head. There has been much research into skull fractures over the past few decades as engineers have attempted to design ever-more-effective seat restraints and helmets. In a 1975 pioneering study on head fractures, a Japanese team found that the force required to produce a first lateral fracture in an unprotected human skull (separations of the parietal-temporal suture) was between 0.136 and 0.385 tons,

---

[1] *The Last Kennedy*, p. 189
[2] http://www.scifighting.com/2013/03/31/1331/bone-crushing-power-force-of-a-fighter/
[3] The calculations can be found in the Appendix, Note 3

with the second (true) fracture occurring at a force of 0.2 to 0.55 tons.[1] As reported by this study as well as by others,[2] it can take as much as twice the force to produce a frontal fracture in a human skull as a lateral one, so let's increase the findings by 100 percent. A clinically significant true frontal skull fracture will occur at a force of between 0.4 and 1.1 tons.

The Japanese study is confirmed by findings cited by the Department of Otolaryngology at the University of Texas Medical Branch in 2010. According to Drs. Martinez and Maeso, a frontal fracture in a human skull will occur in car crashes, industrial and recreational accidents, assaults and the like at a force of between 0.4 and 1.1 tons.[3] Today, these numbers are considered standard when discussing, interpreting, or anticipating human frontal skull fractures.

An average human head weighs between 3.5 and 4 kg and can be covered by flesh up to one cm thick. Although the center of mass of Kennedy's vehicle impacted the bottom of the channel at a speed of at least four mph, the car was also rotating sideways around its longitudinal axis as it descended through the water, causing the driver side to impact the sand at a higher velocity. Dr. Cross has calculated that the driver would have experienced an impact speed of 10 mph or more. Assuming the driver-side head impacted the windshield or roof, decreasing from 10 mph to zero over a distance of 0.5 cm of evenly compressed flesh, the peak impact force on the skull would have been between 1.6 and 1.8 tons.[4] The driver's head would have experienced a force at least 40 percent greater than that required to produce a true human frontal skull fracture 100 percent of the time.

This is why Arena was so surprised by the physical appearance of Kennedy, and this is why Dr. Mills and Frieh, the undertaker, spent much of their time looking for fractures on the head and body of Mary Jo. The accident should have caused any number of cuts, marks, bruises, and fractures to both persons. But unaccountably, it didn't.

Summary

As found on the internet, the following are facts worth noting.

Some 11,000 cars plunge into bodies of water each year in the United States. Florida accounts for most of these with approximately 4,800 crashes ending up with a car in the water. The sheer number of these types of accidents year in and year out

---

[1] Matsui T, Kihira M, Kobayashi H, *Experimental Studies of Skull Fracture in the Temporal Region*, No Shinkei Geka; 1975 Feb;3(2):123-9

[2] P. Reilly, *Head Injury, Pathophysiology & Management*, 2nd Ed, CRC Press, 2005, p. 31, sec. 2.3.2

[3] http://www.utmb.edu/otoref/Grnds/sinus-fx-front-2010-12-17/sinus-fx-pic-2010-12.pdf

[4] The calculation can be found in the Appendix, Note 3

allows researchers to make very accurate predictions about how likely it will be for a person to survive one. From insurance settlements to vehicle design, crash analysis is big business and critical to industries worth billions of dollars. Crash specialists are highly competent and paid well.

Crash researcher Professor Cordon Ciesbrecht says that vehicle submersion is the most deadly type of single-vehicle accident, with between 250 and 300 vehicle submersion events involving one or more fatalities occurring in the US each year. In fact, the mortality rate for submerged vehicle crashes is higher than the rate for head-on collisions. The majority of deaths from submerged car accidents are due to injury rather than drowning, with the chances of injury and unconsciousness rising dramatically if the driver or passenger is unsecured by a seatbelt. Once the edge of a car door has become submerged below the surface by as much as one foot it can be all but impossible to open it until the inside air pressure has equaled the weight of the water pressing in from the outside exactly, which can often be long after it appears that the water has stopped rising in the interior, and it can be equally difficult to climb out of an open window against the force of water cascading into the interior once the water has reached the level of the windows, or if the vehicle has overturned. The type of single-car submersion most likely to result in a fatality, *by far*, is the one that occurs when the vehicle comes to rest upside down in water.

These statistics would also apply to the accident at Dike Bridge:

• Rollover single-car crashes are more likely to cause casualties and more likely to cause serious casualties.[1]
• "Low-G" rollover accidents, where the forward speed of the vehicle is basically irrelevant, are responsible for about one third of all vehicle fatalities.[2] Tests by General Motors in 1985 found that most of the injuries in rollover accidents occurred when the roof struck the ground before the roof collapsed.[3]
• As can be expected, serious injury rises dramatically in rollover accidents if the occupants are unsecured by a seatbelt. A study found that 23 bus rollover accidents in 13 European countries resulted in 116 light injuries, 207 severe injuries, and 245 fatalities.[4]
• Seatbelts reduce the risk of death by 45 percent and cut the risk of serious injury by 50 percent.[5]

---

[1] AJ McLean, CH Kloeden, G Ponte, MRH Baldock, VL Lindsay, AL van den Berg, Centre for Automotive Safety Research, 2005
[2] Robert Eichler, *The Causes of Injury in Rollover Accidents*, 2003
[3] Kenneth Orlowski et al., *The Influence of Roof Strength on Injury Mechanics*, General Motors, Corp, 1985
[4] Hungarian delegate of GRSG, *Unusual Statistics about Rollover Accidents of Buses*, 2001
[5] http://www.cdc.gov/motorvehiclesafety/seatbeltbrief/

After countless hours of research into submerged automobile accidents, backed up by plenty of evidence, the conclusions reached are consistent, and clear. Without the benefit of immediate emergency help it is highly unlikely that Kennedy could have found his way out of the overturned vehicle. And even if he could, the likelihood that either he or his passenger could have survived the fall off Dike Bridge without any noticeable injuries to the face, skull, or body, unrestrained as they were by any belt or harness, is virtually impossible.

It can therefore be assumed, with a high degree of confidence, that neither Kennedy, Kopechne, *nor anyone else* was in the car when it plunged into the pond that night. The vehicle was driven off the bridge with nobody in it.

Why might Mary Jo have been inserted into the vehicle after it was driven off the bridge? Why not place her behind the steering wheel on land? If you think about it the answer is obvious, and entirely predictable.[1]

Objection to the theory

Farrar was told of the theory that Mary Jo's body may have been pushed through a front window after the Oldsmobile was on the bottom. He found the idea no less than ludicrous. Farrar believes that it would have been all-but-impossible for a couple of lawyers to insert a body through a car window five feet or so underwater with a four-knot current at night without the assistance of trained personnel with SCUBA equipment. Farrar cited Chief Arena as an example. Farrar told me, "You would need teams of divers to accomplish the feat. To lug her body around. To accomplish all this. It could not be done by a few drunk lawyers. You are out of your mind."

But I note that Arena, by his own admission, was "a lousy underwater swimmer"[2] and perhaps not overly inclined to risk injury with professional help just moments away. So in the summer of 2014, with my wife and several others as witnesses, I decided to see how difficult the feat might actually be.

On a moonless night at half tide, with a hundred-pound burlap bag filled with wet seaweed, I waded and then swam into the middle of Dike Channel with no SCUBA, mask, snorkel, or flippers. My equipment consisted of a pair of sneakers and gloves to protect my feet and hands from barnacles and a shirt and trousers to protect my chest, arms, and legs. I floated down with the current to a barnacle-encrusted bridge piling at the middle of the bridge, and grabbed on. Holding my breath and working blind, I worked myself down to the sandy bottom of the channel, then pushed my burlap bag three times around the piling before resurfacing, and then did it twice again. I found the whole exercise surprisingly easy since I was holding onto a piling rather than

---

[1] If you can't figure it out, wait a while and it will be explained.
[2] As confessed by Arena himself in the BBC documentary of 1994.

attempting to swim against the flow, and could have continued descending and resurfacing with my bag many times more.

In desperate times, people are able to accomplish desperate feats. I was not desperate, I was 68 years old, and I am way out of shape. I do believe that a reasonably fit swimmer in his thirties could have accomplished the task that night with no equipment, if he was reasonably at home in the water and had a mind to.

Unequal tides

Farrar told Dinis at the exhumation hearing that when he entered the water, the current was flowing at "approximately four knots." Dinis asked, "What significance would that have, four knots?" Farrar replied, "As far as my ability to swim against it, or anyone's ability, very difficult, sir. A four-knot current is very difficult to swim against for any sustained period of time. For many people, it's impossible to swim against."

Farrar testified at the exhumation hearing that he entered the water below Dike Bridge at about 8:50 on the morning of July 19. At 8:50 a.m., just 10 minutes past the midpoint of the two slack tides, the current would have been running at very near its maximum speed. And it would have continued to run at near maximum throughout his time in the water because Farrar also testified at the exhumation hearing that the entire recovery process took just 10 minutes.

But what Farrar may have overlooked is that due to a number of factors, semidiurnal tides are rarely the same height on any specific day. One tide is almost always higher or lower than the other. As all sailors know, boats entering inlets over a shallow bar will often be able to enter on just one high tide each 24 hours, 50½ minutes rather than both.

According to data sent to me by NOAA, the range of tide in Edgartown corresponding to the low at Dike Bridge around 10:40 p.m. on July 18 and the high around 5:30 a.m. on July 19, 1969, was 5½ percent less than the range between the high at 5:30 a.m. and the low at around 11:05 later that morning. Moreover, it took 410 minutes to fill up the pond but just 335 minutes to empty it. A 5½ percent decrease in the range of tide at Dike Bridge combined with a 22.4 percent increase in time would translate to a 22.8 percent decrease in the speed of the current.[1] Assuming Farrar experienced a 4-knot current at 8:50 a.m., 10 minutes after the maximum velocity that morning, the speed would have been reduced to about 3.1 knots at 2:18 earlier that morning, 12 minutes[2] before the maximum current flow at the previous tidal cycle.

---

[1] The calculations can be found in the Appendix, Note 4.
[2] Twelve minutes rather than ten minutes because it took longer that night to fill up the pond than to empty it.

But, of course, this is not the end of the story because Kennedy and his friends would not have entered the water at 2:18 a.m. Kennedy had already returned to the Shiretown Inn by that time. If the accident was staged, Kennedy would probably have entered the water at about 1:15 a.m., a half hour after Look saw the vehicle and about 45 minutes before Gargan and Markham returned to Lawrence Cottage. The current would have been running about 75 percent as quickly as it was at 2.18 a.m., or approximately 2.3 knots.

The difference between 2.3 and 4 knots is huge. The force of current on a body, otherwise known as the drag force, increases or decreases by the square of the velocity in much the same way that the force on a vessel's sail increases or decreases by the square of the wind speed. Even a very slight drop in current becomes a significant gain to a swimmer or diver fighting against it. The relative drag force difference on a body subjected to the same fluid at two dissimilar velocities can be represented by the formula $F_D = (V_V / V_A)^2$, where V_V is the higher speed and V_A is the lower one.

Doing the math, the velocity of the current experienced by Farrar when he first entered the water, *whatever it was,* would have been about 1.74 times greater than that experienced by Kennedy, Gargan, and Markham. This would have represented a relative drag force increase of 1.74^2, or 302 percent. In other words, if the accident was staged (or even if it wasn't), Farrar fought against a current about *three times stronger* than the current experienced by Kennedy, Gargan, and Markham. Of course the current was decreasing for Farrar whereas it would have been increasing for Kennedy, but nevertheless, each of them would have had to contend with a far different challenge.

Chrome trim at the bottom of both passenger-side doors

In a 1995 article for the MATAI journal, Fischer pointed out that although the chrome strip on the bottom of the rear passenger-side door of the Oldsmobile is missing, on the front door it isn't. Fischer believed this would prove that the door damage was caused by "hydraulic shock."

In fact, both chrome strips survived. Farrar can be seen with the missing trim in his hand as he is exiting the water, and the trim is not even bent. Farrar told Nelson that he found the section of trim "at the bottom of the channel close to the wreck."[1]

If the accident was staged, how could those chrome strips have survived an accident on land?

---

[1] *Chappaquiddick Tragedy*, p. 146

Kappel assumed the Oldsmobile slid into trees. But what if that object was a section of farm or construction equipment on wheels? Construction equipment, raised off the ground by a few feet, could be shaped like most anything. The impact could have caused the vertical dents in both doors while sparing the chrome trim.

In 1954, Mary Storer, a good friend of my grandmother, purchased a three-acre parcel of land that became the nucleus of a distinctive Japanese garden called Mytoi on the north (left) side of Dike Road and much acreage for a summer home on the south side of the road around Poucha Pond. She built a distinctive Japanese home designed by Edgartown architect Hugh Jones, set back from the right side of Dike Road at the end of a long driveway.

I visited Mrs. Storer with my grandmother many times in the '60s and remember seeing construction equipment parked close to the side of the road at Mytoi. The equipment was especially noticeable in the immediate years after 1966 when a decision was made to significantly upgrade the landscaping and expand the gardens which Mary Storer, then Mary Wakeman, donated to the Trustees of Reservations in 1976.

Mytoi is located about a quarter of a mile from Dike Bridge and about half a mile from the Dike Road intersection. Its location can be seen on the map of Dike Road found in Chapter 1 of this book. If the vehicle's passenger side slid into equipment parked at Mytoi, it would suggest that Kennedy was driving back from a tryst at East Beach rather than toward it when the accident occurred. This could explain why Mary Jo wore no panties when examined the next morning. They were lost in the ocean or on the beach. It would imply that although the accident on Dike Road had indeed occurred soon after 11:15 p.m., Kennedy and Mary Jo must have left the party well before that time.

The loosened chrome strip from the rear door found in the water near the vehicle by Farrar might have fallen off the side as the car impacted the sand at the bottom of the channel; or it might have fallen off the car at the accident on Dike Road and been thrown into the channel near the Oldsmobile after the accident was staged.

Alcohol level

Assuming the accident was staged, we can now make a reasonable guess as to the alcohol level in Mary Jo's blood at the time she left Lawrence Cottage. If her last drink was at 10:30 p.m., with death occurring at about 1:15 a.m., her kidneys would have had about 2 hours, 45 minutes to filter alcohol out of her system. Mary Jo would have left the party with a blood alcohol level of somewhere between 0.12 and 0.14 percent. *Wikipedia* defines 0.12 to 0.14 percent as "impairment of reflexes, reaction time, and gross motor control causing staggering and slurred speech."

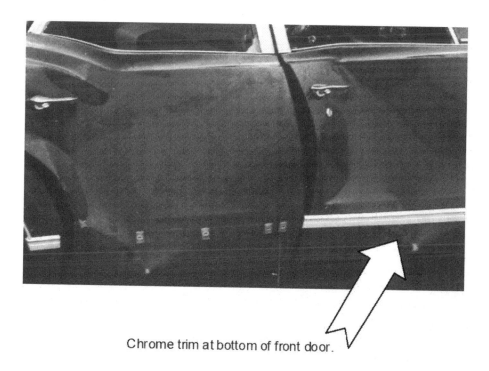

Chrome trim at bottom of front door.

Farrar has the missing chrome trim from the rear door in his hand as he is exiting the water. Photos Jack Hubbard

18

Skid Marks

George Kennedy, supervisor of the Registry of Motor Vehicles stationed in Oak Bluffs on Martha's Vineyard, arrived at the scene of the accident shortly after meeting Chief Arena at the Edgartown dock at 10:15 a.m. on July 19. Kennedy testified that the Oldsmobile had been hauled to within a few feet of the western shore by the time he arrived. Kennedy said that he immediately began to measure the distance of the tire marks with Inspector Molla, his assistant. Kennedy said he found a skid mark attributable to the right side of the vehicle extending 18 feet from the start of the bridge to a scuff mark on the rub rail where the right tires had gone over the bridge; and a skid mark from the left side of the vehicle extending 33 feet 2 inches from start of the bridge to the rail. Kennedy's measurements are included on Arena's sketch of the accident scene which had been submitted to the court at the exhumation hearing the previous October.

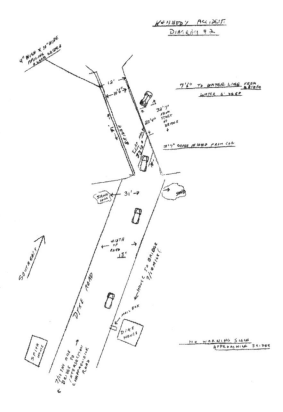

Kennedy, who testified he had been a registry inspector for 15 years and had examined between 100 and 200 accidents during that period, was asked to give his opinion as to the speed of the vehicle required to make skid marks of the length he observed. Kennedy told the court: "20 to 22 mph." That approach speed is also found in Inspector Kennedy's official accident report.

The approach speed was wildly under-estimated. This is how Kennedy said he came to his opinion of 20 to 22 mph:

"All right, a car operating at 20 miles per hour has a reaction time of any person operating approximately three-quarters of a second before a person removes his foot from the gas and applies the brake; approximately 22 feet in the three-quarters of a second for the reaction time. Then, a vehicle after the brakes have been applied at 20 miles an hour, then the vehicle should stop in 25 feet. Now, there is a distance of 25, 22, [for a total of] 47 feet." Questioned twice more, Kennedy repeated that a car traveling 20 mph would stop within 25 feet after braking.

However, both tire marks observed by Kennedy began at the foot of the bridge when, presumably, the brakes of the vehicle had already been applied. According to Kennedy's calculations, a vehicle moving at 20 mph would skid for 25 feet after the driver stepped on the brakes. But the distance from the foot of the wood bridge to the end of the gouge mark in the rub rail was almost 33 feet, as shown in Hubbard's photos. Even if the surface was quite slippery, that might be just enough distance to travel all the way up the bridge and possibly tip over it, but certainly not enough to fly through the air a significant distance before landing in the water, especially since the bridge sloped upward and there was a four-inch-high rub rail to arrest the vehicle's momentum. Chief Arena had run his own experiment on a 1969 Chevrolet driven at 20 mph, locking the brakes at the start of the bridge. The vehicle skidded up the bridge for 31 feet.[1]

Braking or acceleration

Perhaps Inspector Kennedy was not looking at the tire marks on the bridge in the right way. When a stationary vehicle equipped with an automatic transmission is shifted into drive with the engine already revved at a high rpm, the automatic transmission compensates for the engine speed somewhat and the wheels take a bit longer to engage than they would with a standard transmission. This prevents the engine from stalling out. Nevertheless, when they do engage the wheels will begin spinning if the vehicle is at a standstill and the engine is powerful.

---

[1] *Senatorial Privilege*, p. 317. Bill Fischer says that it was not Arena who did the test but rather the Arthur D. Little Company hired by Kennedy's attorneys.

The Delmont 88 was one of the hottest muscle cars of the '60s in an American era of very powerful, gas-guzzling Detroit speedsters. It became the platform for the Oldsmobile police package. Like the Cutlass, the 98, the Toronado, and similar Oldsmobile models of that era, the Delmont 88 was all about torque. Torque is what makes a heavy car nimble.

In 1967, the Delmont 88 came standard with a 330-cubic-inch V8 that could be upgraded to a 425-cubic-inch model. The absence of a 425 emblem on the driver-side front fender suggests that Kennedy owned the 330. Fitted with a 260-HP 90-degree V8 Jetfire Rocket engine coupled with a three-speed Turbo Hydra-Matic automatic transmission geared at 3:23; boasting a two-barrel carburetor able to deliver a massive 550 cubic feet of air instantaneously; the standard 330 could produce a hefty torque of 335 foot-pounds at just 2,800 rpm. It was so powerful it didn't need a very low gear to get up to speed very quickly and could cruise at over 100 mph with ease.

If Kennedy's vehicle was shifted into drive with its engine running at high rpm's, the rear wheels would have begun spinning in the gravel and should have continued to lay rubber all the way up the bridge until the vehicle flew off it. The tire marks in the wood seen by Inspector Kennedy and his associate can be explained equally well by an accelerating vehicle as by a decelerating one. This might also explain Chief Arena's puzzling description of the tire marks at the exhumation hearing: "There were marks that were, they resembled – it's hard to say, like they were scuff marks, in a way they weren't really what you would call skid marks, they were marks that would probably be brought up, be brought about by a tire going sideways, sliding a bit, more like skidding into something."

The approach speed of 35 to 40 mph calculated by the Massachusetts Registry of Motor Vehicles was based on the assumption that brakes were applied on or just before the vehicle reached the bridge because that is what George Kennedy indicated in his accident report. But what would the speed need to be if the brakes were never applied at all and the vehicle was accelerating up the bridge? In other words, what speed would the vehicle need to be traveling when it *left* the bridge?

As all school children know, an object accelerates toward the earth, or decelerates away from it, at 32 feet per second per second, irrespective of its mass. This means that after one second an object dropped from a height will be traveling at 32 feet per second and will have traveled 16 feet during that period. Its velocity will increase by an additional 32 feet per second every second thereafter. The effects of earth's gravity on an object in a vacuum can be boiled down to $d = 16t^2$, where d is expressed in feet and t in seconds. So, to determine the final speed at launch, all we really need to know is the slope of the bridge, the distance "flown" by the vehicle's center of mass (CM), from the point the CM began falling off the bridge to the point it slammed into the channel, and the distance from the bridge to the water in respect to the vehicle's CM.

But exactly where would the CM begin falling off the bridge? And exactly where did it land? Would the rub rail have had an effect on the vehicle's flight? Do the skid marks even make sense?

At the author's request, the accident was studied by Dr. Rod Cross, professor of physics at Sydney University and an expert on plasma physics (fusion). Since his retirement, Dr. Cross has become one of the world's foremost authorities on falling objects, especially as they apply to sport. He has examined numerous vehicle accidents and falling fatalities for the New South Wales Police and is the author of a large number of books and articles – many of which can be found on the internet. For almost two years, Dr. Cross filmed toy cars in slow motion falling off a ramp built to scale and then slogged through the mathematical calculations. He found that the vehicle left the bridge at a speed of just 15 mph.

Cross's very interesting conclusions concerning the accident damage, the skid marks, and an analysis of the physics will be found in the following three chapters.

Other speed estimates

Bill Fischer, an accident specialist consulted by the BBC in 1994, determined that the car left the bridge at 28.8 mph. Raymond McHenry of the *Reader's Digest* calculated that the speed of the car had been reduced by the braking action to a speed of about 25 mph when it went off the bridge. Donald Nelson, a physicist and author of *Chappaquiddick Tragedy: Kennedy's Second Passenger Revealed*, calculated that the vehicle launched itself off the bridge at 30.3 mph.[1]

These numbers are far higher than Dr. Cross's findings. Dr. Cross wrote to me, "I have read car accident reports by accident investigators before. They often get the physics wrong and don't understand that Newton's laws apply to the center of mass motion." After questioning Dr. Cross, these are some of the common errors accident investigators make when attempting to compute the launch speed of a vehicle that has fallen from a height into water. I mention them here because a brief explanation now might make it easier to follow Dr. Cross' explanations later, especially those found in his third chapter.

a) Both the vertical and horizontal distances of flight must be calculated in respect to the vehicle's center of mass while the car is in *free fall*. Free fall means after every part of the vehicle has left the ramp and before any part of the vehicle has touched the water.

b) The vertical and horizontal distances of flight depend on both the orientation of the vehicle at the beginning of free fall as well as its orientation at impact. At Dike

---

[1] *Chappaquiddick Tragedy*, pp. 146-147

Bridge, if the vehicle entered free fall in a horizontal position but impacted the water on its side, the CM would have dropped five feet rather than seven. If it pitched forward 90 degrees so as to hit the water on its nose, the CM would have dropped just four to five inches. Likewise, the horizontal distance of flight will be much less if the vehicle lands flat than if it lands at an angle nose down.

c) When a speeding vehicle lands front-first into water from a height it will usually move forward under the water for a certain distance before coming to rest. One cannot assume that the position of a vehicle's CM on the bottom of a channel will be the same position of the CM when the vehicle impacted the water's surface. The forward underwater distance should be determined using toy models that are suitably scaled.

d) The forward parabolic curve followed by the CM from a positively sloping ramp rises up for some distance before falling back down. The time to reach the point of impact increases, and since velocity is indirectly proportional to time, the initial velocity decreases. This is another way of saying that the horizontal component of velocity is always less than the initial velocity if there is a positive slope to the ramp.

e) The forward parabolic curve followed by the center of mass of the vehicle when the front or side wheels leave a ramp will not be the same *ballistic* parabolic curve after all the wheels leave the ramp and the vehicle becomes airborne and enters free fall. The parabolic curve before free fall projects much further forward and rises higher in the same amount of time, as indicated by the illustration on the opposite page. Solving for the equations that determine the spatial x/y location, attack angle, and vector velocity of the CM at the moment of free fall can be time-consuming and tedious, but if they are not worked out by the accident specialist, the launch speed will be assumed to be substantially higher than it actually is.[1]

There is one further critical factor at Dike Bridge that previous accident investigators have ignored completely: the rub rail. Fischer, in his MATAI report, said that the rub rail would have had no effect on the physics of the accident since the vehicle's springs would have absorbed the impact. Fischer was incorrect. The average vertical speed of the car would have decreased as parts of the vehicle's undercarriage clipped the rail on the way down, arresting the car's descent momentarily, and the impact would have had a significant effect on the rotational speeds of the vehicle around both its longitudinal and lateral axes. This will be made apparent in the following chapters.

---

[1] For those interested, the formulas are found in the Appendix, Note 5.

Difference in Parabolic Curves

The forward parabolic trajectory of the CM "A," after the front wheels leave the ramp, is not the same curve as the forward ballistic trajectory of the CM "B," after the rear wheels leave the ramp and the vehicle enters free fall.

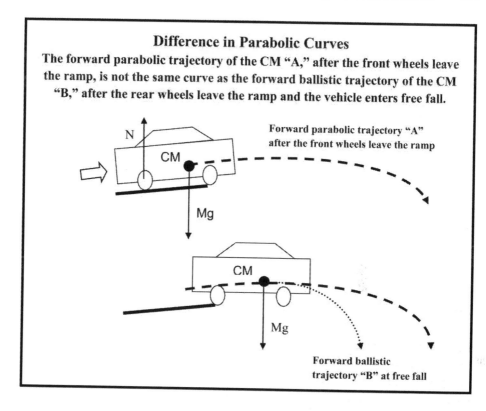

John Farrar

In a conversation with the author in 2013, John Farrar could not accept that someone who was not an expert or stunt person could get a car to drive off a bridge near its apex. In John's opinion it couldn't have been done, especially by people who were obviously drunk.

I am not sure I see the difficulty in getting a car equipped with an automatic transmission, as Kennedy's car was, to drive off a bridge near its apex at a final speed of just 15 mph. Assuming there was sufficient distance from start to launch at the acceleration potential of the empty vehicle, all it would take is a short piece of rope, a rock, and the determination to do it. Rocks are easy to come by on Chappaquiddick, and there must have been rope in at least one of the several boats pulled up on the marsh that night on the southwest side of the bridge.

No one knows just how much alcohol these people consumed, and simply stating they were drunk does not mean they were. And, of course, if they *were* drunk, it might explain why they decided to try.

19

Physics of the Accident at Dike Bridge
by Prof. Rod Cross, Physics Department,
Sydney University

*I*n January of 2015, Bill Pinney asked me if I could have a look at a 1960s vehicle accident in the US since he was writing a book about it. He gave me only a few sketchy details and did not even mention Kennedy's name or the location of the accident. I wrote back immediately to tell him that I didn't know what happened, but I could tell him the name of the driver. The accident made headlines around the world. Local newspapers tend to drop foreign news very quickly so I was not aware that Kennedy's explanation of the accident was subsequently subject to widespread disbelief in the US. The accident itself was completely overshadowed two days later when Neil Armstrong and Buzz Aldrin landed on the moon.

I have fond memories of America. In 1984, I spent six months at the University of Texas at Austin in their physics department. Before I left I sent $5,000 ahead so I would have an account and some money when I got there. When I arrived I discovered that the bank in Austin no longer existed. So I went to another bank to ask if they could help find my money. The woman I spoke to gave me $1,000 cash to help me out. I asked if I needed to sign anything. She said no, because in Texas they trust people, and if I didn't return the money they would just come and shoot me. I was very impressed.

Pinney contacted me since I had written an article in the October 2011 issue of the *Physics Teacher* about a similar accident that occurred in Sydney.[1] My article was based on a report that I had prepared for the police. I am not a traffic accident investigator by profession, but I know about the physics of moving objects, having taught physics at Sydney University since 1967 and having conducted many experiments and written many papers and several books on the physics of sport. Since my retirement in 2003, I have also conducted many investigations for the coroner and the police and have appeared numerous times as an expert witness in court, primarily involving falling fatalities, but also involving traffic accidents. It doesn't matter whether it is a person or a vehicle or a baseball colliding with another object or falling through the air, the basic physics is the same and is governed by Newton's laws of motion. Useful information can also be obtained by conducting simulation experiments to check the physics and to measure the relevant parameters involved in the calculations.

---

[1] R. Cross, *Launch of a Vehicle from a Ramp*, The Physics Teacher, October, 2011, Vol. 49, pp. 410-411

It turned out that in Pinney's case there was very little information available on the accident itself since the accident was never as thoroughly investigated as it should have been. Furthermore, the available information from the exhumation and inquest testimonies was very unreliable. Pinney suspected that I could work out whether Kennedy's vehicle was accelerating or decelerating when it left the bridge, but I doubted that it would be possible to figure that out. If a vehicle leaves a bridge at, say, 30 mph, then it is fairly easy to work out the subsequent trajectory through the air. It is more difficult to work out the trajectory through the water below the bridge and even more difficult to work out the acceleration before leaving the bridge.

Nevertheless, experts trained to interpret tire tracks can usually distinguish between braking and acceleration, at least if the tracks are relatively clear and if both left and right tracks are visible. In Kennedy's case, both tracks were not visible. The left tire track stopped suddenly before it got to the edge of the bridge and the right tire track was missing entirely. As explained below, that was enough to suggest to me that the vehicle was accelerating rather than braking. Other evidence would back this up.

The vehicle also left several distinctive marks and gouges on the four-inch-high wood rub rail at the edge of the bridge. Inspectors at the scene said it left no tire marks on the road immediately before the bridge, but I located a tire mark running through the left side of a large pile of dirt near the front of the bridge that appears to have been left by Kennedy's vehicle. It can be seen clearly in aerial photographs shot by Fred Ward immediately after the accident and is found in my following chapter, Section 1.

The fact that Kennedy's vehicle landed in the water below suggests either that the driver was drunk or otherwise incapacitated at the time, or the driver was driving too fast to negotiate a careful approach onto the bridge, or the driver was not actually watching or could not see where he was going while approaching the bridge.

Alternatively, the accident was staged. That is, the vehicle started from rest near the start of the bridge, was angled towards the right side of the bridge, and was allowed to accelerate over the side of the bridge. That is why Pinney wanted to know if I could determine whether the vehicle was accelerating or decelerating as it left the bridge.

Accident scene evidence indicated that during the fall, the center of mass of the vehicle traveled a distance of about 17 feet horizontally through the air and fell about 5 feet vertically. It left the bridge at a point where the slope of the bridge was 5 degrees. From that information, I was able to determine that the horizontal launch speed was about 15 mph and that the vehicle landed in the water at a vertical impact speed of about 11.4 mph. These estimates could be in error by a few percent, but even relatively large errors would not change the central conclusions regarding this accident.

The calculated launch speed of 15 mph is significantly lower than the value estimated previously by others. This is mostly because the horizontal free fall distance has been overestimated, as described in Sections 4 and 5 of this chapter, and partly because the influence of the rub rail has been generally ignored. As explained in my third chapter, collision with the rub rail during the vehicle's descent extended the fall time, thereby allowing the vehicle to travel a longer horizontal distance at a lower launch speed.

Outline

The primary evidence regarding the accident itself concerns the following:

• tire and gouge marks on the bridge
• damage to the vehicle and injuries to the occupants
• the weight and dimensions of the vehicle
• the landing point and orientation of the vehicle in the water below the bridge
• the dimensions of the bridge and height above the water

The more technical aspects of the evidence and its interpretation are described in my third chapter. However, the first item of primary evidence, the tire and gouge marks on the bridge, will be examined in Section 1 of this chapter since it is easily understood, and because it indicates conclusively that the vehicle was accelerated up the bridge from a standing start. In Section 2, an estimate is made of the distance required to accelerate the vehicle from a standing start to its final launch speed of 15 mph off the edge of the bridge.

Damage to the vehicle has been described by Pinney in earlier chapters; however, the damage to the passenger-side doors, the passenger-side windows, the windscreen, and the roof has particular relevance to a staged-accident scenario and will be discussed in Section 3.

Potential injury to the occupants will be discussed in Section 4.

Despite the availability of the accident scene evidence for almost 50 years, and despite being one of the most famous vehicle accidents ever to have occurred, there has been only one previous detailed technical report published on the accident itself. It was written by Bill Fischer and appeared in the 1995 journal of the MATAI (Midwest Association of Technical Accident Investigators). Fischer investigated the accident as part of a 1994 BBC documentary on the accident. He had good access to the evidence listed above but came to different conclusions from those of the present author. He concluded that the vehicle a) approached the bridge at a speed of at least 33 mph; b) braked on the bridge; c) traveled 31 feet horizontally through the air; and d) landed flatly in the water on the passenger side, thereby denting the passenger-side doors and blowing in the windows.

His report was well researched, but I disagree with his conclusions since he got some of his physics wrong, he did not estimate the impact force on the doors and windows or the actual strength of the doors and windows, he made no attempt to explain the damage to the roof and front windscreen, and he did not account for the gouge mark in the rub rail, the shortened left skid mark, or the absence of a right skid mark. He also did not identify what parts of the Oldsmobile's undercarriage were responsible for the marks on the rub rail. Fischer's accident report will be discussed in Section 5.

An earlier report on the accident was commissioned by the *Reader's Digest* for their February 1980 issue. The report was prepared by Raymond McHenry, a traffic accident expert. It was based on the same data as that used by Fischer and he came to similar conclusions to Fischer, as described in Section 6.

My conclusions about the accident will be presented in Section 7.

SECTION 1. TIRE AND GOUGE MARKS ON THE BRIDGE

After careful examination of photographs of the tire marks and impact damage on the bridge providentially recorded by photographers Jack Hubbard and Fred Ward, and after a thorough review of the very inadequate sketches and exhumation and inquest testimonies provided by Martha's Vineyard Registry Inspector George Kennedy and Edgartown Police Chief Dominick Arena, I was able to piece together an accurate picture of the accident scene. It is shown in Fig. 1 and is similar to the accident scene diagrams provided by Bill Fischer in his MATAI report.

Kennedy's vehicle approached the right side of the bridge at an angle of about 15 degrees, collided with the rub rail at the edge of the bridge, and then veered left to continue its approach at an angle of about 10 degrees. The path of the left wheels on the bridge is clearly visible in several photographs but the path of the right wheels is not visible on the bridge in any of the photographs. The calculated path of the right wheels is shown by two dashed lines in Fig. 1, located at the known track distance of 5.25 feet from the left wheels.

Marks and gouges

An interesting feature of the marks on the rail is that there are so few of them. As the vehicle fell or slid over the side of the bridge, the undercarriage could have damaged long sections of the rail as the vehicle moved forward. Instead, the vehicle was projected over the rail with minimal contact with it.

The first marks on the rail, nearest the start of the bridge, consist of two parallel splinters of wood, about 6 inches long, protruding from the outside edge of the rub rail at the angle of the left track and 5.25 feet to the right of it. The splinters define the path of the right wheels as they went over the bridge.

The next damage to the rail consists of two parallel scratch marks, about 1.5 inches apart, followed a short distance beyond by a broad scuff mark. Massachusetts automobile repair specialist Jim Crandall, a collector and longtime nationally recognized expert on classic Oldsmobile cars and the owner of a Delmont 88, was asked to view the marks. Jim instantly identified the scratches as marks from the tailpipe of a Delmont 88 which is angled down under the rear bumper and is slash-cut at a 45-degree angle on the bottom edge. This creates two sharp edges less than two inches apart which tend to cut into a surface just to the right of the gas tank when the rear of the vehicle bottoms out. The scuff mark was probably left by the differential, which in a Delmont 88 is the lowest point in the undercarriage and is located at the rear axle equidistant from the two rear wheels. Alternatively, the scuff mark may have been created by the gas tank, which is closer to the rear of the vehicle and which may have contacted the rail just before the left front wheel impacted the rub rail. Both the front and rear right wheels were already off the bridge when the scuff mark and parallel scratches were created.

Inspector Kennedy assumed that the scuff mark on the rail was created by friction from a right tire without recognizing that it was only 2 feet 6 inches from the left tire track. He testified at the inquest that the right tire track was 18 feet long, as indicated by the dashed arrow in Fig. 1, although there was no actual tire mark to measure. His mistake is described in more detail in the following Chapter. He also testified that the left track was 33 feet 2 inches long without mentioning that it came to a stop long before it reached the rub rail.

The last mark on the bridge is the three-foot seven-inch-long gouge mark just to the right of the extrapolated end of the left skid mark, shown in Photo A1(a). The mark begins a few inches past the inner edge of the rub rail. It starts at a shallow angle, rapidly increases in depth over the next few inches, then maintains that approximate depth in a straight line, parallel to the left skid mark, to the outer edge of the rail. The vehicle must have been tilted only slightly as it created the gouge. If the vehicle had already tilted substantially to the right, the gouge would have begun at the inner edge of the rub rail rather than several inches past it.

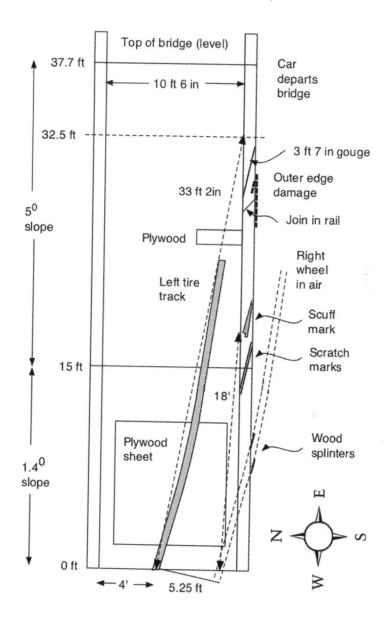

Fig. 1. Accident scene diagram drawn by the author to scale showing the left tire mark on the bridge and other marks on the right rub rail. The path of the right wheels is shown as two dashed lines located 5.25 feet from the left tire track. The bridge was orientated a few degrees south of east in 1969; however, to lessen confusion in these chapters, I have assumed the bridge ran directly west/east, as also assumed by Pinney for this same reason elsewhere in the book.

As shown in Fig. 1 and Photo A1(b), damage to the outer edge of the rail occurred to the right of the gouge mark extending over a length of about four feet. The damage occurred as the rear end of the undercarriage scraped the rail as the vehicle fell off the bridge into the water, as explained in the following chapter.

Photos A1(a) and (b). Photo (a) shows the three-foot seven-inch-long gouge mark in the 10-inch-wide rub rail at the right edge of the bridge (*You, the Jury*, p. 378, Fig 9). The gouge mark, which begins a few inches past the inner edge of the rail, defines the path of the vehicle as it went over the bridge. Photo (b) shows scarring to the outer edge of the rail to the right of the gouge. This photo was shot a day after the accident (photo **Fred Ward**).

Shortened left skid mark

Other than the absence of a right tire track, the most revealing aspect of the marks on the bridge is the fact that the left tire track comes to an abrupt stop about 10 feet short of its projected impact point on the rub rail. Ten feet corresponds almost exactly to the ten-foot three-inch distance between the front and rear axles. This is a critical observation and warrants close inspection.

Two possibilities are indicated in Fig. 2 showing the location of the vehicle when the left track ended, assuming that it was either the left front tire or the left rear tire that created the left track.

Suppose that it was the left front tire that created the left track, as shown in Fig. 2(a), and for some reason or other the left side of the vehicle lifted up just where the left track ended. Neither of the left wheels had collided with the rub rail or anything else on the bridge, so what could that reason be?

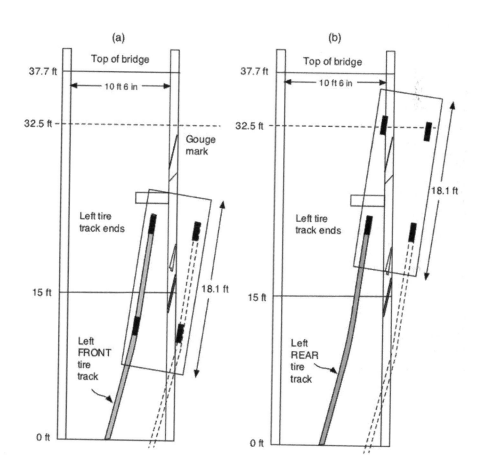

Fig. 2. Location of the vehicle when the left track ended, assuming that the left tire track was laid down by (a) the left front tire or (b) the left rear tire. The drawing is to scale.

An obvious possibility is that the right rear wheel had just fallen over the edge, meaning that both right wheels had fallen off the bridge, causing the vehicle to tilt to the right. However, because more than half the weight of the vehicle would still be located to the left of the outer edge of the rub rail, that would mean simply that both left wheels would remain on the bridge while the vehicle's undercarriage fell onto the rail. In order for the left side of the vehicle to tilt up, more than half the weight of the vehicle would need to be located to the *right* of the outer edge of the rub rail.

More important, the vehicle must have remained horizontal, or at most slightly tilted, for some distance past the point in Fig. 2(a) in order for the front end to cut the three-foot seven-inch horizontal gouge in the top of the rub rail, and in order for the exhaust pipe to cut the two scratches in the rub rail after the vehicle moved a wheelbase further forward. The vehicle could theoretically have remained nearly horizontal, supported only by the rub rail and with all four wheels in the air, but if that had occurred, there would have been deep scars all along the top of the rub rail, starting well back from the scuff mark and extending all the way up the bridge to the gouge. As shown in Photo A2, that type of scarring is not seen in any of Hubbard's or Ward's many photographs. The possibility considered in Fig. 2(a) is therefore inconsistent with the observed damage to the bridge.

Now consider the situation shown in Fig. 2(b) where it is assumed that the left rear tire created the left track. At the point where the left track ended, the left front wheel had just started to rise over the rub rail, lifting the left side of the vehicle off the bridge. Furthermore, more than half the weight of the vehicle was then located on the right side of the outer edge of the rub rail. The combined effect of the collision with the rub rail and the shift in weight over the edge would then result in a strong tilt to the right and a sudden (but not instantaneous) vertical fall of the whole vehicle, ending the left track. Just prior to that time, while the vehicle was still approximately horizontal, something near the front of the car on its left side began cutting the long gouge in the top of the rub rail, starting a few inches past the inner edge of it, as shown in Photo A1.

That "something" was identified by Jim Crandall as the lower control arm, sometimes referred to as an A frame or A arm because it is shaped like an "A." In a Delmont 88 it supports the bottom of the coil spring and keeps the front wheel in place. The lower control arm is aligned with the front axle and is angled down to a rounded point 6-3/8 inches from the ground and 10 inches from the inner edge of the left tire. It is the lowest point at the front end of the undercarriage.

Photo A2. A young girl examines the two parallel scratch marks on the rub rail a day after the accident (the scratch marks run between her two arms). Although difficult to discern in this B&W rendition, the original color photo shows no scarring on the rail between the scratches and the light damage to the outside lip of the rail further up the bridge, just to the right of the gouge mark (at the upper left corner of this photo). The color version shows this clearly because fresh scarring exposes the original yellow wood beneath the weathered surface. Other photos show no scarring between the scratch marks and the two parallel splinters close to the start of the bridge. Photo Fred Ward

Assuming the gouge was about one-half-inch deep, simple trigonometry indicates that the vehicle was inclined to the right about 13 degrees when it first began cutting the groove, and then tilted another degree or so as the groove deepened. The geometry is shown in Figs. 3 (a), (b), and (c). However, the force between the control arm and the rub rail did not cause the vehicle to launch itself off the bridge, given that the left rear wheel did not lift off the bridge until the left front wheel impacted the rub rail. Rapid rotation of the vehicle off the bridge commenced only when the left front wheel hit the rail and lifted the whole left side of the vehicle off the bridge, ending the left track.

The scenario just described was duplicated closely using tests with a toy vehicle, as described and photographed in the following chapter, illustrating the dynamics of the fall. At the calculated launch speed of Kennedy's vehicle, tests showed that after striking the rub rail, the Oldsmobile would have continued traveling up the bridge for at least one wheelbase before tipping over the side.

Braking vs. acceleration

When a vehicle is braking, the friction force acting backward on the tires causes the vehicle to slow down and to rotate forwards. The front end therefore dips down as weight is shifted onto the front tires. Furthermore, vehicles are generally designed to provide about 60 percent of the power to the front brakes and only about 40 percent to the rear ones. As a result, braking skid marks are laid down primarily by the front tires and are always much darker than the fainter rear tire marks which overlap the front ones a wheelbase behind.

Therefore, even if a surface is not conducive to showing marks from both front and rear tires, if skid marks are present from a braking vehicle, they will always show the rubber residue from the front tires, at least, unless the front tires have lost all tread or unless the front brakes have failed.

On the other hand, when a vehicle is accelerating, the friction force on the tires acts forward, causing the vehicle to accelerate and to rotate backwards. As a result, the front end rises and weight is transferred to the rear wheels. Meanwhile, the front tires rotate freely and provide very little friction resistance. Acceleration skid marks are therefore generated almost exclusively by the rear tires.

At the inquest, Inspector Kennedy said the tread on all four tires was good. In fact, the tread on the front tires was excellent, as can be seen from many close-up photographs shot by Hubbard as the vehicle was pulled from the channel and later when the vehicle was on the shore. And it is very unlikely that the front brakes of Kennedy's vehicle had failed. The brakes were examined superficially by Inspector Kennedy at the scene and found to be in good working order. Dr. McHugh, Director of the Massachusetts State Police Crime Lab, examined the vehicle much more thoroughly several months later. The vehicle was then examined and tested by the prestigious Arthur D. Little Company engineering firm, hired by Kennedy's attorneys. Any one of these three parties would have brought failed brakes to the attention of the inquest court, most notably the latter as it would have exonerated Kennedy of any possible wrongdoing.

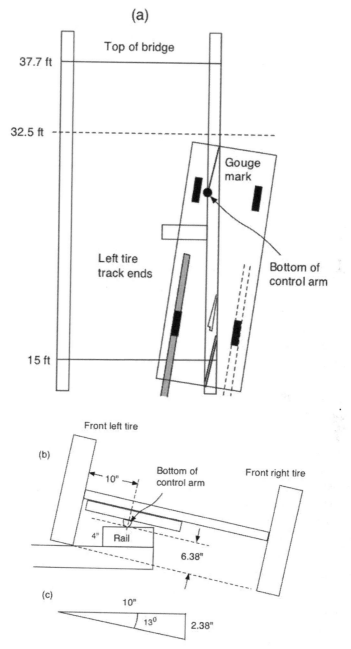

Fig. 3 (a), (b), and (c), to scale. The lower control arm of Kennedy's vehicle, located 10 inches from the inner edge of the left front tire, began cutting the gouge about 4 feet before the left front wheel struck the rub rail, ending the left track.

Absence of a right track

Tests were undertaken by Jim Crandall to determine what would occur when the right front tire of a Delmont 88 struck a four-inch-high rub rail at 15 mph and at an angle of 15 degrees. It was found that due to the vehicle's suspension, the right rear tire would remain firmly on the road and not lift up. How, then, to account for the absence of a right track had the vehicle been accelerating up the bridge?

The Delmont 88 came standard with an open differential. An open differential is designed to deliver an equal amount of torque to each wheel, always, regardless of the circumstances. This allows the outside rear wheel to rotate faster when the vehicle makes a turn. However, it also means that when one drive wheel begins to "spin out" on a surface and its torque drops, the torque on the opposite drive wheel will also drop by that same amount The result is the typical one-wheel acceleration burnout characteristic of the open differential. With an open differential, both rear wheels will rarely spin out at the same time except in very unusual circumstances.

At Dike Bridge, the left rear wheel probably began spinning out at the moment it transited from the gravel road to the slicker wood surface. But when that occurred, the right rear wheel was still on the gravel road, two feet back from the start of the bridge. From that point onward, and while it was rolling up the bridge, there could be no acceleration skid track from the right rear wheel.

When the right rear wheel dropped off the right side of the bridge, its torque would decrease to near zero, resulting in a sharp reduction in torque to the left rear wheel. However, this would not be instantaneous. Slow motion video confirmed that it would take 1 second, to an accuracy of 0.05 seconds, for a wheel revved to just 30 mph to stop spinning out on a wood surface once the opposite drive wheel began spinning in the air. This would be twice the time needed to lay down the remaining 10 feet of left acceleration track had the vehicle been moving forward up the bridge at 15 mph.

The absence of a right track also refutes the argument that Kennedy's foot might have been jolted off the brake pedal at the moment the right rear tire impacted the rub rail, with the vehicle's front tires thereafter leaving no left skid track on the bridge for the following 10 feet as it continued to roll up the bridge until tipping over the side at the gouge mark. Had the vehicle been braking, there would be a right skid mark from the start of the bridge to the right rub rail, mirroring the left skid mark, irrespective of whether the brakes were released a wheelbase after that. Likewise, even if the front tires were bald, and even if the front brakes had failed, had the vehicle been braking, there would nevertheless be a right skid mark on the bridge mirroring the left one – in this case from the right rear braking tire.

Straight left skid mark

Immediately following the right rear wheel impact on the rub rail, the observed left track and its projected extension run straight for about another 20 feet to the gouge at the inner edge of the rail. If the car had been accelerating with the right wheels off the bridge, the force exerted by the accelerating left rear wheel acting around the vehicle's center of mass should have created a clockwise torque, curving the track to the right. Conversely, if the vehicle had been braking, a strong counterclockwise torque would act about the center of mass, curving the track to the left. Why, then, does the track run straight?

When the right front wheel struck the rub rail, the impact must have wrenched the front wheels to the left. The left front wheel, now steering the car to the left as it drove up the bridge, must have counteracted the torque induced by the accelerating left rear wheel attempting to turn the car to the right. The two torques canceled out and the track ran straight. Even had the steering wheel been tied off to the driver-side mirror so as to keep the front wheels from turning to the right or left, at some point the mirror gave way. It would be more likely that the mirror's front fastener would fail on the impact of the right front tire on the rub rail rather than the left front tire because the right front wheel struck the rail at a larger angle than the left front one did.

Steering opposite to the direction of a spinout is an effective steering maneuver when a vehicle is accelerating. On the other hand, steering is ineffective, to either side, when a car is braking and its wheels are locked. The straight left skid mark is further evidence that the vehicle was accelerating and not braking.

Skid mark conclusion

The pertinent observations are these: the scratch marks from the vehicle's tailpipe; the shortened left tire mark with a gouge mark in the rub rail a wheelbase further forward; the absence of a right tire mark; the absence of deep scarring all along the top of the rail; the extrapolated straight left tire mark; excellent tread on the front tires. These observations, when considered together, provide conclusive evidence that the vehicle was accelerated up the bridge. The evidence is inconsistent with sudden braking.

SECTION 2. ACCELERATION UP THE BRIDGE

The evidence presented in this and the following chapter indicates that the vehicle was accelerated up the bridge. Since the launch speed off the edge of the bridge was relatively low, the vehicle could not have left acceleration marks (burned rubber) if acceleration had begun while the vehicle was already in motion as it approached the bridge. This means that the vehicle was accelerated from rest at a point near the start of the bridge, which in turn implies that acceleration was intentional. Reaching the calculated launch speed of about 15 mph would depend on how quickly the empty vehicle would accelerate on the gravel and wood surfaces and where the vehicle was positioned before the gearshift was yanked into drive.

The acceleration potential of Kennedy's empty vehicle, assuming it was fitted with the standard 330-cubic-inch engine and not the more powerful upgrade, was about 3.23 m/sec^2, or 10.6 ft/sec^2. However, an acceleration of 10.6 ft/sec^2 would have occurred only in ideal conditions. The acceleration would have been reduced to an expected 7.4 ft/sec^2 over the hard-packed gravel surface and to about 4.3 ft/sec^2 on the wood surface.[1]

The left skid mark on the bridge was 23 feet long when it came to an end. No right track was visible, but the right front wheel traveled eight feet over the bridge and onto the rail before it went over the side. This means that the vehicle could not have begun accelerating with its rear wheels close to the start of the bridge; if it had, the front right wheel would already have been hard up against the rail. More likely it started accelerating as far back as seemed reasonable to assure that the car would accelerate up the five-degree incline, jump over the rub rail, and land in the water near the middle of the channel. The right tire track in a pile of dirt, shown in Ward's photos in the following chapter (photo composite A7), indicates that the vehicle was probably accelerating for at least one car length before it reached the bridge.

The launch speed could be reached if the vehicle's front bumper was positioned about a car length from the foot of the bridge, as shown in Fig. 4. At that position, the car would have accelerated for 32 feet on the gravel road before the left drive wheel ran onto the bridge and began spinning out.

Starting from rest at an acceleration of 7.4 ft/sec^2, the vehicle would have reached a speed of 21.8 ft/sec (14.8 mph) after traveling the first 32 feet with both rear wheels providing thrust on the gravel surface. Assuming the right rear wheel acceleration decreased by 50 percent for the remaining 2 feet on the road and 8 feet on the bridge, and the left rear wheel acceleration also decreased by 50 percent for the remaining 23 feet on the bridge, then there would be a small increase in speed to 16.3 mph before the car launched itself over the side at the gouge mark. Given that the vehicle would have slowed slightly as three of its tires and the rear of the undercarriage struck the rub rail before it became airborne, the estimated launch speed of 15 mph is consistent with these calculations.

It should be noted that the 50 percent reduction in acceleration from both drive wheels is a reasonable estimate based on experiment; however, even if the actual

---

[1] These accelerations assume a coefficient of friction (COF) of 1.0 for the Delmont 88 factory test runs. The average COF on a hard-packed dirt/gravel surface is about 0.70 for a vehicle traveling at less than 30 mph. Fischer, referencing a test car skidded up Dike Bridge at 20 mph, calculated a COF of 0.404 on the wood surface.

reduction was a bit more or less, it would not affect the launch speed calculation in any appreciable way since the increase in speed following the left rear wheel spinout is minimal.

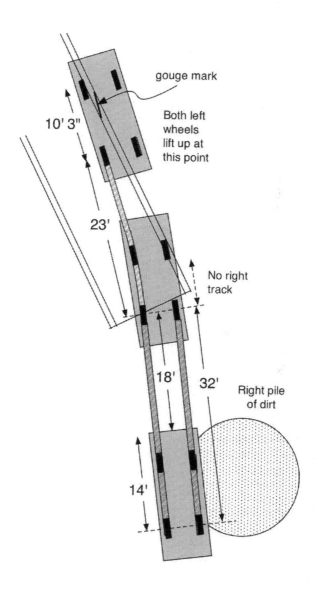

Fig. 4. Acceleration distances. The hashed tire tracks show the distances traveled by the left and right rear wheels. The drawing is to scale.

SECTION 3. STRENGTH OF DOORS, WINDOWS, ROOF, & WINDSCREEN

As explained in the following two chapters, the impact speed of the vehicle on the water in the vertical direction was about 5.08 m/sec (11.4 mph) and the impact speed in the horizontal direction was about 15 mph. The impact force would depend on the orientation of the vehicle as it struck the water and which part of the car struck the water first, but if we are concerned with the maximum possible impact on the doors and windows or on the roof, it will occur when the vehicle lands on the water "flat," in which case the horizontal speed is irrelevant. If we assume a dead flat impact, as Fischer did, the pressure on the vehicle can be calculated from the drag force, which is a function of the impact speed. At 11.4 mph, the maximum pressure on the doors and windows or on the roof would be 1.9 psi.

The pressure here represents only the force acting in a direction opposite the direction of motion of the vehicle. It does not represent the force on the sides adjacent and opposite to the impact surface since water flows directly into the contact area and then around the sides of the vehicle. High speed flow along the sides of an object can actually reduce the pressure acting on the sides, which is partly the reason that airplanes don't fall out of the sky.

Engineering calculations were privately commissioned on the strength of the front and rear doors and the side windows.[1] The doors were constructed from 0.0375-inch (0.95 mm)-thick sheet steel. It was found that the front door would be permanently dented if a uniform pressure of 15 psi or more were applied to the door and the rear door would be permanently dented at a pressure of 27 psi or more. The front passenger-side window would fracture at a 10 psi load and the rear one at 9 psi. It was also found that the pressure required to fracture the curved front windscreen was 40 psi or more, assuming that the outer perimeters of the window remained fixed. In fact, the front edge of the roof of the vehicle was visibly dented, meaning that the perimeter of the windscreen did not remain fixed. One can therefore assume that a localized impact at the top edge of the windscreen resulted in the roof being dented and the windscreen being shattered by the impact rather than by the drag force or pressure of the water acting uniformly on the whole windscreen. For example, the roof may have dented if the front edge of the roof collided with firm, wet sand at the bottom of the pond.

The strength calculations showed that the doors were comparable in strength to a 44-gallon steel drum. A popular classroom physics demonstration is to connect a 44-gallon drum to a vacuum pump to remove the air. Atmospheric pressure is equal to 14.7 psi. Nothing happens until almost all the air is removed, at which point the drum

---

[1] Guglielmo Cacciatore, Raul Ochoa, *Structural Analysis of the Doors of a Delmont 88*, privately commissioned, November 7, 2015 (see the Appendix, Note 6); Raul Ochoa, *Structural Analysis of the Side Windows and Front Windshield of a Delmont 88*, privately commissioned, November 15, 2015 (see the Appendix, Note 7)

suddenly collapses to about half its original size. A uniform pressure of about 14.7 psi is therefore sufficient to severely dent a steel drum.

It can be concluded that the passenger-side doors and windows were not damaged by impact with the water, as assumed by Fischer. Even at 15 psi, the front door would have been only slightly dented. In fact, the front door was deeply and sharply dented as if it had collided with a rock or a tree rather than water. A maximum pressure of 1.9 psi, which would have occurred had the vehicle landed flat on its side in the water, is roughly equivalent to pressing firmly on the side of the front door with two hands, given that the area of two hands is about 35 square inches and the force exerted by two hands could be about 70 lbs. All that would happen in that case is that the side of the door would bend slightly and then pop back into place when the hands were removed. There is no way that a person pushing on the front door could have created the deep dents shown in earlier pages of this book.

Given that the front door panel area was actually 40 inches wide and 25.4 inches high, the panel area was 1016 square inches. A uniform pressure of 1.9 psi would result only if there were 27 pairs of hands pushing on the panel. The hands near the perimeter of the door would have almost no effect at all while the hands near the middle of the panel would have maximum effect in bending the door inwards. Even so, the engineering strength calculations showed that the door would not suffer any permanent deformation.

It is not easy for a lay person to appreciate by intuition alone that the doors would suffer no damage. However, suppose that one of the doors was removed from the vehicle and just the door itself was dropped off the bridge into the water. Suppose also that the door landed flat on the water. Obviously it would make a big splash, but I doubt that anyone would seriously believe that a 1-mm-thick steel door would be deeply dented by the impact, especially if it was dropped from only a few feet. Nevertheless, exactly the same force would be exerted on the door even if a 4,000-pound block of steel was attached to the back of the door. Being much heavier, the door would not slow down through the water as quickly, but the impact force on the door when impacting a fluid flat depends only on its area and its speed. And the impact speed would be the same when dropped from the same height, regardless of whether it was a 100-pound door or a 4,000-pound door. In order to dent the front door even slightly, it would have to be dropped from a height of at least 34 feet and land flat at a speed of at least 32 mph in order to generate a pressure of 15 psi or more.

A different result would arise if the door impacted on a solid surface or on wet sand since a solid does not flow like a liquid. In that case, the impact force on the door would increase with the mass of the door, with the stiffness of the door and the surface, and with the impact speed. You can drop a tennis ball on your head without any discomfort. If you drop a golf ball on your head from the same height, it will probably hurt, even though a golf ball is lighter than a tennis ball. The reason is that a golf ball is much stiffer than a tennis ball so the impact force is much greater.

It can be concluded that *none* of the damage to the vehicle arose from impact with the water itself and significant damage could only have occurred as a result of impact with the sand or with a much harder object such as a rock or a tree.

Engineering calculations on the strength of the roof were performed assuming that the roof was 0.037 inch (0.94 mm) thick and a localized force was applied over an area of 2 feet x 3 feet in the middle of the roof.[1] Roof stiffeners were inserted in the CAD modeling at the known locations of a Delmont 88. A force of 16,200 lbs. (corresponding to a pressure of 19 psi) resulted in permanent deformation of the roof to a depth of 3.4 inches. A force of 5,780 lbs. was sufficient to shatter the front windscreen. A similar calculation was performed by applying a localized force to the brim of the front windscreen. In that case, the windscreen shattered at a force of 2,250 lbs.

A calculation was also performed assuming that a force was applied over the entire roof area to simulate a dead flat roof impact on the sand, or a situation in which the slope of the roof happened to be the same as the slope of the sand. In that event, a force of 21,000 lbs. would result in permanent deformation of the roof to a depth of 3.2 inches.

These results indicate that the roof and windscreen damage resulted from an impact with the sand, described as "hard-packed" by Farrar. The average force exerted on the vehicle by the sand can be estimated by assuming that the vertical speed of the vehicle decreases from a value V to zero while the sand compresses over a vertical distance S. If a constant force F acts over that distance, then FS is equal to $0.5MV^2$ since the work done by the force is equal to the kinetic energy of the vehicle.

Suppose that the vehicle impacted the sand on its roof at a vertical speed V = 4 mph (1.8 m/sec), having slowed to that speed from an initial vertical entry speed of 11.4 mph. That would be equivalent to dropping the vehicle in air onto its roof from a height of 6.5 inches. The actual impact speed may well have been greater than 4 mph but is unlikely to have been smaller than 4 mph. Assuming M = 1800 kg and S = 2 inches (0.051 m), then F = 57,180 Newton = 12,850 lbs., three times the weight of the vehicle. However, this is just the average force during the impact. In practice the force increases to a maximum value of about twice the average value during an impact of this sort, starting at zero, increasing to a maximum, then decreasing again. The maximum pressure on a 24-inch x 36-inch section of the roof would then be about 30 psi, more than enough to severely dent the roof and shatter the windscreen.

---

[1] Raul Ochoa, *Structural Analysis of the Roof and Front Windshield of a Delmont 88*, privately commissioned, February 11, 2016 (see the Appendix, Note 8).

The estimates here are consistent with published data on the properties of dense packed sand where Young's modulus is typically about 50 to 80 MPa. As anyone who has walked on sand knows, wet sand is harder and stiffer than dry sand. And wet or moist sandcastles are easier to build than dry sandcastles. That is because water gets between the sand grains and pulls them together by surface tension.

Suppose that a force F is applied over an area A on a rectangular block of sand of depth D. Then the block will compress by a distance S given by E = Stress/Strain = (F/A)/(S/D) = (FD)/(AS), where E is Young's modulus. The two-inch compression assumed above is consistent with this formula when the sand is at least one or two feet deep.

SECTION 4. POTENTIAL INJURIES

When the vehicle fell off the bridge, it rotated sideways to a near upside-down position even before it landed in the water. During this stage of the fall, the passenger side of the rotating vehicle would accelerate downward faster than the acceleration of gravity, so the passenger's head would strike the roof. The car then landed nose first into the water at 11.4 mph in a vertical direction and 15 mph in a horizontal direction, resulting in a combined speed of 18.8 mph. Even though the vehicle would then slow down quickly in the first one or two feet of water, the passengers were unrestrained and would have collided with the windscreen at a relative speed of 8.5 mph or more. The vehicle then struck hard-packed sand at the bottom as it suddenly came to a stop, again throwing the occupants violently against the windscreen and the roof, this time into shattered glass.

Rollover accidents like this can be fatal, even at low speed. I have investigated similar cases before. In one instance, a young man was killed when he was hit on the head with a light piece of wood and suffered a fractured skull. In another, a group of young drunks rolled their van by turning a corner too sharply at low speed. Every one of the occupants suffered noticeable injuries.

Suppose that Kennedy and Mary Jo impacted the windscreen or roof at just 4 mph (1.8 m/sec) when the vehicle hit the sand. Studies have confirmed that the impact energy required to cause a skull fracture is between 14 and 68 joules, depending on the impact point on the head.[1] If Mary Jo weighed 70 kg, her kinetic energy at 1.8 m/sec was 113 joules. If Kennedy weighed 100 kg, his kinetic energy was 162 joules.

---

[1] See Motherway et al, *The Mechanical Properties of Cranial Bone, Journal of Biomechanics*, 42, 2009, pp. 2129-2135; D. Raymond et al, *Tolerance of the Skull to Blunt Ballistic Tempero-parietal Impact, Journal of Biomechanics*, 42, 2009, pp. 2479-2485; N. Yoganandan et al, *Biomechanics of Skull Fracture, Journal of Neurotrauma*, 12, 1995, pp. 659-668.

Consequently, there was more than enough energy available to fracture the skull and/or to cause less-serious injuries to the face, arms, and legs, especially for the driver-side passenger who could have experienced an impact speed of around 10 mph or more as the vehicle rotated sideways through the water and struck the bottom of the channel heavily.

SECTION 5. FISCHER'S SPEED ESTIMATE

A very different result was obtained by Fischer for the speed of the car on the bridge. He estimated that Kennedy's vehicle approached the bridge at a speed of at least 33 mph, skidded as a result of applying the brakes, and then left the bridge at a speed of 28.8 mph and at an angle of 4.12 degrees above the horizontal. He estimated that the center of mass of the vehicle traveled 31 feet horizontally while it fell through a vertical distance of 6.25 feet. The vertical distance was estimated assuming that the vehicle landed flat on the passenger side.

To arrive at his 31-foot horizontal distance, Fischer cites an accident report written by Inspector Kennedy which reads, "From the position of the car in the water to the beginning of the bridge was 51 feet." I have been unable to track down that report. The distance from the foot of the bridge to the east side of the center span was exactly 51 feet; however, Hubbard's photos show that the vehicle came to rest at the eastern edge of the channel, well past the center span and well past the deepest portion of the channel. The 51-foot distance is therefore incorrect. As calculated in Section 2 of the following chapter, and as shown in Fig. 5 on the opposite page, the actual distance from the start of the bridge to the car was 55 feet 11 inches.

Fischer also confused the two parallel scratch marks left by the Oldsmobile's tailpipe with the actual gouge mark at the extrapolated end of the left tire mark, as depicted in Fig. 1 of this chapter. Fischer wrote, "There is a gouge mark passing diagonally across the south rub rail directly beneath Molla's left knee. This mark defines the angle of deviation from the centerline of the bridge as the car went over the edge. It occurs at a joint in the rub rail which defines its position on the bridge."

As shown in Photos A4 and A5 in Section 1 of the following chapter, Fischer's "gouge" under Molla's left knee, where Fischer assumed the car left the bridge, refers to the scratch marks passing through the join in the rub rail. The scratch marks are located between the scuff mark and the start of the bridge and are about 40 feet from the car in the water. However, at the inquest, Inspector Kennedy said that the gouge was located "between" the two tire marks (in other words, between the scuff mark, which Kennedy believed marked the end of the right track, and the extrapolated end of the left tire mark), and at the exhumation hearing, Arena said, "From the gouge in the wood, the car landed in the water about 23 feet up and about five feet out."

As a result of those two mistakes, Fischer assumed the car launched off the bridge at the position shown in Fig. 2(a) where the left tire track ended, the center of mass of the vehicle being located next to the scratch marks. Fischer assumed also that the vehicle was braking and that it was the left front wheel that created the left tire track. In making those assumptions, he completely ignored the gouge mark and additional damage further along the rub rail (these are not mentioned in his article), he did not attempt to determine what part of the vehicle's undercarriage might have created the scratch marks, and he made no attempt to explain the absence of a right skid track.

Fischer further assumed that the vehicle landed in the water at a point directly above its final resting point at the bottom of the channel, ignoring any horizontal motion through the water as the vehicle fell to the bottom. Falling from rest from a height of 6.25 feet would take 0.623 seconds to fall, but if the vehicle was projected upward at 4.12 degrees above the horizontal, it would take 0.734 seconds to fall. Fischer's horizontal speed estimate was therefore 31 ft/0.734 sec = 42.2 ft/sec = 28.8 mph.

My own speed estimate is considerably less since the center of mass would have traveled a wheelbase forward, or 10.25 feet, before the left front wheel struck the rub rail, and since the vehicle traveled horizontally through the water as it sank, as indicated in Fig. 5. In other words, the free-fall horizontal distance was about 17.0 feet rather than Fischer's estimated 31 feet. The rub rail would also have affected the flight by extending the fall time.

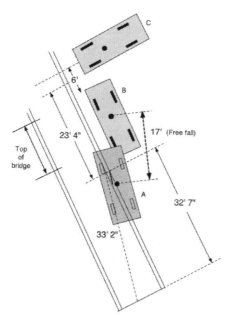

Fig. 5. The fall to scale viewed from above. The vehicle left the bridge at position A, landed in the water at position B, and sank to the bottom at position C. The black dot denotes the center of mass of the vehicle.

Fischer made another significant mistake when estimating the rotation speed of the vehicle through the air. He assumed that the angular velocity increases at a constant rate during free fall. On that basis, he calculated that the vehicle would rotate 107 degrees sideways during free fall and land flat on the passenger side.

The problem with that calculation is that there is no increase in angular velocity during free fall since there is no torque on the vehicle during free fall. The vertical linear velocity increases at a constant rate, but the angular velocity remains constant and is determined by the torque acting only while the vehicle remains in contact with the bridge. A small torque could arise while the vehicle is airborne, due to air resistance, but the effect would be negligible at low vehicle speeds. The drag force is proportional to the speed squared and would be significant only at speeds above about 80 mph.

Fischer was fully aware of the problem concerning the deep dents in both the doors and the roof. He commented that, "All the damage could not have been caused simultaneously from a single impact as a result of falling from the bridge. A rational explanation has to be found to explain why the car was damaged both on the passenger side and the roof." He made that comment in the winter 1995 issue of the MATAI journal. In the following summer issue, where he presented most of his calculations, he makes no mention of the problem, presumably because he was unable to find a satisfactory explanation. However, he did make the strong suggestion that Kennedy was not the driver, commenting that, "It seems unlikely that *anyone* in that car could have escaped after it went off the bridge." In the BBC documentary it was suggested that Mary Jo was the driver and that Kennedy was not in the vehicle.

SECTION 6. McHENRY'S SPEED ESTIMATE

The February 1980 issue of the *Reader's Digest* contained a lengthy article on the accident and included an analysis provided by Raymond McHenry, a traffic accident expert. McHenry figured that the horizontal distance from the center of the gouge mark to the center of the submerged vehicle was about 35 feet, measured directly from one point to the other rather than along the bridge. He then assumed that the center of mass traveled 35 feet horizontally while it fell about 14.5 feet from the bridge to the sand below. A 14.5-foot fall through the air would take 0.95 seconds, so he estimated that the speed of the vehicle off the bridge was 36.7 ft/sec or 25 mph, and the approach speed onto the bridge was about 34 mph, allowing for braking on the bridge. He also assumed that the vehicle rolled through the air and landed on the passenger side.

McHenry may have been deceived by misleading inquest testimony. McHenry appears to have assumed that Inspector Kennedy's description of the gouge mark lying "between" both tire tracks meant that the gouge was located "midway" between the marks. He also accepted Inspector Kennedy's length of 18 feet for the right tire track.

The actual distance from the center of the gouge mark to the centerline of the submerged vehicle was about 28.5 feet rather than McHenry's estimated 35 feet.

Another problem with McHenry's analysis is that the vertical acceleration is equal to the acceleration of gravity only during the free-fall stage. While one or more wheels of the vehicle were still on the bridge, the vertical acceleration was much lower due to the vertical force acting up on the vehicle, and while the vehicle traveled through the water, the vertical acceleration was also reduced due to the drag and the buoyant force. If the total fall time was, say, 1.4 seconds rather than 0.95 seconds, then McHenry's horizontal speed estimate would have been 17.0 mph, closer to my own estimate.

SECTION 7. CONCLUSIONS

Bill Pinney first approached me with the firm belief that Kennedy's accident was staged and was clearly looking for support in terms of further evidence from the accident itself. I told him that I would not do that since that is not what physicists do. I was happy to look at the evidence but would come to my own conclusions, based only on the physical evidence and the physics involved.

When a physicist writes a report or a paper for publication the usual procedure is to have it refereed by others in order to eliminate potential errors. This was not done in the present case since Pinney asked that I not disclose my conclusions prior to publication. Nevertheless, I paid particular care to get the facts straight and to ensure that the physics was correct. In order to do that, I spent almost two years on the problem, looking at every conceivable explanation and examining all the evidence one step at a time.

The biggest hurdle was how to distinguish fact from fiction in the official inquest evidence. Inconsistent and confusing testimony and amateurish if not wholly misleading accident diagrams led to frequent journeys up blind alleys. Countless hours were wasted unnecessarily. Fortunately, photographers descended on the scene and captured valuable evidence even before the official evidence was collected. These photographs provided sufficiently high-quality accident scene evidence to piece together the sequence of events that occurred as Kennedy's vehicle rolled off the bridge.

No doubt others will find fault, since they always do, particularly since some of the facts of the case are not known with certainty. For that reason, I needed to estimate several of the parameters as best I could in order to determine approximate answers and to determine the uncertainties involved in those answers. Nevertheless, approximate values could be estimated, and it was found that the dents to the passenger doors and the shattered windows could not possibly have been caused by impact with water since the impact speed and the impact force were much too small to damage them.

Based on the measurements and calculations described in this and the following two chapters, I concluded that:

1. Kennedy's vehicle approached the start of the bridge at an initial angle of about 15 degrees, then left the edge of the bridge at an angle of about 10 degrees and at a launch speed of about 15 mph.

2. The vehicle was accelerated from rest near the start of the bridge given that the straight left skid track was laid down by the rear left tire rather than the front left tire and there was no track from the right front tire.

3. There was sufficient distance from a point near the start of the bridge for the vehicle to have accelerated from rest over the right side of the bridge and to land where it did.

4. Even if the vehicle landed in the channel flat on the passenger side, the impact force due to the water would have been insufficient to create deep dents in the front and rear doors or shatter the windows. The dents in the passenger-side doors and the shattered side windows were therefore caused by a previous accident before the vehicle was driven off the bridge.

5. The vehicle rotated rapidly through the air and landed on the water about 17 feet from launch at a vertical speed of about 11.4 mph. The roof was dented and the front windscreen shattered when the vehicle impacted hard-packed sand at the bottom of the channel after traveling horizontally through the water for about another 6 feet.

6. The accident was staged given that a) the vehicle was accelerated up the bridge from a standing start (proved by photographic evidence); b) the passenger-side damage could not possibly have been caused by the fall off Dike Bridge; and c) neither Edward Kennedy nor Mary Jo Kopechne suffered any noticeable injury when the vehicle left the bridge, rotated through the air, slammed into the water, and then impacted the sand upside down with sufficient force to dent the roof to a depth of at least three inches and shatter the windscreen. Each of these events would have caused unrestrained occupants to impact the windscreen and roof at sufficient speed, and on three separate occasions, to result in observable physical injuries if not major ones.

20

Evidence Concerning the Accident
by Prof. Rod Cross, Physics Department, Sydney University

In preparing this chapter, I examined closely all the evidence on the accident that I could gather. I have come to the conclusion that the original evidence provided by Inspector Kennedy and Chief Arena, presented at the exhumation hearing and subsequent inquest, is of such poor quality, and so ambiguous, that it can be almost entirely disregarded if not discredited. Some of it is useful, but most of it is quite misleading. The main problems are summarized in Sections 1 and 2.

SECTION 1. TIRE AND GOUGE MARKS ON THE BRIDGE

Skid marks

On the morning of the accident, many photographs were taken by Jack Hubbard. Hubbard, already an accomplished professional photographer in 1969, was on vacation on Chappaquiddick, staying at the residence of Rev. Hal Tilghman, an uncle of Bill Pinney, author of this book. He was advised of the accident at an early hour by Ann (Hoar) Floyd whose father owned Tom's Neck Farm on Dike Road and whose brother, Roddy, owned the rowboat that was found in a different place and tied with a different knot later that morning. Hubbard arrived at the scene well before Inspector Kennedy did. In respect to the skid marks, his two most relevant photographs are Photos A3 and A4 showing Inspector Kennedy and his assistant, Robert Molla, taking their measurements.

The startling significance of Hubbard's collection of skid mark photos has been overlooked by everyone. As explained in my first chapter, Hubbard's photos prove conclusively that Kennedy's vehicle was accelerated up the bridge from a standing start.

Photo A3 shows Kennedy and Molla measuring the right track. However, the right track is not visible. All that is visible is a scuff mark near Molla's left knee. The scuff mark can be seen more clearly in Photo A4, just after the join in the rub rail. Photo A4 shows Kennedy and Molla measuring the left track. The left track is visible near the foot of the bridge, starting from a point near the middle of it, but ends just before a small rectangular piece of plywood against the right rail. The left track is also visible in Photo A5 taken earlier that morning.

The tracks in these three photos have been slightly darkened for clarity, but no pixels have been added or deleted from the original images.

Photo A3. Inspector Kennedy measuring the length of the supposed right track, which is not visible and could not end where he thought it did at the start of the scuff mark under Molla's left knee, just 2.5 feet from the left skid mark. Two splinters of wood protruding from the outside edge of the rub rail (white arrow and detail to the right), oriented parallel to the left skid mark and 5.25 feet from it, indicate where the right wheels actually went over the bridge. Chief Arena is standing on the left track in bare feet, dressed in a bathing suit taking notes. Photo Jack Hubbard

Detail from Photo A3. There is no skid mark where Inspector Kennedy is holding his tape measure. Eight other photos in Hubbard's collection, several revealing far greater detail, show no skid mark at this location.

Photo A4. Inspector Kennedy and Robert Molla measuring the extrapolated length of the left track which ends about 10 feet, or one Delmont 88 wheelbase, from the right rub rail. The gouge mark, and the damaged outside edge of the rub rail just to the right of it, extend past Molla's pad of paper. The scuff mark and parallel scratches can be seen further down the bridge near the break in the rub rail. Photo Jack Hubbard

Detail from Photo A4. The left track ends abruptly 1½ plank widths from a small sheet of plywood butted up against the right rub rail.

Details from Photo A4 showing the scratch and scuff marks (left) and the gouge mark and damage to the outer edge of the rub rail (right). Other than these marks, and the two parallel splinters shown as a detail in Photo A3, there is no other damage to the rail that could be attributed to the accident.

Photo A5 (Inquest Exhibit #10). Chief Arena sitting on the submerged vehicle, unaware that Mary Jo is inside. The left track starts 4 feet from the left rub rail, heading to the right then curving to the left. There is no right track on the bridge. The scuff mark in the rub rail (white arrow), which Inspector Kennedy assumed marked the end of the right track, starts just after the break in the rail where the bridge begins to slope upwards at 5 degrees and is just 2.5 feet from the left track.

Analysis of photographic evidence

There is no visible right track in any of Hubbard's many photographs, all of which were taken at high resolution. Inspector Kennedy measured the length of the right track starting at a point about 5 feet to the right of the left track, approximating the vehicle track width of 5.25 feet. He then interpreted a scuff mark on the rub rail as having occurred from the friction of the right front tire passing over the rail, measuring the straight line distance (18 feet) from the start of the bridge to the start of the scuff mark, as indicated in Photo A4 and in my first chapter, Fig. 1.

The scuff mark was the first of Inspector Kennedy's mistakes. It could not possibly be a mark from the right front tire since it is only about 2 feet 6 inches from the left tire track rather than a full track width of 5.25 feet. Consequently, the scuff mark was created by something else, most likely the differential or the gas tank.

The left track starts out on a curve toward the rail, but just before the scuff mark then runs straight toward the gouge mark on the rub rail. Inspector Kennedy extrapolated the left track to the inside edge of the rail to get his 33-foot 2-inch distance. It ended at a point just past the end of the 3 feet 7 inch gouge mark, as shown in my first chapter, Fig. 1. The extrapolated length of the visible track to the rub rail was measured correctly, judging from Photo A4, and is also copied to scale in my previous chapter, Fig. 1.

Chief Arena and Inspector Kennedy's accident scene drawings

At the exhumation hearing three months after the accident, Chief Arena entered a drawing into the court record. Arena testified that his drawing included Inspector Kennedy's measurements. A detail of that drawing is shown as Fig. 6(a).

Three months after the exhumation hearing, Inspector Kennedy recorded his own observations about the skid marks in a sketch that he presented at the inquest, but the sketch was never released as part of the inquest report. It was submitted into evidence, most likely as Exhibit No. 6. It ended up with Chief Arena, who gave a copy 25 years later to Bill Fischer to assist him with his work on the BBC documentary. Fischer, in turn, gave a copy to me another 20 years later. It is shown as Fig. 6(b). As far as I am aware, it has never previously been published.

(a)   (b)

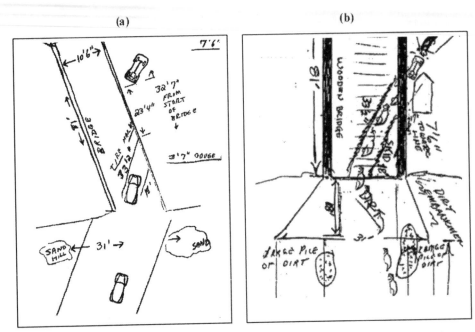

Fig 6(a), a detail of Chief Arena's accident scene drawing entered into the exhumation hearing record; and Fig 6(b), Inspector Kennedy's inquest accident drawing, probably Exhibit No. 6.

In both sketches, the tracks have been shifted well to the left of the tracks measured by Inspector Kennedy on July 19. In fact, the shorter right track, which was actually invisible, starts at around the same place as the longer left track does in Hubbard's photos. It appears that at least by the exhumation hearing, both men had come to the conclusion that the left track marked the beginning of the right one and it was the left skid mark that was invisible.

At the inquest, Inspector Kennedy testified as follows:

Inspector Kennedy (pointing to a photo, "Exhibit 11"): This was the skid mark of the right front wheel going over the rub rail. [This is] the large gouge between the two skid marks, *and the left skid mark does not show in the photo.*

There is a likely reason for their confusion.

Kennedy may have tried to draw the tracks to scale on a sheet of paper. The extrapolated length of the left track, measuring 33 feet 2 inches, began 4 feet from the left rub rail, as shown in Hubbard's photos and as indicated in Fig. 1 of my previous Chapter. The right track, measuring 18 feet, would be 5 feet 3 inches to the right of it.

However, at the scuff mark on the rub rail, where Kennedy assumed the right wheels had left a mark, the track width would be only about half the distance of a Delmont 88 track since the scuff mark was not caused by a right wheel, it was created by the differential or the gas tank at the centerline of the car. The tracks would converge, as indicated in Fig. 7(a).

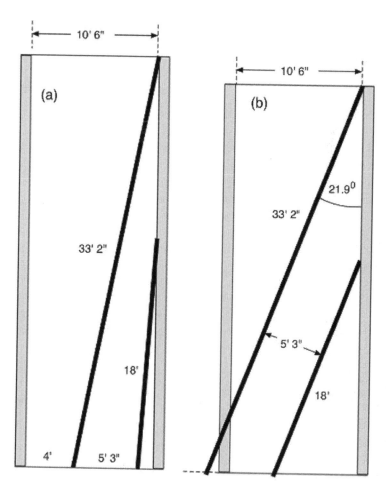

Figs. 7. The tracks would converge if Kennedy attempted to draw two tracks 18 feet and 33 feet 2 inches long, with the left track starting 4 feet from the left rub rail, as shown in Fig. 7(a). Shifting the tracks to the left opens the launch angle. Even so, the track lengths measured by Inspector Kennedy will not fit onto the bridge at the known Delmont 88 track width of 5 feet 3 inches. As depicted in Fig. 7(b), the left track would extend over the left rub rail. The drawing is to scale.

Unable to imagine that the scuff mark was caused by anything other than a right tire, Kennedy would have found that the only way to get close to the correct Delmont track width would be to shift the tracks well to the left since that opens up the launch angle. Even so, the correct track width of 5 feet 3 inches cannot be made to fit into the known 10 foot 6 inch width of the bridge, even with the left track placed as far left as it can go. The left track would extend *over* the left rub rail, as shown in Fig. 7(b).

This should have told Arena and Kennedy that the scuff mark could not possibly have been caused by a right tire impact; and the left skid mark could not possibly mark the start of a right one; however, it did not.

Their modified tracks have another problem.

Inspector Kennedy's sketch 6(b) shows two large piles of dirt near the front of the bridge, clearly visible in aerial photographs of the scene taken a day after the accident by another photographer, Fred Ward. The left pile of dirt is directly in line with Kennedy's modified tracks, and the distance from that pile of dirt to the bridge is only a Delmont 88 car length away, so how did Inspector Kennedy get around this obvious predicament?

In Inspector Kennedy's sketch, a very small vehicle, about 6 feet long, is drawn approaching the bridge along the right side of Dike Road. It then veers left before making a hard right turn to drive between the two tire tracks up the bridge. Inspector Kennedy's diagram appears to be an attempt to explain how Ted Kennedy avoided the left pile of dirt. Inspector Kennedy's track would be possible if the vehicle approached at, say, 5 mph or less, or was actually 6 feet long, but not if it was 18 feet long and approached at 20 mph or more.

Arena handled the problem in a different way. In Fig. 6(a), the two "large piles of dirt" in front of the bridge have been replaced by two small sand hills, with the left sand hill shifted well out of the way of the assumed (but incorrect) track of the vehicle leading to the bridge.

Arena's 31-foot measurement between his sand hills is also incorrect since that measurement actually refers to the distance between the outside edge of the parking lot on the left and the outside edge of Dike Road on the right, well past both piles of dirt, as shown in Inspector Kennedy's sketch 6(b). As can be seen in Ward's aerial photos, the actual distance between the two piles of dirt was about 16 feet, with the left pile of dirt about three times the size and more than twice the height of the right one. Shifting the left pile of dirt further to the left by 15 feet would place it in Dike Channel

In other words, it appears both accident scene sketches were deliberately fudged.

There is one final casualty of their modified tracks, and it is a fatal one. Opening the launch angle makes it impossible to account for the two parallel scratch marks since those marks intercept the rub rail about three feet further down the bridge than the scuff mark.

In that regard, it is noteworthy that the scratch marks are not mentioned or described anywhere in Arena or Kennedy's exhumation or inquest testimonies.

Inspector Kennedy testified further as follows:

Q (by Mr. Fernandes): Now, Mr. Kennedy, prior to going back to the police station with your conversation with Mr. Kennedy, Mr. Markham, Mr. Gargan, you had rendered an opinion of 20 to 22 miles per hour based on the skid marks.
A: I did.
Q: And at the break, we had a conversation about braking, did we not?
A: We did.
Q: Now, for the record, is it your understanding that a car traveling at 20 miles an hour requires 25 feet to stop?
A: That is correct.

In order to tell the truth, the whole truth, and nothing but the truth, Kennedy should have added, "It depends on the type and condition of the road surface, the condition of the tires, and the braking force. It also takes about 25 feet to accelerate from rest to 20 mph." He could also have added, "The 20- to 22-mph braking estimate is irrelevant since the vehicle did not just skid up the bridge for 25 feet and stop. After 25 feet, it still had sufficient speed to jump over the rub rail, launch itself off the bridge, and travel a significant distance through the air before landing in the water."

Skid marks on the road

Inspector Kennedy testified at the inquest that he saw no skid marks on the gravel road leading up to the start of the bridge. However, he also testified that he noticed the skid marks "starting at the edge of the bridge on the dirt" and that he could not measure the marks on the gravel "very well" because of possible heavy traffic over the bridge before he arrived. Consequently, it is not clear from his testimony if there were tire tracks from Kennedy's vehicle on the road, or not.

Fresh tire marks on the road can be seen in Fred Ward's aerial photographs, shot either on the morning of the accident or the day after. One photo clearly shows recent tracks where vehicles had turned off the road into the dirt car park just before the bridge. Others (Photo composite A7) show a clear track running through the edge of a dirt pile about 16 feet before the start of the bridge, directly in line with the right track of the Oldsmobile's wheels up the bridge, but it was not mentioned by Inspector Kennedy. The same dirt pile can also be seen in Photos A3 and A4 shot by Hubbard on the morning of the accident.

Photo composite A7. Details of two aerials shot by Fred Ward. Ward (now deceased) dated his aerials of Dike Bridge, all of which show the same persons and vehicles, as "July 19, or 20th at the latest, 1969." The dirt pile, which can also be seen in Hubbard's Photos A4 and A5, is about 16 feet from the bridge at its closest edge. The tire track in the original (left) color photo can be seen to run perfectly straight, with no left deviation, to at least the left sneaker of the man in white slacks standing near the sawhorse, and is directly in line with the two parallel splinters on the outside lip of the rub rail which define the track of the Oldsmobile's right tires.

The absence of clear tracks on the gravel road itself cannot be taken to mean that there weren't any such tracks. Regardless of whether Kennedy's vehicle braked or accelerated on the bridge, it is safe to assume the vehicle left tracks on the gravel road, but they were not clearly evident to Inspector Kennedy.

SECTION 2. THE LANDING POINT

At the exhumation hearing, Police Chief Dominick Arena provided a sketch of the final resting point of Kennedy's vehicle. A detail is shown in Fig. 8(a). It is quite misleading since the diagram is not to scale; the tracks do not reflect what was actually observed, photographed, and measured on the morning of July 19; and it does not show the final orientation of the vehicle accurately. However, it does contain two measurements of interest.

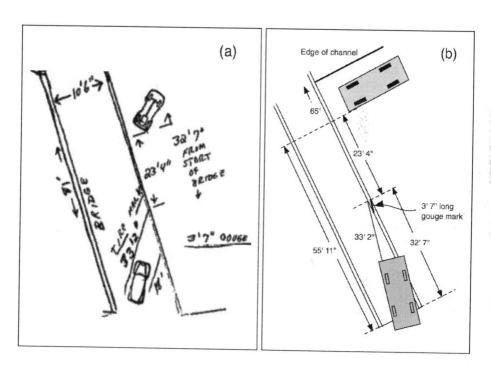

Fig 8(a) a detail of the accident sketch drawn by Chief Arena, and (b) a corrected version drawn by the author to scale showing the final resting position of the vehicle.

The distance between the end of the left tire track and the submerged vehicle is indicated as being 23 feet 4 inches in Arena's sketch. That distance is clearly labeled. The distance from the start of the bridge to the submerged vehicle is labeled as 32 feet 7 inches in Arena's drawing. However, that distance is inconsistent with the 33-foot 2-inch left tire track plus the 23-foot 4-inch distance from the left tire mark to the vehicle. The 32-foot 7-inch distance must therefore be the distance along the rail from the start of the bridge to the end of the gouge mark (or the projected end of the left tire track, which ends at almost the same place). The latter distance is accurately consistent with the fact that the left tire track starts 6 feet 6 inches from the right rub rail (as indicated by the 10-foot 6-inch and 4-foot distances in Fig. 1 of my previous chapter), forming the base of a right-angled triangle.

The following testimony concerning the landing position was given at the exhumation hearing:

Assistant District Attorney Fernandes: With reference to this bridge, can you describe the position of the car with reference to the bridge?

Arena: Well, the front end of the car was no more than six or seven feet away from the actual closest point of the bridge. I have taken measurements and I believe at the time *it was about 23 feet 7 inches away from the gouge on the wood. From the gouge in the wood, the closest point of the car landed in the water about 23 feet up and about five feet out.*

Fernandes: From the shore?

Arena: *From the exit point on that bridge, that gouge in the wood.*

Fernandes: All right, have you the exhibits there?

Arena: My measurements are attached to that accident report.

Flanagan, attorney for the Kopechnes: When did you make those measurements, sir?

Arena: I made the measurements after the car had been removed from the water, but I was given measurements from the registry inspectors who were at the scene conducting a simultaneous investigation and their measurements were approximately the same as mine.

Fig. 8(b) is a corrected version of Arena's sketch, drawn by the author. The final resting point of the vehicle was 55 feet 11 inches from the start of the bridge, placing it well past the end of the horizontal top section of the bridge and part way down the inclined section on the other side, as shown in photos included in Chapter 13 of this book. The vehicle ended up on its roof, located very close to the vertical edge of the channel dredged under the bridge. The diver, Farrar, testified that it was difficult to maneuver around the vehicle on the east side of the car due to the rapidly sloping bank. The east bank of the channel can be seen clearly in the BBC documentary *Chappaquiddick*.

Distance traveled by the vehicle over and through the water

Given the relatively large distance between the gouge mark and the final resting position of the vehicle in the water, as indicated in Fig. 8(b), it is obvious that the vehicle did not come to a complete stop and fall vertically off the bridge at the position defined by the gouge mark. After the left front wheel hit the rub rail, near where the gouge mark ended, the vehicle tilted to the right and hence the left track came to an end, but the vehicle had sufficient momentum to carry it well past the top section of the bridge. As shown by the simulation experiments in the following section, and as expected from the physics of the problem, the vehicle would have continued forward and downward until the undercarriage at the rear of the car on its left side, and then the left rear tire, clipped the rub rail, rolling the vehicle to the right rapidly, pitching it forward slightly, and projecting the vehicle off the bridge.

It can be seen in Fig. 8(b) that the gouge mark ended at a point 23 feet 4 inches from the point at which the near side of the vehicle ended up at the bottom of the channel. The horizontal distance traveled through the water is unknown, but a reasonable estimate, based on experiments with a toy vehicle, is about 6 feet, in which case the vehicle traveled about 17 feet horizontally through the air before it impacted the water. Fischer estimated, incorrectly, that the vehicle traveled 31 feet through the air, as described in Section 5 of my first chapter.

SECTION 3. EXPERIMENTS WITH A TOY VEHICLE

It is possible to simulate the behavior of a real vehicle using smaller models, provided the results are suitably scaled. I have described the scaling problem generally in Sections 1 and 3 of my third chapter, and more thoroughly in two peer-reviewed scientific papers.[1] In the present case, the toy vehicle will replicate the motion of Kennedy's vehicle, both through the air and through the water, if it rotates through about the same angle after falling a vertical distance equal to half its length.

The toy vehicle weighed 416 grams and was 202 mm long. It was filmed as it was pushed off the edge of a horizontal ramp at an approach angle of 15 degrees. A 4 mm high rubber rail was attached to the side of the ramp to simulate the impact of rubber tires on the rail since the toy vehicle was fitted with hard plastic wheels rather than rubber wheels. No attempt was made to simulate a braking or accelerating approach since the primary objective was to determine the behavior of a vehicle as it falls off the side of a ramp and the effects of collision with the rub rail.

---

[1] R. Cross, *Launch of a Vehicle from a Ramp*, The Physics Teacher, 2011, Vol. 49, pp. 410-411; R. Cross, *The Chappaquiddick Incident*, The Physics Teacher, 2016, Vol. 54, pp. 520-522

A typical video sequence is shown in Fig. 9. Differences were observed in the initial bounce height, depending on the approach speed, but the sequence in Fig. 9 was quite reproducible and is consistent with the actual tire tracks and rub rail marks observed in the accident photographs.

In particular, it can be seen that:

a) When the right front wheel ran over the rub rail, the vehicle tilted slightly to the right.

b) After both right wheels fell off the ramp, and just before the left front wheel reached the rail, the vehicle tilted further to the right, with the result that parts of the undercarriage came into contact with the rail. Both left wheels remained in contact with the ramp at this time.

c) When the front left wheel hit the rail, the whole left side of the vehicle tilted up, with the result that the left rear wheel lost contact with the ramp and the vehicle tilted further to the right.

d) The whole vehicle rotated clockwise off the bridge and became airborne until the undercarriage and then the left rear wheel clipped the rail. The left front wheel impact followed by the impacts of the undercarriage and left rear wheel in succession generated a rapid sideways rotation of the whole vehicle as well as a slight forward pitch. The observed damage to the outer edge of the rail near the gouge mark, shown in my first chapter, Fig. 1, is consistent with this behavior.

R front wheel rolls over rub rail   R rear wheel rolls over rub rail

Vehicle tilts slightly to right   L side lifts up as L front wheel hits rail

Vehicle starts falling   Rapid roll when L rear wheel hits rail

Fig. 9. Simulation of Kennedy's accident using a toy vehicle.

A side-on view is shown in Fig. 10 where the toy vehicle was launched off the side of an inclined ramp into a container of water. A rub rail was attached to the side of the ramp to simulate the actual rail. The sequence of events was the same as that in Fig. 9, showing that the toy vehicle fell nose down onto its roof rather than the passenger side, impacting the bottom of the water container heavily. The impact force on the roof of the vehicle was much larger when the roof impacted the bottom of the water container than when it impacted the water surface itself. A similar effect would be evident if a person dove head first into water. An injury would be much more likely when jumping or diving into shallow water than in deep water.

In Fig. 10, the rear section of the roof slammed into the bottom of the container as a result of the counterclockwise torque generated by the drag force on the front end. The effect is described further in Section 3 of the following chapter. The horizontal distance traveled through the water was about one third of one car length, the horizontal speed being slightly greater than the vertical impact speed. This would correspond to a horizontal distance through the water of about 6 feet for Kennedy's Oldsmobile.

Unlike a high-speed highway accident, Kennedy's vehicle was not extensively damaged by multiple impacts as it bounced and rolled along the highway. In Kennedy's case, there were only two separate impacts: one on the roof and one on the passenger-side doors. The simulations shown in Figs. 9 and 10 indicate that the roof rather than the passenger-side doors was damaged during the accident at the bridge.

The toy vehicle approached the edge of the ramp at only 2.8 mph. It rotated at a faster rate than Kennedy's vehicle and fell through a smaller height, but the scaling indicates that it rotated through a similar angle. An exact scaling from the toy vehicle result to Kennedy's vehicle would not be appropriate since the effect of the impact of each wheel on the rub rail may not have scaled correctly. Nevertheless, the qualitative features of the simulation experiments are entirely consistent with the tire tracks and other marks observed on the bridge and provide a simple explanation for the roof damage.

Other water entry scenarios were filmed using the toy vehicle, both with and without the ramp. Many different outcomes were observed, but the ramp launch results in Figs. 9 and 10 come closest to explaining both the roof damage and the complete absence of any damage to the front end. In the toy vehicle simulation in Fig. 10, it was the rear end of the roof that slammed into the bottom of the container. In Kennedy's case, the channel at the bottom of the pond sloped upward at about 6.5 degrees as it neared the far eastern edge, in which case the front end of the roof probably slammed into the sand before the rear end did. That would explain the damage to the front end of the roof and the shattering of the front windscreen. Alternatively, the whole roof may have impacted the sand, damaging the front and rear ends simultaneously.

Fig. 10. Entry of a toy vehicle into water when the vehicle is launched off the side of a ramp.

SECTION 4. TRAJECTORY AND LAUNCH SPEED

Kennedy's accident was possibly the most complicated single-vehicle accident that any investigator would ever have to deal with, involving at least six separate stages. There was the approach to the bridge along Dike Road; the path up the bridge while all four wheels remained on the bridge; then a short period where all four wheels left the bridge one at a time; then the flight through the air; then entry into water; and, finally, impact with the sand at the bottom. Each stage needs to be considered separately, but in this section we will examine only the trajectory and launch speed.

When calculating the trajectory and the speed of a vehicle launched off a ramp into water there are three separate stages to consider. This becomes obvious when it is pointed out, but neither of the two experienced accident investigators (Fischer and McHenry) appeared to be aware of the problem. Both of them estimated the horizontal distance traveled by the vehicle starting from a point on the bridge and ending with a point on the sand in order to calculate the speed through the air. The problem with that approach is that the correct speed can only be determined starting from a point in the air and ending with another point in the air. The time in the air can then be calculated from the fall time through the air, knowing the acceleration due to gravity.

Before the free-fall stage, part of the vehicle was in the air but part was still in contact with the bridge. In that case, the trajectory and fall time would depend on the bridge force acting "up" as well as the force due to gravity acting "down." For example, if the two front wheels had fallen off the bridge but the other two were still traveling along it, then the vehicle's center of mass would accelerate vertically at less than g. Meanwhile, a torque generated by the force on the rear wheels as the front ones were falling would cause the vehicle to rotate about its center of mass at increasing speed, until the rear wheels followed the front ones off the bridge.

The second stage involves free fall where the only or the dominant force on the object is that due to gravity. Air resistance is always present when an object is moving through the air, but it is typically a lot smaller than the force due to gravity, especially if the object is moving at a relatively low speed. For example, the free-fall stage in Fig. 9 extends from the fourth to the sixth frame, just after the left-side wheels leave the ramp and just before the front end would have entered the water.

During free fall, the vehicle will rotate about its center of mass at a constant speed, travel in the horizontal direction at a constant speed, and accelerate in the vertical direction at g. The toy car experiment shown in Fig. 9 indicates that the free-fall stage was interrupted momentarily when the rear left wheel clipped the rub rail. The effect of that impact on the vertical free-fall trajectory is estimated in Section 1 of the following chapter.

It appears in Fig. 9 that the undercarriage of the vehicle might still be in contact with the ramp in frames 4 and 5, but this was not the case in Kennedy's accident since there was no scarring along the rail during this part of the fall. The only scarring that was observed was that next to the gouge mark, which occurred when the vehicle was falling off the bridge, and which corresponds to the position of the toy car in frame 5 of Fig. 9. Since that scarring was relatively light, it would have only a very minor effect on the horizontal free-fall trajectory.

Just after the free-fall stage, part of the vehicle was still in the air but part had made contact with the water. The vehicle did not come to a sudden stop at that point. In the case of a vehicle impacting with water, gravity will cause the vehicle to continue falling into the water, but the water will push upward and backward on the vehicle resulting in a reduction in the vertical acceleration, a reduction in the horizontal speed, and a change in the rotation speed of the vehicle.

A warning sign was placed at the approach to Dike Bridge soon after the accident. The events have been shrouded in mystery to this day. Accident investigators solve puzzles like this one by conducting a rigorous examination of the crash scene evidence, a process that was never seriously attempted in 1969. Photo Jack Hubbard

The free-fall stage is the easiest to calculate so we will consider it first. However, it is first necessary to estimate when the free-fall phase started and when it ended. Carefully considered estimates are shown in Figs. 11(a) and 11(b), viewing the fall from above and also side-on. The vehicle is shown at three different times, the letters A, B, and C denoting the position of the vehicle at each of those times. At time A, all four wheels have just left the bridge and the vehicle has just commenced the free-fall phase. At B, the vehicle has just entered the water, marking the end of the free-fall phase. At C, the vehicle has come to rest at the bottom of the channel and is at right angles to the bridge.

The position of the vehicle on the bottom of the channel, perpendicular to the bridge, was observed the morning after the accident. The vehicle probably rotated to that position during the night as a result of the fast-moving flood current, with most of that rotation probably occurring while the rear end was still relatively buoyant from the air in the trunk. Also, immediately after the vehicle hit the sand at the bottom, it may have bounced up slightly and then rotated on its roof due to swirling water displaced by the vehicle. Both of these effects were observed in the toy vehicle simulation experiments.

If Kennedy's vehicle rolled sideways off the bridge and landed on its roof as in Fig. 10, then the free-fall phase of the fall would be approximately as shown in Figs. 11a and 11b. The estimated free fall horizontal distance is 17 feet and the estimated free fall vertical distance is 5 feet. The 17-foot horizontal distance allows for an additional 6 feet of travel underwater before the vehicle came to rest on the bottom.

The 5-foot vertical drop was calculated assuming a 7-foot drop from the bridge deck to the water, plus the 21.2-inch height of the center of mass of the vehicle, less the 7-inch drop when the vehicle rotated 13 degrees as it carved the gouge, less about 38 inches if the vehicle landed in the water inclined at an angle of about 10 degrees to the water's surface.

At Dike Bridge, the vehicle began to roll sideways off the bridge when the right rear wheel left the bridge. Rotation of the vehicle is a separate issue to free fall distance and is considered in more detail in Section 1 of the following chapter.

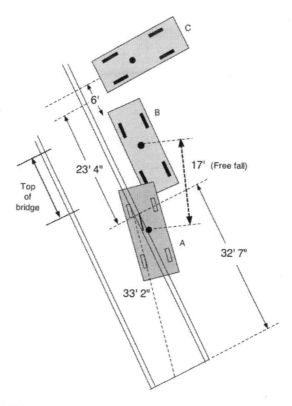

Fig. 11(a). Free fall into water, viewed to scale from above.

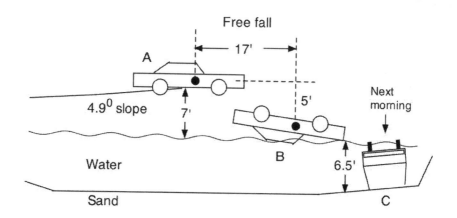

Fig. 11(b). Free fall viewed from the side. The depth of the water at impact on the far eastern edge of the channel was about 6.5 feet at the time of the accident.

21

Technical Aspects of the Accident
by Prof. Rod Cross, Physics Department,
Sydney University

The present chapter is more technical than the previous two and is concerned with evidence at the accident scene and the interpretation of that evidence, including estimates of the rotational speed, launch speed, the trajectory through the air and the water, and estimates of the impact force on the vehicle. It can be skipped over by all but the most curious or technically inclined.

*D*ike Bridge in 1969 was a narrow, one-lane wood bridge on Chappaquiddick Island in the town of Edgartown, Massachusetts. It spanned a channel into an inland body of water known as Poucha Pond. As shown in Photo A8, the bridge sloped upward at 1.4 degrees at the start, increased in slope to about 5 degrees towards the top of the bridge, was level at maximum height, and sloped downward on the other side. The length of the bridge was 81 feet and its width was 10.5 feet plus a rub rail on each side.

Evidence was presented at the inquest that the rub rails were 10 inches wide and 4 inches high, although other evidence suggests that the rails may have been only 9 inches wide, given that the total width of the bridge, including the two rails, was 12 feet. In Fischer's report, he presents a case that the rails were probably 9.5 inches wide and 5 inches high, but the difference is not particularly significant and I have assumed that the rails were 10" x 4".

At the inquest, Inspector Kennedy testified that the distance from the bridge to the water, shown on his accident diagram as 7 feet 6 inches, was the distance measured at 10:30 a.m., about 35 minutes before low tide. This would also have been around the same distance from the bridge at 11:15 p.m. the previous evening, 35 minutes after low tide. However, the accident appears to have occurred sometime between 12:45 and 1:30 a.m. – perhaps two hours later than 11:15 p.m. With a range of slightly less than 22 inches that evening between low and high water, the distance from the bridge to the water at the time of the accident would have been about 7 feet.

Registry Inspector Robert Molla told Bill Fischer that the 7.5-foot measurement represented the distance "from where the car left the bridge deck to the water." Since the horizontal distance from the bridge to the vehicle was measured from the end of the gouge mark, the bridge height must have been measured from that location, too.

Photo A8. Dike Bridge looking west after the vehicle was hauled from the water. Photo Jack Hubbard

The depth of the water varies with the tide but would have been about 6.5 feet deep around the vehicle at the time of the accident. When observed the next morning, the easternmost rear tire was 7 inches higher than the westernmost one over a track distance of 5.25 feet. This indicates that the bottom sloped upward at about 6.5 degrees at the far eastern side of the channel. Since the channel under the bridge had recently been dredged, there were no large rocks where the vehicle came to rest, just water and hard-packed sand.

The vehicle left the bridge on the 5-degree slope and landed in the water on the downward side of the bridge. Since the vehicle left the edge of the bridge at an angle of about 10 degrees to the rail, the actual slope of the bridge in the launch direction was 4.9 degrees rather than 5. However, the 0.1-degree difference is of no real consequence, especially since the slope of the bridge is not known to an accuracy of 0.5 degrees.

Kennedy's vehicle

The vehicle involved in the accident was Kennedy's 1967 model Oldsmobile Delmont 88 four-door sedan, probably fitted with the standard 330-cubic-inch engine. Its dimensions were: length 217 inches (18.1 feet); width 80 inches (6.67 feet); height 55.5 inches (4.62 feet); track width (center of tires) 63 inches (5.25 feet); wheelbase 123 inches (10.25 feet).

The weight, assuming no air conditioner, was 3970 pounds (1800 kg) empty or about 4300 pounds (1950 kg) with Kennedy and Mary Jo as passengers. Height of CM (Center of Mass): 21.2 inches. Weight distribution: 53.4 percent to the front.

Maximum acceleration, assuming the 330-cubic-inch engine and no air conditioner, was 9.8 ft/sec^2 with two passengers (3.0 m/sec^2) and approximately 10.6 ft/sec^2 empty (3.23 m/sec^2).

SECTION 1. ROTATION OF THE VEHICLE

The evidence provided by the marks on Dike Bridge, as well as the toy vehicle simulations, indicate that just before it fell off the bridge, Kennedy's vehicle had rotated sideways through an angle of 13 degrees before the control arm began carving a gouge in the rub rail. Since the control arm supports the coil spring, the arm would depress as the car moved forward, meaning that rotation would continue at roughly the same rate while the gouge was being carved and while the left rear wheel continued to leave a track on the bridge. Since the left tire track came to a sudden end when the left front wheel hit the rub rail, the whole left side must have lifted off the bridge as a result of sudden rotation of the vehicle to the right.

Rotation of the vehicle off the bridge would have commenced at around the same time even if there had been no left front wheel impact on the rail. As shown in Fig. 11(a), the center of mass passed beyond the outside edge of the rail at about the same time that the left front wheel impacted the rail. The vehicle would therefore have rotated off the bridge even without the assistance of the left front wheel impact. The impact not only increased the rate of rotation but acted to project the whole vehicle off the bridge.

The scarring to the rub rail just to the right of the gouge mark, extending over a distance of about 4 feet, indicates that the left rear wheel must have impacted the rub rail on its way down, as depicted in the last image of Fig. 9. The damage occurred as a short length of frame on the undercarriage just in front of the left rear wheel scraped the outer edge of the rail as the vehicle was moving forward and downward. The toy vehicle simulations, as well as the physics of the problem, indicate that the impact of the left rear wheel on the rail would have increased the rotation rate significantly.

The rate of rotation of Kennedy's vehicle cannot be known precisely, but the impact damage to both the roof and the bridge suggests strongly that the vehicle must have rotated in a manner similar to that in the toy vehicle simulations. In that case, reasonable estimates can be obtained concerning the effects on rotation speed of the two impacts with the rub rail, first by the left front wheel and then by the left rear wheel. Those estimates, when combined with the 17-foot free fall horizontal distance, indicate that the vehicle was projected off the bridge at a horizontal speed of 15 mph, landing in the water 0.76 seconds later.

The resulting trajectory of the center of mass is shown in Fig. 12. The trajectory starts with the center of mass at a height of 5 feet and ends when the vehicle first impacts the water, as shown in Fig. 11(b). The fall height is 5 feet and the horizontal distance traveled from the bridge to the water is 17 feet. The vehicle was projected off the bridge at an angle of 5 degrees above the horizontal, while the impact of the left rear wheel acted to reduce the vertical fall speed temporarily (see Fig. 13), thereby increasing the time taken for the vehicle to fall into the water and increasing the rate of rotation as the vehicle fell through the air.

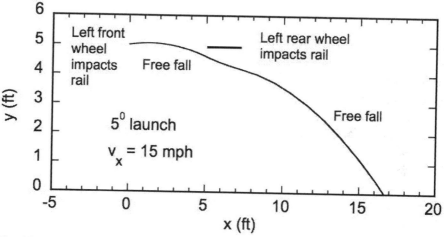

Fig. 12. Trajectory of the center of mass

The calculations and the evidence leading to the result shown in Fig. 12 are based on the rate of rotation, as well as the free fall distances, and are outlined in the remainder of this section.

Calculations

The initial rate of rotation would depend on the vertical force, F, that was exerted on the left front wheel when it impacted the rail. That force would exert a torque, FD, about a rotation axis passing through the center of mass of the vehicle, the axis being located at a distance D = 0.8 m from the left front wheel. If Icm is the moment of inertia of the vehicle about that axis, and ω is the angular velocity of rotation, then

$$FD = Icm \, d\omega/dt.$$

For rotation about the long axis of the vehicle, Icm is approximately $M(H^2 + W^2)/12$, where H is the height of the vehicle and W is its width. For Kennedy's vehicle, H = 55.5 inches (1.41 m), W = 80 inches (2.03 m), and M = 1800 kg. However, most of the weight of the vehicle is in the lower half of the vehicle. If we take H to be 1.0 m rather than 1.41 m, then Icm = 766 kg.m^2.

Suppose that the vehicle rotated through an angle of 150 degrees during the 0.76-second fall time in the manner shown in Fig. 9. The angle and time here may have been slightly different but are approximately correct, given that the vehicle came to rest on its roof. Then ω = 150/0.76 = 197 degrees/sec = 3.4 rad/sec. Suppose also that the left front wheel remained in contact with the rub rail for 0.1 seconds until it lifted off the rail. The estimated contact time is consistent with a relatively long impact involving a heavy car and a soft rubber tire. In that case, ω increased from zero to 3.4 rad/sec in 0.1 sec, giving $d\omega/dt$ = 34 rad/sec^2, and hence

$$F = 766 \times 34 / 0.76 = 34,200 \text{ Newton.}$$

The weight of the vehicle was Mg = 1800 x 9.8 = 17,640 N, so the estimated impact force on the front wheel is 1.9 Mg, or slightly less than twice the weight of the vehicle.

A vertical force of that magnitude is larger than expected for a low-speed, horizontal collision between a wheel and the rub rail. Alternatively, a vertical force of this magnitude could easily arise if the vehicle fell vertically onto the rub rail. Whenever an object falls vertically onto a hard surface, the impact force is typically many times larger than the weight of the object, and can even be 100 times larger depending on the stiffness of the object and the impact speed. A force equal to twice the weight would represent a soft, low speed impact, while a 0.1-second duration impact would represent the impact of an object that is both soft and very heavy.

Consequently, it is more likely that rapid rotation of the vehicle resulted not from the impact of the left front wheel on the rail but from the impact of the left rear wheel with the rail when the vehicle was falling off the bridge, or by the combined effects of both impacts.

A vertical impact force 1.9 times larger than the vehicle weight would not only result in rapid rotation of the vehicle but would also act to decrease the vertical fall speed. The vertical impulse on the vehicle is given by FT, where F = 0.9 Mg, the total force acting up on the vehicle (Mg down and 1.9 Mg up), and T = 0.1 seconds, the time over which F acts on the vehicle. Since the impulse is equal to the change in momentum, the vehicle speed would decrease in the vertical direction by an amount V given by FT = MV, and hence V = FT/M = 0.9gT = 0.88 m/sec.

Even though the impact of the falling rear left wheel with the rub rail might exert a greater vertical force than the impact of the left front wheel, the impact of the front wheel would also have had a significant effect. It was the impact that lifted the left side of the vehicle off the bridge and that launched the vehicle off the bridge. Suppose that the vertical force on the left front wheel was F = Mg/2 and it lasted a time T = 0.1 seconds while the tire compressed and expanded and while the left side of the vehicle was lifted up.

Based on the previously estimated rotation rate, the effect of the front wheel impact would be to rotate the vehicle sideways at about 1 rad/sec by the end of the impact, or through an angle of about 3 degrees after 0.1 seconds. During the impact, the rotation speed increased from zero to 1 rad/sec, so the average rotation speed was 0.5 rad/sec, or about 30 degrees/sec. Rotation at 60 degrees/sec would then continue until the left rear wheel hit the rail about 0.3 seconds later, meaning that the left rear wheel would hit the rail after the vehicle had rotated through a total angle of about 30 degrees, including the initial 13 degrees of sideways tilt.

A different result was obtained in the toy vehicle simulation where the rear left wheel impacted the rail at a time when the vehicle had rotated by about 60 degrees rather the 30-degree tilt just calculated. A simple explanation is that the vertical force on the left front wheel contributed only about half of the total torque on the vehicle while the left front wheel was still in contact with the rail. The other half was due to the fact that the vehicle commenced rotating to the right around its longitudinal axis when its right rear wheel rolled over the rub rail close to the start of the bridge. The impact of the left front wheel with the rail simply added to that rate of rotation.

Impact of the left rear wheel with the rail would have occurred when the center of mass of the vehicle had fallen about 0.12 meters (0.4 feet) below the bridge surface, as indicated in Fig. 13.

If the vehicle was launched at 5 degrees above the horizontal, and the left rear wheel had impacted the rub rail on the way down, then trajectory calculations for a 17-foot horizontal landing distance show that the car would have impacted the water at 11.4 mph in the vertical direction and 15 mph in the horizontal direction, as shown in Figs. 12 and 13.

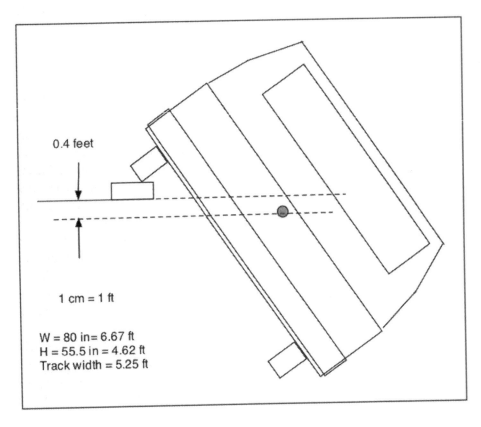

Fig. 13. Impact of the left rear wheel with the rub rail

SECTION 2. IMPACT FORCE ON THE VEHICLE

The main force on an object moving quickly through water is usually the force of the water itself on the object, commonly known as the drag force, represented by the formula $F = 0.5\ C_D\ \rho\ A\ v^2$, where C_D is a number called the drag coefficient, about equal to 1 for a flat surface moving through water or 0.5 for a surface angled at 45 degrees through the water; ρ is the density of water, about 1000 kg/m³ (or 1027 kg/m³ for saltwater); A is the cross-sectional area of the object in contact with the water; and v is the speed of the object through the water. In addition, there is a buoyant force that acts vertically upwards and the gravitational force that acts vertically downwards. The last two forces tend to cancel, but if they don't cancel, then the object will either sink to the bottom or rise and float.

Fischer argued that water does not compress and for that reason it is hard and will damage a vehicle entering water even at moderate speeds. However, any slight increase in water pressure at the point of entry will cause the water to flow around the sides of the vehicle, thereby limiting the increase in pressure on the impact surface. As the vehicle sinks, the buoyant force will increase at first until the vehicle is fully submerged, but will then decrease as the vehicle fills with water. However, the drag force decreases at an even faster rate as the vehicle sinks since it is proportional to the velocity squared. Consequently, the impact force is greatest when the vehicle first strikes the water, and maximum force will occur when the vehicle lands on the water "flat."

The pressure on the surface is given by $p = F/A$, where A is the impact surface area. For a flat surface striking the water at a right angle, the pressure is then given by $p = 0.5\ \rho\ v^2$, where v is the impact speed. At v = 11.4 mph, p = 1.9 psi. As described in my first chapter, the pressure is much too small to cause any damage to the vehicle. A much more likely cause of damage would be an impact with hard sand at the bottom of the channel.

The impact speed at the bottom of the channel is difficult to estimate precisely since it would depend on the impact angle on the water's surface and on the buoyant force, neither of which are known. The buoyant force would depend on how rapidly the vehicle filled with water. All that is known with certainty is that the vehicle sank to the bottom of the pond and that both the passenger side and the roof were severely dented. Regardless of whether the vehicle entered the water on its side or on its roof, the vehicle would slow down rapidly through the water due to the initially large drag force and the buoyant force. Both of those forces would decrease as the vehicle speed decreased and as the vehicle filled with water.

The vehicle entered the water with estimated center of mass speeds $v_x = 15$ mph and $v_y = 11.4$ mph, indicating that the center of mass approached the water surface at a combined or resultant speed of 18.8 mph and at an angle of 37 degrees to the horizontal. The actual orientation of the vehicle as it entered the water would depend on the forward pitch through the air during free fall, but it was probably similar to that shown in the third frame of Fig. 10 where the toy vehicle has just entered the water.

The vehicle was 18 feet long whereas the water depth was just 6.5 feet. If the vehicle had entered the water oriented at 37 degrees to the horizontal, parallel to the velocity vector, it would have speared in a straight line to the bottom, impacting directly on the front end. Since there was no damage to the front end, it can be assumed that the pitch angle was only about 10 or 20 degrees, as it was with the toy vehicle simulation in Figs. 9 and 10. In that case, the drag force acting vertically upward on the front end would exert a strong torque on the vehicle, rotating the rear end rapidly into the water. It would also decelerate the vehicle in a vertical direction. The horizontal force on the front end would act to decelerate the vehicle in a horizontal direction.

A reasonable estimate of the vertical impact speed at the bottom of the channel, consistent with observations of water entry of the toy vehicle, is that it was at least 4 mph due to the combined effects of the increased vertical entry speed of the rear end into the water and the decrease in vertical speed through the water. An impact speed of 4 mph would be sufficient to severely dent the roof or the passenger-side doors, but not both at the same time. Further details are described in Section 3 where an estimate is made of the terminal velocity of the vehicle.

SECTION 3. TERMINAL VELOCITY

It is not immediately obvious that a toy vehicle can reliably be used to simulate the fall of a real vehicle in water. However, a simple calculation shows that it can.

The acceleration due to gravity is the same in both cases. How about the drag force? In order to simplify the problem, suppose that a vehicle falls vertically into water without any horizontal motion and that the only vertical force on the vehicle is the drag force. That is a good approximation if the impact speed is large enough for the drag force to be much larger than the gravitational force. Then the equation of motion in the vertical direction is $M\, dv/dt = -k_0 v^2$, where $k_0 = 0.5\, C_D\, r\, A$. Alternatively, $dv/dt = -kv^2$, where $k = k_0/M$. This equation has a simple solution given by

$$v = v_0 / (1 + kv_0 t),$$

where v_0 is the initial speed and t is the time. The speed will therefore drop by a factor of two when $t = 1/(kv_0) = 2M / (C_D\, \rho\, A\, v_0)$. The time for the speed to drop by half therefore depends on the initial speed, v_0, in addition to the mass and area of the vehicle. That makes it easy to compare real vehicles with toy vehicles.

If y is the vertical distance below the water's surface, then v = dy/dt, which can easily be solved to show that

$$y = \ln (1 + k\, v_0\, t) / k.$$

As the vehicle falls through the water, it slows down quickly at first, so the drag force decreases with time and the velocity then decreases more slowly. For Kennedy's vehicle, M = 1800 kg and A = 11 m^2, representing the maximum possible area when the vehicle happened to land flat on its roof. In that case, k = 3.05 and the vehicle speed would drop from 12 mph to 4 mph in only 0.122 seconds, having fallen through a distance of only 0.36 meters.

However, the above calculation ignores the downward force due to gravity. When the drag force is equal and opposite to the gravitational force, the total force is zero and the vehicle will sink at a constant speed called the terminal velocity. That happens when Mg = $k_0 v^2$, or when v = 4 mph in Kennedy's case. In that case, the vertical speed would drop quickly from 12 mph to 6 mph and then decrease much more slowly to a speed slightly greater than 4 mph after sinking through 6.5 feet of water to the bottom, assuming that the vehicle landed flat on its roof.

The toy vehicle had a mass M = 0.416 kg and a maximum surface area A = 0.016 m^2, so k = 19.2. At an entry speed of 2 m/sec in Fig 8, the vehicle would have reached its terminal velocity of 0.71 m/sec, having fallen through a distance of 0.064 meters in 0.06 seconds according to the above approximate formulas.

In both cases, the two vehicles would reach a terminal speed about three times smaller than the entry speed in a distance less than the length of the vehicle, meaning that the toy vehicle results provide a useful guide to the behavior of Kennedy's vehicle, even in water. The actual terminal speed is complicated by several other factors. The terminal speed would increase if A was smaller, or if the vehicle entered the water nose down or partly on its side, and would decrease if air did not escape from the vehicle and acted to generate a large buoyant force. In Kennedy's case, the vehicle sank, and so did the toy vehicle, since both vehicles filled with water through open windows.

In Fig. 10, the toy vehicle slowed down through the water as a result of the drag force, but the impact speed at the bottom of the container was significantly larger than the terminal velocity calculated above for several reasons. One is that it did not impact the water flat on its roof. It entered nose down and partly on its side. Consequently, the speed through the water remained relatively high until just before the impact on the bottom when the vehicle rotated onto its roof. A second reason is that the vehicle was rotating sideways as it fell through the air, and continued to rotate sideways through the water. As a result, the driver's side (nearest the camera) impacted the bottom of the container at a speed greater than that of the center of mass and greater than that on the passenger side. Similar results would be expected with Kennedy's vehicle: that is, the vertical impact speed on the sand would have been greater than 4 mph, especially on the driver's side.

An additional effect observed in the toy vehicle simulations is shown in Fig. 15. If the front end enters the water nose down, the drag force acting up on the front end exerts a torque about the center of mass. If the front end entered the water nose down, it could potentially spear straight through the water to the bottom and strike the sand at a relatively high speed on its front end. However, if the vehicle is rotating sideways around its longitudinal axis as it enters the water, the surface area underneath the vehicle increases as the vehicle sinks, thereby increasing the drag force acting vertically upwards. The drag force acting up on the hood around its lateral axis exerts a torque about the center of mass. As a result, the rear end swings down rapidly and impacts the sand at a speed greater than that at the front end.

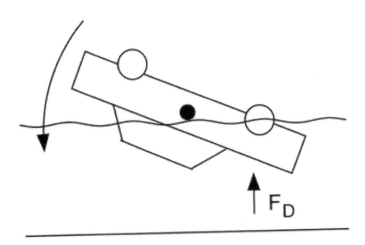

Fig. 15. Rotation of rear end due to drag force on front end

Conversions

1 m = 3.28 ft

1 kg = 2.2 lb

1 m/sec = 3.281 ft/sec = 2.237 mph

10 mph = 4.470 m/sec

1 psi = 6,895 N/m^2

1 degree = 6.28 radian

1 J = 1 N-m = .74 ft lb f

1 ft = .305 m

1 lb = .45 kg

1 mph = 0.4470 m/sec = 1.467 ft/sec

1 ft/sec = 0.3048 m/sec = 0.6818 mph

1 N = 0.2248 lb-force

1 atmosphere = 1.33 kPa

22

From Speculation to Certainty

*D*r. Cross has determined that the vehicle door dents and the shattered side windows could never have occurred from impact on water. The maximum pressure that the doors and windows could have sustained would be just 1.9 psi, and that pressure would be insufficient to cause the damage that was observed by Farrar before the vehicle was hauled from the channel. Dr. Cross has therefore concluded that there were two separate high-impact crash events, and that the damage to the passenger-side doors and windows occurred *before* the vehicle was driven off the bridge.

Is Dr. Cross correct? I put this question to Raul Ochoa, an aerospace mechanical engineer in Los Angeles with over 15 years of experience in the design and development of flight-worthy hardware, and to Guglielmo Cacciatore, a naval architect and marine engineer in Pozzallo, Italy. Cacciatore has a Masters degree in structural engineering from UCLA and has spent more than 15 years examining and analyzing dents and structural failure from ship and submarine collisions. Ochoa and Cacciatore performed a structural analysis on the passenger-side doors using the "finite element analysis" method. Their collaborative report is found in the Appendix, Note 6.

Ochoa and Cacciatore found that the front door of Kennedy's Oldsmobile would sustain permanent deformation at 15.1 psi of pressure and the rear door at 27.3 psi. In other words, the force required to create just tiny, permanent dents in the passenger-side doors would have surpassed the maximum possible force that could have been delivered from a drop into Dike Channel by a factor of 14⅓. The stress/strain curve after fracture is bilinear. To create dents 4.5 inches deep on the front door, which is less than actually occurred, the pressure jumps to 100 psi. That represents a Newton force of 101,200 spread out over the surface of the front door.

The speed, v, that would create a Newton force of 101,200 on the side of the front door from a drop to saltwater, assuming the door hit the water dead flat, can be determined by the formula $v = \sqrt{(N \div \frac{1}{2} \rho A)}$, where v is in meters/second, ρ is the density of saltwater in kg/m^3, and A is the cross-sectional area of the door in m^2. To create dents 4.5 inches deep in the front door, the vehicle would need to reach a speed of 17.41 m/sec, or 39 mph, before impact. That represents a dead-flat drop of 52 feet, or a fall of about five stories. That obviously could not have occurred at Dike Bridge.

Nor would the side windows have fractured, either. Ochoa performed a structural analysis on the side windows and found that the front window would fracture with a 10 psi load and the rear one at 9 psi; in other words, 5¼ times the maximum pressure that could have occurred from a dead-flat impact on water at Dike Bridge. That analysis can be found in the Appendix, Note 7.

It is important to point out that an impact pressure of 1.9 psi would be the maximum possible pressure the passenger-side doors and windows could have encountered at whatever speed the vehicle left the bridge and at whatever angle it struck the water. For instance, Donald Nelson, a physicist and author of *Chappaquiddick Tragedy: Kennedy's Second Passenger Revealed*, has speculated that the car left the bridge at 30.3 mph on a four-degree slope, then dropped six feet before landing flat on its passenger side. This is the highest launch speed that any author or accident specialist has ever suggested for Kennedy's accident. A car traveling that speed launched at that slope dropping that distance would strike the water at 15.6 mph in the vertical direction and 30.2 mph in the horizontal direction, for a combined speed impact of 34 mph.

Even if Nelson is correct, the only relevant impact speed for the doors and windows would be the 15.6 mph one since the horizontal component of velocity could not add any impact pressure to the underside of a car that lands in the water flat or nose down. In fact, if the car landed in the water nose down, which it must have done to account for the dented roof and shattered front windshield, the higher horizontal component of velocity would create a vacuum under the car as it moved forward through the water which would tend to reduce the pressure on the doors and windows.

This means that a car launched off Dike Bridge at Dr. Cross' lower speed should generate more pressure on the doors and windows than a car launched at a higher one. And, of course, the 1.9 psi pressure is a maximum. It can only reach that level if the vehicle lands perfectly flat on the water. With an angled entry, the pressure generated by the vertical component of velocity would be reduced by the abrupt deceleration of the car as its front end hit the water well before the forward door could.[1] Moreover, the impact on the doors and windows would no longer be flat. The impact pressure, already significantly diminished by the front-end entry, would be further reduced by an amount directly proportional to the so-called drag coefficient, or C_D, a fraction which is mostly a function of the impact angle.

Hydraulic shock, as an explanation for the door and window damage, *can be definitively and forever ruled out.*

Now what?

So what's left? What if, after impact on its roof on the bottom of the channel, the vehicle had somehow come to rest on its side over rocks before rolling back over onto its roof again? Irrespective of inquest testimony which states that the vehicle was found

---

[1] With an angled entry, the doors and windows will also incur pressure from the buoyant force once these are submerged, but this would not compensate for the loss of pressure from the drag force since the drag force decreases by the square of the velocity.

resting on hard-packed sand, and in spite the author's observation that no large rocks can be found at the eastern side of the channel today, could two large rocks have caused the vertical dents in the doors?

Cacciatore, the dent expert, sent this e-mail to me:

"The vertical dents in the doors were due to the buckling that is characteristic of a material subjected to a sudden, high-compressive stress. The side windows were fractured due to the stress on the edges of the doors that were adjacent to the glass when that impact occurred. But the shapes of the dents are not compatible with either impact on water or a point source like a rock. They would be compatible with cylindrical elements. I'm wondering if there was a pair of poles, pylons, tree trunks, or something cylindrical in shape spaced about one meter apart when the car dropped onto the sand? Or, could the vehicle have collided with a pair of bridge pilings as it was falling toward the water?"

Farrar noticed nothing like that on the bottom of the channel, and there is no chance the vehicle could have collided with a pair of bridge pilings a meter apart. Moreover, according to Cacciatore, the shape of those dents indicates that the impact on cylindrical elements was sudden – in physics terms a *dynamic* or "shock" force rather than a *static* or "slow and steady" one. Due to the wave propagation speed of steel, dynamic loads will cause far greater localized deformation than static ones, as shown in the following illustration and photos.

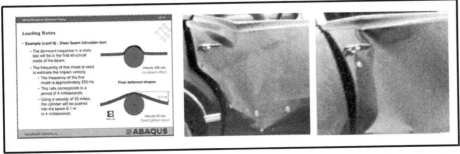

Illustration depicting a dynamic load (top) and static load (bottom); and photos showing dynamic dents to both passenger-side doors.

For dynamic dents to occur, the passenger side would have had to impact the bottom of the channel with substantial force. But if the vehicle had impacted the bottom with sufficient force to create dynamic dents in the passenger-side doors, where does that leave the roof? A dynamic impact on the bottom could account for damage to one or the other, but not both.

But what if Cacciatore is wrong about cylindrical objects and a dynamic force? Suppose the damage to the doors occurred as the vehicle sank slowly onto its side over a pair of very sharp, elongated rocks? Or, suppose the vertical dents occurred as the vehicle swiveled over two large rocks as the rear of the car shifted back and forth with the currents?

Even if the vehicle had somehow come to rest on its passenger side after impacting the sand on its roof (and then afterwards rolled back onto its roof again), rocks could never explain the passenger-side window damage. Those windows might indeed have been fractured as the vehicle swiveled over rocks or settled onto them slowly, with most, or all, of the shattered glass then dropping onto the sand. But there could not have been enough force to propel that glass throughout the interior of the car, as actually occurred.

Olsen says that when Farrar opened one of the doors on the side of the channel and went inside "he saw that there was glass all over the floor, indicating that the windows had blown inward on impact with the water."[1] At the inquest, Farrar said, "I noted that the two windows on the right-hand doors were blown out with the glass smashed and most of the glass shattered and spread throughout the car, as if from impact." Farrar and Batten told me the floor and seats were littered with small shards of glass from the passenger-side windows when the Oldsmobile was examined on the shore and later when it was parked at the Depot station. This is why hydraulic shock, until now, has always seemed like the obvious explanation for the passenger-side damage.

Now consider those doors and those windows, and the deeply dented roof and shattered front windshield, in the context of the semi-detached, driver-side mirror once more. In the absence of even the slightest scratch or dent on the driver side or the slightest damage to the mirror frame or the mirror glass, there is no logical way to account for the failure of the mirror's front fastener other than the obvious one: the steering wheel was tied off to the mirror post. Consider the absence of facial injuries, bruises, or fractures to two front-seat passengers, unsecured by seatbelts, subjected to a sudden vehicular deceleration into the shattered front windshield. Consider the extreme difficulty of a 220-pound driver exiting the upside-down Oldsmobile through the driver-side window without outside assistance. Consider the high level of carbon monoxide in the blood of a woman who did not smoke. *Consider Dr. Cross' certainty that the vehicle was accelerated up the bridge from a standing start.*

Especially, consider the vehicle damage in the context of the blood evidence, and the impossibility that the bloodstains on the shirt could have occurred as Mary Jo lay submerged underwater. It would have taken a substantial amount of time on land for blood to have saturated the back and both sleeves of the blouse of a victim with no obvious, visible wound. This rules out the possibility that Kennedy might have crashed into something soon after Look saw the vehicle, then in his panic drove straight off the bridge by accident.

---

[1] *The Bridge at Chappaquiddick*, p. 148

Finally, consider the vehicle damage and the conclusions of Dr. Cross, Ochoa, and Cacciatore in the context of Carol Jones's sighting at 11:35 p.m.

The passenger-side door and window damage must have occurred from an accident long before the vehicle was driven off the bridge. There is no other plausible explanation. The accident, as described by Kennedy or as imagined by most, is overruled by the forensic evidence.

The Chappaquiddick picture has changed. The reader will be asked to view the remaining evidence in this book with that understanding in mind. Unless one chooses to dismiss the findings of medical doctors, crash experts, engineers, and physicists altogether, it really leaves an objective thinker with no other choice.

The "investigation" of 1969

I am left wondering how any of this could have escaped the notice of crash experts in 1969. The science was there; it just had to be applied. But, of course, it did not escape notice. It was ignored. Assistant District Attorney Fernandes attempted to introduce the passenger-side doors into evidence at the inquest after having been alerted by Dr. McHugh of the Massachusetts crime lab. He was prevented by Judge Boyle. But if District Attorney Dinis, Fernandes's boss, read anything sinister in those doors, as he must have, he could have raised the possibility of a previous accident with any reporter. After all, convinced he was dealing with foul play, Dinis had already leaked the discovery of bloodstains on the back of Mary Jo's blouse to the *Boston Herald Traveler* on September 19, a month before the exhumation hearing. If he had done the same with the doors, the staged-accident theory, and the photos of the accident damage, would have gone from obscurity to mainstream and certainly examined more critically by crash experts, engineers, and authors in the years that followed. There might never have been a Chappaquiddick mystery at all.

Dinis never did. Any suspicions Dinis had were suppressed. By the time the inquest was concluded on January 8, 1970, Dinis, a Democrat, had thrown in the towel. Resistance was futile and damaging his chances of reelection. By the following March, when Leslie Leland was attempting to convene a grand jury, Dinis was firmly in the Kennedy camp and actively working to frustrate the process. He succeeded. As Dinis admitted later, "There's no question in my mind the grand jury would have indicted Ted Kennedy with involuntary manslaughter, if I had given them the case."[1]

The conclusion is inescapable. The Kennedy name was far more important to Massachusetts prosecutors than a search for the truth, or justice for Mary Jo. The agenda was, and always has been, to give the senator a free pass.

---

[1] *Senatorial Privilege*, pp. 391-392

PART 4: ANALYSIS

23
Questions with Answers

The accumulation of evidence in Part 3 paints a grim picture: the accident was staged. There is no real way to get around it, or any clear way to dispute it. Especially, Dr. Cross's three chapters demonstrate conclusively, with the help of original photographic evidence, that a) the vehicle was accelerated up the bridge from a standing start; b) the passenger-side door and window damage occurred from a previous accident on land; and c) no one could reasonably have been in that car without exhibiting noticeable physical injuries if not major ones.

Of secondary interest, Mary Jo drowned. Farrar's suffocation theory is physically (i.e. scientifically) impossible. Therefore, the staging almost certainly led to her death.

With Kappel's theory confirmed, it is time to ask some questions and see if there are some obvious answers.

Is there other evidence that the injury to Mary Jo occurred before Look saw the Oldsmobile at 12:40 a.m.?

The *Boston Herald Traveler* reported on July 24, 1969, that Mrs. Sydney K. Lawrence had told them there was no telephone at the cottage, just a jack for a telephone which was kept in the locked, detached building in the backyard used as her private painting studio. Esther Newberg also told the *Traveler* that there was no phone at the cottage. "No one was worried or concerned [about where Mary Jo was]. I suppose if there had been a telephone in the cottage we would have called to check, but there wasn't." But George Lardner Jr. of the *Washington Post* wrote that "there was a phone, apparently in working order, when investigators went to the cottage later."[1] The investigator, cited by Lardner, almost certainly refers to Tony Ulasewicz, President Nixon's "private eye."

At Nixon's request, Ulasewicz visited Lawrence Cottage on the evening of July 19, less than 12 hours after the accident had been reported to the police, and found it

---

[1] *The Last Kennedy*, p. 94.

"plucked clean" and unoccupied. Ulasewicz describes the painting studio this way: "Around the back of the cottage I discovered a small hideaway studio I thought might have been used by a writer or an artist. It was separated from the main house by a fence. I looked through the windows of the studio but saw nothing important, except a telephone."[1]

Ulasewicz's observation was confirmed on October 6, 1969, when Ralph Clifford, Editor/Publisher of the *New York Graphic,* listed three calls made from (617) 627-4020 on Kennedy's credit card, a number registered to Mr. Sydney Lawrence on Chappaquiddick, owner of Lawrence Cottage. Someone must have gone into Mrs. Lawrence's private studio, used the phone inside, and then carefully locked the studio door behind him afterwards. According to the *Graphic,* a total of 17 calls were made on Kennedy's credit card from Chappaquiddick and Edgartown but they were only describing 12 of them.

The first call from the studio was made at 11:57 p.m. on Friday, July 18, to (212) 935-8790, a number registered to Theodore Sorensen, special assistant to President John F. Kennedy who was to script Ted Kennedy's ill-fated and much criticized speech to the nation on TV at Hyannis Port a week later. The call lasted two minutes.

The second call from the studio was made at 12:04 a.m. on Saturday, July 19, to (617) 775-4732, the unlisted number at 165 Greenwood Ave., Hyannis Port, a house used by the Kennedy family as an office facility. The call lasted six minutes.

The third call was made at 12:12 a.m. on Saturday, July 19, to the same number at Hyannis Port and lasted 18 minutes.

These three calls, dialed one after the other – the first beginning at 11:57 p.m. and the last ending at precisely 12:30 a.m. – appear to have been made after the group had concluded that Mary Jo was dead, and when Kennedy, Gargan, and Markham had returned to Lawrence Cottage in the Oldsmobile with the body of Mary Jo. According to the *Graphic,* no further calls were made on Kennedy's credit card until 2:45 a.m., when a call was made to the Washington D.C. headquarters of Marshall & Hamilton, the office of Kennedy's attorney Burke Marshall, from the public phone at the Shiretown Inn in Edgartown.

According to the Manchester *Union Leader,* two other calls were made from Lawrence Cottage on Kennedy's credit card "before midnight" and twelve from the Shiretown Inn later that morning. However, only nine of the twelve Shiretown calls were detailed by the *Graphic,* and it has subsequently become known that Kennedy made several calls that night to his mistress Helga Wagner, at least one of those from the Shiretown Inn.

It appears Kennedy may have made five calls to Wagner that weekend but the number was never revealed to protect the privacy of Wagner, Kennedy, and/or Kennedy's wife. The two undisclosed calls from Lawrence Cottage before midnight

---

[1] *The President's Private Eye,* p. 190

may have been made to Helga Wagner earlier that day. At the inquest, Kennedy testified he joined the others for a swim at East Beach shortly after 1:00 p.m. on July 18, visiting Lawrence Cottage two separate times to change into and out of his bathing suit. On the first occasion, at least, he was alone. And when he arrived back at Lawrence Cottage at 7:30 p.m. for the cookout later that evening, he said he was the first to arrive. Kennedy testified that he took that opportunity to relax and take a bath before Markham arrived at 8:00 p.m.

Gargan testified at the inquest that he had personally arranged the rental of Lawrence Cottage. Steve Gentle, Mr. Lawrence's rental agent, may have given Gargan the key to the private painting studio so that Kennedy would have access to a phone if needed.[1]

Could the Valiant seen by Carol at 11:35 p.m. have left Kennedy off at the ferry so he would not be involved in the ensuing events at Dike Bridge?

No. No ferry operator recalled seeing Kennedy around 11:35 p.m., or after. Furthermore, calls were made continuously on Kennedy's credit card at Lawrence Cottage from 11:57 p.m. to 12:30 a.m., after Carol's sighting. Esther Newberg testified she was certain Gargan and Markham were at Lawrence Cottage continuously from midnight to 12:30 a.m., suggesting that Kennedy must have been making those calls himself from the private painting studio.

Q: At twelve o'clock, what was your activity as you best remember it? Who was there at twelve o'clock that you can remember?
Newberg: Everyone in the party, except Senator Kennedy and Mary Jo.
Q: So, I understand it now, the party continued between midnight and 12:30, essentially as it had been going on prior to Mr. Kennedy leaving, everyone in the living room for the most part and discussing whatever was discussed?
Newberg: That is right.
Q: Between midnight and 12:30, do you recall Mr. Markham and Mr. Gargan being present, and Mr. Crimmins?
Newberg: Yes, they were all there.

---

[1] Mr. Lawrence could not have given Kennedy the key. Sydney Lawrence told investigator Tony Ulasewicz that he was not aware that Kennedy would be renting the cottage. Lawrence knew only that "a Mr. Joseph Gargan left his phone number with the rental agent [Steve Gentle] who handled his summer rentals" (*The President's Private Eye*, p. 204).

What was the plan of the persons within the vehicle seen by Carol?

Their plan was, initially, to attempt to save the life of Mary Jo. After arriving at the conclusion that Mary Jo was beyond help, the plan was, as Kappel suggests, to save the career of Edward Kennedy by making it appear as if Mary Jo, driving an unfamiliar car, drove off the bridge on her own.

What about the American-type car seen at the ferry landing soon after 12:30 a.m.?

Someone needed to drive back to the ferry landing to arrange transportation between Chappaquiddick and Edgartown. After staging the accident, Kennedy would need to get back to Edgartown to establish his alibi. The sailing boat seen by Ballou was, as suggested by Kappel, Kennedy's own racing boat, the *Victura*.

The person who arranged the transportation might have been Kennedy's cousin Gargan, a knowledgeable yachtsman. Gargan might also have found the boat used to rendezvous with their racing boat – probably the small powerboat seen by Ballou and later abandoned near Memorial Wharf. Gargan might have found that boat on the Edgartown side using Roddy Hoar's rowboat which was tied up with a different knot and in a different place on Chappaquiddick the next morning. The powerboat may have been secured to the Chappaquiddick Beach Club dock in the outer harbor where Lansing Burns heard activity around 1:30 a.m.

The last call at Lawrence Cottage ended at 12:30 a.m. A car was observed at the ferry landing soon after 12:30 a.m. The Oldsmobile was seen by Look at the Dike Road intersection around 12:40 a.m. The timeline suggests that the car seen by the couple at the lighthouse was the rented white Valiant and not the Oldsmobile.

When asked about their conversation with Gargan and Markham after their return to the cottage at about 2:00 a.m., Mary Ellen Lyons said:

M. Lyons: We, you know, when they arrived, we asked them, you know, where they had been; what had happened. Oh, it was just, "Oh, don't even ask us, we have been looking for boats." It was confused.
Q: That they had been looking for boats, they said that?
M. Lyons: That was one of the things they said.

Nance Lyons, when questioned why Kennedy decided to swim across the channel when boats were available (presumably the Chappaquiddick ferry), replied.

N. Lyons: They said that they had been looking for a boat and couldn't find one.
Q: Had been looking for a boat?
N. Lyons: Yes.
Q: But not Mr. Kennedy?

N. Lyons: I don't – you know, they just said, you know, "We were looking for a boat."

Q: Was the purpose of the boat to assist the people at the party to get across, did you know?

N. Lyons: No, I would assume that this was among *the three involved.*

This testimony suggests that Kennedy, Gargan, and Markham were in the Valiant observed at the ferry landing soon after 12:30 a.m.

What about the man and a woman seen by Look at 12:40 a.m.?

While boat transportation was being arranged at the ferry landing, a man and a woman left Lawrence Cottage in Kennedy's Oldsmobile. Moving from the cottage back toward Dike Bridge, the man and woman met up with Look's vehicle at the intersection between School House Road and Chappaquiddick Road at about 12:40 a.m. Their first thought was to pull into Cemetery Road until the car passed. *They were attempting to hide.* Seeing Look's brake lights go on, they backed up before Look could reach them, then drove at a moderate speed down Dike Road.

Kappel suggests that the woman seen by Look was the comatose body of Mary Jo herself, propped up by the driver. I do not believe it at all likely. No one would be expected to prop up what he thought was a dead body on a dark, deserted road at night. If he had a body, he would be more likely to place it on the back seat or in the trunk.

The woman passenger seen by Look in the front seat was not Mary Jo – she was one of the Boiler Room Girls.

What about the shadow seen by Look in the back of the car?

Look said he saw "a person, a bag, or a shadow of some kind" on the rear seat. This was either Rosemary Keogh's bag, found in the front seat area when the car was first examined underwater by Farrar; Mary Jo, if she was not in the trunk; and/or another person attempting to hide.

Could it indeed have been the body of Mary Jo?

Yes, she could have been placed on the back seat of the Oldsmobile after she was found by the group of persons seen by Carol at 11:35 p.m.

Chris Look, Huck's son, told me that his father had always leaned toward the belief that what he saw on the back seat was a person. Huck might later have admitted that it could have been a bag when one was found in the Oldsmobile. At the inquest, Look said that when Arena asked him if he knew who was driving the car, he told him, "I hadn't the slightest idea, only from what I told him, it appeared to be a man and a woman and somebody else." The *Boston Herald Traveler* reported on July 24, 1969, "Christopher Look Jr., a deputy sheriff of Dukes County, has said he thought he saw two girls in the car with Kennedy at the point where the senator's car made a wrong turn and followed a road leading to the bridge." The *Evening Standard* of New Bedford in their edition of October 3, 1969, reported that Look had told them, "It looked as if there might have been two girls in it. "

In fact, what is generally overlooked is that Look, until the exhumation hearing, had always maintained there might have been two girls in the car. Zad Rust writes that Look had told him "he saw a girl who, was seated next to the driver, who was a man. There may have been another person in the rear seat; this, [Look] says, *could only have been another girl*, or an outstretched garment."[1]

Look's sighting of the Oldsmobile was given short shift at the inquest. Look was brought in, asked a few quick questions, and dismissed. His eyewitness account, which disputed Kennedy's timeline, was an acute embarrassment to a judge, district attorney, and police chief who were united in their desire to whitewash the affair.

Judge Boyle, who decided to take over the interrogation from prosecutor Fernandes, attempted to steer Look toward admitting that what he thought he had seen on the back seat that night, if he had even seen the Oldsmobile at all, was Keough's bag. But Huck would have none of it.

Judge Boyle: Now, I am speculating a bit, but it looks as though the car on the rear has, as many cars do, sort of a little shelf?
Look: Yes, sir.
Judge Boyle: And I take it was on that shelf where you saw what you thought might be a person or a bag or some clothing?
   Boyle obviously knew that a "person" could not fit on that "little shelf."
Look: Clothing on that side of the car, yes sir.
Judge Boyle: A sweater or clothing or a bag upon the seat, you wouldn't be able to see?
Look: No, sir.
Judge Boyle: All right, then.
Fernandes: If Your Honor please, I have no further questions of Mr. Look.

Look stated at the inquest that he saw something on the back seat of the vehicle and was absolutely certain the vehicle he had seen at the Dike Road intersection was the same car he saw pulled out of the pond the next morning. Nevertheless, notice how Judge Boyle chose to sum up Look's testimony in his official written report:

"[Huck Look] saw two persons in the front seat and a shadow *on the shelf back of the rear seat which he thought could have been a bag, article of clothing, or a third*

---

[1] *Teddy Bare*, p. 22; p. 89

person. Later that morning, he saw the Kennedy Oldsmobile when it was towed to shore, *but he cannot positively identify it as the same car he saw at 12:45."*

Boyle blatantly misrepresented Look's testimony when he said that Look had seen something on the "shelf back of the rear seat." But he was able to say that Look could never positively identify the Oldsmobile because Boyle had asked him if he could positively say the vehicle he had observed that night was black rather than a dark color of green or blue, and if he was able to identify all the numbers on the license plate. Look said, "No," so Boyle said, "Well, you are unable to positively identify this car taken out of the water as the identical same car you saw the previous night?" Huck replied, "In my opinion −." Boyle interrupted, "No, I'm talking about the *positive* identification." Huck was forced to say, "No, I can't."

This is just one of countless instances of Boyle manipulating the inquest in Kennedy's favor. For one thing, the human eye cannot detect colors at night − it can only detect shades of gray. Boyle obviously knew this. If Look had replied yes to Boyle's question, Boyle could have called Look a liar and have established grounds for discrediting Look's entire testimony. When Look said no, Boyle could at least claim that the identification was uncertain. Look was the victim of a logic trap. If enough parameters are introduced, absolutely nothing can be known with 100 percent certainty.

What other evidence might suggest that Mary Jo had been lying on the back seat of the Oldsmobile before it was seen by Look?

Dr. McHugh found blood on the back seat of the Oldsmobile.

If there was blood on Mary Jo Kopechne's blouse, why was none seen by Farrar, Dr. Mills, or Frieh, the undertaker?

John Farrar suggests that the blood may have come from the blood-tinged froth observed exuding from Mary Jo's nose, from broken fingernails, or from swirling water contaminated by blood. Others have suggested a wound to the back of the head when the Oldsmobile went into the water. All suggest that these traces of blood could have been washed away by the water as Mary Jo lay immersed in it.

Irrespective of the certainty that none of the blood could have pooled onto a specific area of her shirt while she was underwater in the Oldsmobile, I've lived on boats most of my life and can attest to the fact that seawater does not wash out much of anything. The only way you can even make a lackluster suds of sorts in seawater is with a good-quality concentrated liquid or powder detergent. It would seem extremely unlikely, if not impossible, for a bloodstain to wash out in seawater if the clothing was merely immersed in it with little to no agitation. When the blood evidence is cited, many suggest that swirling water might have removed it. But after a matter of a minute or so, there would have been little or no current at all in the interior of the Oldsmobile between the bottom of the windows and the footwell. So where is this swirling water supposed to have come from?

It appears no one, other than Kappel, has imagined that Mary Jo might have been involved in an accident before the Oldsmobile plunged off the bridge. If the real accident occurred before the car went over the bridge, and the accident at the bridge was staged, a bloody blouse would be a dead giveaway. Someone might have attempted to scrub the blood out of that blouse before Mary Jo was placed in the Oldsmobile.

One should keep in mind that the usual reason a forensic technician tests substances with the Benzidine test[1] or looks at them under ultraviolet light is because law enforcement is all too aware that criminals have a nasty habit of trying to remove blood evidence by washing it away. Almost invariably, if a crime scene tests positive for blood using these tests, it is because someone was trying to hide it. Blood, even when fresh, does not wash away easily from fabric without some scrubbing, especially in saltwater. At the inquest, McHugh characterized the bloodstains as *washed out*.

If Mary Jo was brought back to the cottage in the Oldsmobile, was she taken inside to be examined more closely?

No. If she was taken into the cottage, she would have been lying in plain sight of the others. This would imply that every one of the remaining 10 guests at the party was a willing participant in the cover-up, and that these participants managed to keep up the semblance of a rousing party until about 1:30 a.m., as confirmed by Foster Silva from his home nearby.

However, would it really be possible for 10 persons, including 5 young girls, to shout, laugh, and whoop it up for an hour and a half with what they thought was the dead body of their colleague lying there in front of them? Perhaps in a movie, but in real life? And why would they make that effort? It wasn't as though there were many around to hear.

The evidence suggests that the events occurring immediately after the accident were known to just a select few. This appears also to be one of the reasons Kennedy kept to his story of leaving the party at 11:15 p.m. His friends and associates, not involved in the immediate cover-up, would know that he left at around that time. Kennedy could face these people in the future and insist, with a (fairly) straight face, that he told the truth.

---

[1] Benzidine, introduced in 1904 as a forensic tool, is highly carcinogenic. It generally has been replaced by luminol.

Likewise, this might have been why one of the Boiler Room Girls, and one of the men, admitted to having been out walking for several hours at the precise time the fateful events were occurring at Dike Bridge. The others would know they were lying if they testified to something else, and question it.

Could Kennedy have killed (or attempted to kill) Mary Jo on purpose?

No. The fact that Carol saw the Valiant pass her at such a high rate of speed with no attempt at concealment suggests that these people were on a rescue attempt to save a life. Their intentions were, at the beginning at least, honorable. The plan went awry and into unchartered waters when they concluded Mary Jo could not be saved and their attention turned to Edward Kennedy.

Could Mary Jo have been saved?

Yes! This is the ultimate tragedy of the affair.

The blood evidence suggests that Mary Jo received a cut in the back of her head before she ever went off the bridge. Blood had settled onto the back of Mary Jo's blouse, especially around the outside rear collar, and blood was found on the back seat of the Oldsmobile.

Although it has been suggested by others that the blood on her blouse may have occurred after she drove off the bridge, the evidence does not support it. The blood appears to have settled on the back of her shirt as she was lying down, bleeding from a small wound at the back of her scalp when the vehicle was out of the water. If she was bleeding, she was alive and might have been saved. There were no bruises, marks, or fractures anywhere on Mary Jo's body, and often even minor scalp wounds bleed profusely. Notice again what *Web*MD has to say about head wounds: "Although this amount of bleeding may be alarming, many times the injury is not severe."

Most important, Mary Jo had a carbon monoxide level in her blood of just under five percent. She must have been in the trunk of the Oldsmobile, alive, for that to have occurred.

Subsequently, Mary Jo drowned. This could only mean two things: either Mary Jo drowned in the car; or she drowned somewhere else. Either way, the horrifying conclusion is this: deliberate decisions and actions by these co-conspirators led to her unnecessary death by drowning.

Why did the Kennedy team fight so hard against the district attorney's call for an autopsy?

I suspect the most important reason, and perhaps the only reason, was because an autopsy would have found a small cut on the back of Mary Jo's scalp which would account for the blood found on the back of her blouse. If the blood came from a wound to the head and settled onto the back of her shirt, it would indicate that Mary Jo could not have been submerged in water for at least some of the time that the bleeding occurred.

This would inevitably lead to the conclusion that the wound to the back of her head occurred either a) before the car plunged into the water; or b) that Mary Jo was sitting upright, alive, within a pocket of air for some period of time (a body does not bleed if dead) – in other words, what Farrar has maintained all along. If a) Kennedy's entire story was a lie; if b) Mary Jo might have been saved had Kennedy reported the accident promptly instead of waiting over 10 hours to do it. A small cut might even have led investigators to reassess their conclusion that the blood found on the rear seat of the Oldsmobile had come from a person searching for souvenirs.

A determination of the extent of the wound compared to the amount of blood found on the shirt and rear seat might even have suggested how long Mary Jo was exposed to air – alive, breathing, and bleeding – before she died.

It seems highly unlikely that the prosecution, determined as they were to protect Kennedy and stubbornly oblivious to the inconsistencies in his testimony, would ever have arrived at the conclusion that Kennedy's story was a lie. Nevertheless, the alternative would have been almost as damaging to Kennedy's interests. The *Welansky* decision had ruled that an omission to act constituted negligence under the law.[1] In Massachusetts, delayed reporting of an accident resulting in death, when there was ample opportunity to seek help and prevent it, would be manslaughter. It would utterly destroy Kennedy's reputation and any chance of seeking the presidency or even remaining in the Senate. It took just 15 minutes from the time Farrar was called at the Edgartown volunteer fire department to reach the scene of the accident at Dike Bridge, fully dressed in SCUBA gear and ready to go.[2]

---

[1] In the *Welansky* case of 1944 (316 Mass. 383), Barnett Welansky was convicted of wanton and reckless conduct for his failure to provide proper exits at the Cocoanut Grove Club of Boston, leading to the deaths of 492 people in the notorious fire of November 28, 1942. Welansky was found guilty of manslaughter and sentenced to not more than 15 and not less than 12 years in prison.

[2] Several books have stated that it took Farrar as long as 25 minutes to arrive on the scene after he received the call. Farrar himself testified at the inquest that he was about 20 minutes in transit. However, Mrs. Malm's call was logged at the Edgartown police station at 8:20 a.m.; Arena testified at the exhumation hearing that he arrived at the bridge between 8:30 and 8:35, and Farrar was on the scene at 8:45 a.m.

Less likely, an autopsy might also have determined that sexual intercourse had occurred within a short time of Mary Jo's death. Dr. Katsas testified at the exhumation hearing in Pennsylvania that finding sperm was remote in exhumed bodies, but each case was different and no one could be absolutely certain until the autopsy was performed.

If Kennedy really did leave the cottage at 11:15 p.m. with sex on his mind, then they never had a chance to do it, since Carol saw the Valiant speed past her only 20 minutes later at 11:35 p.m. But it is by no means certain that Kennedy left the party at exactly 11:15 p.m. As explained in Chapter 17, the intact chrome strips at the bottom of both deeply dented passenger-side doors suggest that this damage occurred at Mytoi, and that Kennedy was driving back from East Beach rather than toward it when the accident occurred. Kennedy's reputation as a philanderer, both before and after the incident, has been well established. And it is certainly true that Mary Jo was not wearing panties when she was examined at the scene by Dr. Mills.

While it might be unlikely to find sperm in exhumed bodies, that would not be the case before burial. This could have been one more reason Kennedy made arrangements to fly the body from the island before he had even talked to Mary Jo's parents or had reported the accident to the police.

And, of course, if Mary Jo was pregnant, an autopsy would have uncovered it, although our theory does not presuppose or suggest that pregnancy had anything to do with the events of that night.

What were they planning to say?

At the inquest, Mary Ellen Lyons was asked, "Did anyone ask where the senator's car was?" Mary Ellen replied, "Well, Mary Jo had taken the car on the last ferry." Dinis asked who had told her this. Mary Ellen replied, "It was Mr. Gargan." Nance Lyons was asked, "Did anyone say, where is the [Oldsmobile]?" Nance replied, "Miss Kopechne had taken the car to the Katama Shores." Esther Newberg was asked, "How did you believe that Miss Kopechne got back to the motel?" Newberg told the court that Gargan had told her Mary Jo "had driven the black car back before midnight." Newberg also told the court that she had overheard Gargan telling the Lyons sisters that same story around 3:00 a.m. All three testified that they had been told by Gargan that Kennedy had decided to swim across the channel after missing the last ferry.

So, if Gargan actually believed Kennedy was going to report the accident as soon as he got back to Edgartown, why would he tell these others that Mary Jo had driven an unfamiliar car back to the Katama Shores Motel by herself just before midnight but Kennedy had swum a dangerous channel? Why invent such a strange tale? If actually true that Gargan had never told the girls what had happened out of fear they might do something rash, why not just say that Kennedy had driven Mary Jo back to Edgartown in the Oldsmobile before the ferry stopped running? Wouldn't that have that have been the logical thing to say, the story that would have raised the least alarm? And doesn't it seem strange that Gargan never gave the girls a reason for Kennedy's behavior? When asked why she thought Kennedy hadn't accompanied Mary Jo back to Edgartown, Mary Ellen said she was never told. "I just decided that for some reason he didn't want to."

In an exclusive interview with Leo Damore in 1983, Gargan confessed that when they were all milling around the ferry landing at around 1:40 a.m., just before Kennedy dove in the water to swim across to Edgartown, Kennedy "was having alternative ideas about the situation." Why couldn't Mary Jo have been driving the Oldsmobile? Why couldn't she have let him off somewhere with intentions of driving to the ferry by herself but made a wrong turn and drove off the bridge by accident? Kennedy suggested "that when he was back at the Shiretown Inn, Gargan could 'discover' the accident and report to the police that Mary Jo had been alone in the car."[1]

Gargan told Damore that he had immediately "rejected that idea out of hand." Irrespective of the fact that it wasn't true, he doubted he could persuade the girls at the party to go along with it. When the group met up at the Shiretown Inn at 8:00 later that morning, upon hearing that Kennedy still planned to say that Mary Jo had driven off the bridge on her own, Gargan warned Kennedy, "There is no way you can say that! You can be placed at the scene!"[2] But isn't it interesting that Gargan had already fed three of the girls that *that very same story?*

Perhaps the lie they planned to sell to the world was as simple as this: Kennedy and Mary Jo got stuck in the sand on the side of Dike Road. Gargan and Markham freed the car, but Kennedy wanted to be by himself for a while. So Mary Jo said she would make her own way back to the Katama Shores Motel in the Oldsmobile. Gargan and Markham returned to Lawrence Cottage at midnight, then left again at 12:30 a.m. to bring Kennedy to the ferry. Kennedy then swam across to Edgartown because the ferry was no longer operating. As an unidentified Boiler Room Girl had told a reporter, the vehicle had become stuck in the sand and Mary Jo "was simply sitting in it." And as Nance Lyons testified at the inquest, Gargan had told her "they looked for boats but couldn't find one."

Sadly, the next morning they all found that Mary Jo had somehow managed to drive off the bridge by accident. She must have been turned around and thought she was headed west on Dike Road instead of east. Intent on making the last midnight ferry, driving much too quickly in an unfamiliar car, she was unable to stop when the bridge loomed up in front of her unexpectedly.

---

[1] *Senatorial Privilege*, p. 81
[2] *Senatorial Privilege*, p. 90

Did the group realize at the time that Look was a police officer?

No. It does not appear they did.

Almost everyone has assumed that the Oldsmobile began backing up *after* Look stepped out of the Oldsmobile and walked toward the car dressed in his uniform, presumably because this would support the widely held premise that Kennedy drove off Dike Bridge in panic after being approached by a deputy sheriff. Damore says, "Look got out of his car and walked toward the other vehicle. He was 25 to 30 feet away when the car started backing up toward him, taillights showing all over the deputy sheriff uniform he was wearing."[1] *Wikipedia* (2017) repeats the error: "Thinking that the occupants of the car might be lost, Look had gotten out of his car and walked toward it. When he was 25 to 30 feet away, the car started backing towards him."

However, the driver of the Oldsmobile did not begin backing up when he saw Huck Look. He began backing up even before Look stopped his car and got out. And Look never said he was 25 to 30 feet away when the car started backing toward him. He said he was about 50 to 60 feet away. The 25- to 30-foot estimate referred to the distance between Look and the vehicle after the car had already turned completely before accelerating down Dike Road.

Notice Look's testimony at the inquest:

Q: Where did it go when it passed in front of you?
Look: It went into a little dirt road maybe 10 feet off the road that is commonly known, I believe, as Cemetery Road, and it stopped, and as it stopped I proceeded around the corner and looked into the mirror of my car and noticed the car started to back up. I stopped when they started to back up towards me and got out of my car and walked back toward the car.
Q: How far away were you from this car when you stopped your car?
Look: Somewhere around 50 or 60 feet.
Q: Now, at your closest point to this car, how far were you from it, at the closest point?
Look: 25 or 30 feet.

Look had also testified at the exhumation hearing that the car was backing up before he stopped his car:

"I had proceeded around the corner a little bit and I was approximately 50 feet away and I observed in my rear view mirror that the car was backing up, and I thought they wanted information; they were lost or something."

---

[1] *Senatorial Privilege*, p. 103

Had the people in the backing Oldsmobile realized Look was a police officer, it does not appear credible they would have continued with the plan. Nor would Kennedy have made it a point to establish a time with the innkeeper when he was in his room at the Shiretown Inn or make the effort to appear as if nothing was amiss the next morning. *Had they known Look was a police officer, these strategic moves by Kennedy would make no sense.*

This also appears to explain why neither Kennedy nor his associates got in touch with the ferry operator who was known to be on call all that evening to take them across to Edgartown, and why Kennedy was careful to sneak into the Shiretown Inn at close to 2:00 a.m. when no one was looking. They wanted to make it appear as if Kennedy had been in Edgartown from the early morning of July 19 to establish an alibi.

As a test, I drove into Cemetery Road (today, Willett Lane) on a dark night in the summer of 2013, asking my wife to start walking toward me from about 50 to 60 feet away, the distance between Look's station wagon and the Oldsmobile in 1969. In reverse, with my backup lights shining, I looked in both the side view mirror and windshield mirror to see if I could make out what clothes my wife was wearing.

I have good eyesight, but I was surprised to find that it was very difficult to see much from the windshield mirror. I could just make out that my wife was wearing a dress from the driver-side mirror, but only if I took my time and looked very carefully. And bear in mind that I have a modern car with excellent mirrors and powerful lights.

I concluded that if I had been backing up in haste and looking back from the side mirror that night, I might have been able to make out the form of a person walking toward me, but little else. If I was looking back using the windshield mirror, there is no way at all I would have been able to see a person, much less a uniform or badge. From Kennedy's Oldsmobile with a far narrower rear window than mine, it must have been even more difficult. It can also be assumed that the identification would be hampered from either mirror if no one was expecting to see a police officer. There are none stationed on Chappaquiddick, and Look's station wagon was unmarked.

For the dubious, try it yourself on a very dark night in the middle of nowhere. You will be surprised, as I was, at how little your vehicle's backup lights will light up anything. Backup lights are designed to warn others that a vehicle is in reverse and to reflect off nearby objects such as curbs and garage walls. Backup lights were never designed to clearly illuminate objects at a significant distance in an open space, nor will they.

I am all but convinced after this experiment that the only way a person would know with certainty that Look was a police officer, or even that there was a person at all, is if he put his head out the window and looked back directly. But Look said this did not happen. At the inquest, he was asked if he saw any of the people look at him. Look's answer: "No, sir."

So if the group did not realize that Look was a police officer, when did they decide to change their plan?

The plan appears to have gone awry when the group realized that Kennedy could be, as Gargan put it, placed at the scene. Sometime after the group returned to Lawrence Cottage at 2:00 a.m., a witness must have caused Gargan and Markham to reassess their story.

There was no phone in Kennedy's room at the Shiretown Inn, and of course no cell phones in 1969, so it would have been impossible to alert Kennedy from Chappaquiddick. According to Gargan, Kennedy was told that he could be placed at the scene when he met up with Gargan, Markham, and Tretter at the Shiretown Inn at 8:00 later that morning. Mrs. Richards told Detective Dunn she was surprised at the coarse and agitated manner in which Gargan announced his presence, demanding to speak to Ted Kennedy at once. Her husband told Dunn that Gargan had dragged Kennedy forcibly inside by his arm and that loud arguments were heard. When all three eventually left the Shiretown Inn, Kennedy "was not the same man" and clearly "upset and excited." He rushed right by them without even acknowledging their presence or saying good-bye, which they found strange.

Nevertheless, when Kennedy, Gargan, and Markham rode the ferry to the Chappaquiddick side just a minute or two later, the ferry operator stated that Kennedy was smiling and appeared completely relaxed and in a jovial mood. However, on the return trip, after the group had heard from several others that the car and body had been found, and after seeing the hearse drive to the bridge, the ferry operator noticed something quite different. Markham was seen berating a slumped-over Kennedy in a low but urgent voice, his arms making emphatic gestures to emphasize points.[1] This time, Kennedy looked worried.

Markham might have been telling Kennedy he would have to man up and take responsibility for the accident. Neither Markham nor Gargan was prepared to sacrifice their lives and their careers over what Ted had done and what all three appear to have staged, even for a Kennedy. Before the ferry had fully docked, Kennedy jumped off and strode to the police station so rapidly that Markham couldn't keep up.

Could Gargan and Markham have decided to change their plan because they found out Huck Look was a police officer after 2:00 a.m.?

On first blush, it would seem reasonable that sometime after 2:00 a.m., Ray LaRosa or the Lyons sisters – the three who were doing a conga line dance on the road that night – might have informed Gargan and Markham that they had talked to a police

---

[1] *The Bridge at Chappaquiddick*, p. 132

officer in a station wagon around 12:45 a.m. The penny dropped, and Gargan and Markham realized that this must have been the same person in a station wagon who walked toward the Oldsmobile at 12:40 a.m. They could be placed at the scene!

But this could not be correct. If Look's sighting of the Oldsmobile at 12:40 a.m. was cause for Gargan and Markham to abandon their plan, it makes no sense that Kennedy would then state in his police report later that morning that he drove off the bridge with Mary Jo Kopechne soon after 11:15 p.m., fully an hour and a half earlier. Instead, he would have wanted to come up with a timeline that would agree with Look's sighting.

It appears Kennedy, Gargan, and Markham had no idea that a police officer had observed the Oldsmobile when Kennedy reported the accident shortly before 10:00 a.m. to the Edgartown police. In fact, they could not have been aware that the Oldsmobile had been sighted at all. If they realized the Oldsmobile had been seen around 12:40 a.m., by anyone, Kennedy would never have said he drove that same Oldsmobile off the bridge soon after 11:15 p.m., no matter what they thought someone else may have witnessed. If they knew the Oldsmobile had been seen at 12:40 a.m., it would have trumped *any other sighting*.

Could Kennedy have said he drove off the bridge soon after 11:15 p.m. because he was worried that the ferry shut down at midnight, as most assume? Could this be the reason he chose to challenge Look's timeline?

No. Kennedy testified in his original statement to Chief Arena on the morning of July 19 that he drove off the bridge in the Oldsmobile with Mary Jo Kopechne soon after 11:15 p.m. Everyone acknowledges this could not be true. But it makes absolutely no sense that Kennedy and Markham would willingly contradict the testimony of a deputy sheriff just because the ferry stopped running at midnight.

Nearly all the witnesses confirmed that they were well aware the ferry could be summoned after midnight from the phone booth on the Chappaquiddick side. At the inquest it was pointed out that there was a notice to that effect on a conspicuous sign on each side of the ferry landing, with the number to call, clearly visible to everyone. In 1969, special service cost only a couple of dollars. Just about everyone on Chappaquiddick in those days used it at one time or another during the summer. When asked at the inquest whether anyone was concerned over the fact that the ferry shut down at midnight, Nance Lyons said, "No one seemed particularly concerned because someone else suggested that boats were accessible and that we could go back at any time." Tretter said, "I understood that while it stopped running at midnight you could always get service." When asked who had told him this, he said, "Mr. Crimmins."

So, if the real accident occurred after Look saw the Oldsmobile at 12:40 a.m., as most assume, and if Kennedy was aware of Look's sighting, which most believe he was, why wouldn't Kennedy just tell the truth and say that he did drive off the bridge after 12:40 a.m. which would perfectly coincide with Look's observation? 12:30 a.m. was not a scandalous time to wind down a party on Chappaquiddick. When you think about it, how could that possibly hurt his story, or his reputation?

In fact, it would not. In fact, had Kennedy said that he drove down School House Road with Mary Jo at around 12:30 a.m. with intentions of calling the ferry operator from the public phone at the ferry landing, but became confused when he arrived at the Dike Road intersection (having never noticed Look walking toward them), his story would have been far more believable to everyone. *The major reason most people are convinced Kennedy's story could not be true is because his timeline conflicts with Look's eyewitness account.*

Strangely, not one author appears to have even considered the possibility that Kennedy was never aware that the Oldsmobile had been seen around 12:40 a.m. Yet from Kennedy's testimony later that morning, this would be the obvious conclusion.

As argued by Lange and DeWitt in **Chappaquiddick: The Real Story,** *could Kennedy have forgotten about Look's sighting because he was confused, in shock, and suffering from traumatic amnesia? Was this why he mistakenly said he drove off the bridge soon after 11:15 p.m.? Did Gargan and Markham confirm Kennedy's timeline so that he would not later be accused of mental instability?*

Not likely. Lange and DeWitt fail to address the fact that Kennedy *and* Markham took about an hour to compose Kennedy's accident report on the morning of July 19 confirming the 11:15 p.m. timeline. If Kennedy was suffering from traumatic amnesia, it means Markham was, too.

So what could have caused them to panic?

There are only two realistic possibilities: either there was another witness to the event who has never stepped forward; or it was Carol Jones's sighting. Since there is no proof of another witness, let's stick with what we know.

Carol observed the Valiant pass her at high speed and drive down Dike Road at 11:35 p.m. with a carload of people. On reflection, after everyone had sobered up, Carol's sighting might have been viewed as a real threat to their story. It wouldn't have been so much the sighting of the Valiant at 11:35 p.m. as it was the excessive speed of the car as it passed Carol's VW bus – a Chappaquiddick event so extraordinary it could never be overlooked or forgotten – coupled with the fact that the Valiant was filled with people. Their plan of claiming that Mary Jo drove off the bridge alone just before midnight, but no one was aware she had, could not be sustained. As the night wore on, and they began to reason it out, it might have led to panic.

Essentially, the group had just 15 minutes to come up with an alternative story, from about 9:30 a.m. when they heard from Tony Bettencourt that the car had been found, to 9:45 a.m. when they returned to the Edgartown side. This might have been why Kennedy's initial police report was so brief, and this also might be the reason it took Kennedy and Markham so long to compose it. They were trying to come up with a believable story on the fly. But when it came to the time of the accident they had to tell the truth because a witness had seen the Valiant drive down Dike Road at high speed around 11:35 p.m., filled with people. So, as yet unaware of Look's sighting, what would be a believable story that would fit with those details? *Kennedy drove off the bridge in the Oldsmobile soon after 11:15 p.m. with Mary Jo. He jogged back to Lawrence Cottage for the help of some of the guests. He and those guests then drove to the bridge at high speed in the Valiant to attempt a rescue.*

And that, in essence, is exactly what Kennedy said.

If someone had actually observed Kennedy at the scene of the car accident on Dike Road, it would be highly unlikely that Kennedy would state in his accident report that he drove off Dike Bridge with Mary Jo. The witness would know that the real accident had occurred before Kennedy ever reached the bridge. And if a witness had actually observed Kennedy at Dike Bridge after Look saw the vehicle, it would be equally unlikely that Kennedy would state that the accident had occurred soon after 11:15 p.m.

It appears the witness who could place Kennedy at the scene never observed the original car accident, or anyone at the bridge. Nevertheless, the witness must have seen enough to cause Gargan and Markham to panic. Carol's sighting fits those unusual parameters. Furthermore, Newberg and the Lyons sisters were told by Gargan around 3:00 a.m. that Mary Jo had driven the Oldsmobile alone to the Katama Shores Motel before the last midnight ferry. This does not suggest that Gargan was told about a witness as soon as he returned to the cottage at 2:00 a.m. It suggests instead that Gargan changed his mind between 3:00 and 8:00 a.m.

Isn't there some *other story Kennedy and Markham could have come up with that would account for Carol's sighting but keep Kennedy out of it?*

Possibly, but what could that be?

They could not say that Mary Jo drove off the bridge alone soon after 11:15 p.m., because how would they have known that she had driven off the bridge unless they had discovered the accident shortly thereafter? But if this was the case, no one could then profess shock and confusion to account for their appalling decision to walk away from an accident without seeking help. Only someone who had actually driven off the bridge with Mary Jo could use that excuse.

On the other hand, if they just ignored the VW bus, or claimed they were driving down to East Beach to look for Mary Jo who had left the party in the Oldsmobile prior to 11:35 p.m., the sighting of the Valiant driven at extreme speed could suggest that a real accident had occurred just before that time and they were on their way to attempt a rescue. They could never afford someone even voicing that thought. They had to say that Kennedy drove off the bridge with Mary Jo, if only to deflect *any possible consideration* that the accident was staged. Once uttered, the staged-accident theory would be investigated and they would run the risk of being found out.

If Kennedy claimed he was responsible for Mary Jo's death, but her death was an accident, he might survive the scandal. But if accident investigators came to the conclusion the accident was staged, Kennedy would be crucified. Several others involved in the hoax would be, too. This would be the overriding concern that morning. This is almost certainly the reason Kennedy claimed he drove off the bridge with Mary Jo when the bridge loomed up in front of him unexpectedly.

Whatever contorted logic was used, Kennedy said he drove off the bridge with Mary Jo to obscure the truth. The strange part is, even after his confession, few believed Kennedy was in the car when it went into the water, yet they still could not imagine what he was trying to hide.

What other evidence would suggest that Carol's sighting was a factor?

Many have commented on the extraordinary fact that Gargan and Markham were only brought into the picture in Kennedy's TV broadcast to the public on July 25, a week after the accident and well after the event had already turned into a media frenzy. Until that time, no one knew these two were involved. Not even the guests at the party had mentioned their participation.

Why would Kennedy's lawyers involve Gargan and Markham at that late date, and far more important than this, why would Gargan and Markham consent to it? Bear in mind that Markham, especially, as the former US Attorney for Massachusetts, had a very great deal to lose by being named as a participant and had the best legal minds in the country to advise him, including his own. Markham was not even Kennedy's lawyer. And yet a week after the incident, Markham admitted aiding Kennedy at Dike Bridge and leaving the scene of the accident without seeking help. The admission did irrevocable harm to his career and destroyed his legacy. "[Markham] started that weekend fair haired, at thirty-eight a personage," writes Hersh. "Three [sic[1]] miserable days later he was all but busted, reduced, singled out nationally beneath the gigantic klieg light of the scandal... hollow cheeked, hollow-voiced, living with what was left of his mangled lawyer's reputation."[2]

Could Gargan and Markham have been named as participants because Carol saw the Valiant filled with people? Kennedy's lawyers would not have known that Carol

---

[1] It was seven days later.
[2] *Edward Kennedy*, p. 350

had identified a woman in the back seat. But the car had held people, and those people would need to be accounted for should Carol step forward after that TV speech, just as Russell Peachey, Todd Ballou, and Roddy Hoar did. In fact, they might have suspected that Carol would be able to identify Kennedy, Markham, and Gargan with certainty. This might explain something that thus far has been inexplicable: why Gargan and Markham would confess to something that they must have known could only lead to public disgrace.

Before Kennedy's TV speech, the attention and criticism were all on him. That changed after July 25 when a wave of condemnation descended upon Gargan and Markham – two persons who could never claim that shock and confusion had delayed their reporting of the accident for over 10 hours.

Look's possible sighting of the Oldsmobile was reported by the police on July 21, three days after the incident, and appeared in the **Boston Herald Traveler** *a day later in their edition of Wednesday, July 22. Why wouldn't Kennedy have mentioned passing a VW bus in his TV speech on July 25 when the driver of the bus would have confirmed his timeline?*

Look's account must have come as a severe shock to Kennedy's attorneys. *Taken together, the observations by Carol and Look would suggest the accident was staged.* But what to do? Kennedy and Markham had already composed an accident report on the morning of July 19 stating that Kennedy had driven off the bridge soon after 11:15 p.m. It would be difficult to alter that timeline after the fact because although Kennedy could claim shock and confusion on the morning following the accident, Markham could not. And even if they did change it, that would solve one problem (Look) but not the other (Carol). It was a classic Catch-22 situation.

The only logical way forward was deny Look's sighting and pray that Carol never spoke up. The public could then either choose to believe Kennedy (Look was mistaken or lying) or believe Look (Kennedy was mistaken about the timeline, was covering up for his "real" companion, was worried about the ferry shutting down at midnight, was never the driver, was suffering from traumatic amnesia, etc.). But what Kennedy could never afford was someone believing both of them. If Carol showed up with her story suggesting that something serious had indeed been going on soon after 11:15 p.m., some bright reporter would put it all together and conclude that the group had engineered the entire episode.

And, of course, until now, just one book makes the case that Look *and* Kennedy's timelines are essentially true. That book is *Chappaquiddick Revealed: What Really Happened*, and having accepted both timelines, and after analyzing the vehicle damage, Kappel concludes that Kennedy and his friends staged the accident themselves. Every other book, and every other theory, no matter how far-fetched, as well as the BBC documentary *Chappaquiddick*, has argued that the accident (or in the case of *You, the Jury,* Mary Jo's murder) took place after Look's sighting and that Kennedy's timeline is false.

In 1983, Gargan told Damore that in the days following the accident he had feared that a witness might appear to say they'd seen the senator and others at Dike Bridge. "There was no way of knowing how many people in the area saw or heard us, how many witnesses were going to come forward to say, 'Oh, I saw Ted Kennedy at the bridge with two other guys, and the lights of the car.' " But Gargan told Damore that his concerns were never realized – the only witness who had ever materialized was Huck Look.[1]

When he made that TV speech, could there be some reason Kennedy would have hopes that Carol's sighting would never become known?

Lula's cousin, who worked at the Kennedy compound, claimed that Carol could be killed if she ever revealed what she had seen. Perhaps Lula had told her cousin about Carol's observation and the cousin had, in all innocence, repeated the story to someone who had brought it to the attention of Kennedy's staff. The cousin was told to warn Lula that if Carol spoke up about her observation she could be killed.

On the other hand, there might never have been a cousin. Lula might have made that up. Clarence, Lula's son, cannot remember any cousin who worked at the Kennedy compound in 1969. Lula may have been approached by a Kennedy staff member directly.

In August 2014, Sylvia Malm, owner of Dyke House, told me she and her mother were visited by Dun Gifford and another Kennedy aide "a few days" after the incident. Sylvia told me she had the impression "they had other visits on Chappaquiddick they intended to make." After digesting that information, I asked Carol if she could pin down when Lula told her she could be killed. Carol told me, "More than a day, but less than a week" after July 19.

Perhaps, a week after the incident, Kennedy had good reason to be confident that Carol would never divulge what she had seen.

Are there any facts which would suggest that Carol's sighting was **not** the reason they panicked?

In Kennedy's original accident report, no. But in his TV speech to the nation a week after the event, Kennedy said, "Instead of looking directly for a telephone after lying exhausted on the grass for an undetermined time, I walked back to the cottage where the party was being held, requested the help of two friends, Joe Gargan and Paul

---

[1] *Senatorial Privilege*, p. 226

Markham, and directed them *to return immediately to the scene with me, it then being sometime after midnight."* Within that one sentence there are two conflicts with Carol's observation.

First, the Valiant passed Carol on the ferry side of the Dike Road intersection. This would appear to conflict with Kennedy's statement that he directed his friends to return immediately to the scene.

Second, Carol saw the Valiant at 11:35 p.m. This would conflict with Kennedy's claim that he returned to the bridge sometime after midnight.

As regards the first conflict, perhaps their reasoning went like this: It's been a week. The witness in the VW bus has never materialized. Perhaps she never will. Why make up some strange story that we may never have to use? And if the witness does appear we'll just say that Kennedy *did* direct his friends to go directly to the bridge but (Markham? Gargan?) was walking toward the ferry at the time and we had to pick him up first. Notice that Kennedy said, "I requested the help of two friends. I directed them to return immediately." Kennedy never actually said that he spoke to both of these friends at the cottage, or that he took a direct route from the cottage back to the bridge.

The second conflict appears fairly easy to resolve. Notice that Kennedy mentioned he had not looked for a phone because he was lying exhausted on the grass. The phone issue had developed into a major problem for Kennedy by July 25. It had been pointed out by reporters that there was a phone at Dyke House that Kennedy never attempted to use. Yet in his original police report, Kennedy said he had driven off Dike Bridge soon after 11:15 p.m., when the Malms were still awake and the daughter was reading at an open window, clearly visible from the bridge, with a light on.

If Kennedy claimed in that TV speech that he had arrived back at the bridge with Gargan and Markham before midnight to attempt an additional rescue, when Sylvia Malm was still reading and her mother was still awake, his story would be that much more difficult to swallow. Although Kennedy could claim to have been in shock after he drove off the bridge, neither Gargan nor Markham could use that excuse. Perhaps Kennedy fudged the time a bit in his TV speech to account for the Malms' sleeping habits *and* Carol's sighting. If Carol ever came forward, Kennedy could say that either he or she was mistaken about the time. Meanwhile, the Malms were the priority because they had already gone on record as saying they had stayed awake, and the daughter had been reading at an open window, until midnight.

If these explanations do not seem convincing, and the reader is still able to swallow the idea that Kennedy and Markham would choose to dispute the timeline of a deputy sheriff because of concern over a ferry schedule, then there is always the possibility that Gargan or Markham was told about a police officer by Ray LaRosa or the Lyons sisters after 2:00 a.m. Or, perhaps there really was another witness who has never come forward.

Whatever it was, something caused the group to panic that night and change their story.

Why, when the whole world – even Kennedy's most ardent supporters – has come to accept that Look saw the Oldsmobile around 12:40 a.m., would Kennedy continue to insist, with utter conviction to the day of his death, that Look had never seen him driving the Oldsmobile down Dike Road?

Because in this case it appears Kennedy was telling the truth. In his testimony at the inquest, Kennedy said, "*I*" did not drive into Cemetery Road. "*I*" did not back the car up. "*I*" saw no one between the cottage and the bridge. "*I*" did not stop the car at any time." Kennedy could probably have passed a lie detector test with those statements.

It appears most everyone has assumed it was Kennedy and Mary Jo who were seen in the Oldsmobile by Look around 12:40 a.m. Every author of every book, excepting Kenneth Kappel, believes this was so. The BBC thought so, too. The Tedrows speak for the majority when they wrote, "If Senator Kennedy and Mary Jo did leave the party at 11:15 p.m., then there is a lost hour and a half to account for. They were seen at about 12:45 by Deputy Look at the intersection of School [House] Road and Cemetery Road."[1]

But were they? At no time was Look able to actually identify anyone in the car. He was only able to identify "a man, a woman, and a shadow of someone or something sticking up on the back seat." Carol's eyewitness account, combined with Kennedy's insistence that the accident occurred soon after 11:15 p.m., suggests that it was not Kennedy driving the Oldsmobile and it was not Mary Jo sitting next to him. Mary Jo must have been injured by the time Look saw the vehicle. Kennedy almost certainly would not have wanted to drive any car after he had been responsible for the apparent death of one of the Boiler Room Girls, nor is it likely that Gargan or Markham would have allowed it.

---

[1] *Death at Chappaquiddick*, p. 34.

24

The Mystery Man and Woman

Who was the woman seen by Carol? Who was the couple seen by Huck Look?

This is one of the most important questions, and of course it is impossible to know for sure. But for the sake of argument, let's look at the behavior and movements, and the testimony, of Charles Tretter, a 30-year-old Boston attorney and Kennedy aide; and 23-year-old Rosemary "Cricket" Keough, the youngest of the Boiler Room Girls.

When Chief Arena called the Katama Shores Motel to speak to Rosemary Keough on the morning of the incident "basically just to find out how to spell Mary Jo's last name," and having identified himself as a police officer, Arena said Keough sounded "wary and suspicious." He "overheard a muffled consultation going on at the other end of the line before Keough finally came back on to spell out Mary Jo Kopechne's name."[1] Olsen says that Arena heard someone say little more than "what does he want?"[2] But Damore, who also interviewed Arena, implies that the muffled conversation was longer and the subject matter not understood. At the inquest, Arena did not mention overhearing any specific conversation. Arena reported only that he "could hear her talking to someone else in the room."

Damore says that Arena couldn't understand Keough's behavior. "She seemed very down in the dumps, like she knew what had happened. I'm thinking: 'She's way out at Katama and I'm down here. How the hell does she know about the accident?' " Only later, after hearing that there had been a party at Lawrence Cottage, did Arena surmise that her strange behavior had been the result of only recently hearing about Mary Jo's death.

But even if Keough had only recently heard about Kopechne's death, why would she be so reluctant to talk to a police officer? For the first week following the incident most of the other girls had no problem talking to reporters. And why would Arena say that she sounded wary and suspicious? Yes, she would be upset, but upset should have sounded a lot different to a police officer than "wary and suspicious."

Who was Keough talking to? Perhaps Charles Tretter. When it became obvious that the Oldsmobile had been found, Tretter had been deputized by Gargan to bring Rosemary Keough and Susan Tannenbaum from Edgartown to the Katama Shores Motel and then to get all of the Boiler Room Girls off the island of Martha's Vineyard as quickly as possible.

---

[1] *Senatorial Privilege*, pp. 29-30
[2] *The Bridge at Chappaquiddick*, p. 166

Charles Tretter testified at the inquest that he had gone off on the first of his two long walks with Rosemary Keough toward the Dike Road intersection around 11:30 p.m. He further stated that at that time the only car remaining at the cottage was the white Valiant. When he returned to the cottage 30 to 40 minutes later, he said no one was there, and no cars. Damore writes, "But Tretter had walked into a time trap. Had the accident occurred when Senator Kennedy said it did, and had he [Kennedy] returned to the cottage at 12:15 a.m. to fetch Gargan and Markham, Kennedy would have encountered Tretter and Keough on their walk toward the intersection." Rust, Rebold, and Sherrill make this same point in *Teddy Bare*, *The Inspector's Opinion*, and *The Last Kennedy*.

Damore continues, "Keough said she had seen the senator and Mary Jo leave the party at 11:30 p.m., having looked at Susan Tannenbaum's watch. But despite her avowal in August to answer all questions 'fully and cooperatively,' she had little else to say. It was clear from his testimony that Tretter hadn't been paying much attention to anything but Rosemary Keough that weekend. Keough and Tretter were suffering a problem unique to Kennedy witnesses. Having gone to the Shiretown Inn to borrow a radio, danced together at the party, disappeared for two midnight walks lasting over two hours, and slept side-by-side on the living room floor, it was clear that a flirtation had blossomed during the weekend. Tretter's wife was reported furious at the episode of dalliance." Gargan told Damore that in preparing Tretter's testimony, it was Dan Daley's idea to "keep him walking to save his marriage."[1]

But was it really a dalliance? Was the marriage really in jeopardy? We have only the word of Gargan who might have had every reason to lie.

Rosemary Keough was the only Boiler Room Girl who admitted leaving the party for very long periods of time. One can legitimately ask, would Tretter and Keough really go for two romantic walks lasting more than two hours on a mosquito- and tick-infested island when they had hotel rooms waiting for them in Edgartown and Katama?

Charles Tretter stated at the inquest that he and Rosemary Keough set out on their first walk toward the Dike Road intersection around 11:30 p.m., which is only five minutes before Carol saw the Valiant hurtling past her from the direction of the ferry landing toward the bridge.

He then said they returned to the cottage about 30 or 40 minutes later. This is exactly when someone began making phone calls from Lawrence Cottage on Kennedy's credit card.

Keough had a difficult time determining when her first walk began. She first said 11:50 p.m., then changed her mind to 12:15 or 12:30 a.m., then corrected it back to 11:40 p.m. Keough said their first walk lasted about 45 minutes. She stated that they then left for their second walk at around 12:15 or 12:30. This is exactly when the

---

[1] *Senatorial Privilege*, pp. 363-365

phone calls at Lawrence Cottage ended, only a few minutes before Nancy McDonald observed a vehicle driving at high speed toward the ferry landing, and not long before Look saw the Oldsmobile at the Dike Road intersection. Both Tretter and Keough testified they returned from their second walk at 2:00 a.m. This is the exact time Markham and Gargan also testified they returned to the cottage.

The timeline fits exactly with Carol's observation and our supposition of what must have happened that night.

Examine carefully Tretter's inquest testimony as he talks about his walks with Keough, remembering that Tretter also testified that when he left the cottage for his first walk with Keough, the Valiant was there.

Q: Did you leave the cottage [on your first walk with Keough]?
Tretter: Yes.
Q: Approximately what time?
Tretter: Oh, after 11:30 perhaps.
Q: You are certain 11:30 was about the time you left?
Tretter: As best as I can recall.
Carol observed the white Valiant passing her at 11:35.
Q: Can you tell the court what you are using as a basis of that being the time?
Tretter: The watch.
Q: So, you looked at your watch and you are pretty sure it was 11:30?
Tretter: Approximately.
Q: Now, you went for a walk [with Miss Keough]. Could you tell us where you went?
Tretter: As best I can recall – well, I couldn't describe it for you specifically, but to the right of the cottage. I walked out of the cottage.
Q: Down the road?
Tretter: Down the road, yes.
Judge Boyle: To your right as you came out of the cottage?
Tretter: Yes.
Q: And you say when you returned at midnight, or did you say 12:40?
Tretter: You asked me how long I was gone. I said approximately half an hour or 40 minutes.
Q: So, approximately 12:15 when you returned?
Tretter: Right.
Tretter said "30 to 40" minutes from the time he left the cottage on his first walk, or midnight to 12:10 a.m. The calls from Lawrence Cottage began at 11:57 p.m. The lawyers suggested "12:15" because that is the time Kennedy had already told the court he returned to the cottage.
Later...
Tretter: When we went on the first walk, it was necessary to step off the road a few times for automobiles, and one of the cars I thought I recognized was the white

Valiant, and I thought we better get back to see what was going on because there goes our car, and when I got back there were no cars at all.

Tretter said he saw the Valiant at the cottage before he left on his first walk, then saw the Valiant pass by him and this caused them to turn around and begin walking back. If Tretter saw the Valiant drive past him during his first walk with Rosemary Keough, between 11:30 p.m. and midnight, it would corroborate Carol's observation exactly.

Later...

Q: So you went out [again, with Keough] to try to find the main body, the other people?

Tretter: In a sense... there was some thought to walking towards the ferry, which after a bit of a distance we just gave up on that.

Q: Did you attempt it?

Tretter: Half attempted it. It was a long walk and I thought I might as well stay here.

Q: You don't know how long a time you had taken at the cottage before you decided to take the second walk?

Tretter: It wasn't long.

Q: A short period of time?

Tretter: Yes.

Q: Where did you go on this [second] walk? How far did you go? Where did you go?

Tretter: Out to the right.

Q: You went towards the ferry?

Tretter: Yes.

Q: Do you know how far down that road you went?

Tretter: I think almost to the point where you would bear left to go to the ferry.

Q: And how long a time would you say this walk lasted?

Tretter: Oh, it must have been an hour – an hour and a half.

Q: Do you know what time you returned to the cottage?

Tretter: I think it was around two o'clock.

Q: And you tell the court that when you returned after the second walk, Mr. Gargan, Mr. Markham, Mr. LaRosa, and various other people, some of the girls, were present?

Tretter: Yes. In short, when I came into the cottage, people were starting to settle down. Mr. Crimmins and Mr. Gargan were talking.

Q: You didn't come in with them? They arrived previously than you?

Tretter: When I got there, they were there.

It appears, in fact, that these two may have been walking toward the ferry landing on their first walk to catch the last scheduled ferry to Edgartown, an easy stroll on level ground of no more than 30 minutes, but were diverted by a desperate plea for help.

Under the circumstances, they might have welcomed the rumors of a dalliance to divert others from questioning the more damning truth.

Tretter testified that he walked toward the Dike Road intersection on his second walk "almost to the point where you would bear left to go to the ferry," then walked right back to the cottage. In other words, Tretter claimed that it took them one and a half hours to walk less than a half mile up the street and less than a half mile back, a walk my wife was able to make in less than eight minutes each way! Granted, Tretter said he was walking without shoes, but that is still a very long time for a stroll of less than a mile on an asphalt road. Remember, you are talking about an island absolutely infested with mosquitoes, ticks, poison ivy, and brambles. In July, the nights are chilly. There were no blankets or cars to snuggle up in. It was pitch black. There were no lawns. What could they possibly have been doing for one and one-half hours on that second walk?

Zad Rust writes, "The entire period of the walks was spent, according to both witnesses, on the portion of the main road between the cottage and the fork where the road turns left to the ferry landing and right to the Dike Bridge. It was over this same stretch of road and during the same interval of time a) that Senator Kennedy trudged back to the cottage from the scene of the accident; b) that five other members of the cookout party also took their night strolls; c) that Markham, Gargan, and Kennedy hurried back to the scene of the accident in the white Valiant; d) that Markham and Gargan, in the same car, drove back to the cottage from the ferry slip; and c) that Huck Look, after seeing the Kennedy car at the crossroads, was driving over when he passed and offered a lift to LaRosa and the Lyons girls. *Nevertheless, during those two-and-a-half hours, nobody met Tretter and Miss Keough, and they met nobody* [emphasis in the original]."[1]

Perhaps tellingly, it was Keough's handbag with her identification and hotel room key which was found in Kennedy's Oldsmobile when it was pulled from the water on the morning of July 19. In fact, Chief Arena believed it was actually Rosemary Keough's body in the submerged car until told otherwise by Kennedy.

Keough was one of the most loyal of all the Boiler Room Girls. Even long after the accident, she said, "I'll do everything I can to help the senator obtain the nomination [for the Presidency]."[2] She told BBC investigators in 1994 that her relationship with Ted Kennedy was based on mutual loyalty and mutual affection. She also appears to have been one of the most reluctant to talk about the incident later. Olsen says that a reporter camped out for an entire night at Rosemary Keough's front door, receiving nothing but silence for his vigilance.[3] Her inquest testimony was short and vague. In the BBC documentary she said nothing of substance.

---

[1] *Teddy Bare*, pp. 234-235

[2] *Senatorial Privilege*, p. 280

[3] *The Bridge at Chappaquiddick*, p. 221

Carol says that the woman in the white compact car was very short with short hair and dwarfed by the two men sitting on either side of her. Carol has repeated that description to many people for 45 years without ever seeing a photo of Rosemary Keough, and in fact she assumed the woman she had seen in the car was Mary Jo. When Carol told me the woman's hair color was not blond, she still had never seen a photo of Keough. Olsen says that Keough, at only five feet tall, was the shortest of the Boiler Room Girls.[1] In *Senatorial Privilege: The Chappaquiddick Cover-up*, Keough appears in a photo with the other girls as they disembarked from their plane to attend the inquest on Martha's Vineyard. In that photo, Keough appears about a head shorter than any of the rest and her hair is cropped short. In the BBC documentary of 1994, color footage was shown of the Boiler Room Girls entering the Edgartown courthouse. Keough's hair is short and a light shade of brown or red.

Tretter was the only other person who came to the meeting with Kennedy, Markham, and Gargan to plan strategy at the Shiretown Inn on the early morning following the incident. Rosemary Keough and Susan Tannenbaum accompanied all three of them to the inn. At the inquest, Keough recalled looking up and seeing Kennedy standing on the porch outside his room.

Gargan appears to have gone out of his way to distance Keough, Tretter, and Tannenbaum from the scene. He told Damore in an interview that he regarded them as excess baggage when the three wanted to come with him to visit Kennedy in Edgartown, but that "he couldn't refuse." He said that Tretter "burst into the room" when he and Markham were talking to Kennedy at the Shiretown Inn, and "furious at the interruption," he told Tretter, "Hey, you! Get out of here!"[2] At the inquest, Tretter testified that he entered Kennedy's room at the Shiretown Inn because he thought he had been invited in but was told that it was a private meeting.

Nevertheless, it was Tretter, Markham, and Gargan who appeared to stick together as a group on the morning after the incident. Tretter was assigned by Gargan to take Rosemary Keough and Susan Tannenbaum to the Katama Shores Motel. It was Tretter who was told by Gargan to get all of the girls "out of here" and off the island[3] and it was Tretter who went to the police station to pick up Keough's bag.

Most interestingly, Gargan told Damore that after cleaning Lawrence Cottage and returning to Edgartown with Ray LaRosa, Esther Newberg, and the Lyons sisters, he asked the girls to make their own way back to the Katama Shores Motel in a taxi while he told Tretter to bring Rosemary Keough and Susan Tannenbaum back to the motel in Ray LaRosa's Mercury. Gargan said he then walked up the street to the police station

---

[1] *The Bridge at Chappaquiddick*, p. 215
[2] *Senatorial Privilege*, p. 90
[3] *Senatorial Privilege*, p. 94

to meet with Kennedy and Markham. Sometime later, Gargan met Tretter at the Shiretown Inn, at which time he informed Tretter about the accident.[1]

This was corroborated by LaRosa at the inquest, who said he heard about the accident from Tretter at the Shiretown Inn.

Q: When did you learn that Mary Jo Kopechne's body had been found?
LaRosa: I learned the details when I went back to the Shiretown.
Q: How did you learn that?
LaRosa: I began to ask some questions of my young associates who were there.
Q: What associates?
LaRosa: Mr. Tretter was there.

But Tretter testified that he had learned of the accident from Gargan at the Katama Shores Motel, not at the Shiretown Inn.

Q: Well, there was a time you learned that she had died?
Tretter: Yes.
Q: When and how? Who told you?
Tretter: Mr. Gargan. At the Dunes [aka Katama Shores Motel on Dunes Road]. It would be after, I believe, 11:00.

However, none of this is what Gargan claimed at the inquest. Notice Gargan's testimony:

Q: Do you know when Mr. Tretter learned of the accident?
Gargan: From my own personal knowledge, to tell you the truth, I don't think I could help you, Mr. Dinis. He may have found out, and I'm only guessing on this, but he may have found out from the girls, the other girls that did know because Miss Keough and Miss Tannenbaum found out from the other girls about it. Mr. Tretter may have found out from the other girls. I don't know.
Q: You did not tell Mr. Tretter?
Gargan: I did not. Of the accident? I did not.

Finally, Gargan told Esther Newberg and the Lyons sisters that Mary Jo had driven the Oldsmobile back to the Katama Shores by herself before the last midnight ferry whereas Kennedy had swum the Edgartown Channel. This is what a person might say if he had helped stage an accident. But strangely, Gargan never fed this fabrication to

---

[1] *Senatorial Privilege*, pp. 92-93

Rosemary Keough. Keough testified at the inquest that Gargan had told her Mary Jo and Kennedy had driven back to Edgartown in the Oldsmobile *together*.[1]

Why would Kennedy, Gargan, and Markham involve two more persons before heading to the scene of the accident on Dike Road?

Perhaps, if two members of the party were walking to the ferry landing to take the last scheduled boat to Edgartown, Markham and Gargan might have preferred to keep everyone sequestered on the island until the situation could be evaluated. According to the testimony of Gargan and Markham, Kennedy told his friends that Mary Jo had been involved in a terrible accident, but little more. It can be assumed that Kennedy was probably drunk and more than a bit incoherent. Gargan and Markham could not be certain Mary Jo was dead, as indicated by their panicked rush to Dike Bridge at 11:35 p.m. If they could revive her, contain the situation, and make sure everyone established their alibis, the world might never be the wiser.

If not, it was more important than ever that everyone be on the same page.

There is also another possibility. Perhaps Kennedy left the party with Mary Jo and Rosemary Keough. Perhaps Charles Tretter was walking to the ferry alone. Remember the email from Clarence Toliver which purported that someone had seen two people cut behind Pimpneymouse Farm that night? Perhaps the group picked up Tretter because Kennedy knew he had seen him driving to the bridge with both of these girls.

Whoever Carol saw, once these others had been direct witnesses to an apparent injury to one of the Boiler Room Girls, but never sought help, they would, by necessity, be willing participants in all that followed.

---

[1] It is unknown what Gargan told Susan Tannenbaum. The prosecution never asked.

25
Was There Another Woman Involved?

Was there another Boiler Room Girl involved when the accident was staged? It appears likely.

In the BBC documentary *Chappaquiddick* released in 1994, investigators concluded that Kennedy must have stepped out of the car somewhere on Dike Road after observing Huck Look at around 12:40 a.m. Mary Jo then drove off Dike Bridge in the Oldsmobile alone with Kennedy none the wiser. Kennedy first heard of the accident the next morning. This, they reasoned, was the only way to account for Kennedy's extraordinary ability to get out of the vehicle on his own, and for the absence of obvious trauma, either physical or mental, only a few hours after the accident occurred.

This was the same theory advanced by State Police Detective Bernie Flynn and published by Olsen in *The Bridge at Chappaquiddick.* Flynn and Olsen assumed that Kennedy first heard of the accident when advised by Tony Bettencourt that the Oldsmobile had been found with a dead girl in it on the Chappaquiddick side after 9:20 a.m. But BBC investigators had discovered that Kennedy aide Dun Gifford had heard about the accident by at least 8:45 a.m., and the strange, agitated behavior exhibited by Gargan, Markham, and Kennedy when they all met up outside the Shiretown Inn at 8:00 a.m. looked very much like Kennedy first heard about the accident then.

Both Ross and Marilyn Richards told detectives that Gargan and Markham were soaking wet when they arrived at the Shiretown Inn at 8:00 a.m. to meet with Kennedy. Mrs. Richards said she was surprised by Gargan's appearance. "Joe looked awful. His clothes were all wrinkled and his hair was sticking out." Ross Richards confirmed their observation to Cutler in 1971 and Marilyn Richards confirmed it to the BBC in 1994. To anyone who has had to deal with hair after immersion in saltwater, this sounds very much like Gargan and Markham had been swimming in the sea.

So Flynn reasoned that after Mary Jo had never arrived back at Lawrence Cottage that night, Gargan and Markham must have gone looking for her at Dike Bridge in the early morning hours, probably around 6:00 to 6:30 a.m. Discovering with alarm the car in the water, the two dove in but were unsuccessful in recovering the body, so they rushed to the ferry landing to take the first ferry over to Edgartown. In their panic and concern, neither had the time or inclination to clean up at Lawrence Cottage before confronting Kennedy at the Shiretown Inn. Flynn told the BBC, "There is no other reason they should be soaking wet," and the BBC agreed.

There are many reasons to suspect that Kennedy was well aware of Mary Jo's fate long before he met up with Gargan and Markham at 8:00 a.m., and Flynn and the BBC ignored all of them. The blood evidence. The phone calls from Lawrence Cottage. Kennedy's decision not to call the ferry operator to get him to Edgartown.

Most important, Kennedy phoned Helga Wagner to tell her that something very serious had happened and to find the number for Stephen Smith. But Stephen Smith was called from the public phone booth at the Shiretown Inn on Kennedy's credit card at 5:43 a.m. in a call that lasted 27 minutes. Why would Kennedy have told Wagner *before* 8:00 a.m. that something very serious had happened if he never knew Mary Jo had driven into the pond by herself until advised by Gargan and Markham *after* 8:00 a.m.? And if true that none of these men had ever known that Mary Jo had driven off the bridge after Look saw the Oldsmobile around 12:40 a.m., why would all three nevertheless claim that they knew about Mary Jo's death by 12:15 a.m. the evening before but had never tried to get help or report the accident for the next 10 hours? That damning admission hurt Markham's career, subjected Gargan to ridicule, and ruined Kennedy's chances of becoming president.

Irrespective of all that, the damage to the Oldsmobile, the complete absence of injuries to Mary Jo, the acceleration marks on the bridge, the partially detached, un-marked side-view mirror, Kennedy's testimony on the morning of July 19, and Carol's observation all suggest that the real accident occurred soon after 11:15 p.m. and the plunge was staged. What actually appears to have taken place is this:

After panicking sometime after 3:00 a.m., Gargan and Markham drove to Dike Bridge in the early morning hours in an attempt to remove Mary Jo's body from the vehicle before it could be discovered by others. But it was one thing to insert a body into a car in the dead of night and quite another to find and drag her out of it while completely exposed in daylight. And the water level would have been much higher, too. Twilight on July 19 was at 4:52 a.m. and sunrise at 5:24. High tide at the Dike that morning occurred at about 5:30. If they returned to the bridge soon after first light, the water in the channel would have been almost a foot higher than what they had experienced the evening before.

And there might have been another problem they could not have foreseen. Mary Jo would have been in the throes of rigor mortis. By 5:30 a.m., her corpse would have been frozen into a sitting position with arms extended out in front of her. It would have been exceedingly difficult, or perhaps impossible, to maneuver Mary Jo's body out of one of the vehicle's side windows without SCUBA.

Giving up, they crossed over to Edgartown at about 8:00 a.m. in their borrowed powerboat so that no ferry operator would notice they were wet, abandoning the boat on a dock less than 200 yards from the Shiretown Inn. After making phone calls before 8:45 a.m. to arrange for Dun Gifford to fly to Martha's Vineyard, Kennedy then proceeded to the Chappaquiddick side at 9:15 a.m., perhaps to wait for Gifford's help before making another attempt. *After realizing they could be placed at the scene, their plan was to remove Mary Jo's body from the vehicle and have Gifford fly it off the island before anyone was the wiser.* The plan was abandoned when they heard from Tony Bettencourt that the vehicle had already been discovered. Gifford had to wait another 27 hours before he could complete his mission.

This is why no ferry operator or deckhand could remember them crossing on an early ferry that morning. And this is why Kennedy looked so terribly worried and distracted when he brushed right by Ross Richards and his wife when leaving the Shiretown Inn at 9:15 a.m., but appeared so relaxed and cheerful on the Chappaquiddick ferry just a minute or two later. Just like his innocuous conversation with the Richardses and Stan Moore earlier that morning, it was all just an act. Until they heard that the Oldsmobile had been discovered, the group still hoped they could pull it off.

But, if Gargan and Markham had spent some time diving on the Oldsmobile in the early morning hours, but never had time to return to Lawrence Cottage to clean up, that line of thought can be pursued to its inevitable conclusion. It means that none of the other persons who made the trip with them over to Edgartown that morning returned to Lawrence Cottage, either. And the "other persons" were Rosemary Keough, Charles Tretter, *and Susan Tannenbaum.* Every one of the other witnesses at the party said that these five persons left Lawrence Cottage in the early morning, but none said they returned after that until Gargan showed up in the Valiant between 9:40 and 10:00 a.m. to take them off the island of Chappaquiddick.

When Gargan, Markham, Tretter, Keough, and Tannenbaum arrived in Edgartown, Gargan and Markham, looking soaking wet and disheveled, strode off to confront Kennedy. But Tretter, Keough, and Tannenbaum went immediately to Tretter's room at the Shiretown Inn. According to Tretter, the two girls wanted to sleep, but Tretter wanted to shower. At the inquest, Tretter said, "I took a shower, shaved, and left the two girls in my room and went up to see where they were and I went up to Senator Kennedy's room."

Susan Tannenbaum

We have noted the odd movements of Keough and Tretter that night. Now let's take a look at Susan Tannenbaum.

Susan Tannenbaum was the very last person to testify at the inquest. Her testimony was the shortest of all the guests at the party consisting mostly of "Yes," "No," "I don't know," and "I don't remember." No one insisted that Tannenbaum expand on those answers because by the end of four days it had become obvious that both the prosecution and defense were utterly sick of the whole business and just wanted to finish it. At the end of it all, Judge Boyle told Tannenbaum disgustedly, "All right, you are excused, and you may leave the courtroom and go, I assume, right to your friends."

One can imagine that Tannenbaum's truculent testimony was the final straw that broke Boyle's back. Boyle had bent over backwards to be lenient to Kennedy and this is how he got paid. Boyle could no longer avoid the obvious: it was all lies, half-truths, evasions, and contempt for the court and everything it stood for. Far from giving Kennedy a ringing endorsement in his summary, Boyle surprised everyone, then and today, by concluding something much different.

Nevertheless, Tannenbaum did divulge one important detail: she made two walks that night from Lawrence Cottage.

Q: Did you remain in the cottage that entire evening?
Tannenbaum: Except for occasional walks I did.
Q: Did you take several walks?
Tannenbaum: Yes?
Q: How many?
Tannenbaum: Two

Tannenbaum testified that her first walk was with Ray LaRosa and the Lyons sisters, well before the Ray LaRosa and the Lyons sisters met Huck Look at 12:45 a.m. But who was Tannenbaum walking with that second time? Where did she go? How long was she gone? Almost unbelievably, the prosecution never asked and Tannenbaum was let off the hook. But what is certain is this: not one of the guests at the party ever said that they made any other walk with Susan Tannenbaum throughout the evening. This is most strange, as the prosecution, until that point, had made a determined effort to pin down each walk, who was walking with whom, when the walks occurred, and where each person went. It appears either Susan Tannenbaum walked alone that second time, or she wasn't really "walking" at all.

Equally strange, not one of the guests ever admitted talking to Susan Tannenbaum between 12:30 and 2:00 a.m., or even seeing her at all during that period. The closest to an admission that Tannenbaum was at the cottage within those hours came from the testimony of Mary Ellen Lyons, who said that after she returned to Lawrence Cottage from her second walk (when she had observed Huck Look on School House Road), "There were some people sitting on the fence; *I think* Miss Tannenbaum and Miss Newburgh and Mr. Crimmins were in the cottage."

Susan Tannenbaum was asked by Judge Boyle what conversations she had with the other girls after all the cars had left. Unaccountably, Tannenbaum couldn't remember any conversation at all.

Judge Boyle: Were you not surprised to find out that without your knowledge all your transportation had gone so you couldn't get back to Edgartown?
Tannenbaum: Yes, I was surprised.
Judge Boyle: And were the other girls surprised, too?
Tannenbaum: I don't know.

Judge Boyle: Was there not some discussion about it between you?

Tannenbaum: I had no discussion that I can remember.

Judge Boyle: Nothing said about, well, gee, this is unusual to leave us stranded here?

Tannenbaum: I thought so.

Judge Boyle: But no discussion between you and your friends?

Tannenbaum: Not that I remember.

Judge Boyle? Not even mentioning it?

Tannenbaum: Not that I remember.

In fact, Susan Tannenbaum didn't seem to know, or remember, much of anything.

Q: Do you know what [Senator Kennedy's] drink was?

Tannenbaum: No.

Q: Do you know what color it was?

Tannenbaum: No, I do not remember.

Q: Pardon?

Tannenbaum: I do not remember.

Q: Now, did Mary Jo have anything to drink?

Tannenbaum: I do not remember.

Q: You do not remember at all?

Tannenbaum: No.

Q: Did you make an inquiry as to [Mary Jo's] failure to return?

Tannenbaum: No.

Q: Did you see the senator return?

Tannenbaum: No.

Q: Now, when Mr. Gargan returned, did you have any conversation with him as to the whereabouts of Mary Jo or the senator?

Tannenbaum: No.

Q: Did you hear Mr. Gargan tell some of the girls what had happened?

Tannenbaum: No.

Q: Did you have any conversation with Mr. Markham?

Tannenbaum: No.

Q: Did [Mr. Markham] give any reason as to why he was tired?

Tannenbaum: No.

Q: And what about Mr. Gargan's appearance, did you make any note of that?

Tannenbaum: No.

Q: Now, do you recall the time that Mr. Gargan and Mr. Markham returned?

Tannenbaum: No.

Q: Would it be 2:00 a.m.?

Tannenbaum: I do not know.

Q: Did Mr. Gargan tell you [that Miss Kopechne was missing, that later the car had been found]?

Tannenbaum: I do not remember.

Q: Did you see Senator Kennedy leave the cottage?

Tannenbaum: No.

Q: Did you learn why Mary Jo was leaving?

Tannenbaum: No.

Q: Did you inquire?

Tannenbaum: No.

Q: Did Mary Jo have any conversation with you as to why she was leaving?

Tannenbaum: No.

Q: Did she complain to you that she wasn't feeling well?

Tannenbaum: No.

Q: Do you know how many minutes she had been gone?

Tannenbaum: No, I do not.

Q: Do you have an opinion as to how much Mary Jo drank that night at the party?

Tannenbaum: No, I do not.

Q: Do you have an opinion as to how much the senator had to drink that night?

Tannenbaum: No.

Judge Boyle: Do you have any belief as to where [Kennedy and Mary Jo] were going?

Tannenbaum: No.

Judge Boyle: Did you not believe that they were coming back to Edgartown? You didn't think they were leaving the party?

Tannenbaum: I didn't know.

Judge Boyle: I am talking about your belief. You presumed they were just going outside as many people were?

Tannenbaum: I don't know.

Judge Boyle: Did you notice Mary Jo's pocketbook?

Tannenbaum: No.

Judge Boyle: That night in the cottage after she had left?

Tannenbaum: No.

Judge Boyle: Was it called to your attention any time that evening after she had left?

Tannenbaum: No.

Judge Boyle: Nothing said about it being peculiar Mary Jo hasn't returned; here is her pocketbook; nothing of that nature said?

Tannenbaum: No, no.

Esther Newberg was asked if the girls had ever discussed among themselves where everyone had gone.

Newberg: Was there any discussion by whom?

Q: By anybody. Conversations.

Newberg: The two Lyons sisters. We were asking each other the question, and when we answered each other it was sort of – we didn't ask any of the men. We asked each other. We determined in our own minds that [Mary Jo] must be back in the motel and she was lucky, she was asleep.

Q: Was this in the presence of Mr. Markham and Mr. Gargan?

Newberg: No.

Q: In whose presence was it?

Newberg: The three of us were in the bedroom.

Q: So, just the three girls made the inquiry?

Newberg: Yes.

But where was Susan Tannenbaum when that conversation was going on? Why was she excluded from it? Was she "walking" with Ray LaRosa or Jack Crimmins? Or walking alone? Who knows? What is known is that as soon as Markham and Gargan returned to Lawrence Cottage, suddenly Susan Tannenbaum was sitting on the couch with Esther Newberg.

Newberg: Mr. Gargan, when he came back we were in the living room on the couch, Miss Tannenbaum and I. Mr. Gargan came in and collapsed.

Q: Either just before Mr. Markham and Mr. Gargan returned, or immediately thereafter, the cottage has all the participants of the party with the exception of Mr. Kennedy and Miss Kopechne, is that right?

Newberg: *After* Mr. Markham and Mr. Gargan returned, everybody was at the cottage, yes.

Both Charles Tretter and Rosemary Keough said they returned to the cottage on their second walk at 2:00 a.m., very shortly after the arrival of Gargan and Markham. However, Newberg said that all the participants were at the cottage before Gargan and Markham returned. Did Susan Tannenbaum return to the cottage with Tretter and Keough? Or perhaps just before them?[1] It appears that maybe she did. Gargan and Markham had already involved one girl in the plot; why not another?

If you remember, Gargan told Damore that he had no wish for Keough, Tretter, or Tannenbaum to accompany him to Edgartown on the morning of July 19 "but that he couldn't refuse." The question Damore might have asked was, "Why not?" As Kennedy's first cousin and closest confidant, Gargan was second in command. Kennedy was responsible for the death of a young girl – a close friend to Rosemary

---

[1] The only statement from Tannenbaum at the inquest that could shed any light on the subject was this one: "I was in the cottage when [Gargan and Markham] returned."

Keough and Susan Tannenbaum. Considering that Gargan and Markham were dealing with a fatality and fully expecting (they claimed) to be walking into a full-blown police investigation the minute they arrived in Edgartown, with reporters shoving microphones into their faces and demanding answers, it makes no sense that Gargan would have allowed three innocent persons, with no idea of what was going on, to join them on that trip. If Gargan and Markham were driving to Edgartown soaking wet, it makes even less sense.

It seems Tretter, Keough, and Tannenbaum must have been fully informed of what was going on before they reached Edgartown. It just does not appear credible they would have been allowed on that trip if they were completely oblivious of the accident at Dike Bridge, and to the death of Mary Jo.

As mentioned in a previous chapter, Gargan testified that Tretter, Keough, and Tannenbaum were the very last guests to hear about the accident.

Q: Do you know when Mr. Tretter learned of the accident?
Gargan: From my own personal knowledge, to tell you the truth, I don't think I could help you, Mr. Dinis. He may have found out, and I'm only guessing on this, but he may have found out from the girls, the other girls that did know because Miss Keough and Miss Tannenbaum found out from the other girls about it. Mr. Tretter may have found out from the other girls. I don't know.
Q: You did not tell Mr. Tretter?
Gargan: I did not. Of the accident? I did not.

But Tretter testified that he had heard the news from Gargan at the Katama Shores Motel. As for the "other girls," Newberg and the Lyons sisters testified they heard the news about the accident from Gargan; Keough said she heard about it from Newberg and the Lyons sisters; whereas Tannenbaum testified that she had, in fact, heard it from Gargan at the Katama Shores Motel!

Why would Gargan swear at the inquest that neither Charles Tretter, Rosemary Keough, nor Susan Tannenbaum had heard about the accident from him? In retrospect it seems suspicious that Gargan took care to single out just these three persons, especially since Gargan later admitted to Damore that he had, in fact, told Tretter about the accident at the Shiretown Inn, a fact that had been backed up by LaRosa's inquest testimony.

The evidence suggests that Susan Tannenbaum might have joined the group when Gargan, Markham, and Kennedy left Lawrence Cottage soon after 12:30 a.m. to arrange boat transportation at the ferry landing and stage the accident at Dike Bridge. She may have been the female passenger in the front seat of the Oldsmobile when it was observed by Look around 12:40 a.m.; or she may have been hiding in the back seat; in other words, the "second female" Look told the *Evening Standard* and others he might have seen in the Oldsmobile that night. She certainly appears to have been with Keough when the men were diving on the car in Poucha Pond the next morning, if that indeed is what happened, and, of course, she was with Gargan, Markham, Tretter, and Keough when they arrived in Edgartown at 8:00 a.m.

Huck Look told Zad Rust that what he had seen in the back seat of the Oldsmobile "could only have been another girl, or an outstretched garment." In order to identify the form as a girl, the outstretched garment must have looked like a dress or skirt. It is unknown what garment Susan Tannenbaum or Rosemary Keough wore to the party. But it is known that Mary Jo wore dark slacks. Moreover, Mary Jo's blood was found to have a carbon monoxide level of just under five percent. This suggests that Mary Jo was in the trunk, breathing a good deal of car exhaust, for much of the time she was in the vehicle.

The evidence implies that the second girl Look might have seen in the back seat was *not* Mary Jo – she was someone else.

Why might Susan Tannenbaum have been asked to help? Maybe the group had no choice. Perhaps Tannenbaum was outside the cottage when the others returned in the Oldsmobile just before midnight. Perhaps she had seen something suspicious, such as damage to the car, Ted Kennedy, or the body of Mary Jo. It is also a good idea to have women around when clandestine matters are afoot. A group of men are often viewed with suspicion at night, but add a woman or two and the perception instantly changes.

Mary Jo's final position within the Oldsmobile

The BBC's theory that Gargan, Markham, and perhaps others were diving on the car during the early hours of July 19 gives us a plausible explanation as to how Mary Jo's uninjured body ended up in the rear-seat area of the vehicle.

Suppose that after deliberately accelerating the vehicle off the bridge, Mary Jo was inserted carefully into the front seat with her hands cupped around the steering wheel so as to suggest that she was the driver. Dealing with a current of about 2.3 knots and a distance of about three and one-half feet from the open front driver-side window to the surface, this would be a relatively easy task. The buoyant body would remain pressed into the upside-down front seat, and there would have been no current flowing through the car between the top of the seatback and the footwell to disturb that position as rigor mortis set in.

Removing the corpse later in the morning would be difficult in the best of circumstances. The body was no longer supple and the tide was about a foot higher than before. Absent underwater breathing apparatus, the job might be almost impossible. One probably would first want to maneuver the body into the rear seat area, which was closer to the surface, and then attempt to extract it from the rear passenger-side window, just as Farrar eventually did.

This could be accomplished by turning the body sideways. Possibly it could be done simply by flipping the body 180 degrees over the front seat since Mary Jo, like Rosemary Keough, was very short and petite. In fact, the body might have ended up in the rear seat area by virtue of random pushing and pulling rather than through any sort of deliberate intent.

However it ended up there, if it subsequently proved impossible to remove Mary Jo's frozen body through the rear window given the size of the opening and the current, the body would later be found in that odd, sitting-down position, with raised arms bent at the elbows and with hands cupped. Exactly as found and drawn by Farrar.

If Mary Jo was positioned carefully on the upside-down front seat with her hands on the steering wheel, rigor mortis would have frozen her into a sitting position within two to six hours. Maneuvered later into the rear seat area where the car was closer to the surface, possibly by simply flipping the body 180 degrees over the front seat, Mary Jo's frozen corpse would be found in that same position, with bent arms extended forward and hands cupped, as drawn by Farrar.

Notice that the rear window opening in Farrar's sketch is substantially smaller than the front one. In a Delmont 88, however, both openings are almost identical since the front window has a valence or quarter glass at the front which restricts its size, and the roof does not slope downward at the back of the rear window as it does in the sketch.

26
The Relay

Almost every Chappaquiddick book has a timeline, and this one will, too. But in this chapter our timeline will concentrate on just one issue: the discrepancy between the time Kennedy said he plunged over the bridge; and the time he said he returned to Lawrence Cottage and notified Gargan and Markham that there had been a terrible accident.

$\mathscr{I}$f you remember, when Kennedy finally stumbled back to Lawrence Cottage, allegedly at 12:15 a.m., he testified that he remained out of sight near the Valiant and called out to LaRosa to find Gargan. When Gargan arrived, Kennedy asked him to find Markham. Malcolm Reybold calls this exchange of messages between Kennedy, LaRosa, Gargan, and Markham the *relay.*

At the inquest, Kennedy testified he was certain he left Lawrence Cottage with Gargan and Markham at 12:15 a.m. because he specifically remembered looking at the Valiant's dashboard clock at the moment he arrived back at Dike Bridge. According to Kennedy, the clock in the Valiant showed the time of their arrival at the bridge as precisely 12:20 a.m. Unfortunately for Kennedy's memory, the Valiant was later examined carefully by investigative reporters and found to have no clock.[1] Markham put the time of the *relay* as "shortly after midnight," whereas Gargan put the time as 12:15 to 12:30 a.m. However, Look saw the Oldsmobile no earlier than 12:40 a.m., which would seem to indicate that the *relay*, if in fact it occurred as the three said it did, must have taken place sometime after that.

The *relay* was a focus of attention at the inquest, but neither LaRosa, Markham, Gargan, nor Kennedy could get it quite right. Notice how Malcolm Reybold describes the inconsistencies in *The Inspector's Opinion:*

"We have now a direct contradiction between the Kennedy, Gargan, and Markham testimony and that of LaRosa and others concerning the *relay* of the Kennedy message and the departure of Gargan and Markham from the cottage. Notice, too, a third conflict in the position of LaRosa during the exchange. Gargan says LaRosa came into the kitchen area and gave him the Kennedy message, then returned to walk outside through the front door. Here, Gargan told LaRosa to get Markham. Now LaRosa goes back inside the door and informs Markham, then steps outside a third time and points out the car to Markham. None of this appears in the testimony of LaRosa or anyone else. LaRosa merely walked into the cottage after speaking with Kennedy, motioned or spoke to Gargan and Markham, then remained inside the house until they drove away

---

[1] *Senatorial Privilege*, p. 354

in the white Valiant. Note, too, the Gargan statement that they entered the car together, while Markham says Gargan was seated in the car when he reached it."[1]

OK, so let's just say they had a hard time remembering the details. But the point is, Kennedy, LaRosa, Markham, and Gargan testified that a relay of messages had taken place after Kennedy arrived back at the cottage, soaking wet, having had no success in rescuing Mary Jo from the submerged Oldsmobile soon after 11:15 p.m.

Now look at the timeline of Kennedy's story as compared to our interpretation of Carol's observation, side by side.

Kennedy

11:15 p.m. Leaves the cottage.
11:20 p.m. Drives off the bridge.
  Spends 15 to 20 minutes diving.
  15 to 20 minutes resting.
  15 minutes walking back to cottage
12:15 a.m.: Walks to Lawrence Cottage.
  Informs Gargan & Markham of
  the accident (the *relay*).
12:20 a.m. Arrives back at bridge.
  45 minutes diving.
  10 minutes driving to ferry.
  A few minutes talking.
1:40 a.m. Swims channel.
2:00 a.m. Arrives Shiretown Inn.

Carol

Before 11:15 p.m. Leaves the cottage.
11:20 p.m. Gets in an accident.
11:30 p.m. Walks to Lawrence Cottage.
  Informs Gargan & Markham.
11:35 p.m. Valiant passes Carol.
11:55 p.m. Group returns to cottage.
11:57 p.m. First telephone call begins.

12:30 a.m. Third telephone call ends.
12:40 a.m. Oldsmobile sighted by Look.
12:45 - 1:45 a.m. Oldsmobile rigged.
  Oldsmobile sent off bridge.
1:50 a.m. Ballou sights exchange of boats.
2:00 a.m. Arrives Shiretown Inn.

The timeline agrees pretty well in some respects. However, Kennedy said that the *relay* occurred at 12:15 a.m., while Look's testimony seems to indicate it took place after 12:40 a.m. Our version, on the other hand, has the *relay* occurring around 11:30 p.m., 45 minutes to an hour and a quarter earlier. That is a major discrepancy that needs to be addressed.

The prosecution never asked whether Gargan and Markham had left the party before 12:15 a.m., because what was the point? Kennedy said he returned to the cottage at 12:15 a.m., so it would seem logical that the *relay* occurred at that time or sometime later, especially since Gargan and Markham said they left between 12:15 and 12:30 a.m., and Huck Look said that he saw the Oldsmobile drive down Dike Road with a male driver and female passenger between 12:40 and 12:45 a.m.

---

[1] *The Inspector's Opinion*, pp. 159-160

From the prosecution's standpoint, Kennedy under-estimated the time he returned to the party by 15 minutes to half an hour or so, which seemed acceptable. But it turns out that Gargan and Markham left the party *two* times, and it was the *first time, not the second time, that the relay occurred!* The prosecution never picked up on this, but it can be proved by the testimony of five witnesses who took three walks that evening on School House Road.

The four witnesses on the first walk were Ray LaRosa, Susan Tannenbaum, Nance Lyons, and Mary Ellen Lyons. The three witnesses on the second walk, which encountered Huck Look, were Ray LaRosa and the Lyons sisters. The witness on the third walk was Charles Tretter.

Ray LaRosa testified that he never saw Kennedy but recognized his voice near the Valiant. On Kennedy's instructions, he told Gargan and Markham that Kennedy needed to see them but couldn't remember the time. He confirmed that Gargan and Markham then left immediately with Kennedy in the Valiant *before his first walk* with Susan Tannenbaum and the two Lyons sisters. He testified that he met Huck Look with the two Lyons sisters at the intersection on his second walk around 12:45 a.m.

Susan Tannenbaum also testified that she saw Gargan and Markham leave *before her first walk* with LaRosa and the others but couldn't remember the time. Susan Tannenbaum was not a member of the second walk which encountered Huck Look.

Nance Lyons testified that she saw Gargan and Markham leave the cottage "at least 20 minutes" *before her first walk* with Ray LaRosa and Susan Tannenbaum. She remembered talking to Huck Look on her second walk. She put the time of the first walk as 12:45 a.m. and the time of the second walk as from 1:30 to 2:00 a.m. As Huck Look saw Nance Lyons around 12:45 a.m., the times are way off. However, it does confirm, once again, that the *relay* occurred before LaRosa and the Lyons sisters' encounter with Huck Look.

So what we really need to do is nail down the time of that first walk. And Mary Ellen Lyons gives us the hammer.

Mary Ellen Lyons was positively chatty compared to the others. Just like the others, she remembered seeing Ray LaRosa relay the message to Markham and Gargan *before her first walk* with Ray LaRosa, Susan Tannenbaum, and his sister. However, unlike the others, she gives us a time: before midnight or 12:15 a.m. And she remembered meeting Look on her second walk toward the intersection with LaRosa and her sister later.

M. Lyons: Before midnight or 12:15, Mr. LaRosa came into the cottage where I was at that time and called for Mr. Markham and Mr. Gargan.
Q: *And this was before midnight or 12:15?*
M. Lyons: *Oh, yes.*
Q: But I believe you said earlier that Mr. Gargan and Mr. Markham left before you took your second walk.

M. Lyons: *Before I took the first one.*

Q: Oh, before you took the first one?

M. Lyons: Yes. *Mr. Markham and Mr. Gargan were gone.*

Q: Did Mr. LaRosa tell you that Senator Kennedy had returned and asked for Mr. Gargan or Mr. Markham?

M. Lyons: Yes, he did.

Q: Mr. LaRosa told you that?

M. Lyons: Yes.

Q: Did he describe the senator in any way?

M. Lyons: No, as I remember it, he said he didn't see him.

Q: What did he say, Mr. LaRosa, to you about that particular question?

M. Lyons: He just said that the senator had – that he was sitting out front and the senator had come back and asked for Mr. Markham and Mr. Gargan. That is all.

Q: Was there any talk about Mary Jo at that time?

M. Lyons: No, we were speculating whether a car had been caught in the sand, or how do you put that, and we –

Q: Was there any conversation as to why these automobiles were in the sand?

M. Lyons: *No. The cars were gone and we were just saying, you know, where is everybody? The only thing we could think of was that a car was stuck in the sand and Mr. Gargan and Mr. Markham had taken the other car to get the first car out of the sand.*

Q: Now, directing your attention to the second walk... did an automobile slow down?

M. Lyons: Yes, it did.

Q: Will you tell the court what happened involving that automobile?

M. Lyons: We were walking – this was coming out of the cottage to the right, and a car passed and just slowed down as it approached us and asked if we needed any help, and we assumed that it was Mr. Gargan or Mr. Markham *who had prior to this time left the cottage.* We thought they were coming back, and I believe that my sister made, you know, a comment, move along, or something to that effect, and then we discovered that it was not Mr. Markham or Mr. Gargan; it was someone we didn't know.

And there we have it! The *relay* did not take place at 12:15 a.m., as Kennedy testified. It did not take place between 12:15 and 12:30 a.m., as Markham and Gargan testified. It did not take place after 12:40 a.m., as implied by Huck Look's testimony. The *relay* took place *before* midnight or 12:15 a.m.

Now let's examine Charles Tretter's first walk.

Tretter testified that when he left on his first walk with Rosemary Keough at 11:30 p.m., the Valiant was there. When he saw the Valiant pass by him toward the ferry landing he was confused as to what this could mean, so he turned back toward the cottage to find out what was going on. But when they arrived back to the cottage around midnight, the Valiant was not there. And neither were Gargan and Markham.

Tretter: As I remember it I didn't really go into the cottage [after my first walk]. I was sort of out on the lawn. Miss Keough went inside and neither of the two cars was there, and when she came out she said everybody seems to be gone.
Judge Boyle: And when you returned from this walk at midnight there were no cars?
Tretter: Correct.
Judge Boyle: When you left [at 11:30 p.m.], what cars were there?
Tretter: Just the white Valiant.

If Tretter's testimony is to be believed, it means Kennedy, Markham, and Gargan were lying. These three all testified that the *relay* could not have taken place before 12:15 a.m., and none of the three admitted driving the Valiant anywhere between 11:30 p.m. and midnight.

Q: Were there any cars left after Mr. Kennedy took the car?
Newberg: Yes.
Q: How many cars were left?
Newberg: I believe one car.
Q: Was this the white Valiant that was outside?
Newberg: Yes.
Q: Did anyone suggest taking the car that was there to the ferry at 11:30 or before midnight?
Newberg: No.

Tretter also said that when they returned from their first walk around midnight, the only person there was Jack Crimmins, who was sleeping. Questioned several times about this, Tretter repeated that except for a sleeping Crimmins, no one was at the cottage, or anywhere near the cottage, when they returned. Crimmins verified that he went to sleep around midnight, or after. But he said that when he went to sleep, Gargan and Markham *were* there.

Esther Newberg also testified she was certain that Gargan and Markham were at the cottage from midnight. *And she was equally certain they remained at the cottage until 12:30 a.m.!*

Q: At twelve o'clock, what was your activity as you best remember it? Who was there at twelve o'clock that you can remember?

Newberg: Everyone in the party except Senator Kennedy and Mary Jo.

Q: So I understand it now, the party continued between midnight and 12:30, essentially as it had been going on prior to Mr. Kennedy leaving, everyone in the living room for the most part and discussing whatever was discussed?

Newberg: That is right.

Q: Between midnight and 12:30, do you recall Mr. Markham and Mr. Gargan being present, and Mr. Crimmins?

Newberg: Yes, *they were all there.*

If neither Tretter nor Keough saw Gargan and Markham when they returned from their first walk at midnight, and the Valiant was not there, but John Crimmins and Esther Newberg clearly remembered seeing Gargan and Markham from midnight to 12:30 a.m., when the Valiant was there, *it could only mean that Gargan and Markham left Lawrence Cottage twice.* And each time they left in the Valiant.

This is not how Markham and Gargan told it. Gargan told Damore he was responsible for the cooking and had an upset stomach that kept him from drinking. He said he and Markham were continuously at the party from around 8:30 p.m. until Kennedy showed up between 12:15 and 12:30 a.m. They then left immediately with Kennedy and never returned to the cottage again until 2:00 a.m. Even if Mary Ellen Lyons was wrong about the time, if Kennedy actually first showed up between 12:15 and 12:30 a.m., it would not allow enough time for Ray LaRosa, Susan Tannenbaum, Nance Lyons, and Mary Ellen Lyons to see Gargan and Markham leave at least 20 minutes before their first walk to the fire station and back, and then for Ray LaRosa, Nance Lyons, and Mary Ellen Lyons to meet Huck Look on their second walk between 12:40 and 12:45 a.m. Two walks implies at least some interval between the two.

And has the reader noticed that Mary Ellen's testimony is almost identical to the story told five months earlier to a reporter by an unidentified Boiler Room Girl? The girl who said that Kennedy had come back to the cottage with the story that he had driven off the road in the Oldsmobile and that Mary Jo was sitting in it? Mary Ellen Lyons was laying out the evidence for everyone to see, but no one was listening. The only real agenda at the inquest was to wrap up the affair and put it to bed. The blinkers were attached and no one cared.

Now let's look at the side by side once more, but this time from the point of view of the witnesses at the party.

Witnesses at party	*Carol*

11:15 p.m. Kennedy leaves cottage according to most witnesses.

Before 11:15 p.m. Kennedy leaves cottage.

11:20 p.m. Kennedy gets in an accident.

About 11:30 p.m. Tretter walks with Keough toward the ferry. Valiant seen at the cottage.

Before 12:00 or 12:15 a.m. Mary Ellen Lyons says Kennedy arrives back at cottage. The *Relay* occurs. Nance Lyons says that Gargan & Markham had already left "at least 20 minutes" before their first walk to the fire station.

11:30 p.m. Kennedy walks back to the cottage. Gargan & Markham leave with Kennedy toward Dike Bridge.

Sometime after 11:30 p.m. Tretter sees the Valiant pass by them toward the ferry landing.

11:35 p.m. Valiant passes Carol from Ferry Landing toward the Dike Road intersection. Valiant drives fast down Dike Road.

Around midnight Tretter & Keough return from their walk. Both Tretter & Keough say no one is at the cottage except Crimmins, who is sleeping, and no Valiant.

12:00 - 12:30 a.m. Gargan & Markham at cottage according to Esther Newberg & John Crimmins. Valiant is also there.

11:55 p.m. Group returns to the cottage.

11:57 p.m. First telephone call begins.

About 12:30 a.m. Tretter & Keough start out on a second walk.

12:30 a.m. Last telephone call ends.

Just after 12:30 a.m. Valiant sighted at ferry.

12:40 a.m. Oldsmobile sighted by Look.

12:45 a.m. Ray LaRosa, Nance Lyons, & Mary Ellen Lyons admit seeing Look on their second walk.

12:45 a.m. Look sees three from the party on School House Road.

12:45 - 1:40 a.m. Accident is staged.

2:00 a.m. Gargan, Markham, Tretter, & Keough return to Lawrence Cottage.

2:00 a.m. The group returns to Lawrence Cottage.

From the point of view of the witnesses, *the timeline is an exact match.* Carol's observation is confirmed.

Analysis

Virtually everyone who has put forth a theory as to what must have happened that night has begun with the premise that any events of importance occurred after Huck Look saw the Oldsmobile around 12:40 a.m. The timeline of the witnesses at the party, which can often conflict with a favorite theory, is ignored. The assumption is made that these witnesses lied. Sherrill even suggests that the strange times cited by the witnesses were part of a calculated strategy by Kennedy's lawyers to leave the public and the press with an impossible job of reconstruction.[1] Damore suggests that the testimony had been deliberately designed by Kennedy's lawyers to support the senator's accident time and to "overwhelm Huck Look's anticipated testimony by a sheer weight of numbers."[2]

A careful examination of the testimony of Ray LaRosa, Nance and Mary Ellen Lyons, Esther Newberg, Jack Crimmins, and Charles Tretter suggests that it isn't that simple. These persons were clearly uncomfortable straying very far from the truth. Yes, they are often fuzzy on the details, many times conveniently so. "I don't remember" is a common refrain. But there is a line each is not prepared to cross. These witnesses appear to have struggled to find a way to be loyal to Kennedy without committing perjury. Some, of course, did a better job at it than others.

The most obvious example is Tretter, whom Hersh describes as "Malleable Charlie Tretter, constitutionally full of smiles, who did a lot of driving and errand running for Ted Kennedy."[3] Almost unique among all the witnesses, Charles Tretter gives us exact times and places. If what happened that night is how we have envisioned it, Tretter's testimony seems enough to place him at the scene.

Rosemary Keough and Susan Tannenbaum were the most obstinate of all the witnesses at the party. Compared with Tretter, getting some morsel of value out of either of them was like pulling teeth.

Esther Newberg's testimony was also much different than the rest. She was clear and concise in her answers and kept her composure throughout her testimony, even after being browbeaten by Judge Boyle. Perhaps in part because she was so articulate, she was the only member of the party to be recalled and was questioned far more than the other girls. Newberg said absolutely nothing in her statements that would conflict

---

[1] *The Last Kennedy*, p. 174
[2] *Senatorial Privilege*, p. 377
[3] *Edward Kennedy*, p. 348

with Carol's observation, and she was certain Gargan had no scrapes or bruises the next morning.

Newberg was also the only Boiler Room Girl who never admitted taking any walks with anyone that night or straying very far from the cottage. Nor did any of the others admit taking any walk with her. Esther Newberg may have been a direct witness to all the activity that took place as groups of persons flowed into and out of the cottage from 11:15 p.m. to 2:00 a.m.

Examine carefully Newberg's testimony concerning the *relay.*

Q: Between midnight and 12:30, do you recall Mr. Markham and Mr. Gargan being present, and Mr. Crimmins?
Newberg: Yes, they were all there.
Elsewhere in her testimony:
Newberg: Mr. LaRosa walked outside for a few minutes.
Q: Do you recall what time that was?
Newberg: It strikes me that it was sometime between – I am not sure exactly, but I would say *after 12:30 or before 12:15.*
Q: After 12:30 or before 12:15?
Newberg: Right.
Q: So it is safe to say it is after 12:30?
Newberg: I am not sure exactly.

Esther Newberg said she was positive Gargan and Markham were at the cottage between midnight and 12:30 a.m. However, when it came time to nail down the time of the *relay*, Newberg started to say "between," then changed that to *after 12:30 or before 12:15.* Even when questioned again, she repeated those times. That is a very strange way to word an answer, and it is obvious from the rest of her testimony that Newberg was intelligent enough to know it. If Newberg was positive that Gargan and Markham were at the cottage between midnight and 12:30 a.m., how could the *relay* have taken place before 12:15 a.m.? It could not, unless Gargan and Markham had left the cottage twice. It appears Esther Newberg was telling the court that she was not sure whether the *relay* occurred when Gargan and Markham left *before* 12:15 a.m.; or whether it occurred when they left *again, after* 12:30 a.m.

So why didn't the prosecution pursue this ambiguity? Because they were fixated on just one time, not two. With that belief they put the words into Newberg's mouth that they wanted to hear:

Q: So, it is safe to say it is after 12:30?
Newberg: I am not sure exactly.
Q: Between 12:30 and quarter of 1:00?
Newberg: Not as late as quarter of 1:00.
Q: You mean 12:45?
Newberg: *I will say* after 12:15.

Newberg appears to have decided that between the two possible times the *relay* could have occurred, it was the second time Gargan and Markham left Lawrence Cottage. Or, perhaps because the prosecution was so obviously fixated on the later time rather than the earlier one, she just went along with it.

The bottom line is that it is apparent that any theory must take the testimony of the witnesses at the party into account, even if it is with a large dose of salt. No one appears to have told the whole truth and much of what they do say could be taken two ways. Obviously, very little information was volunteered. For instance, Newberg could certainly have told the prosecution, "Look, there were two times Markham and Gargan left the cottage, OK? Do you get it now? How would I know whether Kennedy was there the first time or the second? I never saw him. You figure it out." However, she preferred to be ambiguous; her way, perhaps, of protecting Kennedy while not committing perjury.

Most important, all theories that begin with the premise that the events of importance that night took place after Huck Look saw the Oldsmobile around 12:40 a.m. will have to be abandoned. Carol's observation does not support it, and not one of the witnesses at the party ever said that the *relay* could have taken place after 12:40 a.m., even though three of these witnesses testified that they had, indeed, met Look as they were walking on the road from the fire station back to the cottage.

27
The Reluctant Witness

he Ted Kennedy Episode was the very first book written about the accident, published well before the inquest in January. In a chapter entitled *The Reluctant Witness*, Hastings says a Chappaquiddick witness was interviewed by an "on the scenes investigator" who then passed on the information to him.[1] The witness told the investigator he had seen a car leave Lawrence Cottage around midnight, then park about 500 feet from the house with just its parking lights glowing. He said his curiosity forced him to wait but not to investigate. About 20 minutes later, the car started up again and proceeded toward the ferry. At the Dike Road intersection it paused briefly before continuing down Dike Road. The witness must have believed the vehicle was Kennedy's Oldsmobile, because he said that immediately afterwards he heard no sound of the car hitting the water or "outcry or call for help, just deep deep quiet."

Later that morning, "maybe an hour after the car episode," the witness was situated close to the ferry landing. There, he said, he was sure he heard an outboard motor, but couldn't tell if the sound came from "the direction of Cape Poge" in the outer harbor "or the yacht club basin near where the ferry crosses." This would be consistent with Todd Ballou's sighting of an outboard-powered launch picking up three persons on a Chappaquiddick beach in the Edgartown outer harbor, then motoring through the Edgartown Channel toward the yacht club at around the same time.

Anonymous witnesses are always suspect, but what makes this account seem genuine is the description of a vehicle parked on the side of the road for 20 minutes starting from around midnight – a quirky detail that does not fit with any of the usual Chappaquiddick theories. If the witness was inventing this story and wanted to be in line with what Kennedy had said and what Look had seen, he might have claimed he saw the car park at the side of the road from about 11:15 p.m. to 12:40 a.m., but certainly not from around midnight.

Assuming the pause at the Dike Road intersection was the Oldsmobile turning into Cemetery Road while passing Huck Look's station wagon, the account makes sense when one realizes that a witness positioned "near the house where the party was held" would not have been able to see the Oldsmobile drive down Dike Road if he was also able to verify that the vehicle left from Lawrence Cottage. He would only have been able to see the glow of its headlights. Nor would the witness have been able to see Look's vehicle at the intersection, either.

Calls were made continuously on Kennedy's credit card from the private studio at Lawrence Cottage from about midnight to 12:30 a.m., while Newberg said she had

---

[1] *The Ted Kennedy Episode*, back cover

observed Gargan and Markham within the cottage itself during those same hours. However, Tretter testified that Keough entered the cottage briefly around midnight after their first walk while he stayed outside, and that neither of them met or talked to any of the guests between their first walk and their second. Our staged-accident theory postulates that the Oldsmobile was hidden out of sight from the guests at the party after Kennedy, Gargan, Markham, and two others returned to the cottage with the body of Mary Jo a few minutes before midnight.

Since the witness saw no one enter the car between the time he observed it and the time it drove off toward the Dike Road intersection, it suggests, once again, that *neither Kennedy, Gargan, nor Markham was in the Oldsmobile when it was observed by Huck Look.* Perhaps, soon after midnight, Tretter, Keough, and Tannenbaum drove the Oldsmobile about 500 feet from the cottage, then parked for about a half hour out of sight while Kennedy was making his phone calls and Gargan and Markham were chatting innocently with the remaining guests. The half hour might have been spent bringing Susan Tannenbaum up to speed. These three, with Mary Jo in the trunk, may then have encountered Huck Look at the Dike Road intersection at about 12:40 a.m.

And notice that the witness said the parking lights were on during the entire time the car was parked at the side of the road. Perhaps the engine was idling, too. If Mary Jo was in the trunk, lying close to the vehicle's exhaust pipe for a half hour, it might explain why carbon monoxide was found in her blood. Although a blood carbon monoxide level of five percent is not, by itself, considered dangerous, when combined with a good deal of alcohol it might have intensified or prolonged her comatose state. This might explain why Mary Jo never regained consciousness before the accident was staged.

Who was this witness? Did he really exist? The witness must have observed the car from inside a house because no one would be expected to remain outside with the mosquitoes for 20 minutes or more patiently watching a parked car. A vehicle parked 500 feet from Lawrence Cottage would place it in the fire station parking lot, and less than 200 feet from Foster Silva's home across the street. Foster was Captain of the Chappaquiddick volunteer fire department. If Foster was in the fire station that night, or in his house, it would have allowed him to see everything.

Tellingly, when asked why he had not gone to the police or the press with his sighting, the witness explained that "his job would be in jeopardy if he did."[1] Foster Silva was the caretaker of Lawrence Cottage. If it became known that Silva had contradicted the timeline of Mr. Lawrence's tenant, a United States senator, it might have led to his dismissal. Foster told Olsen that he was still awake at 1:30 a.m., having had no success sleeping with all the noise, and it can be assumed he would have been keeping a wary eye on Lawrence Cottage, especially with a raucous party going on, as

---

[1] *The Ted Kennedy Episode*, pp. 53-54

the cottage was under his care. Dodie, Foster's wife, was awake long into the night, too. Dodie told state detectives Flynn and Killen that she had stayed awake until 2:30 a.m. and had immediately recognized the car pulled from Poucha Pond as the same car she had seen driving up and down School House Road the previous day and into the evening, driven by a middle-aged man with gray hair.[1] She told Tony Ulasewicz that she also had seen a young girl driving the Oldsmobile earlier in the day.[2]

For those of us who knew Foster, this account sounds very much like it came from him. Foster was an "inquisitive" man, poking his nose into this and that, always with a twinkle in his eye. He was a full-time resident and Chappaquiddick icon, a watchman for the Trustees of Reservations which maintained a wildlife refuge on East Beach on the ocean side of Dike Bridge, and also a winter caretaker for more than 50 summer cottages. His responsibilities as a cottage caretaker on a busy holiday weekend with strangers about could explain his presence at Katama Bay near the ferry landing around 1:30 a.m. In 1969, the most expensive Chappaquiddick summer homes were located there.

It seems there might have been more to the witness's reluctance to divulge his identity than just his fear of losing a job. When pressed, the witness was adamant that he would "not reveal [his] identity to the authorities," telling the investigator that "you can't buy a good night's sleep" and "as long as Kennedy and I don't meet, it will be fine for both of us."[3] Dodie and Foster were friends of my parents, and I was told by my father that in the immediate days following the incident a cousin and one other friend were threatened with tax audits if they spoke up about anything they might have seen that night.

Dodie and Foster Silva had no problem telling the press and police about the noise at the party, but they might have been intimidated from saying more. Interestingly, by July 27, the Silvas had softened their tone. "When we went out to quiet the dogs, we could hear normal, happy people at the cottage," Dodie told reporter Joseph Lowry of the *Philadelphia Bulletin*. "There was laughing and singing *a little*."[4] And according to his obituary in the *Boston Globe* of January 28, 1981, Foster Silva was said to be "a longtime friend of the Kennedy family."

Where did this information come from? Hastings said he received his information from an on the scenes *investigator*, not an investigative reporter. It appears his investigator was Tony Ulasewicz, a former detective at the Bureau of Special Service and Investigation (BOSSI) in New York City and hard-nosed undercover PI under President Nixon. Ulasewicz is more popularly recognized as Nixon's bagman during the Watergate scandal of 1972. At the president's request, Ulasewicz arrived on Chappaquiddick in the late afternoon of July 19, the same day Kennedy reported the

---

[1] *Senatorial Privilege*, p. 105

[2] *The President's Private Eye*, p. 204

[3] *The Ted Kennedy Episode*, p. 3; p. 53

[4] *The Last Kennedy*, p. 199

accident to the police, and stayed there off and on through the following January. Ulasewicz says he talked to Dodie Silva on July 20.[1]

As a fictional reporter named Ed Ferguson working for an equally fictitious feature writer's association he made up, and recognizing that as a cop he was "miles ahead" of the others, Ulasewicz fed the information he collected from Chappaquiddick and Edgartown witnesses directly to reporters and authors covering the story. His job, as he saw it, was to nudge reporters in the right direction and to recognize the inaccuracies handed out to the press for what they really were: a clumsy attempt by Chief Arena to give the senator a free pass. Many of his discoveries can be recognized within the pages of *The Bridge at Chappaquiddick* and *Senatorial Privilege*, as well as in newspaper and magazine articles that appeared soon after the incident. None of those reports have ever been found to be inaccurate. As Ulasewicz explains, "I was no longer thinking about this case as an investigator for a president. What was important to me as an investigator was the accuracy in reporting what I had found."[2] His most memorable scoop was the unearthing, in collaboration with Arthur Egan of the *Union Leader,* of the 17 phone calls from Lawrence Cottage and the Shiretown Inn charged to Kennedy's credit card.

---

[1] *The President's Private Eye*, p. 204
[2] *The President's Private Eye*, p. 212

28

The Malms

The author interviewed Sylvia Malm on August 23, 2014. In a series of emails over the following eleven days, I encouraged Sylvia to edit her responses to my interview questions so that they would reflect her thoughts and memories of that time as accurately as possible. However, in response to follow-up questions on May 15, 2015, Sylvia informed me she would prefer that I not repeat anything she had said.

In deference to a neighbor, I will disclose only that Sylvia told me her mother had actually heard two cars at the bridge after midnight, in addition to the car she had heard before midnight (a detail that had already been divulged by Jerry Jeffers); that following publication of a Life *magazine article in August 1969, her mother thereafter refused to talk to authors or reporters because she felt Brock Brower had portrayed Chappaquiddick in an unflattering way;[1] and that she and her mother were visited by Kennedy aide Dun Gifford and another Kennedy associate several days after the accident. Sylvia described that visit as "cordial," and that she had the impression the two men had other visits on Chappaquiddick they intended to make.*

*Q*rena testified at the exhumation hearing that on the morning of July 19, when he asked Mrs. Malm if she had heard anything earlier, she said she hadn't that morning but had heard an engine the night previous. At the inquest hearing, Arena said Mrs. Malm had told him she heard a car going "unusually fast on Dike Road close to around midnight" but didn't hear "any sound of anything hitting the water or anything like that" and "that is the only thing she said." At the inquest, when asked who he had questioned at the scene, Inspector George Kennedy said, "So I went up to Mrs. Malm's house and she said that she had been bothered so much that she had no comment to make; that she did hear a car at night [around midnight] but heard nothing else, and that is all she would comment on."

Tony Ulasewicz interviewed Mrs. Malm in the early morning of the next day, July 20. Mrs. Malm told Ulasewicz she was reading upstairs in bed until midnight and heard a sound of a car "traveling rather fast as it headed for the bridge." She didn't hear it return, then went to sleep at midnight. She said she had two dogs which would have barked if anyone had approached the house, but they never did.[2]

---

[1] I cannot find anything in the *Life* article that would seem to paint Chappaquiddick in an unflattering way.

[2] *The President's Private Eye*, p. 197

Olsen says that questioned by Arena later, Mrs. Malm "wasn't so sure about the time."[1] Damore says that on Wednesday, five days after the accident, Mrs. Malm was visited by Arena once more at which time Arena was able to secure a written statement from Mrs. Malm.[2] This was read to the court by Arena at the inquest. In that statement, Mrs. Malm said she had heard a car going "faster than usual" toward Dike Bridge. She wrote, "*I have no idea of the time.* I think I went to sleep sometime between 11:30 and midnight, *but I do not know the time. I heard nothing during the night.* We have two dogs, and a light was burning all night." Arena also read a statement from Mrs. Malm's daughter, which Sylvia told me he had also received on July 23. Sylvia wrote, "I read in bed underneath an open window which faces east from 11:00 p.m. to midnight, looking at the clock just before I turned my light out. Between 11:15 and 11:45, I heard a car going fairly fast on Dike Road. I thought it was heading toward the Dike. I heard nothing further that night."

Life magazine, in their edition of August 1, 1969, had this to say about their interview with the Malms: "Anyhow, Sylvia, Mrs. Pierre Malm's 21-year-old daughter, lives in Dyke House, can't be more than 100 yards from the bridge, *saw it* [the Oldsmobile] at 11:30 [p.m.] and told her mother. So next morning, when two kids came and told Mrs. Malm there was a car wheel sticking upside-down out of Poucha Pond, she had that feeling. 'You couldn't see what it was in the water, but I knew when they got it out it was going to be that black car.' "

Dyke House was built and owned by Tony Bettencourt who had used it in his younger days as a duck gunning cottage. Sylvia told me her parents entered into negotiations to purchase Dyke House soon after the incident, but the title had issues. Court records show that Tony Bettencourt died in March 1970 and his death resulted in an ownership quarrel between Tony's children and estranged wife, Edna. This was exasperated by a lawsuit with Marvin Taylor, which Skip Bettencourt, Tony's son, told me had to do with a land dispute with a neighbor. The dispute with Taylor was finally resolved on June 29, 1973, and Mr. and Mrs. Pierre Malm purchased the cottage and one and one-quarter acres of upland and marsh four days later on July 3.[3]

Analysis

Dyke House lies only 450 feet from the foot of Dike Bridge. Photographs from that time, taken from the bridge, show that there was an unobstructed view of the front of

---

[1] *The Bridge at Chappaquiddick*, p. 92

[2] *Senatorial Privilege*, p.163

[3] Dukes County Probate Court, Docket 7/4371; 362, Mass. 1; Dukes County Registry of Deeds, Book 309, pp. 401-406; Dukes County Superior Court, Docket No. 1567.

the house, from the ground to the roof, as well as a clear view of the second-story bedroom window on its east side.

The activity at Dike Bridge, whatever it was, whenever it occurred, and however many individuals were involved, must have taken up a substantial amount of time and generated considerable noise. The lower control arm on the front of the car's undercarriage must have made a loud screech as it ripped through three and one-half feet of rub rail. The engine would have been revved to a high pitch, whether the accident was staged or not. If the tires were burning rubber or the wheels were locked as the car skidded up the bridge for 23 feet, the sound should have woken the dead. The vehicle would have made a loud splash as it hit the water. There would have been activity and noise if Gargan and Markham, and perhaps others, had returned in the Valiant to Dike Bridge at first light to dive on the car. It seems reasonable to assume that at least one of the dogs would have heard some of that commotion and let out a startled "woof."

Even if the accident had occurred as Kennedy said it had, someone at Dyke House should have heard some noise. Imagine the scene: men, with nothing to hide, yelling instructions back and forth as they attempted to determine if Mary Jo was still in the car. Sylvia Malm told the BBC that the evening was exceptionally calm. Olsen writes that "the night had been still and windless; earlier visitors to the bridge had heard fish jumping a half mile down the lagoon."[1] Arena told Damore, "Nobody ever heard a car hit the water. *It seems amazing they couldn't hear anything.*"[2]

And if the accident was indeed staged, how could these people have had the nerve to go through with their plan when they could not be certain their every movement was not being watched closely from that open, upstairs window? The burning light in the front yard, as conspicuous as a lighthouse on such a black night, would have indicated to them that the cottage was occupied. If a dog had barked, it would have added to the certainty. It just does not seem plausible they would attempt to pull off such an audacious stunt involving so much noise and so much time, with such dire consequences if they were apprehended, without being absolutely sure they would never be challenged. There was a phone in the cottage. If the police showed up unexpectedly, they were boxed in. There was no place to run.

So would this be good evidence that the accident was never engineered? But then look at the alternative. If Mrs. Malm heard two cars at the Dike after midnight – which two persons insist she did – why wouldn't she admit to this at the scene? Why would she tell Arena, Inspector Kennedy, and Tony Ulasewicz she had heard just one car "around midnight?" When Arena approached her the following Wednesday, why would she give him a written statement that said she had heard only one car but "had no idea of the time;" that she went to bed between 11:30 p.m. and midnight but "heard

---

[1] *The Bridge at Chappaquiddick*, p. 261
[2] *Senatorial Privilege*, p. 5; p 163

nothing during the night?" And why wouldn't she have mentioned Dun Gifford's visit? Wouldn't that visit have been of interest to the chief of police?

Could Mrs. Malm have been aware, long before the Oldsmobile went off the bridge, that the "black car" belonged to Kennedy? *Life* magazine reported that Mrs. Malm had seen the Oldsmobile several times earlier that day. "But this black Oldsmobile was barreling back and forth over Dike Bridge on Friday, the day of the accident – two, maybe three times during the day, different drivers nobody recognized. It was going faster than any beach buggy ever did. It tore through again about 11:30 that night, heading toward the bridge."

At the inquest, neither Arena nor Inspector Kennedy mentioned being informed by Mrs. Malm that the Oldsmobile had been seen running up and down Dike Road at high speed the previous morning. Nor did Olsen or Damore mention hearing it from Arena. Mrs. Malm never mentioned it to Ulasewicz on July 20. Neither Mrs. Malm nor her daughter saw fit to mention it in their written statements. This was the first time the world would hear that Kennedy and his party had visited East Beach before the accident. No other newspaper or magazine had reported it before August 1, none of the guests had mentioned it, and Kennedy had said nothing to the press about it, either.

Before August 1, Kennedy's insistence that he made a wrong turn down Dike Road due to his unfamiliarity with Chappaquiddick roads made sense to those unfamiliar with the island; after August 1, not so much.

Timeline

These are the sequence of events, and the reader can make of it what she will.

1) The Valiant passed Carol at high speed at 11:35 p.m. on July 18 with at least three men and a woman, then proceeded rapidly down Dike Road without stopping or slowing.

2) Gargan confessed to Damore that around 1:30 on the morning of July 19, just before the Edgartown Channel swim, Kennedy told him that he was planning to say that Mary Jo drove off the bridge alone. Gargan was to discover the car later in the morning. If Kennedy had actually gone to the police with this story, there would have been no mention of subsequent diving on the vehicle, or indeed any mention of activity at the bridge by any of them, after the ferry shut down at midnight.

Gargan told Damore that he had immediately rejected Kennedy's story out of hand because it wasn't true.

3) Nevertheless, according to inquest testimony, Gargan told Esther Newberg and the Lyons sisters around 3:00 a.m. that Mary Jo had driven the Oldsmobile back to the Katama Shores Motel alone on the last ferry before midnight but that Kennedy had

decided to swim the Edgartown Channel because they could find no boats to take him across.

4) At the Shiretown Inn at 8:00 on the morning of July 19, an agitated and soaking-wet Gargan pulled Kennedy forcibly into his room. Markham was soaking wet, too. Loud arguments were heard. Gargan told Kennedy that there was no way he could say that Mary Jo drove off the bridge alone, he could be placed at the scene.

5) At 8:30 on the morning of July 19, Mrs. Malm told Chief Arena that she heard a car drive *unusually fast* past their house toward the Dike *around midnight* and *nothing else.* Inspector George Kennedy was told the same thing by Mrs. Malm soon after 10:15 a.m. Coincidentally, "around midnight" was the time Gargan told Esther Newberg and the Lyons sisters that Mary Jo decided to drive to the ferry alone in the Oldsmobile to take the last scheduled boat back to Edgartown, "unusually fast" would have described someone intent on catching a last ferry, and "nothing else" would have described the activity at Dike Bridge by Kennedy, Gargan, and Markham had Mary Jo driven off the bridge alone.

No mention was made to either Chief Arena or Inspector Kennedy of hearing any other car or any other sound either before or after midnight. Neither was told that Mrs. Malm had seen that same car on the road several times the previous morning. When Inspector Kennedy asked Mrs. Malm for more details he was rebuffed because "she had been bothered so much," even though just two hours had elapsed since Mrs. Malm had heard there was a vehicle in the channel with a dead girl in it, and even though Mrs. Malm had been questioned briefly by just one other person.

6) After eventually showing up at the police station around 10:00 on the morning of July 19, two hours after Kennedy had been informed that he could be placed at the scene, Kennedy and Markham took about an hour to compose a short accident report which purported that Kennedy had driven off the bridge with Mary Jo Kopechne soon after 11:15 p.m. Kennedy then went into seclusion at the compound in Hyannis Port and refused to talk to reporters.

7) Early the following morning, July 20, Mrs. Malm told Tony Ulasewicz that she had heard a car traveling rather fast toward the Dike around midnight while she was reading in bed upstairs. She had gone to sleep at midnight and heard nothing thereafter. Her two dogs had never barked.

Just as with Arena and Inspector Kennedy, Ulasewicz was never told that Mrs. Malm had seen that same car the previous morning. He was never told that Mrs. Malm had heard two other cars after midnight. It could be assumed that dogs would never bark if Mary Jo had driven into the pond by herself, and if there was no subsequent rescue by anyone.

8) On July 22, four days after the incident, it was reported by the press that Huck Look might have seen the Oldsmobile at the Dike Road intersection around 12:40 a.m. on the morning of July 19.

9) "Several days" after the incident, the Malms were visited by Kennedy aide Dun Gifford and an associate. The visit was cordial and the two appeared unconcerned when they left. Sylvia Malm had the impression that they had other visits on Chappaquiddick they intended to make.

10) Coincidentally, in the immediate days after the incident, several persons on Chappaquiddick were intimidated by Kennedy aides if they spoke up about what they may have seen. One of these included a cousin, and another a friend of my father.

11) "Several days" after the incident, Lula told Carol that if she spoke up about her sighting, she could be killed.

12) "Several days" after the incident, Leslie Leland, foreman of the grand jury, was intimidated by Chief Arena and Walter Steele, the Dukes County prosecutor, on a drive around the back roads of Martha's Vineyard.

13) On Wednesday, July 23, five days after the incident and only a day after Look's sighting had been revealed by the press, Arena decided to visit the Malms once more. Mrs. Malm gave a written statement to Arena in which she said she had heard a car drive past their cottage in the direction of the Dike. However, although certain it was around midnight on the morning of July 19 *before* Kennedy went to the police, she now claimed to have *no idea of the time.* Instead, it was the daughter who was certain of a much earlier time. A statement from Sylvia said that said she heard a car drive past the cottage toward the Dike sometime between 11:15 to 11:45 p.m., a timeline that would agree with Kennedy's police report on the morning of July 19, *after* Kennedy went to the police. Whereas the mother had told Ulasewicz that she had been reading upstairs in bed until midnight, now it was the daughter who was reading upstairs until midnight.

There was no mention in either statement of any other cars or a bark from a dog or even the slightest sound after midnight. There was no mention of Dun Gifford's visit. There was no mention of having seen that same car the previous morning.

This was the very first time police officials became aware that the daughter was a witness, or was even at the cottage. At the inquest, when questioned about the daughter, Arena insisted, "I didn't even know the daughter was at the house." Both Arena and Inspector Kennedy were emphatic that Mrs. Malm had told them she heard a car driving unusually fast past her house around midnight and "nothing else."

At the exhumation hearing, Arena testified that he had entered Dyke House to change into a borrowed bathing suit in order to swim out to the car. It might be expected that the daughter would have made her presence known at that time. But she never did.

Could Sylvia have remained deliberately sequestered in her room and out of sight while all the activity at Dike Bridge was going on that morning? If so, why? It seems unlikely it was because Mrs. Malm had been told the accident involved Ted Kennedy. When Arena first talked to Mrs. Malm, he had no idea who owned the vehicle. On the other hand, if Sylvia was not averse to having her presence known, why wouldn't she have introduced herself to Arena or Inspector Kennedy to tell them what she had seen or heard? Bearing in mind that the accident involved a fatality, why would she choose to say nothing? At 21 years old in 1969, Sylvia was an adult, not a child.

14) On July 27, a week after the incident, in a deal negotiated by Chief Arena and Dukes County Prosecutor Walter Steele, Kennedy pled guilty to leaving the scene of an accident and received a suspended sentence and a year's probation. His worries appeared to be over. All was wrapped up, signed, sealed, and delivered. The only detail left was for Kennedy to give a fuller explanation to the public of what had taken place and he could resume his march to the presidency.

Later that evening, Kennedy gave a nationally televised TV speech in which he reiterated he drove off the bridge soon after 11:15 p.m. He said he had rested on the bank of the channel for an undetermined time, returned to Lawrence Cottage to fetch Gargan and Markham, and then had been driven back to Dike Bridge sometime *after midnight*.

Ironically, it was this speech, and its failure to address the many inconsistencies, which would eventually lead to an exhumation hearing, an inquest, and the convening of a grand jury.

15) On August 1, two weeks after the accident, Look's sighting of the Oldsmobile was still not accepted as genuine by most reporters. *Life* wrote, "Then again, near one o'clock in the morning, Deputy Sheriff Christopher S. Look Jr. thought he saw it, a car like it anyway, go off Main Street down Dike Road. He even tried to talk to the driver who wouldn't talk to him."

16) In that same *Life* magazine article, Mrs. Malm told Brock Brower that she had a premonition the car discovered lying upside down in the channel was the same black car she had seen traveling several times up and down Dike Road at high speed the previous morning, and the same car her daughter had "seen" tearing down Dike Road again at 11:30 p.m. later that evening. No mention was made to Brower of hearing any other car or any other sound after midnight. No mention was made of Dun Gifford's visit. Nevertheless, in one short interview, Brower had elicited more information from the Malms than the Edgartown chief of police or the Martha's Vineyard inspector of motor vehicles.

It seems Mrs. Malm may have regretted revealing as much as she did because she subsequently refused to talk to reporters or authors and was uncomfortable even talking about it to anyone. Other than one short conversation with Tony Ulasewicz, the interview with *Life* magazine, and a later appearance in the BBC documentary *Chappaquiddick* by the daughter, I have been unable to find one author or reporter who has had any success talking to either of them. These include Jack Olsen and Leo Damore, two authors who made extraordinary efforts to interview everyone involved in the incident. I have been unable to find one book or article that has ever revealed that

Mrs. Malm heard two other vehicles at the bridge after midnight,[1] or that the Malms had been visited by Dun Gifford and another aide a few days after the accident.

Unaccountably, District Attorney Dinis never asked the Malms to testify in person at the inquest, even though they had been sleeping just 450 feet from the bridge when Kennedy's car went off it and when two supposed rescue attempts had occurred. This seems utterly baffling because their interview with *Life* magazine many months earlier would have indicated to Dinis and Arena that the Malms knew much more about what went on that night than they had ever revealed to government officials.

At the inquest, Gargan testified that during the second alleged rescue attempt he had positioned the Valiant on the east side of the bridge with the headlights "*not* shining in the water because of the position they were in, they were shining *across* the water in the direction of Dyke House." Markham testified to this as well. The bank on the east side of Dike Channel was at the level of the foot of the bridge. If Gargan and Markham were telling the truth, those headlights would have been shining all over the front of Dyke House and right into Sylvia Malm's bedroom window.

Detective Flynn told Damore, "Dyke House was so close to the bridge. There's no way you could go down that road and not see that house. It stuck out like a sore thumb."[2] Nevertheless, when asked by the prosecution whether he realized there was a house near the bridge, Gargan insisted, "I have never seen the Dyke House. I didn't notice it during the daylight or at night, but I understand it is there." As for Kennedy and Markham, Dinis must have decided the question was too embarrassing to ask because the subject was never brought up.

17) Look's sighting of the Oldsmobile gained substantial credibility after his exhumation testimony was made available to the public on November 3, 1969.

18) *The Bridge at Chappaquiddick* was published in early January 1970, just days before the inquest. Persuaded over lunch at an Edgartown restaurant by Detective Bernie Flynn,[3] Olsen argued that Kennedy must have stepped out of the car into the bushes on the side of Dike Road after observing Huck Look at around 12:40 a.m. Kennedy never realized that Mary Jo had driven off the bridge alone until advised of that fact later that morning. In other words, Kennedy was innocent. When he published his theory, Olsen had no idea that Flynn would soon be exposed as a Kennedy snitch.

---

[1] The *Vineyard Gazette* ran a story on July 22 claiming that on the morning of July 19, Mrs. Malm had told police she had heard a car go past her house "between midnight and 1:00 a.m." The *Gazette* got it wrong. Mrs. Malm told Arena and Inspector Kennedy on July 19 and Tony Ulasewicz on July 20 that she heard a car "around midnight," just before she had gone to sleep; and in a written statement to Arena on July 23, just a day after the *Gazette* story, she said she had heard a car but had no idea of the time, then had gone to sleep "between 11:30 and midnight" and heard nothing thereafter.

[2] *Senatorial Privilege*, p. 104

[3] *Senatorial Privilege*, p. 307

Sylvia Malm said she was reading at this open window on the second story of Dyke House the night the incident occurred. Sylvia told me that in 1969 the trees to the left were much lower allowing an unobstructed view of Dike Bridge, and indeed, photographs from that time show this to be true.

19) By the time the inquest testimony was released to the public in April 1970, the entire world had come to accept that Kennedy's Oldsmobile had been seen by Look in the early morning of July 19 and that Kennedy's timeline was somehow in error. Two theories were imagined to explain the discrepancy: Kennedy, Gargan, and Markham lied about the time because the ferry shut down at midnight (first advanced by *McCall's* in their edition of August 1974 and later published by the Tedrows in 1976); Kennedy was suffering from traumatic amnesia and Gargan and Markham backed up his timeline so that Kennedy could not later be accused of mental instability (suggested by Lange and DeWitt in 1992).

Of course, in 1989, Kappel had argued that the real accident occurred soon after 11:15 p.m., just as Kennedy and his friends had always said, and there was no actual discrepancy between the two timelines at all. Kappel's theory was mostly overlooked or laughed off.

20) Sometime before her death in 1996, Mrs. Malm revealed to her daughter, and to Jerry Jeffers, that she had actually heard two additional cars at the Dike after midnight.

29

The Accident

There are a number of reasons to assume that Mary Jo might have been injured in a car accident that night before the vehicle was driven off the bridge.

irst, of course, is Kennedy's driving record. By his own admission, Kennedy was a terrible driver. As one author put it, he was simply incapable of taking a speed limit, stop sign, or stoplight seriously. Cited numerous times for driving irresponsibly, Kennedy had resorted to having himself chauffeured everywhere. Kennedy's license had expired by July 18 and he might have deliberately decided not to renew it so that he would not be tempted to get behind the wheel. On the night of the incident, Kennedy's chauffeur was John Crimmins; however, when Kennedy left the party with Mary Jo, ostensibly at 11:15 p.m., he said he did not ask his chauffeur to drive him because Crimmins was preoccupied cooking for others and he had no wish to disturb him. More likely, of course, is the probability that Crimmins would be a third wheel in the type of activity Kennedy had in mind.

Second, Kennedy was known to be a heavy drinker, especially in the months following the assassination of his brother Bobby. Irrespective of claiming that he had little to drink and was dead sober when the accident occurred, there is plenty of evidence to the contrary. That is one story, at least, that few have swallowed.

Third, one of the Boiler Room Girls is said to have told a reporter that Kennedy appeared at the cottage stunned and incoherent with the story that he had driven off the road with Mary Jo in the Oldsmobile and that she was simply sitting in it.

Fourth, blood was found on the back of Mary Jo's blouse and on the rear seat of the Oldsmobile, and a car accident would be the most obvious reason to explain it.

Fifth, the deep, vertical dents and blown-in windows on both passenger-side doors could never have occurred from the fall off Dike Bridge.

Sixth, two doors from the Oldsmobile were brought to the inquest by the state police lab but never allowed into testimony by a judge doing everything in his power to whitewash the affair. It seems logical to assume that at least one of these was a passenger-side door. Dr. McHugh, who would have had far more than a photograph to work with, might have had good reason to suspect that the Oldsmobile must have been involved in an accident before it went off the bridge.

Seventh, Dike Road was unpaved and very narrow in 1969. At night, with no moon, a car driven quickly and erratically would be at great risk.

Eighth, if the Oldsmobile did indeed slam up against a hard object on the passenger side, it might explain why Mary Jo was injured while Kennedy was not.

Finally, Kennedy must have left his Oldsmobile at the place where Mary Jo was first injured because otherwise why would a group of persons drive the rented Valiant to Dike Bridge at around 11:35 p.m. at high speed? The rented Valiant had no damage to it when it was returned and apparently no blood on the seat, either. Why would Kennedy leave the Oldsmobile somewhere near Dike Bridge and walk back to Lawrence Cottage if the vehicle was operable?

However, this leads to one perplexing question: If there was a car accident before the Oldsmobile was seen by Look at around 12:40 a.m., where could it have occurred? Sylvia Malm said that she heard a car driving unusually fast on Dike Road between 11:15 and 11:45 p.m. Both Mrs. Malm and her daughter said they thought the car sounded like it was headed in the direction of the Dike. If this was the sound of Kennedy's Oldsmobile soon after 11:15 p.m., or the sound of the rented white Valiant on a rescue mission observed by Carol around 11:35 p.m., it suggests that the accident occurred between Dyke House and East Beach. *But this does not appear possible!*

Immediately after passing Dyke House, photos taken at the time show that there were a few low bushes on the south side of the road just a few yards from the cottage. The Oldsmobile might have been scratched if it ran into that vegetation, but it certainly could not have been seriously damaged. So what's left? *After passing those bushes, there is absolutely nothing substantial a car could have hit, all the way to the island of Nantucket.* In the '60s, there was not a tree or other structure to mar the view between those few bushes and Dike Bridge. The bridge itself had no guard rails higher than four inches in 1969, and once on the other side there was nothing a car could have run into before the road turned to sand.

Could the Oldsmobile have skidded at high speed and turned over onto its roof, as Kappel suggests, perhaps on the east side of the bridge where the road ends?

My own experience suggests that it would have been difficult to right the Oldsmobile had it flipped completely onto its roof. Against every physical law known to man, my 17-year-old nephew Andrew, who was "not going at all fast really," found a way to flip my Subaru onto its roof on a Chappaquiddick joyride with a friend at the extreme end of North Neck Road in 2000. North Neck Road is a narrow dirt road filled with potholes that normally limit speed to 10 mph, and to less than 5 mph where accident occurred. The accident resulted in bruises to my nephew and a broken arm for his friend.

Trying to right the car before Uncle Bill was the wiser, the two teenagers found a friend with a tractor and chain who proceeded to pull the car 100 feet on its roof before giving up. A tow truck was eventually summoned, but by that time the car was a total wreck and had to be scrapped. To my everlasting dismay, four recently purchased books of ferry tickets hidden in a seat pocket compartment were scrapped along with it.

My Subaru weighed 2,350 pounds. Kennedy's Oldsmobile weighted 3,970 pounds. If two and one-half very fit teenagers were unable right my Subaru with a tractor, what would be the chance of four older men righting a far heavier Oldsmobile with a Valiant?

I don't know the answer to that, and perhaps no one does save the persons who were there.[1] But, of course, it is unnecessary for the Oldsmobile to have rolled over onto its roof. It might simply have become stuck in the sand. Kennedy might have had to leave the Oldsmobile on the east side of the bridge with an injured Mary Jo inside because he was incapable of getting the car free without help. This is what several of the Boiler Room Girls suspected after Gargan and Markham left with Kennedy.

Today, only vehicles with four-wheel drive are allowed to cross over the bridge. But in the '60s, you were allowed to cross over with any car, and we all did. But you had to be careful, because immediately after the bridge the road turns progressively to ever deepening sand. It was impossible to drive more than about 300 feet from the bridge unless the car you were driving was a jeep or some other vehicle equipped to handle the conditions. As a teenager, I remember getting stuck at least twice on the east side of the bridge before getting the message. Carol remembers getting stuck, too. Once mired in the sand, getting out was not easy. It meant hunting for driftwood to shove under the rear wheels, letting the air out of the tires, and generally feeling stupid while onlookers sneered.

Perhaps Kennedy told Gargan, Markham, and the two others that Mary Jo got out of the car when the Oldsmobile became stuck, fell back, and hit her head on the car. Or, perhaps he said she fell back against one of the short posts that line the Dike. Or maybe he told them she fell back onto a rock in the water. Maybe he said they were fooling around when the accident occurred and the car got stuck later. A difficult story to believe, but maybe that's why Kennedy needed their help to stage something more convincing. Who would ever believe that it was really an accident?

But then there is the evidence of those passenger doors with the deep, vertical dents and undamaged chrome strips at the bottom. Could an accident have occurred between the intersection and Dike Bridge? The distance from the intersection to Dike Bridge is close to seven-tenths of a mile, and it could be expected that no one would have noticed damage to an object closer to the main road, especially if they were not looking for it. And if that object was some type of construction equipment already exposed to a lifetime of hard knocks, it would be very difficult to identify damage even if someone *was* looking for it.

Did the accident occur on Dike Road?

Kennedy said the accident occurred soon after 11:15 p.m. This is supported by Carol's sighting. Assuming Kennedy was telling the truth, it would not seem to leave enough time for Kennedy to walk from East Beach over Dike Bridge past Dyke House all the way to Lawrence Cottage, ask for the help of Gargan and Markham, drive toward the ferry landing to find two others, then drive past Carol at 11:35 p.m. State

---

[1] My nephew says, "No way in hell!"

detectives Flynn and Killen said they were unable to make the walk from Dyke House to Lawrence Cottage in less than 21 minutes.[1] However, if Kennedy's accident occurred closer to the intersection with Chappaquiddick Road, and if the two others they picked up in the Valiant had not walked very far toward the ferry landing, the timeline might fit. It could also explain the puzzling fact that no accident was ever heard by Mrs. Malm or her daughter Sylvia while they were still awake before midnight.

Could Kennedy's walk and drive be accomplished in less than 20 minutes? I decided to find out. My knees are not what they used to be, so I asked my wife if she would walk quickly, but not jog, from the driveway at Tom's Neck Farm, a little over 200 yards down Dike Road, to Lawrence Cottage. Happy for the exercise, she made the walk in 7 minutes, 45 seconds. I then drove from Lawrence Cottage to the turnoff at North Neck Road, a mile from the Dike Road intersection and almost half way from the intersection to the ferry landing, turned around, and drove back to the place in the road where the Valiant passed Carol. Keeping the speed under 35 mph the entire time, the drive lasted 4 minutes, 45 seconds. The walk and the drive together had taken only 12½ minutes!

If Kennedy had been jogging rather than walking, as he testified he was, and if the Valiant had been traveling at more than 35 mph, as it was when Carol saw it, the whole thing could have been done in less than 20 minutes easily, even if it took Gargan and Markham a little time to react, and even if Kennedy and the two other persons had walked much further. Gargan told Damore that he didn't waste a second after hearing there was an accident. "He didn't bark out orders or anything. He made it clear he was driving the car and Mary Jo was with him. He didn't say how the accident happened. All he said was, 'There's been an accident.' That's all I needed to know. The only thing that hit my mind was: 'Go to the bridge as quickly as possible.' Gargan then gunned the Valiant down Chappaquiddick Road [sic] to the intersection."[2] At the inquest, Markham said, "I don't think there was anything said from the time that he said that he was in an accident until we got there. We went there at a rather high rate of speed, very high rate of speed."

If the Oldsmobile was indeed heard (or seen) driving very fast toward Dike Bridge by Mrs. Malm or her daughter, perhaps close to 11:45 p.m., it might have been heading to the bridge parking lot after it had been freed from the sand. Dike Road was narrow with very few driveways in 1969. If a car was pointed toward the bridge, it would have been the easiest place to turn around.

If the accident was staged, there would have been two cars at the bridge at around 1:15 a.m.

---

[1] *Senatorial Privilege*, p. 104
[2] *Senatorial Privilege*, p. 77. Gargan gunned the Valiant down *School House Road*.

30
Dike Road and the Edgartown Channel

$\mathcal{I}$ was out of the country when the incident occurred, working as an investigative reporter in South America, but I remember reading about it in the *New York Times*. A very short report of a paragraph or two the first day turned into full-page headlines the next. I remember laughing out loud when reading that Kennedy made a wrong turn onto Dike Road because he thought it was the main route to the ferry.

No one could make that mistake! It wasn't just the fact that there was an arrow pointing the right way to the ferry, or that the main road was paved and banked to the left, or that you would have to come almost to a complete stop before proceeding that way, or even because you couldn't even see the lane from School House Road because it was hidden by bushes;[1] it was because Dike Road was so clearly wrong, especially in 1969.

Visitors today will find a wide, graded dirt road leading to the bridge. You can drive on it at speed if so inclined, and if you can tolerate the horrendous vibration over the washboard surface and the dust. But in the '60s that road was rough, narrow, and littered with potholes. In 1969, Dike Road was little more than a one-lane track with room to pass another car only if both cars crowded over to their respective sides. You took that road slow, unless you didn't care about damaging your springs or shocks or didn't care whether you drove off it. Where Dike Road left the main road there was a pronounced drop from pavement to dirt, and that had to be taken slowly, too. Tall trees grew very close to the road in those days, in contrast to the main road leading to the ferry, and even on a dark night those trees could never be overlooked. Brock Brower wrote in *Life*'s edition of August 1, 1969, "You got to be mighty confused, you got to *hunt* to turn wrong down Dike Road, and it washboards enough to let you know you aren't on any hot top."

In *The Bridge at Chappaquiddick*, Olsen paints a realistic picture of the approach to Dike Bridge in 1969: "Moreover, Dike Road provides the discerning motorist with ample warnings of other kinds. As one drives down the road, trees and bushes that have crowded the edges suddenly disappear, and one passes a few cottages and comes into an open area, all at a range of some 600 feet [sic[2]] from the bridge. Plainly, a

---

[1] Dike Road was invisible from School House Road in 1969 until *after* a vehicle had begun to make the turn onto Chappaquiddick Road. See *Death at Chappaquiddick*, p. 33, and *The President's Private Eye*, p. 190.

[2] Dyke House, where the road begins to widen, is 450 feet from the bridge.

change is coming. One knows that the sea is somewhere ahead and that this road cannot go on much farther. Now the road widens into a parking area; the ripples increase in depth, and at 70 feet from the bridge there is a pronounced hole in the roadway made by previous drivers applying their brakes. Another such hole jounces the car at 50 feet from the bridge. Even if the driver refuses to believe the sight that has been so clearly visible through his windshield for 300 to 400 feet, he has been warned by the changes in scenery, by the bumpiness of the road, by the parking area, and by the two deep ruts. If, after all these natural warnings, he drives up and off the side of the bridge, he has made a driving error so grandiose as to defy the imagination. And if he is traveling at a speed of only twenty miles an hour, as Ted Kennedy claimed later, *no amount of driving error seems to explain the accident* [emphasis in the original]. It becomes, apparently, unexplainable."[1] Kennedy's accident at Dike Bridge was the first ever recorded there since the bridge was constructed in 1951.

Kennedy testified he spent about 15 to 20 minutes resting on a bank of Dike Channel before jogging back to Lawrence Cottage. Unless you had spent time on Chappaquiddick you would never know how absurd that would be. In July, the nights can be chilly. In wet clothes, it would be even more uncomfortable. But the big problem would be the mosquitoes. Poucha Pond, with its extensive marshes, is a breeding ground for the pests and the voraciousness of Chappaquiddick mosquitoes would have to be experienced to be believed. At night they come out in force around Poucha Pond and salty skin seems to drive them into a feeding frenzy. Anyone who has spent some time swimming at East Beach in the summer and has had the bad luck to walk back in the evening can attest to this. No one not lathered from head to toe in mosquito repellant could survive for long at night in that place. Resting on the bank of Dike Channel for 15 to 20 minutes in salty wet clothes around midnight in July with Chappaquiddick mosquitoes for company would be nothing less than a living hell, and had Kennedy actually spent all that time lying on the bank, the swellings and marks around his face and arms would have been clearly visible the next morning.

Olsen says that when Foster Silva visited Dike Bridge in the early evening of July 18 with his wife, Dodie, "The clammy air was thick with mosquitoes."[2] A cousin, who wishes to remain anonymous, confessed to me that she and her husband had driven to East Beach on the late afternoon of July 18, intending to spend a romantic night on the dunes. However, the normal onshore breeze was absent, and the mosquitoes flooding in from the marsh became so unbearable, even with bug repellant, that they were forced to depart in the early evening for a different beach on the Katama side of Chappaquiddick. If it hadn't been for the mosquitoes, they would have been in the immediate vicinity when Kennedy's accident occurred, and perhaps I would have been writing about their observation in this book rather than Carol's.

---

[1] *The Bridge at Chappaquiddick*, pp. 256-257
[2] *The Bridge at Chappaquiddick*, p. 91

As for the Edgartown channel swim, forget it! Unless one was blind drunk, fleeing from terrorists, or a deranged dog, you wouldn't think about attempting it. I and several cousins always talked about doing it, but even as cocky teenagers loaded with testosterone I don't remember any of us ever trying. The current could absolutely boil through that channel, but that could be managed if we timed the tides right. It was the powerboats we were most afraid of. Even in daylight, you could not be sure that you would be seen. At night, you'd be in the hands of fate.

Even though there was less traffic in 1969 it does not mean there was none, and the small decrease in traffic was more than made up by the fact that speed limits were rarely enforced. Long before 1969, I remember walking down to the ferry landing and seeing a Boston Whaler sitting high and dry on top of an Edgartown dock. Some kid (and we all knew who he was) had "borrowed" and then driven that boat at high speed into Edgartown Channel the night before just a bit too close to the Edgartown side. Jared Grant, the Chappaquiddick ferry owner in 1969, testified at the inquest that there were boats running back and forth through the channel when he shut down the ferry at 1:00 a.m. The *Boston Herald Traveler* reported on July 27, 1969, that Farrar had told their reporter, "I think he subjected himself to a great danger because of the plying of high speed motorboats through the channel."

After the accident, a swim was staged by Farrar in front of TV cameras and the press to determine how difficult the swim might actually be. The *Boston Herald Traveler* in their edition of July 27, 1969, reported that Farrar got across in the remarkable time of only six minutes, but you can be sure that no recreational boat was allowed to be near him while he was in the water. Farrar, who said he ran two miles each day and was in excellent shape, made the swim in a pair of trousers but with no shoes or shirt. A number of other people also attempted the swim, but only a few managed to get across without assistance. Farrar reported in the August 1974 edition of *McCall's* that it would have been "virtually impossible" for Kennedy to have accomplished it in a weakened condition and back brace. When asked whether he thought Kennedy could do it with clothes and a back brace, Dick Hewitt, a Chappaquiddick ferry operator more familiar than most with the currents and conditions, said, "If he were here now, I'd call him a liar to his face."[1]

Zad Rust asks, "Stand on the ferry wharf on the Chappaquiddick side of the Martha's Vineyard Channel; look again at that powerfully running expanse of cold, dark water, and see the efforts the oncoming ferry has to put forth to cross it in a straight line. Imagine yourself standing there at night, exhausted, in a state of shock, with two devoted friends beside you and the emergency telephone, which could bring the ferry to your side of the channel in just a few minutes, at arm's length – would *you*

---

[1] *The Last Kennedy*, p. 117

choose instead to dive headlong into that channel and swim across it? Would your friends let you do it?"[1]

In the BBC documentary *Chappaquiddick* released in 1994, investigators concluded that Kennedy was unaware that Mary Jo had been in an accident until advised by Gargan and Markham at 8:00 the following morning. In that context, the channel swim, or Kennedy's credibility gap as others have called it, is germane to the story as it applies to Mary Jo because if not true, it means that Kennedy had something to hide long before 8:00 a.m. And that "something" was probably himself. As Chief Arena said, "For the senator to have walked from the [lighthouse] to the Shiretown Inn unseen on a regatta night suggested a deliberate avoidance of witnesses."

Many have suggested that Kennedy insisted he swam the channel because borrowing a boat was stealing. However, borrowing a boat, while probably technically illegal, was not something that anyone ever worried anything about. On Chappaquiddick in those days it had about the same weight as a parking ticket. A cheap parking ticket. In my whole life I have never heard of anyone being given so much as a warning for borrowing a rowboat after midnight in the '60s. If Kennedy thought he could get away with not reporting an accident involving a fatality for over 10 hours, he surely was not worried about being chastised for borrowing someone's boat when that was the most convenient way of returning to Edgartown at that hour.

Hersh, Kennedy's biographer, describes Kennedy's state of mind before and after finally collapsing at the Shiretown Inn this way: "...he began to be wracked, as soon as he could pull together enough of whatever was still working in his mind, to consider the practical, by premonitions of his fearful responsibility to the family of the poor drowned girl... shaking with chill, he stripped, his headache throbbing, neck torn, back half out, desolated, confused. Tossing, pacing, he was unable to budge his shattered emotions from their fixated need..."[2] Pretty dramatic stuff, but was it really like this?

Swimming the Edgartown Channel has always been something that has seemed particularly incredible to me, as it was to Leslie Leland, so let's spend a little more time fleshing it out. If we look closely, we'll find that the way it must have occurred is embedded in Kennedy's own inquest testimony.

Kennedy's statement at the inquest addressing the channel swim seems almost ludicrously puerile for an individual of supposed intelligence, and from a person who Gargan testified could swim that channel easily "five or six times both ways."

Kennedy: With the court's indulgence to prevent this, if the court would permit me, I would like to be able to relate to the court the immediate period following the time that Mr. Gargan, Mr. Markham, and I got back in the car.

---

[1] *Teddy Bare*, pp. 87-88. The public phone at the Chappaquiddick ferry landing was known to all of them.
[2] *Edward Kennedy*, pp. 360-364

Judge Boyle: I have no objection.
Mr. Dinis: I have no objection.

And this is what Kennedy said:

"I just wondered how all of this could possibly have happened. I also had sort of a thought and the wish and desire and the hope that suddenly this whole accident would disappear, and they reiterated that this has to be reported, and I understood at the time I left that ferryboat, left the slip where the ferry was, that it had to be reported, and I had full intention of reporting it, and I mentioned to Gargan and Markham something like, 'You take care of the girls, I will take care of the accident,' that is what I said and I dove into the water.

"Now, I started to swim out into the tide and the tide suddenly became – felt an extraordinary shove and almost pulling me down again, the water pulling me down, and suddenly I realized at that time, even as I failed to realize before I dove into the water, that I was in a weakened condition, although as I had looked over that distance between the ferry slip and the other side it seemed to me an inconsequential swim; but the water got colder, the tide began to draw me out, and for the second time that evening I knew I was going to drown and the strength continued to leave me. By that time I was probably 50 yards off the shore and I remember being swept down toward the direction of the Edgartown light and well out into darkness, and I continued to attempt to swim, tried to swim at a slower pace to be able to regain whatever kind of strength that was left in me.

"And sometime after, I think it was about the middle of the channel, a little further than that, the tide was much calmer, gentler, and I began to get my – make some progress and finally was able to reach the other shore and all the nightmares before me again. And when I was able to gain this shore, this Edgartown side, I pulled myself on the beach and then attempted to gain some strength."

Hersh, Kennedy's biographer, says, "Halfway over, the tide grabbed him and dragged him toward the Edgartown light and the undertow began to suck him down irresistibly when the tide apparently turned..."[1] Really? Unless you are swimming in strong surf with an undertow or trapped in Edgar Allen Poe's mythical Maelström, water never pulls you down. An experienced swimmer knows this. An experienced swimmer never expends so much energy that he almost drowns. If there is a current against him, he swims at right angles to it. If he is tired, he swims more slowly. A strong swimmer rests (pauses) just enough between each stroke so that he never loses his rhythm or stamina. Kennedy was both an experienced and strong swimmer, yet this account infers that he was little more than a novice or scared little boy. It was written by a speechwriter who was dumbing down to what he hoped was a gullible public.

---

[1] *Edward Kennedy*, p. 364

Kennedy claimed that he impulsively dove into the channel and began swimming across. One wonders where this intelligent yachtsman, who knew Edgartown Harbor and its approaches exceptionally well, thought he could climb out on the Edgartown side. If the current was running swiftly to the north, there was the beach at the lighthouse. But if there was a strong northerly set, as Kennedy insisted there was, a tired swimmer, dressed in clothes and contending with a back brace, could easily miss it and be pulled a good distance out into the harbor.

On the other hand, when the current sets the other way, the swim becomes no less daunting. From the lighthouse south, all around the channel through downtown Edgartown to Katama Bay, the coast on the Edgartown side is lined with private docks and pilings encrusted with barnacles. Worse, pier pilings in Edgartown and Chappaquiddick in the '60s were also covered with razor-sharp mussels – bivalves that have all-but-disappeared today due to infestations of starfish and pea crabs. If you did manage to climb out onto one of those docks without slicing your hands and feet to shreds, you would have to contend with the gardens and locked gates of the private houses behind them.

In fact, there would only be one place south of the lighthouse you could really expect to climb out of the water and walk to a street easily – the narrow beach, only 25 feet wide, to the south of Memorial Wharf where rowboats could always be found pulled up onto the sand. But what would be the chance that the current would take you exactly there?

Finally, when you factor in that Kennedy was supposed to have willingly made that swim fully clothed, shoes and all, with a back brace too, dead sober, and then have walked from the lighthouse down North Water Street, the most upmarket thoroughfare in Edgartown, soaking wet from the hair at the top of his head to his squishy shoes, all the way to the Shiretown Inn near the center of town without being seen by so much as one person and without leaving so much as a puddle on the Shiretown lobby floor, his credibility, as well as the credibility of Markham and Gargan who also testified to the veracity of that cockamamie story, is completely undone.

The distance from the edge of the water at the beach near the lighthouse to the Shiretown Inn is a walk of at least half a mile, depending on exactly where Kennedy floated up. If he washed up at the lighthouse itself, it would be a walk of eight-tenths of a mile. Even at 2:00 a.m., a person walking that distance, conspicuous in soaking wet clothes, should have been seen by someone on a busy regatta weekend. Jared Grant, the Chappaquiddick ferry owner, testified that at 1:00 a.m. when he shut the ferry down and went home, "There were a lot of people in the area [of the ferry landing on the Edgartown side]. It was the night of the regatta. There were people on the dock; there were some people fishing off the dock. There were boats running back and forth in the harbor."

On the other hand, the distance from the small patch of sand in Edgartown where rowboats were landed and could always be found in those days, to the Shiretown Inn only one-and-a-half blocks away, was a short stroll of just 525 feet. If Kennedy was in dry clothes at the time, he could make that walk easily without being recognized.

Examine the supposed walk from the lighthouse to the Shiretown Inn as described by Kennedy as he continued his monologue:

"After that, I walked up one of the streets in the direction of the Shiretown Inn. By walking up one of the streets, I walked into a parking lot that was adjacent to the inn and I can remember almost having no further strength to continue, and leaning against a tree for a length of time, walking through the parking lot, trying to really gather some kind of idea as to what happened and feeling that I just had to go to my room at that time, which I did by walking through the front entrance of the Shiretown Inn up the stairs."

The small beach next to Memorial Wharf as it looks today. Chappaquiddick is in the background. In 1969, this beach was used as a rowboat landing place and was only 525 feet from the Shiretown Inn.

Kennedy said he walked from the beach near the lighthouse "up one of the streets" in the direction of the Shiretown Inn. This doesn't make sense. The only path from the lighthouse leads to North Water Street. The Shiretown Inn, since torn down, was located on the west side of North Water Street between Daggett and Kelly Streets. If Kennedy walked along North Water Street to the Shiretown Inn, he would have walked "down" a pronounced slope the entire way. There was no other route available to him.

Not just this, but why would Kennedy say he walked up "one of the streets" instead of North Water Street? North and South Water Streets are the most fashionable streets in Edgartown. For over 40 years, the Kennedys had always booked accommodation on one or the other of those streets, usually staying at the Harborside Inn on South Water Street. But the previous summer, Ted and his guests had taken up a whole floor of the Harbor View Hotel. *The Harbor View Hotel is located on North Water Street, directly across from the path that leads to the lighthouse.* Even if Kennedy was confused and disoriented at the time he made that walk, he surely wasn't confused five months later. Kennedy was attempting to mislead the court into believing he was unfamiliar with Edgartown.

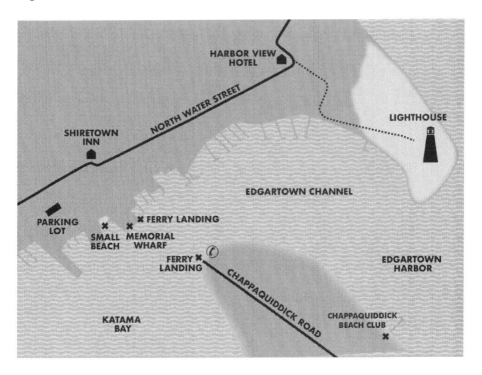

Kennedy's supposed route from the lighthouse down North Water Street to the Shiretown Inn.

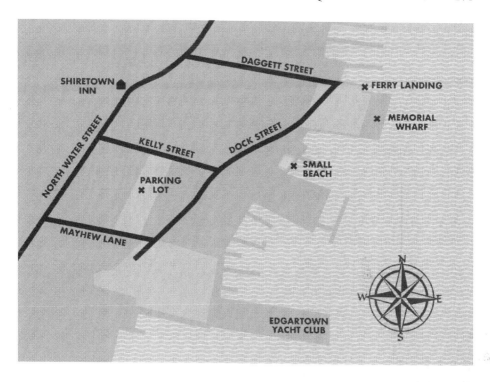

Route from the small dinghy beach past the public parking lot to the Shiretown Inn.

Kennedy said he walked through the front entrance of the Shiretown Inn. What he doesn't mention is that his room had a rear staircase to an outside porch. Gargan and Markham entered his room that way when they met Kennedy the next morning at 8:00 a.m. What is much more interesting is that Kennedy took care to mention a parking lot adjacent to the Shiretown Inn, twice, even though he failed to mention any other landmark between the lighthouse and the Shiretown. But that parking lot is not located between the Shiretown Inn and the lighthouse. The only parking lot near the Shiretown Inn is the public lot sandwiched between Mayhew Lane and Kelly Street, a half block past the Shiretown Inn and a half block east of it, *directly between the small dinghy beach and the Shiretown.* The public parking lot has trees on its east side, toward the water, and from the small dinghy beach you would indeed walk "up" a pronounced slope on Kelly Street to the Shiretown Inn.

It appears Kennedy mentioned leaning against a tree in the parking lot for some time in case someone had actually seen him walking up Kelly Street to the inn. Kennedy's lawyers were attempting to cover all bases in case a witness ever appeared.

So, what appears more likely? That Kennedy stumbled, cold, exhausted, and soaking wet, through the confusing labyrinth of Edgartown streets (when he knew very well there was only one street) without ever being seen by anyone, passed the Shiretown Inn without noticing it, took a wrong left turn on Kelly Street a half block later (well, he had taken a wrong right turn onto Dike Road... was Kennedy dyslexic?), walked another half block down toward the water to the public parking lot, rested for several minutes against a tree on its east side, finally decided he just had to go to his room, walked back up alongside the parking lot on Kelly Street to North Water Street, retraced his steps north to the Shiretown Inn, walked boldly through the front lobby at the exact time nobody happened to be looking, took a bath, dressed in clean clothes, then walked downstairs to complain, according to Russell Peachey, about some noise that had awakened him (although Kennedy testified at the inquest that he hadn't slept at all that night), asked for the time because his watch wasn't working, appeared entirely normal to the innkeeper, rejected Peachey's offer of help because he was confused and disoriented, and then, with his mind still fixated on "his fearful responsibility to the family of the poor drowned girl," began making telephone calls to his mistress and lawyers that lasted all night?

Or... after stepping onto the dock near the dinghy beach, Kennedy dashed across Dock Street to the public parking lot on Kelly Street just a few dozen feet away, hid behind a tree for a while to make sure the coast was clear, slinked through the shadows to the Shiretown Inn a half block up the street and a half block to the north, climbed up the back stairs to the porch in his room, bathed, washed, and walked downstairs to establish his alibi, refused Peachey's offer of help because he never had any intention of reporting the accident, then mentioned the parking lot twice at the inquest because his lawyers told him he should?

But these observations and questions are moot anyway. Carol's eyewitness account and Look's testimony prove that Kennedy's story of driving off Dike Bridge in the Oldsmobile with Mary Jo Kopechne soon after 11:15 p.m. on July 18 was a lie. Research into the state of the tide on the morning of July 19 proves that the strong northerly currents Kennedy told the court he experienced while swimming the Edgartown Channel did not exist.

Kennedy had no problem lying about these details. He had no problem lying about the phone calls, his driving record, his valid driver's license, the clock in the Valiant, the time Dun Gifford was told about the accident, his familiarity with Chappaquiddick, or his drinking. He had no problem lying when he testified that he returned to Lawrence Cottage just once. And therefore it can be reasonably assumed that he would have had no problem lying about much if not all of the rest of his testimony, too.

PART 5: AUTHOR'S OBSERVATIONS

31
Rochester

In Senatorial Privilege: The Chappaquiddick Cover-up, *Leo Damore recounts an amusing story about a dog.*

C hief of Police Arena told reporters "about a dog we used to see every day downtown that was soaking wet and bothering people. Finally, one of my officers grabbed it and looked at his collar. The dog belonged to somebody on Chappaquiddick. Apparently, every day the dog would jump in the water and swim to Edgartown, have his fun, then swim back at night. And we chuckled about that at the police station. We figured: If the dog could do it, Ted Kennedy could do it."[1]

That dog was our family dog Rochester.

Rochester was a black mutt who was the smartest dog I've ever encountered, and absolutely fearless. He was sired by Midnight, my grandfather's dog, who roamed the island from my grandfather's farm in Edgartown looking for conquests. A week wouldn't go by without some farmer calling from Chilmark or some other remote place to report that "your damn dog Midnight is here again." Rochester was a chip off the old block, if there ever was one, and it was said in those days that half the dogs on the Vineyard were sired by one of those two.

There weren't many female dogs to court on Chappaquiddick in the '60s, so every morning at daybreak, Rochester would bound up, bushy tail held high, eyes bright with anticipation, and lope the mile and a quarter from our home on Chappaquiddick down to the ferry landing. Without hesitation, he would plunge in and make the long swim to Edgartown where he would win the heart of any bitch in heat he came across, and woe to the competition that got in his way.

And every evening at sundown, Rochester would come limping back home, tail dragging, tongue hanging out, wet, bloodied, and bruised and flop down in front of the fireplace, absolutely spent. A hot poker wouldn't move him.

---

[1] *Senatorial Privilege*, p. 217

And the next morning he would do it all over again, and continued doing it to the day he died, rain or shine, calm or storm. Tony Bettencourt, who often ran the ferry in those days and witnessed Rochester swimming the channel each morning and evening, would joke about it with my father all the time.[1] Everyone on Chappaquiddick knew about Rochester, the dog who swam the channel and could never "get enough."

And so Arena was making a comparison to Kennedy that was more apt then perhaps he realized.

---

[1] Tony Bettencourt would allow Rochester to ride the ferry from Edgartown back to Chappaquiddick free of charge if Rochester was so inclined, which in his later years he often was.

32
The Failed Autopsy

*D*r. Mills was a very sweet man. Mills never had a bad word to say about anyone. He answered every phone call from reporters and was polite when they weren't. He was also honest, even at his own expense. At the inquest, Mills took care not embellish his actions or to defend his diagnosis. In spite of much criticism of his determination of death by drowning which had reached a crescendo in the five months that had elapsed since the incident, Mills admitted he spent very little time examining the body. He testified that Mary Jo's arms were extended out from her body and her hands were shaped into a claw − observations which some might interpret as evidence that Mary Jo had spent a good deal of time alive in a pocket of air.

Nevertheless, having to decide by himself whether or not to order an autopsy on Mary Jo, Dr. Mills was not up to the task. He waffled, and he looked for guidance, but never finding it was incapable of making the right choice. Worse, even after being highly criticized for his initial decision he refused to budge or admit a mistake. At the exhumation hearing, Mills argued that an autopsy would be unnecessary.

Dr. Mills might not even have been aware of some of the symptoms of drowning. When Mills pressed on Mary Jo's chest and water poured out of her mouth, Frieh, the undertaker, said, "That looks like it's coming from her stomach." However, Dr. Mills, who was convinced he was dealing with a drowning, rebuked him saying, "No, it is coming from her lungs." Yet in a drowning, considerable water should be found in the stomach while sometimes none at all will be found in the lungs.

It was only bad timing that Mills was called to the scene that morning rather than Dr. Nevin who was off on weekends. Dr. Nevin was the Dukes County Medical Examiner in 1969. Dr. Nevin co-signed the petition for exhumation and autopsy "because I've favored an autopsy all along. An autopsy would have been distinctly to the advantage of Senator Kennedy by putting an end to a lot of shabby rumors and thrown light on many obscure and debated facts." In the BBC documentary *Chappaquiddick*, he said, "Things were sort of being hinted and said, 'People die. Don't obstruct the Kennedys. Play the game and there won't be any problems.' I felt an autopsy would be in order. I felt that certain inevitable questions were going to be asked and I would feel happier and more comfortable if they were answered appropriately, and the only appropriate way I knew of was an autopsy. I think the facts have borne me out."

In a public statement, Nevin said, "We don't know if the girl died of a heart attack, a stroke, or from drowning." Nevin said he would have asked the state police to send a pathologist to Edgartown. "I wouldn't have let that autopsy go. I would have gone to

Washington if I had to. It wasn't too late when Dr. Mills learned the entire story around 2:30 p.m. The corpse had been embalmed; the presence of formalin couldn't change the picture."[1] The *Handbook for Massachusetts Medical Examiners* says: 1) "If you are wondering whether you should do an autopsy or not, you had probably better do one," and 2) "Death occurring following motor vehicle accidents should be autopsied if there is *any question* as to whether the accident caused the death."

I talked to Dr. Nevin, who was the family doctor for all our cousins on Chappaquiddick in those days, several times after 1969, and once specifically about the incident at his office in 1980. Dr. Nevin always maintained that he would have ordered an autopsy on Mary Jo before pronouncing death in such a circumstance. He found it irresponsible that one had not been performed. Dr. Nevin is reported to have described Dr. Mills as "a sweet, gentle, kind person who hooks rugs and plays the organ. He won't take a stand unless pushed."[2] The two doctors never had a good relationship after the incident.

When discussing the autopsy issue as it relates to the Chappaquiddick cover-up, many books concentrate on the medical reasons for arguing that an autopsy is the only real way to make a determination of death by drowning. The Tedrows, for instance, in *Death at Chappaquiddick*, list the tests that are required in an autopsy to make a determination of drowning:[3]

1) Examining for hemorrhages of the inner ear, present in over 70 percent of all drowning cases.

2) Look for swelling of the lungs because the lungs are large with water and the water will exude on the cut surface.

3) The presence of diatoms and algae in remote parts of the body.

4) The presence or absence of foreign material deep in the airway and the bronchi.

5) Considerable quantities of water in the stomach.

6) The presence of above average chloride content in the left side of the heart in saltwater drownings.

7) And the various negative findings: that death was not caused by any obvious wound or means, or by skull or spinal fracture, rupture of the aorta, or other internal injury.

These tests are made routinely in an autopsy and it is telling that none of these were performed on the body of Mary Jo. And with that said, I'll digress to a short story.

In 2003, while sailing my schooner across the Indian Ocean, I dropped anchor in a bay in Madagascar off a town called, appropriately as it turned out, Hell-Ville. When

---

[1] *Senatorial Privilege*, p. 175
[2] *Senatorial Privilege*, p. 268
[3] *Death at Chappaquiddick*, p. 213

attempting to leave, the anchor became stuck in some cable on the bottom and Chogin, my Indonesian deckhand, jumped in with his mask and snorkel to free it. Chogin never came up. About 20 minutes later, I was able to find him, lying on his back on the mud.

Then followed a nightmare of negotiating the bureaucratic ins and outs of dealing with a death in a foreign country, notifying the grieving parents, arranging for burial, and generally feeling mortified and tremendously saddened by the needless death of a very good person and friend.

But what I remember from that experience, as it applies to Chappaquiddick, was sitting out in the sun for over three hours while an autopsy was performed on Chogin to determine the cause of death. It was absolutely obvious to me, and to the police officials, that Chogin drowned, but nonetheless, an autopsy was performed *to be sure.*

So I've always wondered: if the doctors knew enough to perform an autopsy on an obvious drowning, in a primitive and poor country, in a very small shack, in a place where outboard motors were virtually unknown and handmade sailboats the norm, surrounded by bugs and flies and kids without clothes, why in God's name, in a modern country, with modern facilities, was one not done here?

33

The Kopechnes

*I*n their later years, the Kopechnes were said to express their bitterness and disillusionment with Ted Kennedy and his associates. They are reported to have said, "The biggest mistake we ever made was not allowing the autopsy."[1] Leslie Leland, who spoke with them many times before their deaths, says the concern which was initially expressed by Ted Kennedy ultimately turned to intimidation. Leland says the Kopechnes came to fear the Kennedys and the power they wielded.

Regrettably, the Kopechnes really had only themselves to blame for much of the mystery that surrounds the death of Mary Jo. Inexplicably passive in the early months, they allowed themselves to be completely controlled by the Kennedy team. When they did become more involved, their actions all but assured that the real story would never emerge.

1) Immediately following the accident, they allowed Kennedy's lawyers to formulate their policy and to speak for them.

2) In the first few years following the accident, they accepted Kennedy's version of the events unconditionally.

3) When it became obvious to almost everyone in the entire country that Kennedy's story was untenable, they never demanded answers and continued to insist for years that Kennedy was not to blame. In 1975, Mrs. Kopechne told journalist Gerald Kelley, "No matter how you look at it, it was an accident." The Kopechnes put all the blame on Markham and Gargan and concluded that Mary Jo must have been asleep in the back seat of the Oldsmobile without Kennedy being aware of it. "I think Kennedy made his statement when he was still confused," opined Gwen. "I do believe he couldn't think clearly. I think he was taking all this bad advice and it just continued for days. He got so deeply involved in it he couldn't back out and tell the truth."[2]

5) They agreed that Mary Jo should be buried without an autopsy.

6) Perhaps worst of all, they vehemently argued against the exhumation of their daughter's body for an autopsy – a procedure which might have answered many if not most of the numerous unexplained mysteries and inconsistencies surrounding the accident. Had they not agreed to contest the exhumation and autopsy, Kennedy would have had no legal basis for opposing it.

---

[1] *Left to Die*, p. 28
[2] *Senatorial Privilege*, p. 414

Mary Jo Kopechne is buried next to her parents, Joseph and Gwen, in Larksville, Pennsylvania.

At first, the Kopechnes were in favor of an autopsy. Nevertheless, by August, Joseph Kopechne vowed that "we'll do everything and anything we have to do in order to prevent an autopsy."[1] Mrs. Kopechne explained to a reporter from *McCall's* in September 1970 why they had opposed it: "We didn't feel that an autopsy would yield new evidence and the thought of it was grossly offensive to us. It would have been like a second funeral." In later years, they confessed that Ted Kennedy had convinced them that the only real purpose of an autopsy was to determine whether their daughter was pregnant.

The Kopechnes never thought it odd that bloodstains were found on the back of their daughter's blouse. They never thought it strange that a deputy sheriff had seen the Oldsmobile drive down Dike Road an hour and a half after Kennedy said he had gone off the bridge with Mary Jo. They never wondered how their daughter could have been found in the back seat of Ted's car without so much as a bruise or scratch. They never read anything sinister into Kennedy's objection to an autopsy. All of this was made

---

[1] *You, the Jury*, p. 29

apparent to them either before the exhumation hearing or during it. Yet when the exhumation was denied, the Kopechnes declared themselves greatly satisfied by the judge's ruling. On the release of the inquest testimony on April 29, 1970, when they read that Judge Boyle had come to the conclusion that Senator Kennedy had lied when he said he had been driving from the cottage to Edgartown with their daughter, they told *McCall's* in September 1970, it "leaves a bad taste in our mouth, and we absolutely reject it and any implications that flow from it."

It is also unfortunate that the Kopechnes insisted that Mary Jo's clothes be destroyed by the police, even though the police argued against it and delayed carrying out the order for as long as they could. The police considered Mary Jo's clothes as case evidence that should be preserved.

In the beginning, the orders emanating from Walter McLaughlin, Chief Justice of the Superior Court, were that Mary Jo's clothes be returned to the Kopechnes. Lieutenant Killen said, "I couldn't figure out what the hell the Kopechnes wanted their daughter's clothes back for in the first place. Whether the clothes actually belonged to Mary Jo Kopechne was debatable. The deceased owned no property rights to exhibits presented by the district attorney's office in a judicial hearing. Standard operating procedure was for evidence to be kept a minimum of five years in storage bins in the basement of the courthouse; longer in cases under appeal or subject to reinvestigation."

Killen was reluctant to carry out the order. He requested a letter of verification from Joseph Flanagan, the Kopechnes' attorney. But now the Kopechnes wanted Mary Jo's clothes to be destroyed. Flanagan wrote to Killen on November 10, 1971, on behalf of Mr. and Mrs. Kopechne, requesting "the specific articles of clothing be destroyed" and for Killen to let him know when the district attorney's office had complied with the request.

Accordingly, Mary Jo's clothes, consisting of one white blouse, one blue slacks, one bra with blue trim, and one pair of leather sandals, were doused with lighter fluid and burned on November 16.[1]

Frustrated by the Kopechnes' steadfast support for Ted Kennedy in the face of mounting evidence against him, many reporters began to wonder if they had been paid to keep quiet. It was pointed out that an insurance settlement totaling $140,943 had included a $90,000 personal contribution from the Kennedys, even though there was no evidence the Kopechnes were aware of this at the time. Some questioned how their second home in the Poconos costing $75,000 to $100,000 was paid, and rumors began circulating that they had accepted as much as half a million dollars for their cooperation[2] – accusations vehemently denied by the couple.

So why the stubborn refusal to assign any blame to Ted Kennedy? The general belief is that the Kopechnes were a remarkably naive couple who clung to the certainty

[1] *Senatorial Privilege*, pp. 401-403
[2] See *McCall's* magazine, August, 1974; *Death at Chappaquiddick*, pp. 196-197.

that Kennedy was a good and just man because the alternative was just too horrifying to contemplate. If Kennedy was responsible for Mary Jo's death, then her life and passion for politics would amount to little more than a meaningless joke, and their own lives, too. That analysis has a solid ring of truth because there is little doubt that the Kopechnes were absolutely devastated over the death of their only child. It has been reported by many that they never fully recovered from it.

If they did allow themselves in the beginning to be seduced by the Kennedys, it could not last forever. Denial eventually turned to understanding, and an acceptance of their mistakes. In the July 1989 issue of the *Ladies Home Journal*, the Kopechnes broke years of silence to rake Kennedy over the coals. Joseph said, "He was worried about himself, not about Mary Jo." The only good thing that had come out of the tragedy is that at least it had kept the senator from becoming president. Gwen said, "I don't believe *anything* I've heard so far. I don't think he seemed upset either time we saw him, and I don't remember him saying he was sorry." The Kopechnes also had harsh words for the Boiler Room Girls, telling the *Journal* that they were angry at every one of them. "They should try to explain," Gwen insisted. "Somebody is hiding something. I think all of them were shut up. I think there was a big cover-up and that everybody was paid off. The hearing, the inquest – it was all a farce. The Kennedys had the upper hand and it's been that way ever since."

It did not take Kennedy long to respond. "I have told everything I know about the accident," explained Ted. "I only wish it were in my power to do something more to ease the continuing pain that I feel and that Mr. and Mrs. Kopechne feel for Mary Jo's loss."

By the following November, the Kopechnes had concluded that the accident was staged. Kappel's theory had convinced them like nothing else ever had. In a bombshell statement read to reporters at the National Press Club in Washington on November 2, the Kopechnes wrote, "We believe that Mr. Kappel's book does present new evidence, and it is worthy of serious attention." The story was picked up by the AP wire service and made headlines in multiple outlets the next day.[1] On November 4, Kennedy spokesperson Paul Donovan fired back a terse comment: "The story is preposterous and absurd. We're not going to comment any further." In a personal letter to Kappel, the Kopechnes characterized Donovan's response as "cavalier" and "a personal insult."

The change in perspective, the bitterness, and the hurt took their toll. Leland writes that Joseph Kopechne soon "grieved himself right into cancer." Coughing up blood, Joe said, with some understatement, "Our girl didn't have to die. They are very bad people. They never told us the truth and they wouldn't let us talk with anyone who could provide accurate information. They manipulated us."[2]

---

[1] See, for instance, the *Sitka Sentinel,* the *Orlando Sentinel, etc.*
[2] *Left to Die*, p. 27

34
Joseph Gargan Jr.

*T*he brilliantly written book, *Senatorial Privilege: The Chappaquiddick Cover-up*, owes much of its success to Joe Gargan – lawyer, Kennedy aide, and first cousin to Ted Kennedy. Gargan chose to break his 14-year silence with exclusive interviews to Leo Damore in 1983, leading to Damore's book becoming a number one bestseller in 1988 and 1989. Damore writes, "This book would not have been possible without the wise counsel of Joseph Gargan Jr."[1]

Many of the facts, and much if not most of the dialogue put into the mouths of the participants in that book, come from Joe Gargan. Damore appears to have accepted most of it. But the evidence suggests that Gargan's claim to have had a falling out with Kennedy was somewhat less than the truth. A careful reading of *Senatorial Privilege* shows that Gargan supported Kennedy's version of the events on virtually every one of the important matters, and conceded that Kennedy might have dissembled on the very few that didn't matter or were obvious anyway.

Gargan affirms that he and Markham tried to rescue Mary Joe after the accident, diving repeatedly in deep water that would not even have been much over their heads at 12:45 a.m. He affirms that Kennedy swam from Chappaquiddick to Edgartown and that he watched him go. He affirms Kennedy's timeline to the minute, from beginning to end. He denies that Look could have seen the Oldsmobile drive down to Dike Bridge and he says there were no rowboats to take Kennedy across to Edgartown. He says, and Kennedy confirmed, that he managed to get all the way into the Oldsmobile, cutting his arms badly, but somehow never managed to touch the body of Mary Jo or convince the witnesses who saw him later that those wounds actually existed. He is portrayed as a hero and leader, and Damore is comfortable reporting all of it with nary a whisper of doubt.

When discussing the testimony from several witnesses who saw no scrapes or wounds on Gargan's arms after the incident, Gargan told Damore that David Burke, Kennedy's administrative assistant, suggested that he have the "deep scratches on his chest and upper arms" photographed as evidence that he had really got into the car. But Gargan told Damore that he dismissed this out of hand because he was "just a witness to a certain aspect of the investigation" and that his injuries "had no bearing on the case at all." Damore relates this supposed conversation as proof that the wounds were in fact there.[2]

---

[1] *Senatorial Privilege*, p. xiv
[2] *Senatorial Privilege*, pp. 111-112

Damore is satisfied that Gargan told the whole truth and nothing but the truth at the inquest. "For all his outrageous garrulousness," Damore writes, "Gargan walked off the witness stand in triumph, neither having betrayed Ted Kennedy *nor having committed perjury*." Damore gives a similar thumbs up to Markham's testimony. At the inquest, Markham was asked, "The reason that you or Mr. Gargan did not seek assistance or notify the police was that you assumed that Mr. Kennedy was going to do so when he arrived in Edgartown after the swim?" Damore describes Markham's answer this way: " 'That is what he told us,' Markham said *truthfully*."[1]

Susan Tannenbaum, one of the Boiler Room Girls, is reported to have asked Joe Gargan, "Would you just do anything the senator asked you to do?" Damore claims that Gargan then "gave her the honest answer: 'If you mean the time of Chappaquiddick, no I would not. I didn't do it then, and I wouldn't do it now.' "[2]

Gargan gave her the honest answer...

After reading *Senatorial Privilege,* I wondered if Gargan might have agreed to talk to Damore on the condition that Damore would question none of what he heard, or at least not in the book. An acceptable price to pay, perhaps, for a potential bestseller. I wondered if Damore might have been more dubious of Gargan's testimony than he let on.

I put this question to Leslie Leland, foreman of the ill-fated grand jury, who had several intimate conversations with Leo Damore before Damore committed suicide in 1995. Leland told me that Damore's interviews had occurred after Gargan had spent years at Alcoholics Anonymous as a recovering alcoholic. Damore was completely convinced that Gargan was telling him the truth about everything because AA had stripped away all deceit and left him an honest man. Damore was impressed with Gargan's obvious sincerity and desire to "get the whole thing off his chest" after so many years of not speaking out and being a laughing stock to his own children. According to Damore, Gargan just wanted "the real story" of the accident to be told.[3]

Leland also found Gargan very convincing. Long after the incident, Leland telephoned Gargan to hear firsthand what happened that night. Leland was particularly doubtful of the claim that Kennedy had swum from Chappaquiddick to the Edgartown side.

In that call, Leland found Gargan very believable and chatty. Gargan confirmed everything that Damore had reported. Gargan had made determined efforts to rescue Mary Jo from the car. He had swum into the car and cut himself on the way out. He freely described the events that unfolded, from the minute Kennedy appeared at Lawrence Cottage to the time he drove Kennedy to the ferry landing. But just as

---

[1] *Senatorial Privilege*, p. 368
[2] *Senatorial Privilege*, p. 376
[3] *Senatorial Privilege*, p. 423

Gargan got to this point in the story, he said there was another phone call coming in and he had to hang up.

About a year and a half later, after the senator had been diagnosed with cancer, Leland decided to call Gargan again. He was unsatisfied that his question about the Edgartown Channel swim had never been answered. But this time it was as if Gargan was a different person – a "Dr. Jekyll and Mr. Hyde," as Leland put it. He raved at Leland, screaming, "Why can't you damn people just leave Chappaquiddick alone, for Christ's sake. Kennedy is sick and all you can think of doing is dredging up ancient history." Gargan carried on venting, screaming, and cussing for several minutes more, and then slammed down the phone.

What to believe? Was Gargan really telling the truth? There seems little doubt that Gargan could charm the socks off a nun if he had a mind to. Gargan appears to have had a good time at the inquest. He was verbose and witty, punctuating his testimony with unsolicited but amusing accounts of his culinary expertise at the cookout, even impressing District Attorney Dinis who confessed later that "he had been disarmed and amused in spite of himself and regaled his staff with Gargan's testimony."[1] *McCall's* had called Gargan's testimony "that one bit of unintentional comic relief" in their edition of August 1976.

In light of what Carol saw that night, and what Dr. Cross has concluded, could *Senatorial Privilege*, so utterly reliant on Gargan's testimony, still be considered the defining book about Chappaquiddick? The reader, as always, is the final judge. But we, as longtime Chappaquiddick insiders, would be inclined to be skeptical.

---

[1] *Senatorial Privilege*, p. 366

35

BBC Documentary *Chappaquiddick*

he British Broadcasting Corporation's documentary *Chappaquiddick,* released in 1994 at the 25th anniversary of the accident at Dike Bridge, was later marketed in the US as *A&E Investigative Reports Chappaquiddick* using an American commentator, Bill Kurtis. By consulting nationally recognized crash specialists, the BBC was the first to analyze the accident itself in any meaningful way. Although their timeline of events could best be described as shaky, they were responsible for one major and one minor scoop: they discovered that Kennedy aide Dun Gifford had been advised of the accident by at least 8:45 on the morning of July 19; and they were able to verify that Gargan and Markham were indeed wet when they confronted Kennedy on the Shiretown Inn porch at 8:00 a.m. earlier that morning, although, apparently unbeknownst to them, that fact had already been ferreted out by Robert Cutler in 1971.

After detailed analysis, crash specialists consulted by the BBC arrived at one clear certainty: Kennedy could not have been in the vehicle when it went over Dike Bridge. First, against all odds, he was able to get out of the car. Second, he had no obvious injuries, scrapes, or marks. Third, his demeanor was atypical of someone who had been in an accident of that kind. And it wasn't as if these observations and behaviors were borderline strange – they were so far off the chart that according to the experts, it could really lead to no other assumption at all.

So, having stated this as fact, there were only two reasonable conclusions the BBC could reach: Kennedy got out of the car and Mary Jo drove off the bridge alone; or Kennedy and his friends had staged the accident. And therein lies the problem because against all logic and in spite of much evidence to the contrary, the BBC chose to believe that Kennedy was an innocent victim of circumstance.

There were at least three damning facts that clearly pointed the other way, and the BBC was aware of each of them.

First, the two crushed doors. Crash analyst Bill Fischer said that when he first looked at the vertical dents in the doors, it appeared to him as if the vehicle had been in a previous accident with a solid object and "he couldn't figure out what was going on." But why not? Fischer was filmed using Cutler's accident diagram to help determine the speed of the vehicle as it approached and then left the bridge, and Cutler was the original inventor of the staged-accident theory. Wouldn't Fischer have had enough curiosity to glance through the book he was toting around all day and read what Cutler had to say about the accident? Granted, Cutler's final analysis was extreme, but his basic assumptions were sound. Cutler had argued, with lucid reasoning, that the two crushed doors, the mirror, the skid marks, and the blood evidence proved that the accident was staged.

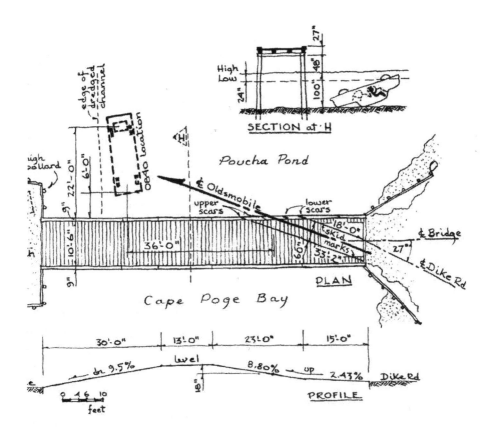

Cutler's accident diagram (*You, the Jury*, p. 374, Fig. 7). Fischer was filmed referring to this diagram as he made his bridge measurements in the BBC documentary. Cutler wrote that his diagram was created from information provided by "Jones, Sullivan, George Kennedy, and John Farrar." As Dr. Cross has pointed out, the skid marks, based on Arena's exhumation accident drawing, are wrong. The final position of the car is not accurate, either.

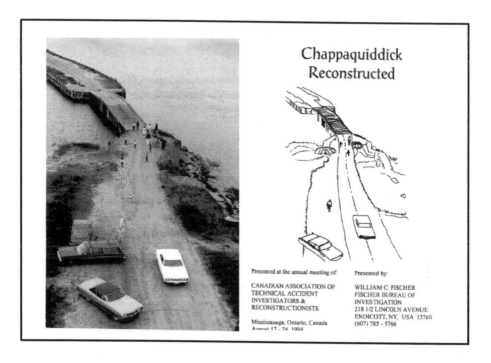

Chappaquiddick
Reconstructed

Presented at the annual meeting of: Presented by:

CANADIAN ASSOCIATION OF   WILLIAM C. FISCHER
TECHNICAL ACCIDENT   FISCHER BUREAU OF
INVESTIGATORS &   INVESTIGATION
RECONSTRUCTIONISTS   218 1/2 LINCOLN AVENUE
                                       ENDICOTT, NY, USA 13760
Mississauga, Ontario, Canada   (607) 785 - 5766
August 17 - 24 1994

This aerial of Dike Bridge, shot by Fred Ward on July 19 or 20, appears in *Chappaquiddick Revealed*. Kappel, the author, argued that the accident was staged. Bill Fischer, who analyzed the accident for the BBC, copied the photo as a sketch for the front cover of a report he presented to accident investigators in 1994.

Notice the size of the left pile of dirt at the front of the bridge compared to the right one. In Arena's accident diagram (Chapter 20, Fig. 6(a)), the left pile of dirt is reduced to a size much smaller the right pile of dirt and shifted 15 feet to the left so as to be out of the way of the assumed, but incorrect, skid tracks up the bridge. A 15-foot shift to the left would place the dirt in Dike Channel.

Not just this, but Fischer included a sketch traced from an aerial photo of Dike Bridge in his report to accident specialists in Canada – a photo that had appeared in just one book: *Chappaquiddick Revealed: What Really Happened*. Kappel, the author of that book, had argued that much of the damage could only have occurred from an accident on land, and his theories had even been backed up by an accident specialist. Yet Fischer came to the conclusion that the Oldsmobile must have landed dead flat on its side, ignoring the crushed windshield, the deeply dented roof, and the absence of injuries to Mary Jo or damage to her clothing which would appear to rule out such a landing.

Fischer even admitted that the passenger-side damage and the deeply dented roof were incompatible with a single crash event and "a rational explanation has to be found." Not finding any, why wouldn't Fischer have at least raised the possibility that the accident might have been engineered? Why the stubborn refusal to even mention it?

Second, crash analyst Robert Dubois said that the absence of dicing marks to Mary Jo's skin or clothing was "simply amazing" and "did not make any sense" to him at all. He concluded that she "must have been somewhere else." Questioned by the BBC about Flynn's theory, Dubois said that if Mary Jo was the driver, it was *conceivable* that she might have been able to survive the plunge with no injuries. But conceivable suggests that Mary Jo, like Kennedy, was never in the vehicle, either. So why wouldn't Dubois even consider that possibility?

Third, the BBC correctly identified Kennedy's admission that he was the driver of the Oldsmobile and responsible for Mary Jo's death as the greatest objection to their theory. But instead of considering the possibility that their premise might be flawed, they proceeded to paper over Kennedy's confession with contorted and fallacious reasoning. But why not at least voice the obvious alternative: that Kennedy *was* driving the car at the time of the accident and *was* responsible for Mary Jo's death, just as he had always maintained, but the real accident had occurred before Look saw the Oldsmobile around 12:40 a.m.? Kappel, who had arrived at that very conclusion, had published his theory just five years before and Cutler, who had argued that the accident was staged, 21 years before. Was the BBC so ill prepared that not one of their analysts had ever bothered to read the existing literature, even superficially? Or was it something else altogether?

When an investigative reporter arrives in unfamiliar territory there are two things she does immediately: visit the local press to get the lay of the land and perhaps a promising lead or two; and interview the locals. While the BBC may have done the former, they certainly never bothered with the latter. If they had, they might have learned something from the families who were on Chappaquiddick that weekend: Self, Jeffers, Silva, Potter, Bettencourt, and many others. At some point, they would have run across some cousins: Gostenhofer, Knight, Pinney, and more. Although I was not on the island in July, my sister was. If a cousin had been interviewed, it would have circulated quickly around to the rest of the family. Someone would have suggested, "Hey, why don't you talk to Carol Jones? She saw something interesting that night."

So why did this never happen? And there is something else which seems peculiar, too. The witnesses given the most time to put forth their opinions were Kennedy insiders or admirers: Walter Steele, Dun Gifford, Rosemary Keough, Jim Arena, Bernie Flynn. Police Detective Bernie Flynn, who had betrayed the public trust by revealing the details of the prosecution's inquest case to the Kennedys, was nevertheless given top billing in *Chappaquiddick.* His theory that Mary Jo had driven the Oldsmobile off the bridge alone while Kennedy was hiding from Huck Look in the bushes at the side of Dike Road was accepted as the best hypothesis to explain the evidence. Flynn comes across as a wise old sage in the film and his appalling conduct as a Kennedy spy is never brought up. It could very well be argued (and will) that Flynn was fed his theory by the Kennedys themselves, which should have made it suspect from the outset, but wasn't.

Even a superficial reading of the inquest testimony should have made it very clear to the BBC that Flynn's treachery was of great importance to Kennedy. Without a heads up from Flynn, Kennedy and his associates might very well have been trapped in numerous lies. For instance, after much legwork, State Police Detective Killen discovered the store in Boston where Crimmins had purchased liquor for the party. The prosecution had a copy of the store invoice with all the details. Hoping to trap Crimmins in a lie, the prosecution asked him if he had purchased a quart or pint of vodka. Crimmins promptly said no, it was three half gallons. When asked if he had purchased it locally on the Vineyard, Crimmins said no, he had purchased it in Boston. These timely preemptions and blithe explanations for suspicious activity occur so frequently in the testimony they are impossible to overlook.

Conspicuously absent in the film were Kennedy skeptics Huck Look and Leslie Leland. John Farrar appears as a minor bit player. Leo Damore, author of *Senatorial Privilege: The Chappaquiddick Cover-up,* managed to get in several sly, sarcastic comments regarding Kennedy's story in the few minutes he was allowed to talk; however, the points Damore did bring up could be explained away if Kennedy never knew about the accident until after 8:00 the next morning. Persuasive objections to Flynn's theory, which Damore had raised in his book, were never presented. Neither Rosemary Keough nor Sylvia Malm was asked to explain the timeline inconsistencies in their inquest testimony, even though these had been abundantly documented by numerous authors.

Toward the very end of the film, the BBC was able to come up with just one possible reason their theory might not be correct. "Critics of the 'Kennedy was not-in-the-car' theory," said Bill Kurtis, *A&E*'s commentator in the US edition, "have pointed to the fact that the senator was examined by his 'personal physician' the following afternoon and found to be suffering from a 'severe concussion.' " Since Dr. Watt, Kennedy's personal physician, never said Kennedy suffered a *severe* concussion, at the inquest or elsewhere (he had actually called it a *slight* concussion before July 22),[1] and in fact later changed his diagnosis to a *possible* concussion, and the words *personal physician* were uttered by Kurtis with a subtle smirk, it certainly did not give the viewer an impression that there could be any serious objection to their theory.

---

[1] See the *Vineyard Gazette*, July 22, 1969

Furthermore, only one book, *Chappaquiddick: The Real Story*, has ever said that Watt's diagnosis was evidence against the "not-in-the-car" theory, principally because few have ever really believed that diagnosis and Watt himself backtracked on most of it after being heavily criticized by reporters and peers.[1] There are far more powerful arguments against the BBC's theory which will be discussed in a later chapter.

The *A&E* version of the film concludes with the following observation by Kurtis, uttered in a solemn tone and, to my ear, with sincere regret: "Events since Chappaquiddick have proven one thing: when Mary Jo Kopechne drowned early one morning in 1969, so did any ambitions and dreams of Edward Moore Kennedy that he one day would be President of the United States."

Crucial evidence was overlooked or explained away by the BBC and normal investigative procedures were ignored. Witnesses allowed the most time to voice their opinions were overwhelmingly on the side of Kennedy. Arguments against Flynn's theory and alternative explanations for some of the more puzzling aspects of the accident are nowhere to be found. Kennedy aides Dun Gifford and Rosemary Keough, who had refused to give interviews to the press before (or since), had no problem talking to the BBC.

So it makes you wonder, was the real intent of this film to provide a whitewash for the senator? Could the crash specialists consulted by the BBC have had suspicions that were never aired? Because between the two possible conclusions the BBC could have reached – Ted Kennedy had no hand in Mary Jo's death; Kennedy staged the accident – there could be little doubt which version Kennedy would have preferred.

---

[1] See *Senatorial Privilege*, p. 49

36
Look & Carol

*I*n 1998, Carol, in company with David Maddox, told Huck Look what she had seen because word had gotten around that Look was writing a book about the incident. Chris Look, Huck's son, confirmed to me that he was. But Look merely listened to Carol's story without saying much, then thanked her for her time, excused himself, and left.

Considering that Look knew Carol by sight and was a friend of Carol's father, this does not make sense. Even if Look was skeptical of Carol's story – even if only to be polite – a friend of the family would be expected to ask a few questions and float a few possibilities. To Carol, the meeting was very strange. Look should have been interested, but wasn't. He should have treated Carol's observation with respect, but didn't.

Or did he? Look was an investigator. He had lived with the evidence for most of his career. He had just retired and *he was writing a book*. Authors hoping to solve a mystery seldom dismiss anything, no matter how far-fetched. They listen, and they consider. This would be especially so in 1998. Carol was the first new witness who had come forward in 30 years.

Chappaquiddick was a defining moment for Look. It had caused him much grief, but it had also made him famous. Over the years, Look must have worried the mystery of Chappaquiddick around in his mind like a tongue explores a chipped tooth. It would never be far from his thoughts. Carol's observation, coupled with his own, should have been a Eureka moment. The dominoes should have fallen into place, one by one, just as they had to me. Listening to Carol, Look should have realized immediately, if he hadn't already, that the accident was staged.

Shortly after Carol's meeting, Look abandoned his book. That's strange enough, but what is even stranger is that on his death in 2011, Look willed his papers and his conclusions about the incident to the succeeding sheriff – a law officer – rather than to the press or his son.

Why would Look do this? After listening to Carol and figuring it out, could Look have gone to the Kennedys and worked out a deal, maybe something that included an end to continuous harassment? Could his papers have been passed on to Mike McCormack because both parties agreed that nothing would ever be revealed, at least not while any of the principals were still alive? Could this also have been the reason Huck's book never got off the ground?

Far-fetched? Perhaps. Maybe Look's papers concerned anecdotes from his time as Sheriff. Maybe they were a collection of cooking recipes. Maybe there aren't any papers at all. But remember, Kappel had discussed his staged-accident theory with Look in 1988, 10 years before Carol had approached him. According to Kappel, Look did not discount that possibility; on the contrary, he was intrigued by it, and especially interested in the photos of the two crushed, passenger-side doors. Look had already told the press and others that he thought he had seen two women in the car, and he knew with absolute certainty, more than anyone else ever could, that Kennedy's claim of plunging over the bridge soon after 11:15 p.m. was a lie.

Look was a very smart man. I wonder, has this book already been written? Are we destined to see it again in a few years, after everyone involved has passed on?

37

John N. Farrar

*J*ohn Farrar attended Brown University and has been characterized by everyone who knew him as "very bright." Farrar was manager of the Turf 'n' Tackle shop in Edgartown and Captain of the Edgartown Fire Department SCUBA Search and Rescue Division when called to the bridge on the morning of July 19. He was 33 years old and had been diving since he was 15. In a radio interview in 1994, John Farrar explained that he left Martha's Vineyard because it was "all downhill" after Kennedy's accident. "Not that I blame Kennedy," Farrar assured his listeners, "but that's just what happens when he touches an area." Today, Farrar makes his home in Brooklin, Maine, a scenic village on a peninsula just to the north of Deer Isle.

I had several cordial talks with Farrar in the early days of researching material for this book. I welcomed his intelligent comments and insights. It made me think, and it helped me anticipate possible objections to the theories I was beginning to develop. Farrar became my devil's advocate. He made me dig deeper, and of course he was able to provide me with valuable insights into the conditions on the bottom of Dike Channel, skid marks, damage to the Oldsmobile, and much other minutiae that I could not find elsewhere.

In our very first conversation, almost before I had properly introduced myself, Farrar told me, "Whatever you've come up with, you have to account for the fact that Mary Jo suffocated. She did not drown." I received the message loud and clear. If I wanted John's help, or his support, I had better be on the same page. But because it did appear to me that Mary Jo did, in fact, suffocate, I let the comment slide. The air-bubble theory appeared sound. The body floated. There was very little water in the lungs. She was found upright, gripping the bottom of the rear seat. Farrar told me her fingernails were torn away. It all seemed reasonable.

But the more the evidence appeared to support the premise that the accident was staged, the more I talked to doctors, the more I poured over testimony from crash specialists, the more I began to question Farrar about the validity of his air-bubble theory. As the direction I was going with my reasoning became obvious, and my questions more pointed, our conversations quickly degenerated into shouting matches and became counterproductive. With some embarrassment, we decided to end them.

John has lived with his bubble theory for nearly half a century. He is a central figure in the story, and in the Kennedy mystique. He has given countless interviews, and his analysis appears never to have wavered once from that first interview in 1969 to his last. The BBC interviewed John Farrar in their 1994 documentary and John helped crash analyst Bill Fischer with his bridge measurements. When discussing Farrar's conviction that Mary Jo lived for an hour or more inside a bubble of air within the vehicle, BBC investigators, who had rejected it, said wryly, "Over time, opinions have become deeply entrenched."

Damore writes, "A summer kid who'd moved to Edgartown in 1965, Farrar had held press conferences at the Turf 'n' Tackle to explain his theories about the accident. No matter how expert his testimony was, Farrar had, by pontificating to such length about the accident, literally talked himself out of any credibility as a witness." Damore quoted Edgartown attorney Dick McCarron as saying, "John was a little screwy on the subject of the accident."[1]

Farrar told me the accident specialists consulted by the BBC got it all wrong. Mary Jo did climb into the rear seat area unaided and she lived for a significant time breathing air trapped in the footwell. Farrar uses as proof the testimony of Dr. Werner Spitz at the exhumation hearing: "So she breathed, that girl, she breathed. You're not going to find a cause for instantaneous death whether you exhume her or you don't." And, indeed, that is how Rust, Willis, and Damore report the quote.[2] What these three failed to include is Spitz's last sentence: *"So she inhaled water."*

Damore says that Spitz's testimony "had medically corroborated John Farrar's long-held opinion – heretofore excluded from testimony – that Mary Jo Kopechne had lived for a time in the submerged car, an admission that, because it came from a 'defense' witness, was especially damaging."[3] However, when viewed in context with the rest of Spitz's testimony – which is detailed and unambiguous – Damore's analysis is clearly wrong.[4] The confusion comes from Spitz's unfortunate choice of the word *breath* rather than the more precise word *inhale.* Spitz was not saying the pink foam exuding from her nose proved that Mary Jo breathed air within the Oldsmobile, which is what Farrar has always maintained. Spitz was telling the court that the evidence of pink foam suggested Mary Jo drowned by breathing seawater, and that this would mean that she could not have been killed instantaneously when the vehicle impacted the water.

---

[1] *Senatorial Privilege*, p. 317

[2] *Teddy Bare*, p.124; *Chappaquiddick Decision*, p. 150; *Senatorial Privilege*, pp. 331-332.

[3] *Senatorial Privilege*, p. 332

[4] It is unclear whether Damore's misinterpretation of Spitz's testimony was deliberate or inadvertent. As has been pointed out several times in this book, Damore was not above embellishing exhumation and inquest dialogue if it suited him.

John Farrar in 1969. Photo Jack Hubbard

As *Web*MD explains it, "The foam is a mixture of water, air, mucus, and surfactant whipped up by respiratory efforts. Thus, it is a vital phenomenon and indicates that *the victim was alive at the time of submersion.*" After observing that pink foam, Mills said, "Whatever had happened in that car, the girl had not been dead when she reached the bottom of Poucha Pond. *She had stayed alive long enough to inhale water and die by drowning.*"[1]

Nevertheless, although Farrar has always maintained to reporters and in interviews that Mary Jo suffocated within the Oldsmobile over a substantial period of time, he brought little of this to the attention of Judge Boyle at the inquest hearing. Sherrill,

---

[1] *The Bridge at Chappaquiddick*, p. 144

who found Farrar's conclusions credible, writes, "Diver Farrar, who seemingly never ceased telling his story about how Miss Kopechne probably stayed alive for hours in an air bubble and very likely could have been saved if he had been called promptly – he had given his report numerous times to reporters – was called to testify at the inquest. But neither Dinis nor Judge Boyle asked him a question even obliquely addressed to the air-bubble theory; the standard Farrar story is missing, every word of it, from the inquest record."

Sherrill cites speculation that Farrar had worked out a deal to keep quiet at the inquest about his theory. "The deal, some believed, was that if Boyle and Dinis wouldn't ask Farrar about his theory, Kennedy's attorneys wouldn't try to force the introduction of an Arthur D. Little Company study that was said to propound the theory that the air would have been forced from the car within a few minutes under the conditions existing at the accident." Sherrill writes that Farrar's failure to bring the air-bubble theory to the attention of the court after espousing it for almost six months at every interview, then declaring to reporters afterwards that we had the opportunity to give everything we had to offer, suggests that the rumors might very well have been true.[1] According to the *Boston Herald Traveler* in their edition of January 5, 1970, Farrar told reporters covering the inquest that Judge Boyle had been "very fair and very thorough. He allowed me to say everything I had to say while answering dozens of questions."

The Arthur D. Little study was cited by the *Boston Herald Traveler* in their edition of September 6, 1969, four months before the inquest and after Dr. McHugh of the Boston police lab had examined the vehicle. "Meanwhile, experts of the Arthur D. Little Company, Inc., a Cambridge research and consulting firm engaged by attorneys for Kennedy and the others, were continuing their evaluation of tests made on the car. The tests include filling the car with water and hoisting it to the upside-down position it was in when it held the victim's body [and] determination of how quickly water replaced air in the car." The study found that the water rushed into the car so quickly that Mary Jo could have remained conscious for no more than "one to four minutes."[2]

Damore, on the other hand, suggests that Farrar was prohibited from expressing his opinions to the court by Fernandes, who instructed Farrar to describe "exactly what you saw" and "not speculate on whether professional rescue efforts, if promptly made at the time of the accident, would have saved Mary Jo's life, or to deliver himself of the opinion, 'She suffocated in her own air void – she didn't drown.' "[3] However, Damore was inventing dialogue to support a premise. The only words from Fernandes at the inquest were, "Well, so we understand each other, you don't know what was done. I want you to describe just exactly what you saw."

---

[1] *The Last Kennedy*, pp. 150-151
[2] *Chappaquiddick Decision*, p. 128
[3] *Senatorial Privilege*, p. 382.

Fernandes was prosecuting Kennedy and on Farrar's side. Before the inquest, Fernandes and Detective Killen had interviewed Farrar. According to Damore, after listening to his theories, both men had concluded, "He's going to make one helluva witness."[1] At the conclusion of Farrar's testimony, Fernandes asked, "Did you make any other observations at the scene, Mr. Farrar?" Farrar replied, "With regard to what, Mr. Fernandes?" "The automobile or the body that you have not yet told us?" "Physical observations?" asked Farrar? "Yes, sir." This is when Farrar might have told the court about his air-bubble theory, how long he believed it took Mary Jo to die, whether she might have died by suffocation rather than by drowning, and whether she might have been saved had Kennedy made an emergency call – all the details he had related to Fernandes and Killen earlier. However, Farrar chose to mention that he saw Dr. Mills examining the body. He was then excused.

According to Farrar, his failure to present his theories at the inquest had nothing to do with Fernandes or any deal with Kennedy's attorneys. Farrar explained to Cutler in 1971, "The stenographer's tape was torn up when Boyle ordered most of the testimony about bubbles bursting around the car stricken from the record. [Jon] Ahlbum, who was to testify particularly about trapped air, dry trunk, and bubbles, was not called as an inquest witness."[2] Later in 2016, Farrar told Nelson he "felt intimidated" and "was sworn to secrecy as to what had happened." Unsure of what right he had to challenge Judge Boyle, "he just decided to put a good face on the situation."[3] However, Farrar's account of air bubbles emanating from the vehicle as it was towed toward the shore *is* included in the inquest testimony. And even if Boyle did strike out some of Farrar's testimony, swear him to secrecy, or intimidate him, while that might explain why his theories do not appear in the inquest record, it would not explain why they are absent in his exhumation testimony, too.

Could Farrar have been aware all along that his bubble theory was untenable but have continued to affirm it anyway? Even though he had characterized the conclusions of the Arthur D. Little study as "worse than useless" in 1969,[4] surely Farrar would have been aware of Fischer's dismissal of the air-bubble theory in the BBC documentary of 1994 because Farrar had appeared in that film and had helped Fischer with his bridge measurements. Why would Farrar continue to insist that a bubble of air could have kept Mary Jo alive for hours when Fischer had pointed out, with irrefutable logic, that the gaps between the passenger-side doors and frame, one extending from the window all the way down to the rocker panel, would have made that impossible? The laws of physics are what they are, and all the wishful thinking in the world will not

---

[1] *Senatorial Privilege*, p. 326

[2] *You, the Jury*, p. 388. See also *Teddy Bare*, p. 155; *Death at Chappaquiddick*, p. 216

[3] *Chappaquiddick Tragedy*, p. 146

[4] *Senatorial Privilege*, p. 316

prevent air from escaping a submerged, overturned vehicle with substantial cracks running up its side.

In truth, the air-bubble theory will not go down easily without a fight, and perhaps never will. It has been accepted as fact, or at least found credible, by every author who has written about the subject, including Kennedy's own biographer, Burton Hersh. It has purportedly been accepted as fact by the new film about the incident, scheduled to appear in early 2018. And this all appears due to the dogged insistence of John Farrar who is married to the theory like a limpet to a rock.

Kappel, for instance, writes, "She was not dead before the car entered the water. Proof of that is the macabre, rigor-mortised condition (clawed hands, tightly gripping the edge of the back seat which aided her in holding her head up to the now upside-down footwell of the auto) of her arms, and the fact that her body was found in the uppermost portion of the upside-down automobile. She did live for a time in that car and then succumbed to asphyxiation by breathing her own expelled carbon dioxide after her air pocket ran out of oxygen. Consequently, her body did not fill up with water as in a normal drowning. It is a well-known fact that bodies that drown sink for 72 to 100 hours before becoming buoyant. Mary Jo's body did not sink to the bottom of the car. *Mary Jo did not drown!* [emphasis in the original]"[1]

The Tedrows, after listing all of Farrar's arguments, affirm this:

"The authors believe it is *clear* that Mary Jo consciously took the position in the uppermost portion of the car to take advantage of the air trapped in that 'top' portion, that she positioned herself and propped her arms and legs and gripped her hands in an effort to hold herself there. She remained in this position for a substantial period of time, perhaps for as long as three or four hours according to medical testimony.[2] She died in this position after exhausting the oxygen in the trapped air pocket. Rigor mortis set in while the body remained in the tense position taken before death. The bent, still body with gritted teeth and clawed hands was found in that position and remained so bent when taken to the surface and examined by Dr. Mills."[3]

I do not believe it is all that *clear* that Mary Jo survived for a substantial period of time within the Oldsmobile. That said, I would love to endorse Farrar's air-bubble theory anyhow. No one wants to be make waves, and it would not materially affect the staged-accident theory at all. For many, it would undoubtedly make this a more titillating story. But if the evidence does not support it, how in the world can we not point that out?

---

[1] *Chappaquiddick Revealed*, pp. 200-201

[2] There is no medical testimony suggesting that Mary Jo remained alive for three or four hours. Mills put the time of death at "six hours *or more*" when he examined the body at 9:30 a.m., or no later than 3:30 a.m. If Kennedy drove off the bridge soon after 12:40 a.m., which the Tedrows believed, it would mean she could not have remained alive within the Oldsmobile for more than 2 hours 45 minutes.

[3] *Death at Chappaquiddick*, p. 218

Farrar believes Kennedy's story is mostly true, except for the timeline. Kennedy drove off the bridge with Mary Jo by accident after observing Huck Look. Kennedy managed to get out, but Mary Jo didn't. Or, perhaps Kennedy leaped out of the Oldsmobile before it went over. Kennedy's only real mistake that night was not running to Lawrence Cottage to get help. If he had, Mary Jo could have been saved because she lived for a good deal of time in the Oldsmobile. And her savior would have been him.

Farrar rejects the notion that it would be possible for a person to insert a body into the Oldsmobile under the known conditions at Dike Bridge that night and he rejects the possibility that it would be possible for a group of partygoers to rig a car to drive off a bridge. According to Farrar, the Valiant observed by Carol at 11:35 p.m. probably held a bunch of people from Lawrence Cottage having a good time in the early evening hours around Dike Bridge. No one at the party told the truth at the inquest, and therefore the testimony from Kennedy and the others that the accident had occurred soon after 11:15 p.m. can be ignored, as can the fact that no one ever admitted taking a joyride that night around 11:35 p.m. in the Valiant. Sure, Kennedy said he was diving in Dike Channel at 11:35 p.m., but that was just a coincidence. Kennedy lied about the time because he was worried about fallout if confessed to driving off the bridge after the ferry had shut down. Even if the vehicle was going very fast when it passed Carol on a blind curve, and even admitting this might have been an extraordinary event on Chappaquiddick in 1969, they were all drunk, so what can you expect? OK, maybe the testimony of the others at the party might make sense if the accident at the bridge was staged, and if several others had been involved, but because all these people lied and were drunk, what difference does it make what they said?

Farrar told me in our last conversation, "No one has *ever* dreamed up a story like yours. It is unbelievable. It will be laughed off, and you will be embarrassed. I sincerely doubt anyone will publish your book, or if they do, it will be because they have not done the proper research." Ouch.

I promised Farrar I would include his objections to the staged-accident theory. I have endeavored to do so throughout these pages. But I wonder, could Farrar's hostility toward the staged-accident theory have more to do with an invested interest than an objective analysis of the evidence? Irrespective of whether there was an air bubble in the vehicle or there wasn't, if the accident was engineered, Farrar would never have had the chance to save Mary Jo because no one would have had any intention of reporting the accident.

Farrar told me he believes the theory set forth in this book is built entirely on supposition, not on facts. However, the facts cited in this book have been submitted by experts in their fields, including Farrar, by investigative reporters, and by actual testimony from the inquest and elsewhere. We have taken care to reference quotes and sources so that these could be verified by others. We have been aware of the objections and alternative theories, and have stated them. We have validated theories by personally recreating the events insofar as possible, and I would venture to say, we are at least as familiar with Chappaquiddick and Edgartown as Farrar is.

Our theory was developed from the evidence and the science, not the other way around, and we are not the first to voice it. Most important, we have nothing invested in it. We are interested only at getting at the truth, and with that one guiding principle before us, we have gone where we believe the evidence has taken us.

John Farrar is one of only a very small handful of persons who had the courage to stand their ground against the Kennedy machine at a time when doing so could not be taken lightly. He has become one of my heroes. But there are at least eight theories and their variants concerning the Chappaquiddick incident, including the possibility that Kennedy told the truth. Any one of these could be true, and every one of them could be wrong. Except for those who were there, no one can say with certainty what *must* have happened that night, and equally, no one can make the absolute claim that they have got it right.

PART 6: THE REAL STORY

38
How it Might Have Occurred

I have presented the evidence and suggested some theories. Now it is time to put it all together.

*C*arol saw a white compact car drive down Dike Road at high speed at 11:35 p.m. on July 18, 1969, filled with people. On the surface, it seems like such a minor thing. Carol was not at the bridge that night. She overheard no conversations. She cannot identify Kennedy or, indeed, any of the principals involved in the incident. Carol saw so very little, but what little she did see turns out to be huge. It changes the traditional narrative and narrows the possibilities. Just as important, it may have caused Kennedy to fabricate a story quite different than the one originally intended, and it may have forced Gargan and Markham to acknowledge their participation.

It is important to point out here that neither Carol nor I have any agenda. We have attempted to arrive at an idea of what *may* have occurred by following the trail of evidence to see how it might fit with Carol's observation. This would seem self-evident except that so many authors have appeared to sift through the evidence with a biased sieve to find just those details that would support a favorite theory. Especially, this is true of the books with a political leaning which, unfortunately, account for many. We would like to make it clear, to those who do not know us, that both of us are liberal Democrats and neither of us is married to the theory set out here. If something else fits better, we'd be more than happy to abandon ours and go with another.

We realize there may be many who will find nothing extraordinary in Carol's observation. But Carol's testimony is unnecessary to uncover the mystery of Chappaquiddick. The answer has always been there right in front of us. It is found in the forensic evidence of the crash itself – evidence that should have been examined critically from the very beginning but never was, and never really has been until now. Carol's sighting can be thought of as a nudge: an invitation to look at the accident in a different way.

Neither Carol nor I can be given credit for the theory that the accident was engineered. Cutler argued that the accident was staged and detailed much of the evidence in *You, the Jury*. Kappel refined Cutler's premise in *Chappaquiddick Revealed: What Really Happened*. What we have provided is an eyewitness account which supports their central argument, and the scientific expertise to back it up. The rest is speculation that conforms to the evidence.

I also feel it is important to commend the work of Dr. John McHugh, Director of the Massachusetts State Police Crime Lab, and to State Police Detective-lieutenant George Killen. In fact, these should be added to the short list of heroes of this story. Neither allowed the Kennedys to intimidate them. They steadfastly did their job while others surrounding them did not.

Dr. McHugh examined Mary Jo's clothing and the Oldsmobile – virtually all he had after much of the evidence was withheld from him. Even so, the suspicious evidence McHugh was able to find: bloodstains on the back of Mary Jo's blouse; two doors from the Oldsmobile; a high level of carbon monoxide in Mary Jo's blood; was contemptuously explained away by Kennedy's attorneys or withheld from the inquest record altogether. Killen, reluctant to devote much time to the case in the beginning, was persuaded to become involved after hearing Kennedy's "foolish" TV talk to the public which "didn't explain a goddamned thing about the accident."[1]

Killen supported the exhumation for an autopsy and interviewed and brought in most of the witnesses to the inquest including Look, who he believed. Killen made sure a blood sample was taken from Mary Jo, discovered the store that had supplied the liquor for the party, determined how many Oldsmobile-like vehicles had license plates beginning with L7, and tracked down and eliminated numerous crack-pot leads. He strongly resisted burning Mary Jo's clothes until direct orders came from Joseph Flanagan, attorney for the Kopechnes.

In short, without the honesty and perseverance of these two men who must have had to contend with considerable opposition from the Kennedy machine, it is doubtful that much of anything could be inferred from the selected amnesia of the participants in this story. To his dying day, Damore says Killen was infuriated about the incident on Chappaquiddick. His inability to bring the case to a successful resolution was the greatest failure of a long and distinguished police career. Damore writes, "Two months before his death in 1979, as he was dying of cancer, Killen decried the injustice of Chappaquiddick; Senator Kennedy, he said, 'killed that girl the same as if he put a gun to her head and pulled the trigger.' "[2]

A harsh accusation, but perhaps not so far off the target.

---

[1] *Senatorial Privilege*, p. 211
[2] *Senatorial Privilege*, p. xiii

Aerial of Dike Bridge and Poucha Pond looking west a few days after the accident. Dyke House, which had a light burning on a front yard post all night, could be seen clearly from the bridge. Likewise, the bridge could be seen clearly from Sylvia's upstairs bedroom window (the uppermost window on the second story under the eaves of the roof). Notice the low bushes on both sides of the road east of Dyke House and the absence of any structure on the bridge that could have damaged the passenger side of the car. At least three small boats, where rope could be found, have been pulled up on the marsh to the south of the bridge. Photo Jack Hubbard

Narrative

Sometime before 11:15 on the evening of July 18, 1969, Kennedy left the party at Lawrence Cottage with Mary Jo Kopechne. Both knew what the deal was: Kennedy was bombed and a serial philanderer, Mary Jo had drunk far more than she was accustomed to, Kennedy was famous, rich, powerful, charming, and handsome, and Mary Jo was young, single, pretty, and blond. A potent cocktail as old as time. Mary Jo left her pocketbook and hotel room key at the cottage. East Beach, with its secluded dunes, was a well-known hangout for lovers in those days,[1] and both had visited the beach earlier that day and were aware of the possibilities. The accident occurred at the height of a new and intoxicating age of sexual freedom when AIDS was unknown and just about anything one could imagine was allowed.

Irrespective of her Catholic upbringing, investigators were able to find credible evidence that Mary Jo had recently begun to question her religious convictions and be far more daring and wild as she approached her 29th birthday, which was only eight days away for her on July 18. In her BBC interview in 1994, Keough said, "People have portrayed Mary Jo as a saint. She was not a saint. She was a red-blooded, normal girl. She wore short skirts like the rest of us." And as Keough had explained in 1969, "All us girls who attended are eligible young women. I think every eligible young woman in America would be thrilled at an invitation to attend that party and would accept in a hurry."[2]

Let's just face it and call a spade a spade: Mary Jo was just as willing as Kennedy was and neither was seriously considering driving to the ferry landing to take the boat back to Edgartown.

Following a tryst at East Beach, Kennedy tore back up Dike Road far too fast for the conditions, sliding and skidding this way and that, juiced up and having a wild time, until the heavy but powerful Oldsmobile took one slide too many. Somewhere between Dike Bridge and Chappaquiddick Road the car skidded off the trail and slammed into construction equipment, probably parked at Mytoi. It would be very difficult to identify an impact on heavy machinery, even if one were looking for it. But, of course, no one was looking for it because in 1969, no one ever imagined that an accident might have taken place before the Oldsmobile landed in the water.

The impact occurred on the passenger side. Seatbelts had not been installed in Kennedy's Oldsmobile[3] and Mary Jo was thrown against the door frame. She was instantly rendered unconscious, with blood pouring from a small cut at the back of her head, possibly caused by a shard of flying glass from the broken passenger-side window.

The Oldsmobile had come to a stop off the side of the road and it was impossible to free it. Perhaps it was stuck in the sand. After placing a bleeding Mary Jo in the back seat, Kennedy jogged back to Lawrence Cottage and asked LaRosa to fetch Gargan and

---

[1] In the summer of 1969, my grandfather was on East Beach with a couple of grandchildren when a reporter looked over and said to his colleague, "There's an old-timer. Maybe he's worth a quote." The reporter stuck a microphone in my grandfather's face and asked if he was familiar with Chappaquiddick. My grandfather replied, "Well, son, I've lived on Chappaquiddick since 1896." The reporter's face lighted up and he asked, "Well, is it true what they say, that Dike Road is known as a local lover's lane?" My grandfather replied, "My boy, in my day they were *all* lover's lanes."

[2] *The Ted Kennedy Episode*, p. 62

[3] *Chappaquiddick: The Real Story*, p. 26

Markham. Gargan, a man long accustomed to dealing with his younger cousin's rash actions, acted promptly. As he stated to Damore, he did not ask questions or waste a second. With Markham and Kennedy as passengers, Gargan "gunned the Valiant down Chappaquiddick Road to the intersection."

All three were lawyers, and lawyers think of the consequences. Their first thought was to pick up two in the party who were walking to the ferry: a man and a woman. If the accident was as bad as Kennedy claimed, it was important to keep everyone together. It would take just a minute or two because Gargan and Markham would know they had only recently left. The two others would have told someone they were leaving the party to return to Edgartown.

Somewhere between the Martin House and the ferry landing, the two others were found and told to get in. They wouldn't have had any say in the matter. The Oldsmobile was turned around and driven back to the intersection at over 45 mph. At 11:35 p.m. it came suddenly upon a slow-moving VW bus and rocketed past. As Markham testified at the inquest, "We went there at a rather high rate of speed, very high rate of speed."

Arriving at the scene of the accident, the five people, still giddy from their uninhibited consumption of alcohol, made the fateful determination that Mary Jo was dead. Perhaps the Oldsmobile was driven rapidly to the bridge parking lot to turn around. It might have been this car that was heard by Mrs. Malm and possibly "seen" by her daughter, Sylvia. By 11:55 p.m., both cars had made their return to Lawrence Cottage. Tretter testified that he remained outside the cottage (with the mosquitoes for company) after his first walk. He said Keough went in but just for a short while. Perhaps she went in for a bathroom break.

From 11:57 p.m. to 12:30 a.m., while Gargan and Markham chatted innocently to others inside the cottage, Kennedy sneaked into Mrs. Lawrence's private painting studio in the backyard, where the phone was located, and made three calls to associates. If Kennedy had made two calls to Helga Wagner earlier that day, he would have known exactly where that phone was located. A plan was devised: the Oldsmobile would be driven off the bridge, making it appear as if Mary Jo was driving the car on her own. Gargan told Damore that it was Kennedy's idea to make it appear as if Mary Jo had driven the vehicle off the bridge by herself, and perhaps it was. No one mentioned to the others at the party what had really taken place.

Meanwhile, the Oldsmobile was driven about 500 feet from the cottage and parked at the fire station with its parking lights glowing and motor running, with Mary Jo in the trunk. This might be the reason Mary Jo's blood had a carbon monoxide level of just under five percent. The driver was the same man picked up by Gargan and Markham earlier that evening on Chappaquiddick Road. The female passenger may have been that man's companion, or perhaps another Boiler Room Girl asked to accompany the other. One of these girls may have been sitting in the back seat.

The strategy called for Kennedy to claim he was never around to know the details. So at 12:30 a.m., Gargan, Markham, and Kennedy drove the Valiant to the ferry landing to arrange transportation. This may have been the American-type car seen traveling at an unusually high speed by Nancy McDonald and her boss from the lighthouse beach across the channel soon after 12:30 a.m. They might have borrowed Roddy Hoar's rowboat to find a small powerboat somewhere along the Edgartown waterfront. The rowboat was returned to a slightly different place and secured with a different knot, but the powerboat was tied to the Chappaquiddick Beach Club dock. There were no occupied houses there in 1969 and it would be a perfect place for a rendezvous.

While the others were busy at the ferry landing arranging boat transportation, the Oldsmobile was started up and driven toward the bridge, with Mary Jo lying unconscious in the trunk. Just before reaching the Dike Road intersection, the persons in the Oldsmobile saw the headlights of Huck Look's car approaching from the left. Not wanting to appear as if they were driving to the bridge, and unwilling to pass that car because their own could be recognized, they drove straight into Cemetery Road and attempted to hide. If there was a passenger in the rear seat, she might have laid down so she wouldn't be noticed. Perhaps, after noticing Look pass through the intersection, the driver of the Oldsmobile backed up and proceeded down Dike Road without ever realizing that Look had stopped his car. Or, maybe the driver observed Look's brake lights but never noticed him. Either way, the group was convinced that their own car had not been recognized.

When the Valiant returned from its mission at the ferry landing and joined the others at Dike Bridge, the persons in the party rolled up their sleeves and got to work. The Oldsmobile was parked near the foot of the bridge and the steering wheel was tied off to the driver-side mirror. A rock was placed on the accelerator pedal, increasing the revs to a high pitch. When all looked perfect, someone leaned in and gave a tug to the gearshift lever. The Oldsmobile took off, reached a speed of about 15 mph, rolled off the right side of the bridge, and landed on its roof on the bottom of the channel. The forward fastener on the driver-side mirror was sheared off at launch and the windshield and roof crushed on impact with the sand.

Someone then waded in to retrieve the rope wrapped around the steering wheel and dump the rock in the pond. At the inquest, Gargan gave an elaborate description of entering the Oldsmobile through one of the windows and "feeling around, feeling around, feeling around." If there had been a rock placed on the accelerator pedal, it would have dropped onto the overturned roof. Someone would have had to enter the Oldsmobile through a window and feel around in the darkness to find it.

Lawrence Cottage in 1969. Notice the detached painting studio in the backyard just visible at the far right. Santi Visalli, Getty Images

Mary Jo was placed in the water and someone attempted to scrub out the bloodstains on the back of her blouse. She was then inserted through a front window and her hands cupped around the steering wheel so as to make it appear as if she was the driver. This may have been why there were no marks, bruises, or fractures on Mary Jo's body. Mary Jo might have drowned as soon she was pushed underwater.

Why might Mary Jo have been inserted into the Oldsmobile after the vehicle was in the channel? Why not place her behind the steering wheel on land? Because the group could not be certain that the residents of Dyke House or the Smith cottage would not hear the noise of the Oldsmobile splashing into the pond. In fact, they might not even have been sure that the Oldsmobile would make it off the side of the bridge. If someone came out of their home to investigate the disturbance, or if a stray car had come down the road and noticed the activity, and if the police were summoned, they would find a corpse in the Oldsmobile with the steering wheel tied off to the outside mirror and a rock on the accelerator pedal. It was vital that those telltale items be removed before the last, final act could be carried out.

As soon as Mary Jo was placed in the Oldsmobile, the group beat a hasty retreat. Dike Road was a cul-de-sac. They would not have wanted to hang around the area even a fraction of a second more than they had to.

Kennedy was driven to the place where the powerboat had been hidden. This might account for the suspicious noise heard by Lansing Burns, an employee of the Chappaquiddick Beach Club, at 1:30 that morning. Kennedy was then transported by Markham and Gargan to Kennedy's racing boat, the *Victura*. It was almost certainly this boat and these three persons seen by Todd Ballou from his Concordia yawl in the Edgartown outer harbor shortly before 2:00 a.m. After making certain the coast was clear, the powerboat proceeded to the Edgartown dock adjacent to the small dinghy beach. In 1969, this would be the only landing near the Shiretown Inn where a person could be confident of stepping ashore unnoticed.

Kennedy then walked to the public parking lot across the street, hung around for a few minutes to make sure the coast was clear, and then dashed from there to the outside stairway leading up to his room. After washing up and changing his clothes, Kennedy walked down to the lobby at 2:25 a.m. to establish his alibi.

After returning the powerboat to the Chappaquiddick Beach Club dock, the four or five remaining persons drove wearily back to Lawrence Cottage. Witnesses testified that Gargan and Markham returned just after 2:00 a.m. Charles Tretter said he returned from his second walk with Rosemary Keough a minute or two later. Esther Newberg told the court that the first words out of Gargan's mouth were, "I am exhausted; if you knew what I had been through, you would let me lie there. Please let me lie there." All found it difficult to sleep. Gargan told Damore that sleep was impossible.[1] Markham testified at the inquest that he couldn't get to sleep and eventually spent most of the night in the Valiant. Rosemary Keough testified that she was awake "pretty much all night." Tretter testified that he "slept terribly. My knee bothered me."

Around 3:00 a.m., Gargan laid the framework for their story when he told Newberg and the Lyons sisters that Mary Jo had driven the Oldsmobile alone back to the Katama Shores Motel just before midnight. Sometime later, Kennedy had swum from Chappaquiddick to Edgartown because they could not find any boats to take him across.

Later that night, after 3:00 a.m., Gargan or Markham, or perhaps both together, came to the conclusion that their plan was untenable. A witness had seen the Valiant drive down Dike Road at high speed, filled with people. Their plan of claiming that Mary Jo, unbeknownst to anyone, drove off Dike Bridge alone just before midnight could not be sustained. In the full light of morning and completely sober, their work of the night before may not have looked quite so clever. In near panic, Gargan and Markham, and perhaps others, raced to the bridge in the early morning hours to dive on the car and retrieve the body of Mary Jo. If they could get her out and fly her off the island in a private plane, no one would ever know that she had died in that car. They would arrange an "accident" somewhere far removed from the senator.

---

[1] *Senatorial Privilege*, p. 86

Edgartown waterfront looking north in 2013. The small dinghy beach, with tracks for hauling boats, can be seen in the bottom left corner. Kennedy might have been transported to the dock adjacent to the dinghy beach (immediate foreground), since it was more private than the public dock at Memorial Wharf (upper right). For the same reason, the powerboat was also probably abandoned at this dock around 8:00 later that morning. In 1969, the Shiretown Inn was located almost directly behind the dinghy beach, only a block and a half away, with the public parking lot sandwiched in between.

But the ebb tide was boiling out of the pond and it couldn't be done in the time they had. They had no snorkels, masks, or flippers to help and the tide was much higher than before. The light was increasing. They were completely exposed. Mary Jo's body was frozen into a sitting position with arms extended out in front of her.

Their efforts were enough to move the body to the higher rear-seat area but were insufficient to extract the body from the vehicle. This might explain why Mary Jo was later found in a sitting position at the back of the car, with her arms extended forward and cupped hands touching the bottom of the rear seat.

Giving up, they rushed to Edgartown in their borrowed powerboat to explain to Kennedy that if Mary Jo's body was found, their carefully thought-out scheme would not work. They had to get Mary Jo's body out of that car and off the island at the first opportunity.

This is why Gargan dragged Kennedy into his room by the arm with such urgency and this is why Gargan and Markham were soaking wet when they met him. By Gargan's own admission, this, too, is when Gargan warned Kennedy, "There is no way you can say that Mary Jo drove off the bridge on her own! You can be placed at the scene!" Kennedy called one of his aides to ask that he phone Dun Gifford in Nantucket to take the short 10-minute flight to the Vineyard to be ready to fly the body off the Vineyard and perhaps to help in the recovery.[1] Maybe Gifford was also instructed to bring a tank of air and a regulator with him. Kennedy, Gargan, and Markham then ran to the ferry landing. In their panic they brushed right by the Richardses without acknowledging their presence, but were careful to act as if nothing at all was amiss on the ferry a minute or so later.

The change in plan might not have been to Kennedy's liking. Ross Richards testified that he heard loud arguments in Kennedy's room. Perhaps Kennedy was protesting that there was no need for panic. Everything was still OK. But if Gargan and Markham were not prepared to go through with their original plan, there would be nothing that Kennedy could do except eventually agree.

Calls were made continuously on Kennedy's credit card from the public phone at the Shiretown Inn, from just fourteen minutes after the arrival of Gargan and Markham to the moment the group rushed from the Shiretown Inn to the ferry. Kennedy, who had recently dressed, must have made those calls himself because Gargan and Markham would have had to shower at the Shiretown before traveling to the Chappaquiddick side. No one noticed that either Gargan or Markham were wet or unkempt after 9:15 a.m.

Kennedy testified that he crossed over to Chappaquiddick to make a call to his Washington lawyer, Burke Marshall, from the public phone booth at the ferry landing. But the ferry operators did not see him using the phone when the ferry was on the Chappaquiddick side, and no call was ever cited by the *New York Graphic* as having been made on Kennedy's credit card after 9:15 a.m. However, Laura Knight, a cousin, was in the ferry line that morning waiting to cross over to Edgartown. Laura told me she clearly saw Kennedy with the phone in his hand talking to someone. Kennedy may have traveled to Chappaquiddick to receive a call rather than make one himself, perhaps because Kennedy or the person called preferred to avoid adding to the paper trail of Shiretown calls.

---

[1] The BBC said Gifford may have been called from the Chappaquiddick landing, but the BBC had not done its homework. Gifford had already been advised of the accident by 8:45 a.m., a half hour *before* 9:15 a.m. when Kennedy, Gargan, and Markham took the ferry to Chappaquiddick.

Whatever they were doing on Chappaquiddick, within a short while, Tony Bettencourt informed Kennedy that his car had been found with a dead girl in it, and the game was up. Kennedy, who was responsible for the death of Mary Jo, would have to say that he was the driver of the Oldsmobile when it went off the bridge. Gargan and Markham were not asking. They were demanding, and they were scared. If it came out that they had staged an accident to cover up Kennedy's involvement in a fatality, it would be the ruin of their lives and careers.

Kennedy's lawyers must have had a hard time dealing with this tale because by the time the inquest took place five months later they already knew exactly what Look had witnessed, and who intended speaking up. But Kennedy and Markham had already composed an accident report stating that Kennedy had driven off the bridge soon after 11:15 p.m., and Kennedy had reiterated that time in his TV speech a week later. Look's sighting would have to be denied. There was no other choice, because if Kennedy claimed he drove off the bridge soon after 11:15 p.m. in the Oldsmobile, that Oldsmobile certainly could not be seen by Huck Look at 12:40 a.m. Deny something long enough and people might believe it. At least that's the theory.

The tire marks found on the bridge by Inspector George Kennedy were an unexpected bonus. All Ted Kennedy would have to do is claim he had braked at the last second before going over the bridge and those marks would be interpreted as braking marks. If they were braking marks, no one would ever suspect that the accident was staged. So at the inquest, that's exactly what Kennedy said, although he had never mentioned braking in his original police report or in his TV speech many months earlier.

Unfortunately, the marks would be interpreted by the registry of motor vehicles as indicating the vehicle was traveling at close to 40 mph before the brakes were applied. But you can't have everything. The higher speed was a small price to pay for the greater good. If Kennedy's lawyers had argued the point, the marks might have been seen for what they really were. And anyway, Boyle was there to obligingly delete the registry's speed estimate from the inquest record so it all worked out fine in the end.

The lawyers must have been very concerned about Carol's distinctive VW bus. The Kennedy team, so thorough in everything, must have been very aware of who it belonged to. But if nothing had been said in the first few days, it was a good bet that the witness would never speak up, or perhaps had never even been aware of the significance of her sighting. Kennedy's lawyers may have finally decided that Carol had never actually seen the vehicle continue down Dike Road. When the Valiant passed Carol near Liz Stephens's house it was still 350 feet away from the intersection and hidden from sight behind trees. On the other hand, they may have instructed Lula's cousin, or even Lula herself, to mention that Carol could be killed if she ever came forward. They might have had good reason to be confident that Carol would never say anything.

In any event, they could at least be certain that Carol's sighting would not become an issue at the inquest because they had an informer in the enemy camp. State Police Detective Bernie Flynn later confessed to leaking what was known by the police to the Kennedys on a periodic basis. Kennedy's lawyers knew every single detail, every crumb of evidence, and what every witness would say before they ever showed up in court. Flynn might not have been the only informer. It was a well-known fact in Edgartown that a pile of money was floating around soon after the incident, and mysteriously, some of the principals sympathetic to the Kennedy cause began making very large purchases soon after.[1]

---

[1] I personally know of two, but I won't say more.

39

Timeline

Kennedy's version

11:15 p.m.: Senator Kennedy and Mary Jo Kopechne leave the cottage for the ferry.

Shortly after 11:15 p.m.: Kennedy drives off Dike Bridge. Kennedy spends the next 15 to 20 minutes diving for Mary Jo; 15 to 20 minutes resting on shore; and 15 minutes walking back to the cottage: total 45 to 55 minutes.

12:15 a.m.: Kennedy arrives back at Lawrence Cottage. Advises Gargan and Markham that there has been a terrible accident.

12:20 a.m.: Kennedy, Gargan, and Markham arrive back at the bridge. Kennedy remembers the exact time because he looked at the clock in the Valiant (later determined to have no clock). Gargan and Markham spend 45 minutes diving for Mary Jo; 10 minutes driving to the ferry landing; a few minutes talking at the landing: total about 60 minutes.

About 1:40 a.m.: Kennedy dives impulsively into the water, begins swimming to Edgartown, and almost drowns. Climbs out on the beach at the Edgartown lighthouse due to the strong northerly set.

Before 2:00 a.m.: Kennedy arrives back at his room at the Shiretown Inn.

About 2:30 a.m.: Kennedy complains about noise and asks the time from the innkeeper at the Shiretown Inn.

Shortly after 8:00 a.m.: Kennedy walks downstairs to the Shiretown lobby, talks to the receptionist, and makes one call to Mr. Stephen Smith from the public phone outside the restaurant at the Shiretown Inn.

8:30 a.m.: Kennedy meets Gargan, Markham, and Tretter "just a few minutes after he met Mr. Moore, probably." Then takes the ferry to Chappaquiddick to call a dear friend Mr. Burke Marshall, but could not reach him. Testifies that these were the only calls he ever made.

Before 10:00 a.m.: After "fully realizing what happened," Kennedy immediately contacts the police.

Our version

Before 11:15 p.m.: Kennedy leaves Lawrence Cottage in his Delmont 88 with a willing Mary Jo for fun on the beach. Mary Jo loses her panties.

Shortly after 11:15 p.m. More than a bit drunk, Kennedy drives off the road and slides into heavy construction equipment, probably parked at Mytoi. The Oldsmobile sustains deep, vertical dents to both passenger doors and the windows are shattered. Mary Jo is knocked unconscious and suffers a small cut at the nape of her neck, possibly from a sliver of glass from the broken passenger-side window.

Around 11:30 p.m.: Kennedy jogs back to Lawrence Cottage leaving Mary Jo bleeding on the rear seat of the Oldsmobile. Finds LaRosa and asks him to fetch Gargan and Markham. Kennedy, Gargan, and Markham rush toward the ferry landing in the Valiant to pick up two of the partygoers – a man and a woman.

11:35 p.m.: Kennedy, Markham, Gargan, and an unidentified couple race by Carol Jones at high speed in the rented white Valiant from the direction of the ferry landing, then speed down Dike Road toward Dike Bridge.

11:55 p.m.: The two cars return to Lawrence Cottage with Mary Jo lying faceup in the trunk. Kennedy, Gargan, and Markham enter the cottage while the Oldsmobile is driven about 500 feet down the road and parked at the fire station with just its parking lights glowing and engine running. The vehicle's passengers include the two persons picked up earlier and perhaps another female guest from the party. Mary Jo breathes carbon monoxide from the car exhaust.

11:57-11:59 p.m.: While Gargan and Markham chat to others inside, Kennedy makes a two-minute call on his credit card to Theodore Sorensen at (212) 935-8790 from the private painting studio at Lawrence Cottage.

12:04-12:10 a.m.: Kennedy makes a six-minute call on his credit card to a Kennedy office facility in Hyannis Port at (617) 775-4732 from the painting studio at Lawrence Cottage.

12:12-12:30 a.m.: Kennedy makes a second call on his credit card lasting 18 minutes to the Kennedy office facility in Hyannis Port from the painting studio at Lawrence Cottage.

Around 12:30 a.m.: The Valiant is sighted driving unusually fast to the Chappaquiddick ferry landing. Gargan, Markham, and Kennedy arrange boat transportation.

12:40 a.m.: The Oldsmobile, with a man and woman passenger in the front seat and perhaps another woman hiding in the back, is spotted by Look driving toward Dike Bridge. The passengers in the Oldsmobile are unaware that their vehicle has been identified.

12:45 a.m.: Huck Look spots Ray LaRosa and the Lyons sisters near the fire station. Talks to Nance Lyons but is brushed off. LaRosa informs Look they are renting the cottage down the road.

12:45-1:30 a.m.: The Valiant joins the others at Dike Bridge. The Oldsmobile is rigged and driven off the bridge. Someone wades in to remove the rope securing the steering wheel and the weight used to hold down the accelerator. Someone attempts to wash the blood out of Mary Jo's blouse. Mary Jo is inserted upside down into the Oldsmobile through a front window and her hands are cupped around the steering wheel. Mary Jo drowns.

About 1:30 a.m.: The Valiant, with Kennedy as a passenger, is driven toward the ferry landing. Lansing Burns, an employee of the Chappaquiddick Beach Club, hears suspicious activity somewhere near where the public phones are located.

1:50 a.m.: Ballou sights boats exchanging passengers between Chappaquiddick and Edgartown. Kennedy is transported to the dinghy beach near Memorial Wharf in the borrowed powerboat. Gargan and Markham return to Chappaquiddick and tie the powerboat to the Chappaquiddick Beach Club dock.

2:00 a.m.: Kennedy sneaks from the dinghy beach to the nearby public parking lot, hangs around for a few minutes until the coast is clear, then dashes to his room at the Shiretown Inn via the outside staircase, bathes and changes clothes.

2:00 a.m. Gargan, Markham, and the two or three others return to Lawrence Cottage in the Valiant. The group settles down and attempts to sleep.

2:25 a.m.: After bathing and dressing in clean clothes, Kennedy asks the time from Russell Peachey at the Shiretown Inn to establish an alibi.

2:54 - 12:58 a.m.: Kennedy makes a four-minute call to the Washington D.C. headquarters of Marshall & Hamilton at (202) 233-9600 on his credit card from the public phone booth at the Shiretown Inn.

3:00 a.m. Newberg and the Lyons sisters are informed by Gargan that Mary Jo drove back to the Shiretown Inn by herself in the Oldsmobile just before midnight, but Kennedy decided to swim the channel. Sometime later, Gargan and Markham decide their plan is untenable.

5:04 - 5:07 a.m.: Kennedy makes a three-minute call to Marshall & Hamilton on his credit card from the public phone booth at the Shiretown Inn.

5:28 - 5:49 a.m.: Kennedy makes a 21-minute call to Theodore Sorensen at (212) 935-8790 on his credit card from the public phone booth at the Shiretown Inn.

5:54 - 6:21 a.m.: Kennedy makes a 27-minute call to Stephen Smith, Kennedy's brother-in-law, at (202) 393-3111 on his credit card from the public phone booth at the Shiretown Inn.

Early morning hours: Gargan, Markham, and Tretter, accompanied by Rosemary Keough and Susan Tannenbaum, race to the bridge at first light to dive on the car. They are able to maneuver the body into the higher rear-seat area but are unsuccessful at extracting the frozen body through the passenger-side window.

6:34 - 6:41 a.m.: Kennedy makes another seven-minute call to Theodore Sorensen on his credit card from the public phone booth at the Shiretown Inn.[1]

6:56 - 6:57 a.m.: Kennedy makes another one-minute call to Washington & Hamilton on his credit card from the public phone booth at the Shiretown Inn.

7:19 - 7:21 a.m.: Kennedy appears in the lobby of the Shiretown Inn and asks the day clerk, Mrs. Stewart, if he can borrow a dime to make a call, then makes a two-minute call to Washington & Hamilton from the public phone booth at the Shiretown Inn, charged to his credit card.[2]

7:30 a.m.: Kennedy meets Ross Richards and Stan Moore in an alley by the Shiretown Inn and innocuous conversation ensues on the Shiretown porch. The group is joined by Marilyn Richards at 7:50 a.m.

8:00 a.m. Joe Gargan, Paul Markham, Charles Tretter, Rosemary Keough, and Susan Tannenbaum drive their borrowed powerboat to the Edgartown side and abandon it at a dock less than 200 yards from the Shiretown Inn. Gargan and Markham, looking soaking wet and unkempt, confront Kennedy on the Shiretown Inn porch and drag him into his room. Kennedy is informed that he can be placed at the scene. Loud talking and arguments are heard. Tretter first showers at his room at the Shiretown Inn, then meets Kennedy in his room nearby. Keough and Tannenbaum shower and take a nap in Tretter's room.

8:14 - 8:56 a.m.: While Gargan and Markham shower at the Shiretown Inn, Kennedy makes a 42-minute phone call to Theodore Sorensen on his credit card from the Shiretown public phone booth.

---

[1] Published by the *New York Graphic* as a 7-minute call beginning at "6:04 a.m.", probably a typo; or, the earlier call to Stephen Smith lasted 7 minutes rather than "27" (a typo) and ended at 6:01 a.m.

[2] Olsen says the time of that call was 8:30 a.m. (*The Bridge at Chappaquiddick*, p. 119) and Lange and DeWitt say it was at 8:00 (*Chappaquiddick: The Real Story*, p. 39); however, Damore says Kennedy made the call just before his meeting with Ross Richards and Stan Moore at 7:30 a.m., a time confirmed by Mrs. Stewart, the Shiretown receptionist (*Senatorial Privilege: The Chappaquiddick Cover-up*, pp. 87-88). Several books have pointed out that there is no proof that Kennedy made these calls himself because anyone could charge a call to his credit card. However, as this call to Washington & Hamilton charged to Kennedy's credit card was definitely made by Kennedy himself at the public phone booth at the Shiretown Inn; and as another call had just been made to Washington & Hamilton on Kennedy's credit card in the early morning hours from the Shiretown Inn; it all-but-proves that all the calls made that night on Kennedy's credit card were made by Kennedy himself. Two other calls were made on Kennedy's credit card from Lawrence Cottage and three others from the Shiretown Inn but never detailed by the *Graphic*. These appear to have been made to Helga Wagner, Kennedy's mistress, who admitted to receiving "several calls" from Kennedy that weekend, at least one from the Shiretown Inn on the early morning of July 19.

9:01 - 9:12 a.m.: Kennedy makes an 11-minute phone call to Stephen Smith on his credit card from the public phone booth at the Shiretown Inn.

9:15 a.m.: Kennedy, Gargan, and Markham dash to the ferry landing just down the road. They cross to the Chappaquiddick side. Kennedy appears distraught when leaving the Shiretown Inn but jovial and unconcerned on the ferry.

9:20 - 9:40 a.m.: Kennedy, Markham, and Gargan mill around the public phone booth at the ferry building on the Chappaquiddick side. Kennedy is seen talking on the phone. They see the hearse on its way to Dike Bridge and hear from Tony Bettencourt and others that Kennedy's Oldsmobile and a body have been found.

9:40 a.m.: Kennedy and Markham board the ferry back to Edgartown. This time, Kennedy looks worried. Markham is seen berating Kennedy as the ferry makes its way to Edgartown. Gargan, meanwhile, rushes back to Lawrence Cottage to remove all evidence with the assistance of Ray LaRosa and the Boiler Room Girls who had remained there.

9:45 a.m.: Kennedy and Markham finally walk to the police station to report the accident.

11:00 a.m.: Gargan transports the remaining guests at Lawrence Cottage from Chappaquiddick to Edgartown. Esther Newberg and the Lyons sisters take a taxi back to the Katama Shores Motel while Ray LaRosa walks to his room at the Shiretown Inn. Gargan instructs Tretter to drive Rosemary Keough and Susan Tannenbaum back to their hotel in LaRosa's Mercury, then walks up the street to join Kennedy and Markham at the police station.

Later that morning: Gargan meets with Tretter at the Shiretown Inn to plan how to break the news of the accident and Kennedy's involvement to the others. LaRosa hears the news from Tretter at the Shiretown Inn.

Later that evening: Tretter rushes the five girls off Martha's Vineyard on the 6:00 p.m. ferry from Vineyard Haven to Woods Hole before they can be questioned.

Thereafter: One of the greatest cover-ups ever seen in this country ensues. This is a partial list of those who participated:

Robert M. McNamara, Secretary of Defense under John Kennedy
Theodore Sorensen, Special Assistant to President Kennedy
Richard Goodwin, lawyer and Special Assistant to President Kennedy
Burke Marshall, Kennedy's Washington attorney and US Attorney General under
        John Kennedy
John Culver, US congressman
Robert Clark, lawyer and district court judge
Robert Clark, III, lawyer
Dun Gifford, friend and aide

Herbert "Jack" Miller, Washington attorney and former head of the criminal division
    of the US Department of Justice under Robert Kennedy
Sargent Shriver, Kennedy's brother-in-law, presidential candidate in 1976
Frank O'Connor, Kennedy's assistant
Dan Daley, lawyer
Paul Redman, lawyer
Paul Markham, lawyer, former US Attorney for Massachusetts
Joseph Gargan, lawyer and Kennedy's first cousin
Milton Gwirtzman, lawyer
John Tunney, US congressman
David Burke, Kennedy's administrative assistant
Edward Hanify, lawyer and Director of the New England Telephone Company
Stephen Smith, Kennedy's brother-in-law
James Smith, Assistant District Attorney and former Kennedy campaign coordinator
Richard McCarron, lawyer
John Driscoll, lawyer
Kenneth O'Donnell, friend
Lamoyne Billings, friend and aide
David Hackett, friend and aide
Frank Mankiewiez, Press Secretary to Robert Kennedy

Help was sought from Senator Abraham Ribicoff, John Kenneth Galbraith, and Arthur Schlesinger. Cynics could add Edgartown Police Chief Dominick Arena, Dukes County Prosecutor Walter Steele, and judges Bernard Brominski, James Boyle, and Wilfred Paquet to the list.

As the Tedrows note, presidents have declared war with less advice and fewer advisers.

Ferry —— Chappaquiddick Road —— Dike Road —— Bridge

School House Road

Cottage

~10:00 p.m.	TK & MJ leave cottage for fun at East Beach. MJ loses her panties.
11:20 p.m.	Driving west on Dike Road, TK slams into construction equipment parked at Mytoi. **Collision**
11:25 p.m.	TK runs back to cottage leaving MJ lying face up and bleeding on rear seat
11:30 p.m.	Valiant heads toward ferry to pick up two guests
11:35 p.m.	Valiant speeds past Carol Jones with 5 passengers
11:35 p.m. to 11:55 p.m.	Oldsmobile extracted from collision site
11:55 p.m.	Both cars return to cottage with wounded MJ in trunk
11:57 p.m. to 12:30 a.m.	TK makes 3 calls from cottage. Valiant, Markham & Gargan at cottage. Oldsmobile parked on School House Road 500 feet from cottage with 2-3 guests and MJ in trunk
12:30 a.m.	Valiant to ferry to arrange transportation between Chappaquiddick and Edgartown
12:40 a.m.	Look spots Oldsmobile + 2-3 passengers
12:45 a.m. to 1:30 a.m.	Accident staged MJ drowns
1:30 a.m.	Valiant returns to ferry with TK, Gargan, Markham + 2-3 guests
2:00 a.m.	TK rows to Edgartown. Gargan, Markham + 2-3 guests return to cottage
After 3:00 a.m.	Gargan & Markham realize their plan is untenable
5:30 a.m.	Gargan, Markham, Tretter, Keough, and Tannenbaum return to the bridge at first light to dive on the car and remove the body
8:00 a.m.	Gargan, Markham & Tretter confront TK at the Shiretown Inn
10:00 a.m.	TK reports the accident to the police

40
The Unthinkable

𝒯hus far the assumption has been made that Kennedy and his friends staged the accident believing that Mary Jo was dead. But, of course, the possibility exists that the accident was engineered knowing full well she was alive. This would presuppose that the group believed Mary Jo's injuries were fatal, or worse, that a wounded Mary Jo would be as much of an embarrassment to Kennedy's ambitions as a dead one.

It is almost unthinkable to me that such a thing would be possible, as I am sure it would be for most persons reading this book. But, to be honest, it is equally unsettling to me that no one thought to call for immediate help after rushing to Mary Jo's side soon after 11:35 p.m. The natural instinct is to do everything possible to save a life, no matter how remote. But these persons appear to have summarily rejected that choice, and that in itself is troubling.

The one question that may have occurred to many, as it has to us, is how at least five, and possibly six, intelligent persons could have arrived at the certainty that a breathing, bleeding body was dead. It isn't as though their assumption was made in haste. Rosemary Keough told the BBC in 1994 that any decisions made that night probably occurred in an instant, but that isn't really true. Considering that these persons must have first examined Mary Jo's body soon after 11:35 p.m., and Ballou saw a boat crossing the channel with three persons in it at 1:50 a.m. (with Markham, Gargan, Tretter, and Keough arriving back at the cottage around 2:00 a.m.), they had about two hours of time to examine the body and reconsider their options.

There is also the anomaly of Mary Jo's death. If she was dragged out to the car and pushed underwater through a window, alive, she should have begun convulsing almost immediately, whether unconscious or not. Surely those convulsions would have been noted by whoever was doing the dragging and pushing? The *Manual of Physiology* describes the process of asphyxia this way:

"As the struggles for air become more severe, the inspiratory muscles lose their power and the expiratory efforts become more and more marked, until finally the entire body is thrown into a general convulsion in which the traces of a rhythm are hardly apparent. This stage of convulsion, called the hypoxic convulsion stage, is short, the expiratory muscles becoming suddenly relaxed by exhaustion."

Could Mary Jo have been dead, in fact, before the accident was staged? Although possible, it seems most unlikely. The bloodstains discovered on the back of her blouse and sleeves is powerful evidence the real accident occurred on land, and that Mary Jo was lying on her back out of the water for a significant period of time. The carbon monoxide level in her blood suggests this, too. Nevertheless, the forensic evidence indicates she died by drowning. This could only mean that she drowned in the car, or drowned somewhere else.

But drowning raises disquieting questions. Tony Ulasewicz, President Nixon's private investigator, visited the Edgartown Funeral Home on July 20 before the body had been flown off the island and when Mary Jo was still in her casket. Eugene Frieh, the funeral director, told Ulasewicz that Dun Gifford, who had been tasked by Kennedy to make the necessary arrangements to send the girl home, "was also very interested in what Mills had to say about the official cause of death." When Ulasewicz asked why, Frieh answered, "I don't know. He left in a hurry."[1]

Was Gifford concerned because the group *needed* Mary Jo to drown? This is an important point to remember. A staged-accident into water presupposes that the victim drowned after the plunge. Because Mary Jo's body was unmarked, any cause of death other than drowning would indicate to authorities that Mary Jo had died before the accident occurred. It would indicate, in fact, that the accident had been engineered.

The pertinent question is this: would at least one person in the group be aware of this fact? Because if so, it makes no sense that an accident would be staged using a dead, unmarked body. The group would know, full well, they'd be exposed. Kennedy would be aware that a successful deception *must* begin with a live woman, and end with a drowned one.

Affirmative: The group believed Mary Jo was dead.

The group probably had a good deal to drink. Alcohol clouds reason and leads to bad choices. Alcohol could obviously have been the culprit, here.

It appears there were at least five people involved in the scheme. It is very difficult to believe that all five would agree to what was, essentially, premeditated murder. One of these persons was a senator. Another was a young woman. This hardly seems like the sort of group that would place someone in a submerged car when they honestly believed there was still some life left in her.

Perhaps, if the current was very strong, it might have masked Mary Jo's death convulsions if the body had, in fact, been inserted into the Oldsmobile after the vehicle was driven off the bridge. As the *Manual of Physiology* points out, the hypoxic convulsions would have been brief.

It was very dark from 8:30 that evening. What little moon there was had set, and they might not have had flashlights or indeed any other light at all to examine Mary Jo closely.

There might have been very little contact with Mary Jo after she was observed soon after 11:35 p.m. It appears Gargan and Markham remained inside Lawrence Cottage

---

[1] *The President's Private Eye*, pp. 198-199

from midnight to 12:30 a.m. while Kennedy made phone calls in the private, backyard studio. It appears Kennedy, Gargan, and Markham then drove to the ferry landing in the Valiant to arrange transportation between Chappaquiddick and Edgartown, leaving others to transport Mary Jo to the bridge in the Oldsmobile. If Mary Jo was bleeding on the back seat during the time Kennedy jogged back to Lawrence Cottage, but was in the trunk of the Oldsmobile thereafter, the body may never have been examined carefully by anyone.

And even if it was known that Mary Jo was alive when the accident was staged, it might not have been known to the entire group. Those aware of it might never have shared their knowledge with others.

Negative: The group knew she was still alive.

Although the group probably did have a lot to drink, they had two hours to sober up. They had two hours to examine the body. They were sober enough to stage an accident, to make phone calls, to find boats. Gargan testified that he drank four cokes before the accident and no liquor at all.

Although it was very dark that night, both vehicles had headlights. If Mary Jo was placed in the Oldsmobile, they had the vehicle's dome light to illuminate her body.

There appear to have been at least five persons who helped stage the accident. It seems unlikely that not one of those five would realize that a dead, unmarked body would put the lie to what they were attempting to accomplish and not relay that insight to the others.

The lofty ambitions of Kennedy, and of his family in those years, can never be overestimated, nor can the near-fanaticism of many of their supporters. You are not dealing with just any career here – you are talking about a US senator with the presidency of the United States at stake. In 1969, Ted Kennedy had an acknowledged lock on the presidential nomination from the Democratic Party whenever he decided to run. As Senator Edmund Muskie said, he could have had the nomination "for the asking."[1] And as Kennedy aide Dun Gifford explained to the BBC in their 1994 documentary, "1969 was an enormously passionate time. It's hard to think back sometimes and remember how intense a time it was." Rosemary Keough told the BBC that no one today can appreciate how politically committed people were in 1969, and of course she and the rest of the girls were at the very center of the political process. Ambition and adoration can lead to unfortunate decisions.

The greatest concern could be Ted Kennedy's character. I am not referring to his long-standing drinking problem, cocaine habit, or his single-minded pursuit of anything in a skirt, so painfully detailed by his biographer, Burton Hersh. Nor am I referring here to his senate record or his passion for the poor and downtrodden.

---

[1] *Senatorial Privilege*, p. 234

Supporters can laud those all they like and they will not find an objection from us. I am referring to Kennedy's personal moral principles which seem to be very much at odds with his public persona, at least before his marriage to Victoria Reggie in 1992.

There were death threats made to several individuals who questioned his story, and while it would be easy to blame these on overzealous fans, one threat stands out.

Leslie Leland was in his pharmacy one day when he received a call. A gruff, uneducated voice told Leland, "You better listen to what I say. I told you not to call the grand jury. And if you think I'm kidding, you're not going to like what will happen to your wife and kids if you go through with this. We don't play games. So get it done and get it done quick or we're going to have to do things you're not going to like." Asked if this was a joke, the voice said, "Believe me, this is no joke, and I'm not kidding. There are people who don't want this grand jury and they are willing to make sure it don't happen. So I'm giving you this warning. And I strongly suggest you take it. 'Cause I know you don't want anything to happen to your wife and kids."

A few evenings later, the phone rang again. This time an urbane, educated voice told Leland, "Mr. Leland, several days ago you received a call from a friend of mine. He suggested that you call off the grand jury investigation and described to you what might happen if you didn't. Do you recall that conversation?" When Leland told the man he was going to hang up, the person continued, "I wouldn't hang up, Mr. Leland. It doesn't matter who I am. I am calling because I want to help you. I don't want to see any harm come to you or your family. But if you don't do what my friend told you to do, I am afraid there will be nothing I can do. Call off the grand jury investigation and all will be forgotten. Now, I'm asking you again. You can get on with your pharmacy business and your family life. You won't hear anything further from my friend, which, believe me, will be a blessing for all of you. With that I'll say good night and I hope you have a wonderful evening."[1]

This type of coordinated threat does not sound like it would come from a crackpot supporter, and the police did not think so, either. They assigned around the clock protection for Leland's family throughout the grand jury period. Several other calls were received by the police at Leland's home, but the person hung up before he could be questioned. A week later, a letter arrived at Leland's home renewing the same threats he had received from the first two phone calls. With further, written proof the police intensified their protection. Huck Look, a county sheriff, had no doubts at all that his death threats came from the Kennedys and took serious measures to protect himself.

Many have commented on Ted Kennedy's extraordinarily cool and collected manner the morning following the accident, and, indeed, this one fact alone has been enough to persuade many that either Kennedy was not aware that Mary Jo was in the

[1] *Left to Die*, pp. 95-97

car when it went over the bridge, or was never the driver. Yet Kennedy testified at the inquest that he was perfectly cognizant of the fact that his passenger had drowned while he was chatting innocently with his friends before meeting with Gargan, Markham, and Tretter in Edgartown at 8:00 a.m. Irrespective of whether the accident was staged, has anyone considered that such sangfroid would be symptomatic of sociopathic behavior?

According to *psychecentral.com*, sociopaths are pathological liars, manipulators, and charmers. They have difficulty accepting responsibility for their actions, struggle to form personal, long-standing attachments – although they can form enduring attachments to a group – and possess an overall lack of empathy. Unlike psychopathy, sociopathy is the result of environmental factors that occur during childhood, such as emotional abuse. When a sociopath engages in antisocial behavior he may do so in an impulsive and largely unplanned, reckless manner with little regard for the risks or consequences of his actions. Whereas psychopaths are unable to experience guilt from their behavior, sociopaths can.

Kennedy supporters will cry foul, but honestly, would anyone find it easy to have a lighthearted conversation for a half hour knowing they were responsible for the death of a young woman just hours before, no matter how or when that death may have occurred? Kennedy showed so little emotion that the three persons he was talking to were never aware that anything at all was amiss, even in retrospect. Hersh, Kennedy's biographer, says Kennedy had that conversation while "operating with a politician's reflexes to select from among the refractions of his splintered consciousness,"[1] but even so, contrast Kennedy's cool and collected conversation with his friends the morning after the incident, and his jovial demeanor on the ferry just a few minutes later, with his supposed tearful lamentation to Gargan as they were driving to the ferry landing before his alleged swim across the Edgartown Channel: "Can you believe it, Joe, can you believe it, I don't believe it, I don't believe this could happen, I just don't believe it." Could such behavior really be considered normal?

Kennedy appears to have helped stage this accident, and Gargan said that it was Kennedy's idea to make it appear as if Mary Jo drove off the bridge alone. But even if he didn't, and it wasn't, would it be normal to just walk away from an accident without doing everything in his power to save a life? To seek immediate help? To wait over 10 hours to report it? There were houses around with their lights on. There was an emergency phone at the fire station. Foster Silva lived just a few yards away from Lawrence Cottage trying to sleep with a whole army of volunteers at his disposal willing to help. Russell Peachey, the Shiretown innkeeper and part owner, had asked if Kennedy needed assistance, but Kennedy said no.

Kennedy's insistence that he was not aware that there was help to be had appears untenable. He was certainly aware enough to get the help of Gargan and Markham at

---

[1] *Edward Kennedy*, pp. 366-367

Lawrence Cottage. But why not walk right into the cottage and ask for the help of everyone? If Kennedy really drove off the bridge by accident as he claimed, why not ask for the help of LaRosa, a trained and sober diver? Why hide like a thief in the Valiant? Why make phone calls from Lawrence Cottage and the Shiretown Inn without asking for assistance for Mary Jo, instead of assistance for him? And if he really was confused, which seems impossible, what about the others? Put yourself in Kennedy's shoes. Would you have acted that way? Would your friends? With a life at stake, *how could every one of them be so cold and unfeeling? So calculating?*

Such questions relate to a person's intrinsic empathy with a fellow human being. Or lack thereof. In a response to an internet discussion concerning Kennedy's failure to seek help for Mary Jo or report the accident promptly, John Denison posted the following comment in 2009:

"I have held people's lives in my hands on a few frightening occasions. No thought of my own safety even entered my mind. I remember the time I pulled someone from the water after he was thrown off our catamaran in high wind and waves. I have never before or since felt that actual physical reaction in the pit of my stomach. I have looked death in the eye on a handful of occasions. Every time it took my breath away. Nothing, let me repeat, NOTHING, has come close to the physical fear I felt as the boat was blown away from my fellow sailor, with me at the helm and him in perilous danger. I know what the term 'gut-wrenching' means. I was so frightened that I still cannot, these many years later, find the words to describe it. Even now as I write this I can feel some of that fear, I can feel my heart racing and my hands are literally shaking. I did everything in my power to save him, and did. Do I consider this act heroic? Not in the least. It was my responsibility, *and I was scared to death every second until he was back on board* [emphasis in the original]."

Denison's reaction to a life-threatening emergency is the healthy one; as *Time* wrote, "The normal instinct to get help quickly."[1] The response to Mary Jo's plight by Kennedy and his friends was not. The question is, if these people had no empathy for a wounded friend, or were able to suppress what little sympathy they did have for what they believed was a greater cause, how far would they be prepared to go? If Kennedy was drunk, and if reporting the accident promptly would have meant a blood test, incarceration, total humiliation, and the certain end of his lofty ambitions, what risk would they be willing to take?

Kennedy supporters claim he was suffering from a blow to the head, but there seems to be little evidence for it. An affidavit at the inquest from Dr. Watt, Kennedy's personal physician, said he found a half-inch scrape above the right ear, a bruise with swelling at the top of the senator's head, and a muscle spasm around the area of the nape of his neck. With these few facts he was able to diagnose "concussion,

---

[1] *The Last Kennedy*, p. 118

contusions, and abrasion of the scalp and acute cervical strain." He said that his determination was predicated "upon objective evidence of injury and the history of the temporary loss of consciousness and retrograde amnesia." Watt later changed his diagnosis to "a possible concussion and acute cervical strain,"[1] and in a later interview with the *Boston Globe*, admitted that much of his diagnosis was based "simply on what Kennedy told him."[2] X-rays at Cape Cod Hospital "found no evidence of fracture or depression" at his neck.[3] Nevertheless, Kennedy was fitted with an orthopedic collar which he was careful to wear at the funeral for Mary Jo. Kennedy next went to Dr. Milton Brougham, chief of neurosurgery at Cape Cod Hospital. With just Kennedy's own description of his amnesia and loss of memory to go on, Brougham testified within his own inquest affidavit that he found "concussion, contusions, and abrasion of the scalp, acute cervical strain" substantiated by X-rays which showed "a loss of the normal cervical lordosis which was due to spasm of the cervical musculature." Brougham recommended an electroencephalogram. The test, conducted by Dr. Robert Feldman of the Boston Neurological Laboratory, found "no abnormalities."[4]

The negative electroencephalogram appeared to call into question the symptoms of memory loss, impairment of judgment, and confused behavior reported by the senator and as diagnosed by Doctors Watt and Brougham. According to medical authorities consulted by the *Boston Globe*, any neurological symptoms or alternations of awareness, levels of consciousness, or memory would show up on an EEG. The *Globe* stated, "It is safe to be dubious about the contention that there was a protracted period when Kennedy was alternately lucid and then terribly confused."[5]

Kennedy was rational enough to make numerous phone calls that night, to chat with his mistress, to ask for the help of Gargan and Markham, to find his room on his own, to appear absolutely normal to everyone the next morning, to dictate a coherent statement to the police which conveniently left out all the important details, to make arrangements to fly Mary Jo's body off the Vineyard before it could be examined closely, to get himself and everyone else off the island before they could be questioned. Does anyone genuinely believe he did not know what he was doing? Hersh, Kennedy's biographer, attempts to justify the calls to Helga Wagner at the Shiretown Inn by suggesting that "hours after the Oldsmobile crashed to the ocean's floor, blood from the hematoma forming on Kennedy's brain was starting to contort his reactions,"[6] but in view of the negative EEG, and noting that Kennedy made a total of 17 calls that night, most of those to his attorneys, could anyone really take that diagnosis seriously?

---

[1] *The Last Kennedy*, p. 95
[2] *Senatorial Privilege*, p. 49
[3] *Senatorial Privilege*, p. 135.
[4] *Senatorial Privilege*, p. 136
[5] *Senatorial Privilege*, p. 136
[6] *Edward Kennedy*, p. 366

And what about Gargan and Markham? Does anyone believe they did not know what they were doing, either?

That Kennedy was perfectly aware of what he was doing can be inferred from his choice of Markham over LaRosa at the *relay*. Markham was not as athletic as LaRosa. He was not an experienced diver. But what Markham possessed, in spades, was a deep knowledge of the law. In at least that one respect, Markham was head and shoulders above all the others. Even as he was jogging back to Lawrence Cottage, Kennedy was considering the legal implications of what had occurred.

Kennedy told so many lies with such conviction for so many years, in spite of being confronted with the inconsistencies again and again and again, that it just does not seem normal.[1] Kennedy's fondness for cracking jokes about Chappaquiddick is legendary, and disturbing.[2] His disregard for the feelings of the numerous women he was sleeping with is well known, and reprehensible. And then there is that troubling fact again: no one made the slightest effort to get help at the instant of gathering at Mary Jo's side soon after 11:35 p.m.; or, for those who refuse to believe the accident could have been staged, after Look saw the Oldsmobile around 12:40 a.m.

None of this bodes well for the theory that Kennedy or anyone else sincerely believed Mary Jo was dead, or that they had any real concern for her when balanced against Kennedy's interests, before she was placed in the Oldsmobile, if that indeed is what happened.

---

[1] The *Boston Globe* attempted to investigate the events in 1974, but Kennedy refused to address the inconsistencies. Nine of ten members of Kennedy's entourage refused to answer *Globe* questions at all. According to the *Globe,* the senator also refused to urge any of these persons to cooperate with the probe. Kennedy also declined to discuss the accident or the inconsistencies with the BBC for their documentary *Chappaquiddick* in 1994.

[2] For the audio: http://hotair.com/archives/2009/08/28/one-of-his-favorite-topics-of-humor-was-indeed-chappaquiddick-itself/

41
Alternative Possibilities

*C*arol saw what she saw. Clearly silhouetted through a large, squared-off rear window of a white compact car were at least two men and a short, non-blond woman with short hair. We have arrived at our version of what might have occurred that night because we cannot imagine any other story that would fit with the facts, although we certainly have tried. This, of course, does not mean that there isn't one.

Let's examine some of the other versions of the Chappaquiddick incident, and some of the possibilities, which we have discussed ad nauseam between us and ultimately rejected before a word of this book was ever written. But first, a caution once more concerning the inquest testimony.

If a question cannot be avoided, the natural instinct of a hostile witness in a court of law is to tell the truth, or at least a version of the truth that could be taken two ways (*I never had sex with that woman*). The penalty for perjury is severe and rarely taken lightly, and no witness can ever be sure that a false statement might never be exposed for what it is, even if long in the future. Nevertheless, virtually every writer has come to the conclusion that the witnesses at the Kennedy party must have been bald-faced liars, willing if not eager to parrot anything at all a Kennedy lawyer lay in front of them. Several writers, such as Rust, Damore, and Sherrill, have come right out and stated it. If these witnesses were liars, their inquest testimony can be ignored, and that is a very convenient supposition to make when it comes to Chappaquiddick theories because every one of them, with the exception of Kappel's staged-accident theory, is very much at odds with the times and recollections of the persons who were actually there.

There are at least five good reasons to be confident that the testimony of the witnesses must be taken seriously.

Huck Look

Kennedy and Gargan had steadfastly maintained that Huck Look was either mistaken or lying about seeing the Oldsmobile around 12:40 a.m. This one point was critical for Kennedy. If the court chose to believe Look, Kennedy was finished. His entire testimony – indeed, his political career and his very freedom – depended on a judge accepting Kennedy's timeline over the word of a deputy sheriff.

To circumvent this predicament, Damore suggests that the testimony of the witnesses had been deliberately designed by Kennedy's attorneys "to support the senator's accident timeline, and to overwhelm Huck Look's anticipated testimony by a sheer weight of numbers." In other words, Kennedy's attorneys were able to persuade the witnesses to swear to an elaborate fabrication. But if this were true, why would Ray LaRosa and the Lyons sisters admit meeting Look around 12:45 a.m.? If they had no problem perjuring themselves for Kennedy, why would these three persons corroborate one half of Look's story? With something so crucial to Kennedy's defense, why not just swear that they never saw, or talked, to Look at all?

Tretter and Keough

Both Tretter and Keough testified that they took walks for two and one-half hours between the cottage and the Dike Road intersection at the precise times Kennedy said the accident and a subsequent rescue attempt occurred. They even admitted arriving back at the cottage at 2:00 a.m. within minutes of Gargan and Markham. As several authors have pointed out, their movements that night were suspicious. Were they having an affair? Were they actively involved in the incident? Speculation concerning their activities could not have been welcomed, and it is obvious from her inquest testimony that Keough, in particular, was very uncomfortable talking about any of it. So why, then, would they admit to these walks?

Gargan told Damore that it was Dan Daley's idea to keep Tretter walking to save his marriage. But this is a very clumsy way to convince a wife there was nothing going on. If the others at the party were comfortable committing perjury, why wouldn't these two just tell the court they spent the entire night at the cottage with their friends and never walked anywhere?

Gargan's injuries

On September 19, a month before the exhumation hearing, District Attorney Dinis leaked to the *Boston Herald Traveler* that the Boston police lab had found bloodstains on Mary Jo's blouse – a discovery that could suggest foul play. It was crucial for Kennedy's lawyers to find an innocent explanation, and after the Kopechnes' lawyer had no success impeaching Dr. McHugh's credibility at the exhumation hearing, both Kennedy and Gargan testified at the inquest three months later that Gargan had cut his arms badly while entering the submerged Oldsmobile. It has been suggested that this might have been an attempt by Kennedy's lawyers to introduce blood into the crime scene.

So, if all the witnesses were willing to lie for Kennedy, why did Esther Newberg and Nance Lyons testify that they never saw any wounds on Gargan's arms, even though they had observed him after his return from the ferry landing at 2:00 a.m. and had been in close proximity to him for an hour when he returned to the cottage from the Shiretown Inn around 10:00 a.m. later that morning wearing a short-sleeved t-shirt?

In fact, why were Kennedy's lawyers unable to find *even one person* at the party who would corroborate Gargan and Kennedy's story?

Esther Newberg and the Lyons sisters

Esther Newberg and the Lyons sisters testified that Gargan had told them Mary Jo had driven the Oldsmobile back to Edgartown by herself just before midnight whereas Kennedy had decided to swim the Edgartown Channel. While Kennedy might have wanted them to believe this on the night of the accident, it certainly would not be something he would want them to divulge at the inquest. Such a revelation could suggest to an intelligent judge or prosecutor that Kennedy was planning to say that Mary Jo drove off the bridge alone and that Kennedy's unconcerned demeanor the following morning was an act. At the very least, it would suggest that Kennedy had an ulterior motive when he was chatting innocently to his friends from 7:30 on the morning of July 19 and that he was not as confused and disoriented as he claimed.

So, if these three girls had willingly rehearsed their stories in advance under the tutelage of Kennedy's attorneys, why would they admit to a conversation that could undermine Kennedy's story? Why wouldn't they just have told the court that Gargan had told them Kennedy and Mary Jo drove back to Edgartown together, just as Rosemary Keough did?

Timeline of LaRosa, the Lyons sisters, Newberg, and Tretter

Kennedy testified that he was certain he returned to Lawrence Cottage from Dike Bridge at 12:15 a.m. to fetch Gargan and Markham, having looked at the clock in the Valiant. Gargan and Markham, on the other hand, said that Kennedy returned between 12:15 and 12:30 a.m. All said that Kennedy returned to Lawrence Cottage just once.

If all the witnesses were comfortable lying for Kennedy, why then would LaRosa and the Lyons sisters, who had admitted seeing Huck Look at 12:45 a.m. on their second walk, all testify that Kennedy left with Gargan and Markham before their first walk, with Nance Lyons saying that Kennedy left with Gargan and Markham at least 20 minutes before that first walk, and Mary Ellen Lyons testifying that Kennedy had left with Gargan and Markham before midnight or 12:15 a.m.? Why would Esther Newberg, who testified she was positive Gargan and Markham were at the cottage between midnight and 12:30 a.m., also testify that Kennedy left with Gargan and Markham after 12:30 a.m. or before 12:15 a.m.?

Even more remarkable, Charles Tretter testified he was certain he left the cottage with Rosemary Keough at 11:30 p.m., having looked at his watch. His sighting of the Valiant driven toward the ferry landing caused him to turn around and begin walking back. Tretter said that when they arrived back at Lawrence Cottage around midnight, neither Gargan, Markham, nor the Valiant was there. Tretter's testimony implies that his sighting of the Valiant occurred midway on that walk, at around 11:45 p.m., 30 to 45 minutes before Kennedy, Gargan, and Markham said that the *relay* could have occurred.

Sherrill argues that the strange times cited by the witnesses were part of a calculated strategy by Kennedy's lawyers to leave the public and the press with an impossible job of reconstruction. Damore says that the strange times were attempts to support the senator's timeline and overwhelm Look's testimony by a sheer weight of numbers. Sherrill and Damore, like most authors, have assumed that the real timeline was subsequent to Huck Look's sighting of the Oldsmobile at 12:40 a.m. But it turns out most have missed the point. The point is not about the witnesses' timeline, or even that it's true. The real surprise is that the witnesses' timeline so obviously contradicts the senator's version. This has been overlooked by everyone.

I believe that any convincing hypothesis must account for the testimony of the witnesses at the party, just as it must account for the rest of the evidence, too. Unfortunately, every one of them, with the exception of Kappel's staged-accident theory, fails significantly at one or the other, or both.

Kennedy got out of the car after observing Huck Look between 12:40 and 12:45 a.m. and it was Mary Jo herself, driving an unfamiliar car, who drove off Dike Bridge. Kennedy first heard of the accident after seeing the hearse and being advised by the ferry operators on the Chappaquiddick side after 9:20 a.m.

This is the version first advanced by State Police Detective Bernie Flynn. Flynn convinced Olsen over lunch at a local restaurant who then published the theory in *The Bridge at Chappaquiddick*, the second book to be written about the incident. The theory was later modified by Malcolm Reybold in *The Inspector's Opinion* and by Larryann Willis in *Chappaquiddick Decision*.

The theory attempts to explain Kennedy's extraordinarily unconcerned demeanor between 7:15 and 8:00 the next morning as well as the odd fact that he had no bruises or scrapes. As Bernie Flynn made efforts to convince Olsen and his fellow police officers in Edgartown that his theory must be correct at about the same time he became a Kennedy informer; and as Flynn admitted discussing his theory with his Kennedy contact, Jack Miller;[1] it appears likely he was fed this story by the Kennedys themselves.

The theory does not explain why Kennedy thought he could fudge an hour and a half from the time he said he went off the bridge to the time he was seen by Look. And because there was no real reason Kennedy should have been concerned over leaving the party after midnight anyway, the theory does not explain why he would want to

---

[1] *Senatorial Privilege*, pp. 256-258; p. 307; p. 312

fudge that hour and a half in the first place. It does not explain why Gargan and Markham would consent to being named as accessories to the rescue attempt if there never was any and admitting to the serious allegation of never making any efforts to find help. It does not account for the blood evidence. It does not explain the vehicle damage to the passenger-side doors. It does not account for the detached mirror. It does not explain why Kennedy never attempted to contact the Chappaquiddick ferry operator at 1:30 a.m. It does not account for the insistent urgings of Gargan and Markham when they met Kennedy outside his room at the Shiretown Inn at 8:00 a.m. It does not account for the telephone calls made from Chappaquiddick and Edgartown on Kennedy's credit card. It does not account for the testimony of pilot Wilfred Rock who was told that Kennedy had been in an accident and asked to make a low pass over Dike Bridge by 8:45 a.m. It does not explain the testimony of Esther Newberg and the Lyons sisters who were told by Gargan at 3:00 a.m. that Mary Jo had taken the Oldsmobile back to Edgartown on the last ferry herself but that Kennedy had swum across the channel. It does not account for the uninjured body of Mary Jo. It does not explain why Helga Wagner would have been told before 5:54 a.m. that Kennedy had been involved in something serious.

In his police report on the morning of July 19, Kennedy testified that "the car turned over and sank into the water and landed on the roof resting on the bottom." How would Kennedy have known that the vehicle turned over and landed on its roof if he was never aware there even was an accident until advised of that fact by the ferry operator? How would Kennedy aide Dun Gifford have known about the accident before 8:45 a.m.?

Most important, of course, the theory does not account for the rented Valiant seen by Carol at 11:35 p.m.

Even without Carol's testimony, it always seemed, to me at least, far more likely that Kennedy's behavior on the morning of July 19 was a deliberate attempt to make it appear he was never aware the car had gone off the bridge. Kennedy asked the time from the innkeeper to establish an alibi. His unconcerned demeanor was an acting job. Kennedy was setting the stage. When the car and Mary Jo were discovered, the plan was for Kennedy to say it was all news to him.

Mary Jo drove off Dike Bridge alone after Huck Look saw the Oldsmobile. Kennedy first heard of the accident from Gargan and Markham at 8:00 the following morning.

Suggested by Flynn in the 1994 BBC documentary *Chappaquiddick,* this is Flynn's original theory all over again but with the timeline moved back an hour and a quarter to explain how Dun Gifford could have heard about the accident before 8:45 a.m.

In this scenario, when Mary Jo never arrived back at the cottage, Gargan and Markham drove to the bridge in the early morning hours to see if they could find her.

Observing the car in the water, they attempted to dive on the vehicle to recover her body. This is why Gargan and Markham were wet and unkempt when observed by the Richardses at 8:00 a.m. The theory attempts to account for Kennedy's unconcerned demeanor from 7:15 to 8:00 a.m., his ability to get out of the vehicle without outside help, the absence of obvious injuries, and the failure of everyone to report the accident immediately to police. But other than explaining how Dun Gifford could have heard about the accident by 8:45 a.m., the BBC's theory has every one of the same problems as Olsen's original.

The most serious deficiency of all with the BBC's theory, and with the three modified versions that preceded it, is this: it would not explain why Kennedy would later admit to the far more serious charge of driving the car off the bridge himself and then waiting over 10 hours to report the accident.

The BBC attempted to address that deficiency by suggesting a legal motive. Their convoluted reasoning goes like this:

If Kennedy was seen leaving the party with Mary Jo at 11:15, but denied being the driver, his story might not be believed, especially with no witnesses to back him up. Kennedy might then be open to the more serious charge of manslaughter. Even if he was found not guilty, such a claim would have damaged his political career. Claiming he was the driver, Kennedy could plead guilty to a lesser charge of leaving the scene of an accident.

OK, think about that. Kennedy has two choices. He can tell the truth (he wasn't the driver); or he can lie (he was the driver).

Telling the truth opens him up to the possibility of not being believed since there are no witnesses to back him up. He risks being accused of leaving the scene of an accident and not seeking professional help until 9:45 the next morning.

So instead, Kennedy lies and says he was the driver. He admits to leaving the scene of an accident and not seeking professional help until 9:45 the next morning.

The first choice carries a risk. The second one seals his fate. Kennedy would not have known at the time that he could successfully plead guilty to a charge of leaving the scene of an accident and be given just a pat on the wrist as punishment. If District Attorney Dinis had acted on Judge Boyle's findings, as he *could* have, Kennedy *might* have been charged with manslaughter or negligent vehicular homicide. If Leland had been allowed to view the inquest testimony and interview witnesses, as he *should* have, Kennedy *would* have been charged with one of those offenses. Dinis later admitted that there was no question in his mind that the grand jury would have indicted Kennedy with involuntary manslaughter, if he had given them the case.

However, if Kennedy tells the truth, he will probably be believed since he has appeared completely normal to everyone that morning, he shows no physical signs that he has been in an accident, and everyone will almost certainly give him the benefit of the doubt because he's a senator.

If you were in Kennedy's shoes, which choice would you make? If you were in Markham's shoes, which choice would you suggest Kennedy make?

Bernie Flynn gave his reasons to the BBC for believing Kennedy said he was the driver:

You have an accident, you become a hero. A lot better, it seems to me, than saying you got out of the car because you were afraid you would be picked up for driving under the influence or driving with a young woman at that hour.

It could certainly be argued that concern about drunk driving or being seen with a young woman might have led Kennedy to step out of the car, but it is difficult to believe that this was the reason he afterwards admitted to the far more serious crime of driving the car off the bridge and waiting over 10 hours to report it, if in fact he did not. There is a fundamental difference between the two concepts. The first attempts to explain why he might have hidden from Huck Look; the second with why he would later wrongfully confess to something altogether different and far more serious. There are a hundred reasons Kennedy could afterwards have said he got out of the car. He had to take a leak. He thought he had a flat tire. He simply wanted to avoid being hassled by a local cop. And after 10 hours he never would have had to admit he was driving under the influence. He never admitted to that, anyway.

It is equally difficult to buy into Flynn's hero theory when one remembers that Kennedy's initial police report was never written by Kennedy alone – it was a joint effort, composed with the help and guidance of the recently retired United States Attorney for Massachusetts. Even if Kennedy, a lawyer, had not been aware of the legal repercussions of such a boastful and self-serving lie, Markham certainly would.

Larryann Willis argues that Kennedy wrongfully confessed to being the driver and took the blame because he wanted to avoid a public trial. She suggests Kennedy also probably felt guilty for not searching longer for the car when he eventually wandered down to East Beach to look for it. But Kennedy had to be convinced by his lawyers to plead guilty to the charge of leaving the scene of an accident after a plea deal had been worked out with the prosecution. It is highly unlikely, on the morning after the accident, that Kennedy would have confessed to being the driver because he was hoping to avoid a public trial when he had no idea at that time how events would play out. And again, Willis's theory does not explain why Gargan and Markham would also claim involvement a week after the incident occurred. Why would these men admit to waiting over 10 hours to report the accident if they hadn't even known that an accident had occurred until late the next morning?

The very fact that Kennedy *did* say he was the driver is what makes it virtually certain he *was* the driver and responsible for Kopechne's death. Unless a person had very compelling reasons, no one in his right mind would claim he was responsible for a death if he was not, especially after waiting so long to report the accident. Nor would an innocent person continue to claim responsibility for the next 40 years, to the very moment of his death, choosing instead to endure unending criticism and snide comments from a large segment of the country's population. One has only to surf the internet to get a taste. And the theory does not account for Kennedy's friends, Gargan and Markham, either. Claiming to this very day that they were fully aware she was in the pond from before midnight, but, like Kennedy, made no attempt to report the accident until late the next morning, has exposed them both to decades of criticism and ridicule. The BBC, Flynn, and Willis are clutching at straws to support a premise.

Kennedy jumped out of the car before it plunged over the bridge.

Zad Rust suggests this in *Teddy Bare: The Last of the Kennedy Clan*, Bruce Roberts suggests it in *The Gemstone File*, and John Farrar endorsed it, too. These are attempts to explain how Kennedy was able to escape the overturned Oldsmobile and why he had no scrapes or bruises the morning after.

However, it really does not seem to explain anything. How could Kennedy have survived the jump onto gravel without so much as a scratch or bruise in a car traveling between 30 and 40 mph or so before the brakes were applied? At the very minimum, one would expect a scrape of some kind somewhere on his body. Yet no scrapes were observed, and Kennedy never mentioned any. A scrape would have supported Kennedy's story and it seems likely he would have brought it to the attention of authorities if he had one. Kennedy's personal physician was unable to find anything more than an abrasion on the top of his head.

If Kennedy had the time to open a door and jump out of a car, he certainly had enough time to brake and stop the vehicle before it plunged over the side. Braking is the instinctive reaction whereas jumping out of a car requires conscious thought. It can take about three-quarters of a second for a driver to step on the brake pedal after observing a danger, but it would take far longer to logically arrive at the conclusion that bailing out of the car would be the better bet, then locate the door latch, open the door, rise off the seat, and leap out.

The theory does not account for the tire marks on the bridge. If Kennedy jumped out of the vehicle before it drove off the bridge, there would have been no one to stamp on the brake or accelerator pedals. And while the theory might attempt to account for Kennedy's lack of injuries, it does not explain how Mary Jo had none, either.

In any event, Carol's testimony rules this out, at least as to how it was envisioned by Rust and Farrar. Kennedy did not jump out of the car at the last minute soon after 12:40 a.m. when the bridge suddenly loomed up in front of him unexpectedly.

Mary Jo, unbeknownst to Kennedy, was asleep in the back seat of the Oldsmobile before it plunged over the bridge.

This rumor surfaced just a few weeks after the accident and was attributed to a hypothetical secret service agent assigned to guard Ted Kennedy. The Kopechnes eventually accepted it by August 1975 after visiting Edgartown for the first time in June. The Tedrows argue that the story appears to have been deliberately planted on behalf of the senator because they were fed it several times from Kennedy insiders as they were conducting interviews for their book in 1975. They point out that if true there would be no possible reason to conceal it as it would be the best defense available. The Tedrows were "satisfied that there is no truth in this one."[1]

Described by *Time* in their edition of August 13, 1969, as "another version in the gossip stage" and "a story that is not so much a measure of truth as an index of how elaborate the speculation has become in the absence of an adequate explanation by Kennedy," the rumor purports that a federal agent secretly assigned to guard Ted Kennedy observed, a weary Mary Jo take a nap in the back of Ted's Oldsmobile. Sometime afterward, the agent saw Kennedy leave the party with Rosemary Keough and drive off toward East Beach. The theory assumes that a sleeping Mary Jo was the person seen by Look in the back seat of the Oldsmobile around 12:40 a.m. Kennedy and Keough managed to get out of the sunken vehicle OK, but neither realized that Mary Jo was also in the car until late the next morning.

This is another attempt to explain Kennedy's unconcerned demeanor on the morning of July 19 and appears to be the current flavor of choice. A story floated around the internet from 2006 alleges that a few years after 1969, an unidentified girl confessed to her close friend Sally Swift, a former editorial director for CBS, that she was Kennedy's real passenger on that night and that neither she nor Kennedy was aware that Mary Jo was also in the car when they went over the bridge, nor even aware that she was dead, until late the next morning. According to Ms. Swift, the reason Huck Look saw only one person in the car was because Mary Jo spent most of her time "puking on the side of Dike Road." For a former CBS editorial director, Ms. Swift was strangely misinformed. Look never said he saw just one person in the car; Look said he saw two people and perhaps three.

Nevertheless, a long and detailed 2009 article in the *Cape Cod Today* by Mary Wentworth argued that "such a theory is the only credible explanation." So convinced was Ms. Wentworth of her reasoning that she begged Kennedy to just admit it: "By telling it now, he can remove a stain from his own legacy as well as from his family's."[2]

---

[1] *Death at Chappaquiddick*, p. 189

[2] See https://www.capecodtoday.com/article/2009/05/22/3806-Mary-Jo-Kopechne-died-40-years-ago-today.

One blog presented these arguments in support of the theory in 2010:[1]

Kennedy had a reputation as a womanizer, but in 1969, an affair with another woman would have been political suicide for him and devastating for his companion's reputation.

Perhaps so. But that argument would support a whole number of theories, not just this one.

People who saw Ted Kennedy after the accident reported him to be in a jovial mood. While the extremely cynical attribute this to a callous attitude toward Mary Jo Kopechne's life, a much simpler explanation would be that he was relieved to have avoided drowning and had protected his (real) companion's identity, as yet unaware of Kopechne's death.

An even simpler explanation is that Kennedy's mood the next morning was an acting job, especially when considered against the fact that Kennedy never attempted to return to Edgartown on the Chappaquiddick ferry. Kennedy, Markham, and Gargan were well aware the ferry was on call with just a phone call from the public phone booth at the ferry landing on the Chappaquiddick side, and in fact Kennedy testified that he made a call from that same phone booth the next morning. As Chief Arena said, "For the senator to have walked from the [lighthouse] to the Shiretown Inn unseen on a regatta night suggested a deliberate avoidance of witnesses."

Believing that Ted Kennedy knew Mary Jo Kopechne was in the car, yet failed to report the accident, makes no sense. It doesn't take a Kennedy fan to recognize that the senator was intelligent and strategically gifted. No one with his sights on the American presidency or even a high-profile career as a United States senator would have failed to report that accident, knowing that Mary Jo Kopechne was missing underwater in his car, presumably drowned.

Affirms the consequent, otherwise known as begging the question. It does make sense if one assumes Kennedy was hoping he would not be involved in the accident at all. It does make sense if Kennedy had staged the accident. It does make sense if Kennedy and his friends believed that Kennedy's career and ambitions took precedence over a life.

---

[1] See http://www.assaultweb.net/forums/showthread.php?t=127852

Mary Jo Kopechne's body was found in the back seat, not the passenger seat, of Ted's car.

Actually, this is a very good argument. But if the perpetrators dove on the vehicle later that morning, Mary Jo could have been maneuvered into the rear seat area. Or, Mary Jo might have been inserted through a rear window rather than a front one because the rear of the car was closer to the surface.

In 1970, Huck Look told Zad Rust that what he had seen in the back seat "could only have been another girl, or an outstretched garment." To be able to identify the form as a girl, the outstretched garment Look saw must have looked like a skirt or dress. However, Mary Jo wore dark slacks. If Look really did see a girl in the rear seat, Huck's description does not suggest it was Mary Jo.

The second passenger theory was proposed by Donald Nelson, a Martha's Vineyard summer resident, in *Chappaquiddick Tragedy: Kennedy's Second Passenger Revealed*, published in 2016. What I find most disappointing about this book is that Nelson, a physicist, makes no attempt to analyze the physics of the crash itself, or any effort to explain the vehicle damage, other than to agree with Fischer that "water does not compress." It would seem that Nelson would have been uniquely qualified for such a role; however, he concentrates almost exclusively on the inquest testimony to make his points.

The second passenger theory does not account for the fact that not one of the other Boiler Room Girls was observed to have so much as a scratch at the funeral for Mary Jo just four days later, nor Kennedy nor the body of Mary Jo, either. As we have seen, the absence of injuries to either Kennedy or Mary Jo is one of the most persuasive reasons the accident doesn't make any sense to crash analysts. Add one more person who survived the accident without a scratch and the odds go from virtually impossible to out of the question. Nor does it explain how Kennedy or his "real" passenger even made it out of the Oldsmobile. According to crash specialists consulted by the BBC in 1994, the chance that Kennedy could have made it out of the vehicle without outside help – taking into account the speed of the car, the overturned position of the vehicle as it landed in the water, the depth of the water, the current, the darkness, and the absence of seat restraints – would have been close to zero. And now there is supposed to have been another person who made it out with no problem, too?

The theory presupposes that Mary Jo could remain asleep while a vehicle traveled seven-tenths of a mile over a very rough road at 20 mph or more for much of it and close to 40 mph at the end, and that she never made a sound when the vehicle went into the pond. Mary Jo had a lot to drink, but in 1969 her blood alcohol level was still not high enough for her to be classified as legally intoxicated in the state of Massachusetts.

The theory presupposes that Kennedy and his lawyers would have concluded that Kennedy's reputation would suffer a greater hit if he admitted to driving off the bridge with his "real" companion, never realizing at the time that someone else was in the car, than it would if he wrongfully confessed to driving off the bridge with Mary Jo, abandoning her in the vehicle, and then waiting over 10 hours to report the accident – a confession that could very well have led to a stint in prison. Since his real companion would have corroborated a story that would have exonerated Kennedy from any possible criminal charges, and since just about everyone assumes Kennedy was driving down to East Beach to have sex with Mary Jo anyway, this supposition seems utterly preposterous.

If Kennedy truly had no reason to suspect that there was another woman in his car until advised by others, why would he not have gone immediately to the police after he woke up before 7:20 on Saturday morning? OK, he may not have realized there had been a fatality, but there was certainly his vehicle in the channel which would need to be explained. The police station was less than a four-minute stroll up the street. Kennedy would have known that the Oldsmobile would be discovered and he would be questioned because his car registration and the weekend lease to Lawrence Cottage were in the glove compartment. Kennedy supporters insist, "No one with his sights on the American presidency or even a high-profile career as a United States senator would have failed to report the accident," but if so, why would Kennedy spend the first part of the morning chatting innocently with his friends, all the while dressed up in yachting clothes for that day's race? Why would he plan to have a leisurely breakfast with these same friends later and only change his mind when Gargan and Markham showed up at 8:00 a.m.? As a "presidential candidate and United States senator" with nothing to hide, why wouldn't Kennedy have reported the accident to the police in a timely manner?

To my mind, the greatest objection to the theory is that it would not explain why Gargan or Markham would agree to be involved and admit to waiting over 10 hours before reporting the accident, thereby exposing themselves to serious charges. If Kennedy and his real passenger were able to get out of the vehicle on their own, but no one realized that Mary Jo was also in the car until sometime later in the morning, there would have been no need for any additional rescue attempt that night by any of them. So why would Gargan and Markham confess to something they did not do? Perhaps it could be argued that Gargan might have agreed to help Kennedy out by throwing himself on his sword for a cousin, but Markham? Markham was just a guest. He had no responsibility to Ted Kennedy at all. He was not even Ted Kennedy's lawyer. Markham would have known what he was getting into. He would have known that his confession would be detrimental to his reputation and career. Reporters had been fastened to Kennedy's jugular for a week before Markham was brought into the picture.

The theory does not explain the blood on the back of Mary Jo's blouse or the back seat of the Oldsmobile. It does not explain the deep, vertical dents to the passenger-side doors or the detached mirror. It does not explain why the vehicle was accelerated up the bridge from a standing start. It does not explain the telephone calls made from Lawrence Cottage from about midnight to 12:30 a.m., well before Look saw the vehicle at the Dike Road intersection. It does not explain Gargan and Markham's panicked behavior when they met Kennedy outside his room at the Shiretown Inn at 8:00 a.m., at least an hour and a quarter before the three were told that Kennedy's vehicle had been found with a body in it. It does not explain the eyewitness account of the Oldsmobile and passengers parked at the fire station from midnight while calls were made on Kennedy's credit card at Lawrence cottage. It does not explain why Dun Gifford would have been told to fly to the Vineyard before 8:45 a.m. It does not explain why Kennedy would appear upset and distracted at 9:15 a.m., but unconcerned and jovial on the ferry just a few minutes later. It does not explain the absence of even the slightest injury to Mary Jo and to every one of the Boiler Room Girls.

Most important, of course, the theory does not explain the Valiant seen by Carol driving at high speed toward the bridge at 11:35 p.m. with at least three men and a woman sandwiched between them.

The second passenger theory appears to be one more example of cherry picking the salient facts to support a favorite hypothesis. As for the alleged confession to Sally Swift, I find it suspicious that a Boiler Room Girl would confide her story to a stranger or friend who had no problem posting it on the internet many years later when not one of the other girls has said anything of substance about these events to anyone in 45 years.

I myself was told a story in confidence by someone who purported to have been at the Kennedy compound in Hyannis Port as a guardian of Jack Kennedy's children on the night of July 18, 1969. According to this stranger, he was minding his own business when Ted Kennedy was driven back to the compound on a Kennedy powerboat. Kennedy was given advice by his lawyers for several hours, fitted with a neck collar to hide bloody scratches around his neck, then transported back in the powerboat to Edgartown. The person who told me this was very believable and I repeated the story to numerous people afterwards, albeit with some skepticism. It was only later that I found that the only time Kennedy was seen with a neck collar from July 18 was at the funeral for Mary Jo, and he was so much criticized for it by the press that he never wore it again.

Many people have a need to invent themselves, and invent stories. It is more prevalent than most realize. This is why I insisted on affidavits before publishing this book.

The accident was staged, using a Kennedy double, by outside forces in an attempt to prevent Kennedy from reaching the White House.

Advanced by Robert Cutler in *You, the Jury*. I would rather just skip over this theory, but because a discouraging number of persons have accepted it, and because this theory and close variants take up so much space on the internet, here are some thoughts that the political conspiracy theorists might mull over.

Cutler's theory requires that every witness at the party was a willing accomplice to the conspiracy and that every one of them lied at the inquest. It means that Helga Wagner was an accomplice, too. The theory presupposes that the perpetrators forced a drugged Kennedy to make calls to Kennedy's Washington lawyer, the Kennedy compound, Kennedy's brother-in-law, and Theodore Sorensen. The theory presupposes that teams of operatives could have successfully accomplished all this on an island and in a town at a time when every stranger stood out like a sore thumb and was fodder for gossip. It presupposes that every one of these Republican operatives could have kept their secret for 45 years.

According to Jane Jones, a cousin who was fishing off Wasque on the evening of July 18, the bluefish were running very strongly that night and large numbers of fisherman could be found pulling in extraordinary catches at Wasque and from one end of East Beach to the other. It would have been nearly impossible for boats of a size capable of transporting large groups of men and personnel to have landed on Chappaquiddick beaches without being noticed by someone. So, if boats never landed on Chappaquiddick beaches, no one reported hearing a helicopter that night, and ferry operators never noticed anything out of the ordinary, either, how could Republican agents and their equipment have gotten onto the island and off it without being seen?

If the accident was staged in the way Cutler envisioned, with teams bashing in the passenger side of the Oldsmobile with sledgehammers, it would be impossible for Mrs. Malm and her daughter not have heard the noise on such a calm night. It seems equally unlikely that professional hit men would have undertaken such an operation without making absolutely sure the occupants of Dyke House were on the same page, or perhaps more likely, eliminated with extreme prejudice. But could anyone really believe that Mrs. Malm and her daughter would have kept silent over an obvious assassination? And if they kept silent because they were intimidated by these operatives, how could Mrs. Malm appear so normal to Arena and Inspector Kennedy the next morning?

But the real question to ask is, why on earth would Republicans have gone to so much trouble, involved so many people, and have stooped to murder, just to keep Kennedy from being offered the presidential nomination from the Democratic Party? Surely a less complicated scheme, with far less chance of error, could have been imagined to accomplish that goal?

For instance, according to Kennedy's biographer, Burton Hersh, it was well known to political insiders in 1969 that Kennedy was bedding every woman he could. "All through the '60s in Washington, everyone heard the stories. Kennedy appreciated fun." His own aides were expected to act as pimps at political fundraisers and later as lookouts while Kennedy "performed" in the lady's bedroom.[1] Kennedy's wife was pregnant in 1969 at a time when infidelity was a serious matter in the public's mind. If the Republican Party was willing to stage an accident and stoop to blackmail and murder, surely they would have had little hesitation in introducing their own female operative to Kennedy and then filming the couple in flagrante delicto? Why not first try something simple like that instead of choosing such a complicated plan almost certain to fail and almost certain to bury the Republican Party when it did?

Cutler's theory and its close variants all have one thing in common: a whole lot of major maybes with precious little evidence offered in support. *Maybe* Mary Jo found out something about John Kennedy. *Maybe* Mary Jo told Robert Kennedy about something. *Maybe* Robert appointed her as his secretary to keep her quiet. *Maybe* Mary Jo found out something incriminating from her roommate. *Maybe* they ambushed Mary Jo and Ted Kennedy after they left the cottage. *Maybe* the conspirators kept Ted Kennedy in line by threatening his children. And not one of these theories explains Markham and Gargan's behavior with any kind of sense. If Kennedy was being blackmailed and he confessed to being responsible for Mary Jo's death because it was a less dangerous alternative than the other (whatever that "other" alternative may have been), why would Gargan and Markham have supported that lie? Why would they have said they spent time at the bridge with Kennedy diving on the car? *Maybe* they were being blackmailed, too? Bear in mind that neither of these men were identified as being involved until Kennedy's TV broadcast to the public on July 25. Nor do these theories have a convincing explanation for the vehicle damage. Why would Republican operatives have bashed in the doors and windows with sledgehammers? What would be the point? Why risk the chance that the police would figure out that the accident had been engineered by a third party?

Cutler and those who subscribe to his theory, or something close to it, believe the accident was staged. We believe they are right. But why the need to dream up complex scenarios, imagine mysterious groups of people with sinister motives, and resort to maybes, when the simplest explanation of all – the one that conforms to the evidence and testimony exactly – is that Kennedy and a few of his friends staged the accident themselves? Admitting that Kennedy might have engineered the accident at Dike Bridge is no condemnation of the Democrats just because he happened to be one. There are bad apples in every political party, and no one man defines it.

---

[1] *Edward Kennedy*, p. 438; p. 462

Kennedy took the rap because he was covering up for his nephew Joseph Kennedy who was also racing in the Edgartown Regatta on another Wianno Senior sloop, the **Resolute.**

This theory has been advanced by some, and it certainly would show Kennedy in a more favorable light if true.[1] However, witnesses observed Joseph Kennedy and some friends in continuous party mode from the early evening of July 18 to 10:30 p.m. at the Shiretown Inn, at the Edgartown Yacht Club, and at the Colonial Inn. Kennedy and his friends then said that they sipped drinks at the Shiretown Inn "for an hour or so," but after that, Joseph Kennedy and 8 to 10 of his friends were observed at the Edgartown Yacht Club to midnight. After that, Kennedy and his friends said they went back to the Shiretown Inn, then walked to the Harborside Inn for a dip in the pool until 1:00 a.m.[2]

This pretty much takes up the entire evening. If Joseph Kennedy was involved in the Chappaquiddick incident, it means that several of his friends lied to investigators. But even if they did, the only time it would be possible for Joseph Kennedy to have been on Chappaquiddick and not seen by independent witnesses was between 10:30 and 11:30 p.m.; and after midnight. However, Carol saw the Valiant at 11:35 p.m., at the very time independent witnesses saw Joseph Kennedy chatting with his friends at the Edgartown Yacht Club dressed in jacket and tie.

The theory does not account for the absence of injuries to either Mary Jo or Joseph Kennedy, or explain how Joseph Kennedy could even have managed to exit the car. It does not account for the blood evidence. It does not account for the vehicle damage or the detached mirror. It also does not explain why Markham would consent to being named as an accessory to the rescue attempt over a family affair, or being involved at all, thus opening himself up to the possibility of serious charges.

Kennedy drove down Dike Road in error while attempting to take a shortcut to the ferry.

This theory has been bandied around Chappaquiddick for years. To those familiar with Chappaquiddick, it is well known that there is another route to the ferry from Lawrence Cottage – a dirt lane called Litchfield Road. If Kennedy had planned to use this route to take Mary Jo back to Edgartown, perhaps because someone at the party had suggested it as a shortcut, he might have turned right from Lawrence Cottage in error rather than left toward Litchfield Road. Arriving at the sharp left turn toward the ferry at the Dike Road intersection, he might have confused it for the sharp left turn

---

[1] The Tedrows' thoughts about this version: "Our only comment here is, 'that will be the day!' " (*Death at Chappaquiddick*, p. 189)

[2] *The Bridge at Chappaquiddick*, pp. 100-102

toward Wasque at a landmark called the Bugle, then turned right on the unpaved Dike Road believing he was turning right onto the unpaved Litchfield Road. He might then have driven over Dike Bridge because he was under the impression it was all clear sailing to the ferry from there on.

It's a tidy theory because all the turns and surfaces match up, and if true, or if Kennedy's advisors had been more knowledgeable of Chappaquiddick roads, one might assume Kennedy would have used it. However, Kennedy did not, and therefore the theory can be dismissed. Moreover, while it could explain why Kennedy drove down Dike Road and went off the bridge, it explains absolutely nothing else. The real mystery has never been about Kennedy's decision to drive down Dike Road, or even how he could have driven off the bridge. The mystery concerns Kennedy's insistence he drove off the bridge soon after 11:15 p.m. when Look had seen the Oldsmobile around 12:40 a.m.; how he could have survived the crash with no apparent injury; his failure to report the accident immediately to the police; and why Kennedy exhibited such strange behavior the morning after.

The car and passengers seen driving down Dike Road at 11:35 p.m. by Carol had nothing to do with Kennedy or Mary Jo.

An extraordinary coincidence if true. It does not explain the high speed of the car as it passed Carol's VW bus. It does not explain why no other such car was known to be on Chappaquiddick on July 18 or why no other such car was seen driving off the island by ferry operators after July 19. It does not explain why at least four witnesses, including a woman, never reported being in the vicinity of the bridge at around the same time Kennedy said he drove off it, if only to contradict Kennedy's story or confirm it. At the moment that car would have reached Dike Bridge, Kennedy said the Oldsmobile was already in the water and he was diving repeatedly in the pond in attempts to save Mary Jo. If Kennedy was really at Dike Bridge at that time, he would have noticed that car, too. It does not explain the testimony of Charles Tretter who observed the Valiant drive past him toward the ferry landing on his walk with Keough after 11:30 p.m. but was not at the cottage when they returned at midnight. It does not account for the testimony of Nance Lyons who confirmed that Kennedy left with Gargan and Markham at least 20 minutes before her first walk with three others, and long before those same three others encountered Huck Look around 12:45 a.m.

Carol did observe the Valiant rented by the Kennedy team that weekend, but her sighting had nothing to do with the "real" accident at the bridge.

This is the avowed belief of John Farrar. The theory assumes that everything of real importance occurred after Huck Look saw the Oldsmobile around 12:40 a.m. Kennedy did drive off the bridge with Mary Jo after observing Huck Look but managed to get out while his passenger did not. Kennedy cooked up the story of leaving with Kopechne at 11:15 p.m. because he was worried about fallout if he confessed to leaving with her after the ferry shut down. According to Farrar, he could have saved Mary Jo if Kennedy had made just one emergency call.

Farrar's theory presupposes that six persons at Lawrence Cottage, several of them attorneys in their late 30s, would pass a car at 45 to 50 mph on a blind curve with a female passenger in their rented Valiant just for fun at the exact time Kennedy said he was diving in Poucha Pond to save Mary Jo, and then continue at high speed down Dike Road. It further assumes that these five persons would fail to bring their innocent joyride to the attention of the inquest court, and lie about driving or riding in the Valiant between 11:30 p.m. and midnight, when such a remarkable observation would be certain to be remembered by the witness. It presupposes that every one of the persons at the party lied at the inquest as to times and events. It presupposes that Kennedy and his lawyers would be concerned about Kennedy leaving the party with Kopechne after midnight when everyone was aware the ferry operator could be summoned with just one call from the ferry landing, and when there could be no scandal associated with a party breaking up at 12:30 a.m. It presupposes that both Kennedy and Mary Jo could have survived the plunge without a scratch and that Kennedy could have gotten out of the car without outside assistance. It presupposes that crash experts consulted by Kappel, the BBC, and the author did not know what they were talking about. It presupposes that the forward fastener on the driver-side rearview mirror could have failed as the vehicle was pulled backward out of the channel on its roof or on its wheels. It presupposes that Mary Jo could have remained conscious for the time it would take to climb into the back seat with a car filling rapidly with water through three open windows and two crushed doors. It ignores the telephone calls from Lawrence Cottage or dismisses them as coincidence. It assigns improbable explanations to the blood evidence.

Basically, this is the "reasonable, conventional" theory advanced by the Tedrows in *Death at Chappaquiddick.* The Tedrows are obliged to dismiss the blood on the back of Mary Jo's blouse as nothing more than grass stains. They find nothing incongruous in the fact that both Kennedy and Mary Jo, unsecured by seat restraints, sustained no serious injuries from the impact. They suggest that the pressure of water gushing in from the imploded passenger-side windows could have pushed Kennedy's 6-foot 2-inch 220-pound frame out of the driver-side window without dicing his passenger's skin or clothing or causing the slightest injury to Kennedy himself. They blithely dismiss virtually all inquest testimony as outright fabrication. They fail to explain how a car landing partially on its passenger side could have sustained deep, vertical dents in the passenger-side doors and deep dents in the roof. They ignore the detached, driver-side mirror. They dismiss the vehicles seen or heard by Mrs. Malm, her daughter Sylvia, and Nancy McDonald as irrelevant. They fail to address the timing or the persons called from a phone at Lawrence Cottage on Kennedy's credit card between midnight and 12:30 a.m., well before Look saw the Oldsmobile around 12:40 a.m. They accept Farrar's bubble theory unconditionally without thinking it through.

A significant accumulation of evidence is dismissed, rejected, or ignored by the Tedrows in order to propound a theory. It raises the obvious question as to whether their theory was derived from the evidence, or the other way around.

Mary Jo was not injured before Look observed the Oldsmobile between 12:40 and 12:45 a.m.

This would not account for Carol's testimony.

No Boiler Room Girl was ever involved.

This would mean that Mary Jo must have taken at least two joyrides that night to Dike Bridge, the second one taking her life. Possible, but improbable, especially when Carol has testified that the woman she observed in the car was not blond and had short hair. Or, it would mean that some other woman was at the party that night who has never been mentioned by the Kennedys. Again, possible, but improbable. Or, it would mean that the Valiant observed by Carol was on a high-speed joyride at 11:35 p.m. with not one of the five passengers ever admitting to it. Possible, but considering all the other evidence, very improbable.

Gargan told nothing but the truth at the inquest and in **Senatorial Privilege: The Chappaquiddick Cover-up.**

Prove it with a lie detector test. Better yet, several of them. Someone who has nothing to hide and has told the truth has no problem going before one. Just step up, and do it.

Every Boiler Room Girl told the truth when they claimed they did not know what happened.

Ditto

Carol Jones and/or Huck Look lied.

Always possible, but very improbable.

The Oldsmobile was never rigged and driven off the bridge deliberately.

OK. Perhaps not. So what did happen, then?

A believable theory must include convincing explanations for the following evidence: the testimony of the guests; Carol's observation at 11:35 p.m.; Look's observation at 12:40 a.m.; the eyewitness accounts of Todd Ballou, Nancy McDonald, Lansing Burns, Foster Silva, Wilfred Rock, Ross and Marilyn Richards, and Stan Moore; Kennedy's confession; Gargan and Markham's confessions; Kennedy's behavior before and after 8:00 a.m. on July 19; the phone calls from Lawrence Cottage and the Shiretown Inn; the blood evidence; the medical evidence; the high level of carbon monoxide in Mary Jo's blood.

Most important of all, a successful theory must account for the accident and impact analysis: the passenger-side door and window damage; the windshield and roof damage; the tire marks; the semidetached driver-side mirror; the absence of visible injuries or fractures to Kennedy, Mary Jo, and to every one of the Boiler Room Girls. Not one book or TV report has ever analyzed that evidence in more than a rudimentary fashion, if at all. And yet this is where an analysis should begin. The key to a successful theory can be found in the forensic details. It can and should be found in the science.

In short, a believable theory must account for all the evidence, not just some of it.

Gargan confessed to Damore that Kennedy had planned to say that Mary Jo had decided to drive the Oldsmobile back to the Shiretown Inn on her own before midnight and that she must have made a wrong turn and driven off the bridge by accident. The plan called for Gargan to discover the car the next morning and report it to the police. This is exactly what the staged-accident theory proposes. According to Gargan, Kennedy told him he still planned to tell the police this lie when they met up at the Shiretown Inn at 8:00 a.m. on July 19 and only changed his mind after being alerted by Gargan that Kennedy could be placed at the scene.

If Kennedy changed his mind at 8:00 a.m., it means that Kennedy spoke with Peachey at 2:25 a.m. to establish an alibi and his innocuous behavior from 7:15 to 9:15 a.m. was an act.

So, if the Oldsmobile was not deliberately driven off the bridge by Kennedy and his friends, *what other scenario would fit the evidence?*

No one still alive knows what actually happened.

As of this writing, Gargan, Markham, Tretter, and every one of the Boiler Room Girls are still alive.[1] Several of the lawyers who prepared Kennedy's testimony are,

---

[1] Gargan died in December 2017.

too. If the reader has perused these pages carefully, it should be fairly obvious to her, as it is to us, that a few of Kennedy's lawyers must have known the real story right down to the smallest detail. Kennedy's testimony is too artfully structured for it to be otherwise.

If one really wished to know the full details, it seems to us that the person to ask is Charles Tretter. Lawyers are taught to keep secrets told to them by clients, and the Boiler Room Girls appear to have made a pact among themselves never to reveal anything at all. However, Tretter was clearly uncomfortable with his role as a Kennedy flunky. His inquest testimony was the most detailed and believable of all the participants by far. Even if he was never directly involved, Tretter spent two and one-half hours in the general area and at the precise times that the events occurred.

None of the principals will ever reveal what actually happened.

OK. But that does not mean the evidence does not speak for itself. I have tried to lay out as much as I could here. It is up to others to draw their own inferences if they are able to imagine something more plausible.

42
Objections to Our Theories

There appear to be four major and one minor objection to conclusions we have reached in this book. As I have poked holes in theories advanced by others, I can similarly find a few holes in ours.

Major problems for the theory

1) It seems unlikely that five or more people would all assume that Mary Jo had not survived the initial accident and was already dead when they staged the plunge.

$\mathcal{F}$ or some, this will be the killer of the staged-accident theory. For some, it will be self-evident that a group of five or more persons could never be so naive as to believe that a breathing, bleeding person was dead, and equally self-evident that Mary Jo could never be placed in the Oldsmobile knowing she was alive. Irrespective of the fact that Kennedy and his friends never thought to ask for help when the real accident occurred, whenever that was, it would be a leap to equate callous inaction with a deliberate intent to cover up Kennedy's mistake with a homicide.

This would be especially true if Mary Jo was placed into the car after the vehicle was in the channel. The violent terminal respiratory convulsions should have been noted just as soon as Mary Jo was pushed underwater.

But if Mary Jo was in the trunk of the Oldsmobile for most of the time these people were occupied at different tasks, she may never have been examined closely by anyone. And even if she began convulsing after the water rose over her face, the extreme darkness might have hidden it from everyone save the person who was holding her. That person might have hesitated before saying anything to the others, believing that events had spiraled well beyond the point of no return. The Oldsmobile was already in the water; Mary Jo was injured; the *relay* had occurred at 11:30 p.m.; no one had ever gone for help. How could that possibly be explained if they revived her now?

On the other hand, if they became aware that she was alive when they opened the trunk, and Mary Jo was comatose, they were in a dilemma. If they came up with an alternative story to account for her injuries, how could they be certain she would repeat that same story to doctors or police when she woke up at the hospital? And there was the vehicle damage to explain, too. How could they recreate that? The only way they could be sure she would never tell an embarrassing story, or would implicate Kennedy, is if she never woke up at all, and if they could make it appear that she had died by her own hand.

2) The staged accident theory makes far more sense if one assumes Mary Jo died at the original car accident on Dike Road.

Unfortunately, the evidence is strong that Mary Jo drowned. The key is the pink foam observed exuding from the nostrils by Arena, Farrar, Mills and Frieh. Although water can enter the lungs of an immersed corpse due to hydrostatic pressure, it will remain in the lungs, and exude, as water, not foam.

Foam, often tinged with blood, is a classic indicator of a drowning. It originates from the violent terminal respiratory actions from breathing water.

Nevertheless, it is possible that Mary Jo died of asphyxiation before she was placed in the car. Suffocation can lead to a pulmonary edema that exudes pink foam. However, while that would, indeed, mean she was already dead when she was placed in the car, it leads to conclusions that are even more repugnant than the other.

There are three key pieces of evidence that must be explained when considering Mary Jo's death: pink foam exuding from her nostrils; blood "all over" the back of the blouse and both sleeves; a blood carbon monoxide level of nearly five percent. A corpse immersed in water does not exude foam; a corpse does not bleed; a corpse does not inhale carbon monoxide. What *is* consistent with these three things: a bleeding, live body placed on its back in a car trunk for a significant period of time; and a subsequent drowning or strangulation/asphyxiation.

3) It would not have been possible to insert a body into an overturned car in the conditions that night at Dike Bridge. If you believe John Farrar, it could not have been done without a team of professional divers.

There are two compelling reasons to believe that Mary Jo was inserted into the Oldsmobile after the vehicle was in the pond: the difficulty in believing the group would insert a body into the driver seat of a rigged car without first removing the evidence that the accident was engineered; and the absence of any obvious injuries or marks to the body.

Every accident specialist who has analyzed the vehicle damage has concluded that Kennedy could never have been in the car without exhibiting noticeable physical injuries. Since Kennedy had no noticeable physical injuries, it follows that he could not have been in the car. Yet, inexplicably, that argument is never applied to Mary Jo. However, if you make that case for Kennedy, you make it for Kopechne, too.

Farrar believes that it would be impossible for just two or three untrained persons to insert a body into the vehicle without SCUBA because it conflicts with the conditions he experienced firsthand at Dike Bridge on the morning of July 19.

However, the current experienced by Kennedy and his friends at Dike Bridge the evening before would not have been the same current experienced by Farrar the morning after. In this case, personal experience could lead to misleading conclusions.

4) A group of non-professionals would never be able to rig a car to drive off a bridge.

If you believe John Farrar, it could not have been accomplished without a crew of professional stunt persons. If it couldn't have been done, then the accident was never staged.

Minor problem for our theories

1) If the witnesses were truthful about the time Gargan, Markham, Tretter, Keough, and Tannenbaum left Lawrence Cottage on the morning of July 19, it would leave no time for diving on the vehicle before meeting Kennedy at the Shiretown Inn at 8:00 a.m.

Esther Newberg testified that these five left Lawrence Cottage for Edgartown just before 8:00 a.m. Nance Lyons testified that she was awoken around 7:45 a.m. by the activity of others leaving the cottage. Mary Ellen Lyons testified that they had already left by the time she awoke at 8:00 a.m. If true, then perhaps no diving was ever attempted on the vehicle in the early morning hours and the unkempt, soaking-wet condition of Gargan and Markham when observed by the Richardses was due to something else.

Or, it might mean that these five were diving on the vehicle much earlier in the morning, returned to Lawrence Cottage around 7:45 a.m., and then in their haste to advise Kennedy at the very earliest opportunity, left again immediately without bathing. This possibility is given credence by the fact that Tretter testified he was awake by 5:10 a.m. that morning, and Keough testified she woke up around 5:30 or 6:00 a.m. but was awake "pretty much all night." Gargan told Damore, "There were a lot of people up at this time, around 5:00 or 5:30 a.m."[1] It appears, in fact, that most everyone was awake in the very early morning hours, with the possible exception of Esther Newberg and the Lyons sisters.

Either way, this is a detail that does not affect the validity of the staged-accident theory. Maybe Mary Jo was found in the back seat because it was easier to insert her through the rear window rather than a front one when the accident was engineered.

---

[1] *Senatorial Privilege*, p. 86

43

The Case for Ted Kennedy's Story

$\mathcal{T}$here are several websites dedicated to restoring a luster to Ted Kennedy's tarnished reputation. In fairness to Kennedy, here are the principal arguments found on one such site in 2015.[1]

Ted Kennedy and Mary Jo were not having an affair.

The website says there is no evidence for it and Kennedy consistently denied it.

Ted Kennedy never murdered Mary Jo to cover up a pregnancy.

The website claims that the doctor at the scene found no evidence of pregnancy, and that Ted Kennedy was not opposed to an autopsy.

Actually, Dr Mills testified at the exhumation hearing that he spent "probably 10 minutes" examining the body. He testified that the extent of his examination for pregnancy consisted of "pushing her slacks down a little ways in order to just run over her tummy, or her, excuse me, abdomen."

No one who has studied the evidence seriously believes that Ted Kennedy ever wanted an autopsy. Ted made arrangements to remove the body of Mary Jo from the island before he had even talked to Chief Arena at the police station in Edgartown or had ever talked to Mary Jo's parents. If Kennedy had really wanted an autopsy, he would have asked for one before making those decisions. Kennedy had no legal basis for opposing the state's request for exhumation for an autopsy so he sent Cardinal Cushing, longtime intimate friend, to the Kopechne home to make his case on religious grounds. After the autopsy was denied, Kennedy said he was happy about the judge's ruling because of what it would mean for the Kopechnes.[2]

In any event, I do not believe the evidence suggests that Mary Jo was murdered to cover up a pregnancy, nor did the Kennedy team fear that an autopsy would uncover one. I suspect that Kennedy's attorneys were worried that an autopsy would find a wound at the back of Mary Jo's head which would lead to embarrassing questions.

---

[1] http://www.sabinabecker.com/2009/08/debunking_the_myths_about_chap.html
[2] *Teddy Bare*, p. 140; *Death at Chappaquiddick*, p. 89

Ted Kennedy was very depressed over Mary Jo death.

The website quotes Gargan's inquest recollections concerning Kennedy's reaction as they were driving to the ferry: "Senator Kennedy was very emotional, extremely upset, very upset, and he was using this expression... 'Can you believe it, Joe, can you believe it, I don't believe it, I don't believe this could happen. I just don't believe it.' Markham told the inquest that Kennedy was 'sobbing and almost actually breaking down and crying.' He said, 'This couldn't have happened, I don't know how it happened... What am I going to do?' "

They ask, "But here's the main thing: would a guy who didn't give a s**t attempt 'seven or eight times,' in the *Boston Globe's* words, to rescue Mary Jo whom he did not even know all that well? And would he be upset and crying, as Kennedy was? Would he have attended her funeral, as Kennedy was photographed doing?"

Ted Kennedy never walked away from the scene of the accident. He sincerely did the best he could to rescue her.

The site says, "Kennedy *did* remain for as long as it took him to realize that he could not get Mary Jo out of the car. After that, he had to rest a moment, then he made his stumbling way back." The site claims that Kennedy was so confused he did not even see the light at Dyke House along the road he had just driven down.

Ted Kennedy never lied.

The site says, "FACT: When you can't remember in precise detail what happened because you've been thumped on the head and had your neck badly wrenched, not to mention that you're in shock and confused, would it be fair to call *you* a liar? NO? Well, then, think of how Ted Kennedy must have felt, being hounded by the media on this point every time he was up for reelection. He recollected the night's events to the best of his ability. Unfortunately, his ability was impaired by the head injury he received. Not receiving proper psychiatric care at that crucial moment can't have helped much, either."

Ted Kennedy never tried to cover up Chappaquiddick

The site claims that any cover-up was entirely the fault of Gargan and Markham who gave Kennedy bad advice.

Conclusion:

The site concludes with this comment:

"Unfortunately, sometimes a cigar is just a cigar, sometimes there's no 'there' there, and sometimes an accident is really just an accident. Chappaquiddick was an accident – terrible, tragic, painful for all those involved – but it really was just an accident. There is nothing to be inferred from it.

"But the fact that it cost Ted Kennedy his larger political ambitions, and relegated him to becoming an undignified sideshow even in death, is without a doubt the real scandal of Chappaquiddick."

PART 7: SUMMARY

44
The Boiler Room Girls

*M*any of the books which discuss the Chappaquiddick incident portray the Boiler Room Girls as innocent bystanders caught up in a conspiracy that was not of their making. Sexually promiscuous, maybe, but this was the late '60s when sexual freedom came of age. In 1969, it was OK to treat sex casually.

Several authors have even given grudging praise to the Boiler Room Girls, if only for their staunch and steadfast refusal to reveal much if anything of what happened that night. *They refused to be snitches.* As the Tedrows put it, "A breath of fresh air in an otherwise shabby masculine performance."[1]

And except as it applies to keeping their mouths shut, not one book has accused one or more of them of being active and willing participants in the events that took place that night.

This book does.

Unless one accepts that Mary Jo Kopechne was an enthusiastic passenger on two joyrides that night on Dike Road, one with a group of at least three men and one with Kennedy, the last ride taking her life; or unless there was another woman in the entourage who has never been mentioned by the Kennedys; it is obvious that at least one of the Boiler Room Girls was a willing hands-on accomplice from the very beginning.

Everyone who has analyzed the inquest testimony of the Boiler Room Girls has been confused over the times and statements of each of them. It just never made sense. But read over that testimony again with the idea that the real accident occurred shortly after 11:15 p.m., that the plunge was staged, that Gargan and Markham left Lawrence Cottage twice, that one or more of the girls were directly involved, and their testimony fits together like a hand in a glove. With a new perspective, the evasions, half-truths, and double entendres can clearly be seen as a clever attempt to protect Kennedy, themselves, and their friends, while never actually resorting to an out-and-out lie. I suspect that at least by the inquest, every one of these girls knew exactly what had really occurred that night.

---

[1] *Death at Chappaquiddick*, p. 194

But say I'm wrong. It would still seem probable that many, if not all, know much more about what happened that night then they have ever revealed. How could they not, with cars and people moving frantically about from just before midnight through the early morning hours of the next day? With more direct evidence at their disposal than I have given here, how could they not have already figured it out?

By Esther Newberg's own admission at the inquest, the Boiler Room Girls were very intelligent. In their edition of August 1974, *McCall's* had called them "frighteningly intelligent, politically astute, capable as all get-out, a little tough, perhaps." Ten years after the incident they were reported to have remained close friends.[1] They would have talked it over. Three of them testified that Gargan and Markham had left the party with Kennedy before their first walk. Nance Lyons said that Gargan and Markham had already left at least 20 minutes before they set out on that first walk, and Mary Ellen Lyons said that the first walk was before midnight or 12:15 a.m. Esther Newberg implied that Gargan and Markham left before 12:15 and then again after 12:30 a.m. They all knew Look was not lying about observing the Oldsmobile at 12:40 a.m. Heck, two of them admitted seeing Look and one of them admitted talking to him. Esther Newberg and both Lyons sisters were told by Gargan around 3:00 a.m. that Mary Jo had gone back to Edgartown alone in the Oldsmobile before midnight but that Kennedy had swum the channel, whereas Keough said Gargan had told her Kennedy and Mary Jo returned to Edgartown in the Oldsmobile together.

With just those few facts alone they could only have come to the same conclusion as we have, or something much like it. But, of course, they had more. One of them will have remembered passing Carol's VW bus at high speed. Several of them will have remembered which girls were at the cottage that night, and which girls weren't. If only because one of their own was featured in it, all of them would have seen the BBC documentary of 1994 in which America's leading crash experts explained why Kennedy could never have been in the vehicle when it plunged over the bridge. For the past 45 years they have had access to the exhumation and inquest testimonies, and they've undoubtedly read each and every book detailing the countless inconsistencies in the senator's story. Just as they'll read this one.

Four of the men at the party were lawyers, and lawyers are expected to treat truth casually. But we hope for something more from young women working for an idealistic cause. All these girls went on to lucrative careers which many have suggested were the result of a leg up by the Kennedys. Three became lawyers themselves, which is perhaps fitting.

Ted Kennedy, who they have consistently supported, or his team, were responsible for harassment, intimidation, and, almost certainly, death threats, too. They made life miserable and frightening for many including, most of all, the Kopechnes. The very few individuals who did have the courage to speak up at the time – John Farrar, Huck

---

[1] As reported by the *Virgin Islands Daily News*, May 31, 1979.

Look, Leslie Leland, a couple of witnesses – lived in fear for their lives and the lives of their families for a long time after.

Mrs. Kopechne told *McCall's* in September 1970 that soon after the accident, one of the girls who was visiting someone nearby dropped in to see her at their home in Berkeley Heights, New Jersey, to assure them that the party was an innocent affair. But after that one visit, the Kopechnes waited in vain from some word from any one of them just to "ease the heartache." Leslie Leland, who spent a good deal of time talking to the Kopechnes over many years, says that the couple made many efforts to talk to the girls who attended the party on the island that weekend in hopes that they might be able to answer some of their questions, but that they were consistently rebuffed. The Kopechnes were always asked to speak to their respective lawyers.[1]

None of the damage, fear, and heartache resulting from Kennedy's actions and the cover up that followed have seemed to matter much to these girls. They haven't *cared.* And therefore, one can reasonably ask, just how culpable are they? Should any real admiration be given them at all? Yes, they had to consider their careers and what was done was done. But Farrar, Look, and Leland stood up and fought back. Was it too much to ask that at least one of these might do the same? Was it the stick or the carrot that mattered most to them?

And for those who might have stood by and done nothing while their friend lay wounded on the side of the road, we ask this:

Did you ever think of going for help? Did you ever look at that light shining brightly from the cottage nearby and even consider running there to knock on the door? Did you even speak up?

At night, do you ever wonder what might have been had you acted differently? Have you persuaded yourself that Mary Jo was dead from the beginning? Has time washed it all away by now, as if it never really happened? Are you still convinced that Ted Kennedy was a deserving recipient of your lifelong devotion and esteem?

Has your silence given you peace?

In those moments of truth, when one must decide whether to step up and accept the consequences or take the easy road, everyone hopes they'll make the right choice. The right choice does not appear to have been made at Chappaquiddick. Is it too much to ask, after all this time, that these women, now in their '60s and '70s, might finally find the courage to come clean? Would the real story be so much worse than what many suspect already?

---

[1] *Left to Die*, p. 27

45

Requiem for Edward Moore Kennedy

Jack Olsen's book, The Bridge at Chappaquiddick, *was published just before the Kopechne inquest on January 5. Perhaps because he had so few facts at his disposal, Olsen fills up the first quarter of his book with a description and analysis of Edward Kennedy's life* before Chappaquiddick.

Olsen paints Kennedy, at least before the incident, as a brother who was more adept than the others at public relations and the business of politics but was far less confident in his abilities as a thinker and writer. Unlike Jack and Bobby, Ted left thinking and speechwriting to others. Kennedy would just mention a subject, such as voting or black rights, and let his writers fill in the blanks. Ted Kennedy took the idea of delegated responsibility to an extreme.

Reading through Olsen's eyes it is hard not to feel more than a bit sorry for Ted. Driven by a family patriarch consumed with ambition, failure was never an option. Just as he was becoming more confident in the senate, he was undone by a miscalculation when he asked President Johnson to nominate his mentor, Judge Francis X. Morrissey, to the federal bench. The nomination was shot down by the rest of the senators, and Kennedy once more retreated to his old ways. And then came the 1968 tragedy in Los Angeles when his brother Bobby was assassinated. Olsen says that his friends had never seen Ted Kennedy in such a deeply depressed state. "He wept, sometimes in public, and fought uncharacteristically for his privacy, even refusing to see close friends who wanted to comfort him."[1]

So when the incident at Chappaquiddick occurred in July of 1969 it was only natural for Ted Kennedy to do what he always had done: allow others to take over. Kennedy let his team determine what should be said and how he should act; in fact, to actually invent a story that would put him in the best light. Most of these august men, all with unblemished reputations, endowed with the best education and the highest moral standards, had no hesitation in bending and even breaking the law for a Kennedy. It was as if a sort of mob hysteria took over, leading some of the most esteemed men of our country to put ethics aside and do things they might never have otherwise considered.

But this is where the sympathy ends, at least for many of us who live on Chappaquiddick. Because Ted Kennedy let it all happen. Worse, he encouraged it. He read the speeches others put before him with a straight face. He stood by while those

---

[1] *The Bridge at Chappaquiddick*, p. 43

who questioned his story were subjected to tax audits and death threats. He never had the guts to say, "Enough!" So, what does that say about the man behind the image?

To the last, Kennedy maintained he was at peace with himself over the Kopechne affair, having done absolutely everything in his power to save her. In a very short while he was cracking jokes about Chappaquiddick, even if no one had brought up the subject. While praise can be given for his ability to find humor in a tragedy, few have been able to find anything particularly funny about it.

Kennedy never admitted that he had dissembled on anything. He never had the fortitude to come clean. He admitted he had made some bad decisions, perhaps, but he had never lied. Long before the inquest, Kennedy said, "I can live with myself. I feel the tragedy of the girl's death. But what I don't have to live with are the whispers and innuendoes and falsehoods. Because these have no basis in fact."[1] In a November 6, 1974, letter to *Time* magazine, Kennedy wrote, "*Time* has said that 'to this day the full truth is obscure.' I submit that the full truth has been told but that it has been confused and obscured by the uncorroborated and groundless speculation of unnamed sources." In 1980, 10 years after the incident, Kennedy told Roger Mudd of *ABC*, "There hasn't been a new fact that has questioned the position that I stated at the time of the tragedy and there will not be and cannot be."[2] He said, "People may not believe me or accept some of my answers, but the idea that the people who were there that night are holding back some secret is just all wrong."[3] In a televised campaign speech in 1980, he claimed, "I testified in court, in detail, under oath, to God, the truth about the accident, the only truth I can tell because that is the way it happened."[4] He told *Newsweek* in their edition of October 7, 1974, and the *Los Angeles Times* in 1979 that no new evidence would ever challenge his sworn testimony "because it doesn't exist."

Well, it does now.

Kennedy is said to have been the conscience of the Democratic Party. He is said to have represented the best of liberal values. He was nicknamed the Lion of the Senate. As a Democrat, and as a resident of Massachusetts, I respect him for this. But Ted Kennedy, like every hero, was not without flaws. It started with a cheating scandal at Harvard in 1951 and it continued with a drunken party in 1991 at the family's ancestral mansion in Palm Beach that led to a charge of rape against Kennedy's nephew William Smith.[5]

Chappaquiddick was just one of many personal lows for Kennedy in a life of professional triumph.

---

[1] *Senatorial Privilege*, p. 264

[2] *Chappaquiddick Revealed*, p. 256

[3] *Senatorial Privilege*, p. 413

[4] Television clip in the 1994 BBC documentary *Chappaquiddick*

[5] William Smith was charged with the rape of Patricia Bowman but was later acquitted.

46
Conclusion

*T*he Kennedy Chappaquiddick incident became a fiasco when the public relations faction within the Kennedy camp butted heads with the Kennedy legal team. One group was concerned with Kennedy's image; the other with keeping Kennedy, Gargan, and Markham out of jail. Kennedy's ill-advised television speech and inquest testimonies were attempts to marry two different concerns into one story. The result was an embarrassing failure that fooled no one.

When reporters were finally allowed to examine the inquest testimony on April 29, 1970, almost a year after the incident, Damore says the report "staggered them." The effort to manage inquest testimony had backfired. That Senator Kennedy had not spoken the truth about the accident was, as reported by the *New Bedford Standard-Times,* "the only finding a jurist of integrity could make."[1] Zad Rust, although he could come up with no theory, appears to have hit the nail on the head in *Teddy Bare: The Last of the Kennedy Clan,* one of the best books written about the incident. "The court could not possibly have believed it, could not have failed to conclude that all the evasions, this fabrication, and this effrontery had only one purpose: *to conceal some damning truth* [emphasis in the original]."[2] Arena, who was involved in the incident from start to finish, told the BBC in 1994, "What I feel about the whole thing is that there is more than has been said."

On the other hand, Lange and DeWitt wrote in 1992, "For over twenty years, jealous citizens, vindictive political rivals, and sensation-mongering journalists have tried to make out that Ted Kennedy got away with something that no one else could have gotten away with. On the contrary, he suffered a much greater series of penalties and misfortunes because of who he was."[3]

There are just two alternatives with the Chappaquiddick story: either Kennedy was in the car when it went over the bridge, or he wasn't. The crash experts are certain he

---

[1] *Senatorial Privilege*, p. 82; p. 393

[2] *Teddy Bare*, p. 214

[3] *Chappaquiddick: The Real Story*, p. 162. One wonders if this was really true. The *Average Citizen* posted this story online in 2005: "Less than a week after the accident at Chappaquiddick, the *Oregonian* (Portland, Oregon, July 24, 1969) reported an accident in Salem, Oregon, in which a car crashed through the chain on a ferry while crossing the Willamette River. A passenger riding in the car had drowned, but the driver escaped from the car and swam to shore. The driver was charged with negligent homicide."

wasn't, and most authors are, too.[1] If he wasn't, there are only two likely scenarios: either Kennedy got out of the car soon after Look saw the vehicle and Mary Jo drove off the bridge alone; or the accident was staged. Since it seems highly unlikely that Kennedy would have confessed to causing the death of Mary Jo if he hadn't, and equally unlikely that a week after Kennedy's confession, Gargan and Markham would admit to being involved in the incident if they weren't, the only reasonable conclusion one can reach is that Kennedy and his friends attempted to pull off an expedient hoax. And this would be the logical conclusion even without Carol's sighting.

Lange and DeWitt, co-authors of one of just three books which argue that Kennedy did drive off the bridge with Mary Jo, wrote, "It would have been against Kennedy's interests to say he was driving if he was not. Perjuring himself to make himself look worse than the truth would have served no purpose."[2] Yes, but perjuring himself to look *better* than the truth, would.

On the other hand, if Kennedy was never in the car, was it really because he stepped out of the vehicle after observing Huck Look? Was Kennedy, in actual fact, an innocent victim of circumstance? The evidence for it is nowhere to be found, and the arguments in support of it are weak. Detective Flynn, who was the first to come up with that theory, told the BBC in 1994 that if Kennedy had known about Mary Jo's death, "he would have called Burke Marshall at 1:00 or 2:00 in the morning and asked for his help. But he didn't do that. The only time he called him was when he heard about the accident, which was at 8:00 in the morning."

Certainly Kennedy *said* he called Marshall from Chappaquiddick after 8:00 on the morning of July 19. But according to the *New York Graphic*, calls were made to Burke Marshall's office on Kennedy's credit card at 2:54 a.m., 5:04 a.m., 6:56 a.m., and at 7:19 a.m.,[3] and no call was made to Burke Marshall on Kennedy's card at 8:00 in the morning or after, either in Edgartown or from Chappaquiddick. Moreover, Marshall was the very first person called after Kennedy arrived back at the Shiretown. According to Kennedy aide Rick Burke, the 17 calls reported by the *Union Leader* had indeed been made on Kennedy's credit card, several to Helga Wagner. So what does that say about Flynn's theory? That Kennedy was in the car, although crash experts are certain he was not? Or that Kennedy staged the accident? Would Flynn have continued to insist that Kennedy stepped out of the vehicle after Huck Look saw it if he had been aware of Carol's sighting?

---

[1] Five of the eight books which advance a theory, and one investigative team (BBC documentary *Chappaquiddick*), conclude that Kennedy could not have been in the vehicle.

[2] *Chappaquiddick: The Real Story*, p. 146

[3] None of the calls to Burke Marshall's office were answered.

Which brings us to an interesting question. What might have happened had Carol gone to the police and told them what she saw? Or what might have transpired had Carol testified at the grand jury?

A Massachusetts lawyer friend and Chappaquiddick resident detailed the probable charges against Kennedy, Markham, Gargan, and others if Carol had spoken up at the time, and if Judge Boyle or the grand jury had come to the conclusion that the accident was engineered. "Assuming the inquest prosecution or grand jury believed the accident had been staged, there would likely be several counts brought against the defendants. One group of charges would be concerned with frauds of various sorts: false statements, insurance fraud, conspiracy; the other group would be concerned with felonies such as negligent and wrongful death and manslaughter. If found to be guilty, the total criminal exposure for what would likely be a half dozen or so charges would probably result in a sentence in the 20-year range with concurrent sentencing. Putting aside the identity of the prime defendant, it might wind up as a 10-year sentence, serving, say, 3 to 5 years and out for good behavior.

"This all, of course, would depend on whether they actually believed that the perpetrators were convinced the woman was dead before staging the accident — otherwise the charge would be murder one."

Would Judge Boyle have ever arrived at the conclusion that the accident was engineered? Considering the way Huck Look's testimony was received, probably not. And because the grand jury was prohibited by Judge Paquet from questioning any witness who had previously testified at the inquest, or even examining the inquest testimony itself, it is very doubtful that anything constructive would have come from Carol running to them, either. The grand jury would not have had enough facts at their disposal to understand what Carol's observation could imply.

Nevertheless, no matter how one chooses to interpret Carol's sighting, one thing is certain: it could not be the way Kennedy, Gargan, and Markham told it. Not one of these admitted driving down Dike Road at high speed with a woman in the rented Valiant at 11:35 p.m., and neither Gargan nor Markham admitted leaving Lawrence Cottage twice.

Although many of the details suggested in this book – the whys, whens and hows – are almost certainly incorrect, the verdict appears certain: the accident was staged. And there seem to have been more persons involved in this tragedy than many have heretofore supposed. In his defense of Kennedy's initial police report, Herbert Croly might have come close to the truth when he wrote in the *New Republic*, "He did not in his statement tell all, but the privacy of even a United States senator is entitled to some respect. Moreover, some of those details might have incriminated people who foolishly and irresponsibly and perhaps culpably helped him during that confused night and in the days thereafter – not only Mr. Gargan and Mr. Markham, but perhaps others, too, including some of the girls."[1]

We believe the evidence suggests that an attempt by at least five persons to conceal Kennedy's involvement in an apparent vehicular homicide resulted in the accidental death of Mary Jo. And that's giving Kennedy and his friends the benefit of considerable doubt. According to Lange and DeWitt, the charge for such a crime under Massachusetts law would be second-degree felony murder.[2] This might explain why, in all this time, not one of these individuals has opened up in spite of the recent death of Edward Kennedy.

Even Judge Boyle, so sympathetic to the Kennedy cause at the inquest, was forced by his conscience to render the following judgment: "I infer a reasonable and probable explanation of the totality of the above facts is that Kennedy and Kopechne did not intend to return to Edgartown at that time, that Kennedy did not intend to drive to the ferry slip, and his turn onto Dike Road was intentional." After that bold statement, and possibly fearing dire consequences from the holy toes he had tread on, Boyle promptly retired.

But in spite of Boyle's damning statement, the only legal punishment ever bestowed on Kennedy, following a hearing that lasted less than 10 minutes, was a two-month suspended sentence and a year's probation.[3] Oh yes, and Kennedy's license, which he didn't even possess at the time of the accident, was suspended for a year.

Nevertheless, the verdict was rendered long ago by public opinion, if not by the courts. Except to the few close to the senator who have chosen to bury their heads in the sand, at least publicly, the question for most has always been not *whether* these people lied, but by *how much*. And, of course, *what the hell actually happened?*

Carol's eyewitness account, after 45 years of secrecy, reveals another small piece of the puzzle. We hope it will not be the last.

---

[1] *The New Republic,* Vol. 161, p. 98, September 20, 1969

[2] *Chappaquiddick: The Real Story*, p. 144

[3] There has been disagreement as to whether Kennedy was also given a year's probation. Olsen says he was not (see *The Bridge at Chappaquiddick*, p. 240, and the prosecution's decision not to ask for a year's probation, p. 225). Damore says he was (*Senatorial Privilege: The Chappaquiddick Cover-up,* p. v), but then says he was not (p. 169; pp. 192-193). The official judgment is included in the exhumation testimony (Exhibit #2) which reads, "Commonwealth on complaint of Dominick J. Arena vs. Edward M. Kennedy, Chapter 90, Section 24, leaving the scene of an accident. Plea, Guilty. Result, 2 mo. House of Correction Barnstable - sentence suspended. *Probation one year.*"

Postscript

In 1994, on the 25th anniversary of the incident, Jeff Jacoby, a columnist for the *Boston Globe*, listed 15 questions that had never been answered satisfactorily by Kennedy or his team. I will endeavor to give my thoughts on each of them.

1) Did Kennedy order [Dun] Gifford to remove the body? *Yes.*

2) Why did Kennedy and Kopechne leave the barbecue? *For the obvious reason.*

3) What time did they leave? *Sometime before 11:15 p.m.*

4) Did Kennedy take a wrong turn without realizing it? *No.*

5) Why didn't Kennedy call for help to rescue Kopechne? *He never drove off the bridge by accident. He never called for help because his only real concern was himself.*

6) How much alcohol had Kennedy drunk that night? *A lot.*

7) If he and Kopechne did leave the barbecue at 11:15, what occupied their time until 12:45 when Deputy Look saw them drive toward the bridge? *Look never saw them drive to the bridge. Between 11:20 and 11:55 p.m., Kennedy occupied his time jogging back to the cottage, summoning help from Gargan and Markham, being driven back to the accident on Dike Road in the Valiant, and then returning to Lawrence Cottage with a wounded Mary Jo. Between 11:55 p.m. and 12:30 a.m., Kennedy made phone calls at the private, detached studio in the backyard of Lawrence Cottage. From 12:30 to 1:40 a.m., Kennedy appears to have spent his time finding boat transportation and staging the accident.*

8) After getting out of the submerged car, why didn't Kennedy walk to the lighted house a few yards away and call for help? Or call from the house with the barbecue? Or from his motel? *Kennedy never was in the submerged car. The accident was staged.*

9) Did he urge Gargan to fabricate a story about Kopechne being alone in the car when it went off the bridge? *Yes.*

10) Did he go to the police only when he realized he would not be able to carry off such an alibi? *Yes.*

11) If, as Kennedy said later, what was uppermost in his mind was "the tragedy and loss of a very devoted friend," why did he summon 19 high-level political advisers to Hyannis the next day? *That was never uppermost in his mind.*

12) Was the prosecutor [Dinis] awarded for not bringing manslaughter or driving-to-endanger charges against Kennedy? *Massachusetts District Attorney Edmund Dinis, a Democrat, appears to have tried to walk a shaky tightrope between doing his job and keeping his Democrat friends happy to win an upcoming election, which he subsequently lost. A better question is whether Edgartown Police Chief Dominick Arena and Dukes County prosecutor Walter Steele were rewarded for failing to undertake any serious investigation, supporting Kennedy's version of the events*

unconditionally, negotiating a plea deal ridiculously favorable to Kennedy, and intimidating those who questioned the truth of Kennedy's story.

13) Why was the grand jury threatened with jail and intimidation by a judge [Paquet] when it tried to look into the tragedy? *Power of the Kennedys.*

14) When an inquest was eventually held, why did Kennedy fight – against all precedent – to keep its proceedings secret? *So the public and press would never hear about the inconsistencies until long after the inquest was over.*

15) Why was Farrar, the diver, barred from telling the inquest and grand jury what he knew? *As regards the inquest (and exhumation hearing), perhaps a deal had been worked out between Farrar and Kennedy's attorneys. As regards the grand jury, Judge Paquet refused to allow the jurors to question anyone who had previously testified at the inquest.*

Jacoby ends with a rhetorical question, one Ted Kennedy himself asked in 1994 after President Nixon was pardoned by President Ford:

Do we operate under a system of equal justice under law, or is there one system for the average citizen and another for the high and mighty?

Appendix

Note 1: Torque Acting About a Pivot Point

Torque (τ) acting around a pivot point when the object is perpendicular to the current.

Given Data

A = cross-sectional area of the side of the car = ~ 4.4 m²
v = assumed velocity of the current at the time of the accident = 2.3 knots = 1.183 m/sec
Θ = assumed angle of the car on the bottom, viewed from the side = 20°
ρ = density of saltwater = 1027 kg/m³
L = length of the vehicle = 18 ft. = 5.49 m

Force (F) = ½ ρ A v^2 = 0.5 * 1027 * 4.4 * 1.4 = 3163 N
Lever arm (X) = (L/2) cos Θ = 2.75 * 0.94 = 2.59
τ = FX = 3163 * 2.59 = 8,192 N-M = 6,042 foot-pounds

Note 2: Air Flow from a Submerged Vehicle

How fast, in cubic feet per minute, would air escape an overturned vehicle submerged in saltwater?

Assume two half-inch-wide gaps, each running for two feet up the side of the car. Both gaps begin three feet below the surface of the water and end one foot from the surface. Calculate the initial flow of air from the car.

Given Data

Width of the gap = ½ in
Number of gaps: 2
The height of the gap = 2 ft.
Surface to end of gap: 3 ft.
Surface to start of gap: 1 ft.
Initial flow of air from the car 3 ft. from surface = ?

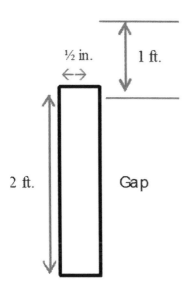

½ in.   1 ft.

2 ft.   Gap

Solution

To calculate Air Flow in Cubic Feet per Minute (CFM) it is necessary to determine the velocity (v) in feet per minute, then multiply this figure by the duct cross-sectional area.

The density of air = 1.184 kg/m³, much less than seawater. The air will be compressed and then escape from the car by some velocity.

The following equation is used to determine the escape velocity of air:
$v = \sqrt{(2gh)}$
where g is 9.8 m/sec² and h is the distance from the surface of the water in meters.
Initial velocity of air, 3 feet from the surface: v = 4.233 m/sec

To determine the Flow Rate (Q), use the equation Q = avk
where a is the area of the combined 2 gaps = 0.015484 m²
v is the velocity of the air in m/sec
k is a constant for this type of gap = 0.85

Initial flow of air:

Q = 4.233 * 0.015484 *0 .85 = 0.055712 m³/sec = 118 CFM

Note 3: Impact Force on a Body and Head

What would be the peak impact force when a 220-lb. human body impacted the roof of a car driven 4 mph into the sand? What would it be for a 110-lb. passenger? What would it be for a head? (Assume the bodies decelerated from 4 mph to zero over a distance of 1 inch, and assume the head decelerated from 10 mph to zero over a distance of .5 cm).

Given Data

Mass of human (1) = 220 lbs	= 99.9 Kg
Mass of human (2) = 110 lbs	= 39.895 kg
Speed at impact = 4 mph	= 1.79 m/sec
Distance covered = 1 in	= 0.0254 m
Mass of human head	= 3.5 - 4 kg
Speed at impact = 10 mph	= 4.47 m/sec
Distance covered = 0.5 cm	= 0.005 m

Case 1: When weight of human is 220 lbs

Kinetic energy of human before impact = $0.5mv^2$

$K.E. = \frac{1}{2} 99.9 * 1.79^2$
$K.E. = 160.0 \, J$

The body struck the roof and decelerated to zero in 1 inch. In effect, the roof "worked" to stop the body and exerted a force on the body. According to the work energy principle

$F * d = 0.5 \, mv^2$
$F = 160.0 / 0.0254$

The average impact force on the body = 6299 Newton or 1416 lbs or 0.7 tons

The impact force begins at zero, rises to a peak at twice the average force, then returns to zero over the distance traveled. Therefore, the peak impact force is 1.4 tons.

Case 2: When weight of human is 110 lbs

Kinetic energy of human body before impact = $0.5mv^2$
$K.E. = \frac{1}{2} 49.9 * 1.79^2$
$K.E. = 80 \, J$

$F = 80 / 0.0254$

The average impact force on the body = 3150 Newton or 0.35 tons
The peak impact force is 0.7 tons

Case 3: When weight of head is 3.5 - 4 kg

Kinetic energy of human head before impact = $0.5mv^2$
$K.E. = \frac{1}{2}\,3.5 * 4.47^2$
$K.E. = 34.97\,J$

$F = 34.97 / 0.005$

The average impact force on the head = 6994 to 7992 Newton, or 0.79 to 0.90 tons
The peak impact force is 1.58 to 1.80 tons

Note 4: Flow Rate of Water from a Pond

a) The Flow Rate (Q) of liquids is directly proportional to the volume (V) of the fluid and inversely proportional to the time, expressed by the formula $Q = V / t$.

b) The Flow Rate (Q) is directly proportional to the speed of the flow (v) if the size of the opening remains constant.

Given Data

Pond A) Average Speed: 4 knots
Height of pond: 23 inches
Time to empty: 335 minutes

Pond B) Average Speed: ?
Height of pond: 21.75 inches
Time to empty: 410 minutes

The length and width of the pond did not change appreciably. Only the height changed.

Therefore: The volume of the pond in B) was 0.945 that of A.
The time of pond B) was 1.224 that of A.

$Q = V/t$ Pond A: 1 unit of volume ÷ 1 units of time = Q of 1.
Pond B: 0.945 units of volume ÷ 1.224 units of time = Q of 0.772

$Q = v$ because the size of the opening is the same for both ponds. Therefore
v of Pond A = 4 knots
v of Pond B = 0.772 x 4 = 3.09 knots

Note 5: Formulas to Determine the State of the CM at the Moment of Free Fall (and from this, the initial velocity of the vehicle as it leaves the ramp)

Caveat: these formulas will not apply perfectly at Dike Bridge because the rub rail complicates the situation.

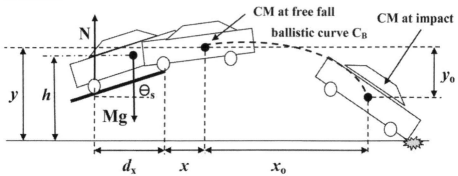

Step 1: Input preliminary data:

V_0:   assumed initial velocity, in m/sec
g: gravitational acceleration (9.81 m/sec^2)
M: mass of vehicle, in kilograms
L: total length of vehicle, in meters
D: horizontal distance from CM to rear axle, in meters
Θ_S: slope of the ramp, in degrees
Θ_L: launch angle of the vehicle off the ramp in respect to its vertical axis, in degrees
Θ_A: angle between rear axle and CM, viewed from the lateral axis, in degrees
Θ_B: angle between a rear wheel and CM, viewed from the vertical axis, in degrees
d: vehicle wheelbase, in meters
h :   vertical height from the CM to the impact surface at the moment the front wheels begin falling off the ramp, in meters

Step 2: Solve for these formulas:

Θ_R: relative ramp slope, in degrees: $\Theta_R = \Theta_S \cos \Theta_L$
I_{CM} :   moment of inertia of vehicle, in kg-m^2: $I_{CM} = ML^2 / 12$
N: Newton force acting up through the rear wheels while both rear wheels remain on the ramp: $N = g \cos \Theta_R / [1 + (MD^2 \cos \Theta_A) / I_{CM})]$
    If only one rear wheel remains on the ramp, the formula is:
    $N = g \cos \Theta_R / [1 + (MD^2 \cos \Theta_A \cos \Theta_B) / I_{CM})]$
a: vertical acceleration acting up through the rear wheels while one or more rear wheels remain on the ramp but the front wheels are airborne, in m/sec^2: $a = g - N \cos \Theta_R$
t: time that vehicle traverses distance d, in seconds: $t = d / V_0$

d_x: horizontal distance traveled by the wheelbase at the slope of the ramp, in meters:
              $d_x = d \cos \Theta_R$

Δh: change in height h at the moment of free fall, in meters:
              $\Delta h = d_x \tan \Theta_R - [a d_x^2 / (2 \, V_0 \cos \Theta_R)^2]$

S_x: horizontal speed of the CM at the moment of free fall, in m/sec: $S_x = d_x / t$

S_y: vertical speed of the CM at the moment of free fall, in m/sec:
              $S_y = V_0 \sin \Theta_R - (a d_x / V_0 \cos \Theta_R)$

Step 3: Solve for the vector velocity, horizontal position, vertical position, and attack angle of the CM at the moment free fall begins, assuming the initial launch velocity V_1:

a) The vector velocity $|v|$ of the CM at the moment of free fall, in m/sec, is given by:
$|v| = \sqrt{(S_x^2 + S_y^2)}$

b) The horizontal distance x from the end of the ramp to the CM at the moment of free fall, in meters, is given by: $x = d_x - D \cos \Theta_R$

c) The vertical height y of the CM at the moment of free fall, in meters, is given by:
$y = h + \Delta h$

d) The attack angle Θ of the CM at the moment of free fall, in degrees, is given by:
$\Theta = \tan^{-1}(S_y / S_x)$

Step 4: Solve for the forward parabolic curve of the CM from the moment of free fall to impact:

Compute the distance x_0 traveled by a projectile launched at velocity $|v|$ at angle Θ and at drop y_0, following a normal ballistic curve C_B at gravity g. Drop y_0 will depend on the orientation of the vehicle at impact. There are several internet sites to help the layman determine the ballistic curve. See http://hyperphysics.phy-astr.gsu.edu/hbase/traj.html#tracon
and http://www.convertalot.com/ballistic_trajectory_calculator.html

The mathematical formula is given by: $x_0 = (|v| \cos \Theta / g)(|v| \sin \Theta + \sqrt{[(|v| \sin \Theta)^2 + 2g \, y_0]})$, where x_0 and y_0 are in meters.

Step 5: Solve for the true initial velocity of the vehicle V_0:

If the measured distance x_0 traveled by the CM of the vehicle, from the moment of free fall to the point of impact, is greater than the calculated distance of x_0 in *Step 4* above, assume a lower initial velocity V_0 and work through the calculations in *Step 3* through *Step 4* again. If the distance is less, assume a higher V_0 and work through the calculations again. And so on until the initial velocity is correct for the actual distance traveled by the CM during free fall. The measured distance x_0 will depend on the orientation of the vehicle at impact.

Note 6: Door Structural Analysis

Guglielmo Cacciatore, Raul Ochoa
Structural Analysis of the Doors of a Delmont 88
November 15, 2015

Outline

- CAD Model Designs: Front and Rear Doors
- Material Properties
- Structural Analysis Loads and Boundary Conditions
- Front Door Analysis Results
- Rear Door Analysis Results
- Summary

Front
Door

Rear
Door

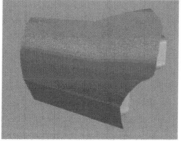

Front Door

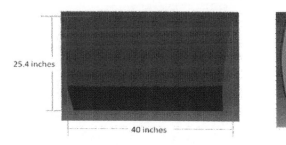

25.4 inches

40 inches

Both external panel and internal frame are **0.0375** inches thick.

Rear Door

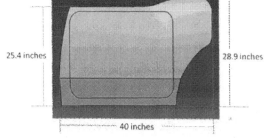

25.4 inches   28.9 inches

40 inches

Both external panel and internal frame are **0.0375** inches thick.

Material Properties

- Properties for Cold Rolled Steel
- Modulus of Elasticity, $E = 29 \times 10^6$ psi
- Poisson Ratio, $\nu = 0.3$
- Density, $\rho = 0.284$ lb/in^3
- Yield Strength, Fty = 44,962 psi
- Stress Strain curve created for non-linear analysis (see next slide)

Stress Strain Curve

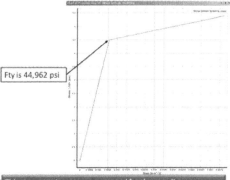

Fty is 44,962 psi

This stress strain curve was created for the non-linear analysis. Notice, after the yield point, the material behavior changes, no longer falling within the elastic range.

Loads and Boundary Conditions

- Structural Analysis of front and rear door panels was performed.
- Pressure loads were applied to find loads required to dent front door panel to approximately 5 inches.
- Pressure loads also applied to rear door panel to check how much load it took to displace a few inches.
- Pressure loads applied to outer skin of door.
- The total surface area of each door – pressure area.
  - Front Door Area = 1012 in^2
  - Rear Door Area = 952 in^2

Uniform pressure applied to sheet metal skin.

Boundary Condition – Front Door

The two side walls of the internal frame were fixed.

Boundary Condition - Rear Door

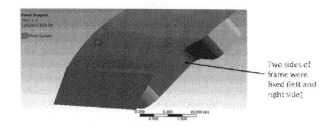

The two side walls of the internal frame were fixed.

Front Door

Load	Max Displacement (inches)	Fty (psi)
15.1 psi	0.17	44,962
100 psi	**4.47**	

Total Surface Area of applied pressure = 1012 in²

At 15.1 psi loading condition is when the door panel will begin permanent deformation.

Front Door Results

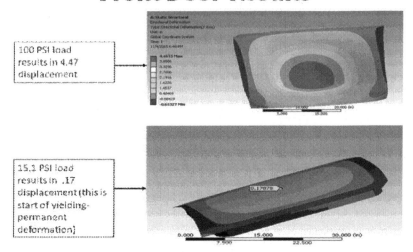

100 PSI load results in 4.47 displacement

15.1 PSI load results in .17 displacement (this is start of yielding-permanent deformation)

Rear Door

Load	Max Displacement (inches)	Fty (psi)
108 psi	1.57	
127.5 psi	1.96	44,962
152 psi	2.36	
27.3 psi	0.1	

Total Surface Area of applied pressure = 952 in²

At 27.3 psi loading condition is when the door panel will begin permanent deformation (0.1 in)

Rear Door Results

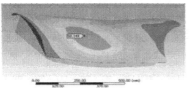

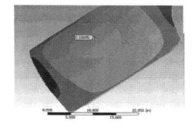

1.57 inches

1.96 inches

Summary

- Structural analysis performed using Finite Element Analysis Method.
- The analysis provided was performed with an approximate door panel design made of cold-rolled steel.
- Loads were applied to identify pressure loading that would create an approximate 5 inch dent in the front door.
- Cold-rolled steel with a Yield Strength of approximately 44,962 psi was considered.
- The non-linear stress strain curve created for the nonlinear structural analysis was assumed to be bilinear after the steel's Yield Point (44,962). This assumption approximates the behavior after the material yields.
- Analysis shows that the front door will have permanent deformation of 15.1 psi. This means that the steel panels will stay deformed (ie, not return to original un-deformed state). The rear door starts permanent deformation with a pressure load of 27.3 psi.
- Furthermore, the front panel will experience a dent of approximately 4.5 inches when the pressure loads reach 100 psi.

Note 7: Side Window & Front Windshield Structural Analysis

Raul Ochoa
Structural Analysis of the Side Windows and Front Windshield
of a Delmont 88
November 15, 2015

Outline

- CAD Model Designs: Driver side windows, front and rear. Front windshield.
- Material properties
- Structural analysis loads and boundary conditions
- Front passenger window results
- Rear passenger window results
- Front windshield window results
- Summary

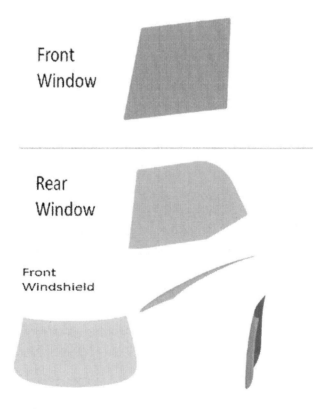

Front Window

Rear Window

Front Windshield

Front Door

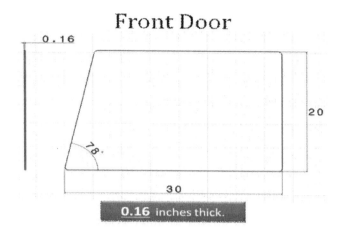

0.16

20

78°

30

0.16 inches thick.

Rear Door

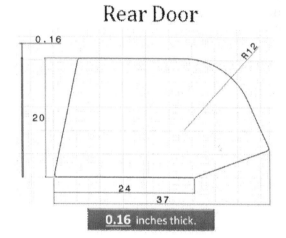

0.16

R12

20

24

37

0.16 inches thick.

Front Windshield

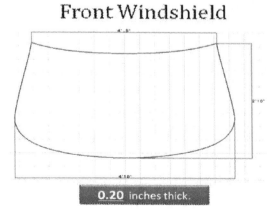

0.20 inches thick.

Material Properties

- Properties for Tempered Glass
- Modulus of Elasticity, $E = 10 \times 10^6$ psi
- Poisson Ratio, $\nu = 0.22$
- Density, $\rho = 0.0903$ lb/in^3
- Fracture (break) Strength = 24,000 psi

- Strength and Elastic Modulus – Reference
  – http://www.makeitfrom.com/material-properties/toughened-tempered-soda-lime-glass/

Loads and Boundary Conditions

- Structural Analysis of the side windows and front windshield were performed.
- Pressure loads were applied to find loads required to fracture the windows.
  – Breaking stress is 24,000 psi.
- Pressure loads applied to outer windows perpendicular to surfaces.
- Outer perimeters of windows were fixed.
- The total surface area of each window – pressure area.
  – Front side window area = 557 in^2
  – Rear side window area = 603 in^2
  – Front windshield area = 1861 in^2

Uniform pressure applied to outer surfaces of windows

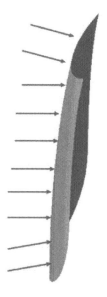

Boundary Condition – All Windows

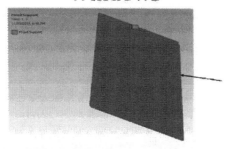

The outer perimeters of the three windows were constrained (fixed).

Front Side Window Results

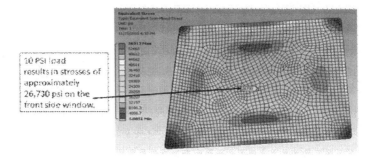

10 PSI load results in stresses of approximately 26,730 psi on the front side window.

10 psi load will break the front side glass window

Rear Side Window Results

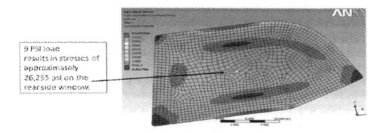

9 PSI load results in stresses of approximately 26,255 psi on the rear side window.

9 psi load will break the front side glass window

Front Windshield Results

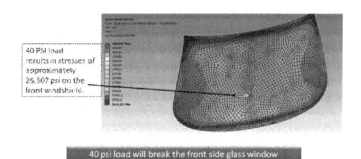

40 PSI load results in stresses of approximately 25,307 psi on the front windshield.

40 psi load will break the front side glass window

Summary

- Structural analysis performed using Finite Element Analysis Method (ANSYS used).
- The analysis provided was performed using approximate 3D models of the side windows and front windshield. Thicknesses of 0.16 and 0.20, side windows and front windshield respectively, were assumed.
- Loads were applied to identify pressure loading that would fracture the glass windows. The breaking stress considered was 24,000 psi.
- Analysis shows that the front side window will fracture with a pressure of approximately 10 psi.
- Analysis shows that the rear side window will fracture with a pressure of approximately 9 psi.
- The front windshield will fracture at about 40 psi. The higher fracture pressure for the front windshield is due to its curvature which provides more cross-sectional inertia. Furthermore, the front windshield is thicker than the side windows (0.20 inches vs 0.16 inches).

Note 8: Roof and Front Windshield Structural Analysis

Raul Ochoa
Structural Analysis of the Roof and Front Windshield
of a Delmont 88
October 2, 2016

Outline

- CAD Model Designs: Roof of Oldsmobile Delmont 88
- Material properties
- Structural analysis loads and boundary conditions
- Roof deformation results
- Windshield stress results
- Summary

Roof CAD Model

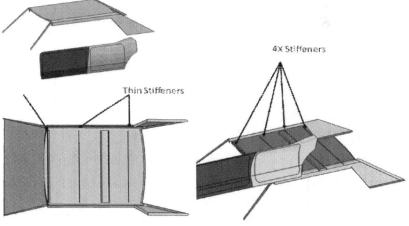

CAD Model with Photos

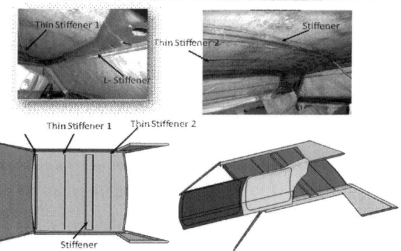

Roof with Windshield

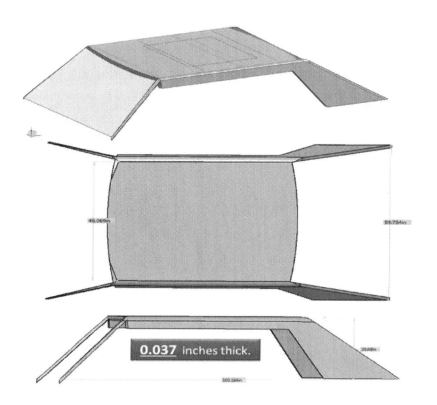

Stiffener

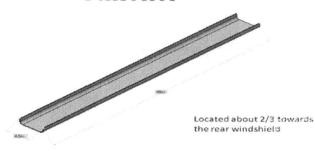

Located about 2/3 towards
the rear windshield

0.037 inches thick.

Thin Stiffener

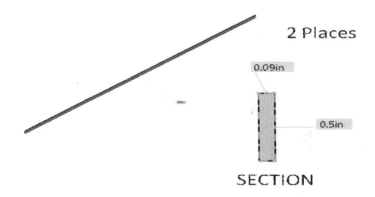

2 Places

0.09in

0.5in

SECTION

L Stiffener

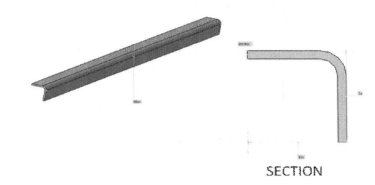

SECTION

Windshield-Tempered Glass

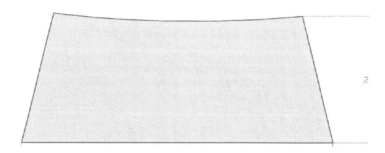

Material Properties

- Properties for Cold Rolled Steel
- Modulus of Elasticity, E= 29 x 10^6 psi
- Poisson Ratio, v = 0.3
- Density, ρ = 0.284 lb/in^3
- Yield Strength, Fty = 44,962 psi
- Stress Strain curve created for non-linear

Stress Strain Curve-Steel

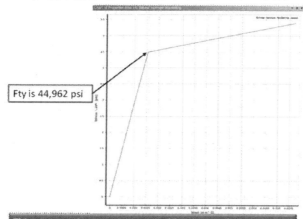

Fty is 44,962 psi

This stress strain curve was created for the non-linear analyses. Notice, after the yield point, the material behavior changes, no longer falling within the elastic range.

Material Properties

- Properties for Tempered Glass
- Modulus of Elasticity, $E = 10 \times 10^6$ psi
- Poisson Ratio, $v = 0.22$
- Density, $\rho = 0.0903$ lb/in^3
- Fracture (break) Strength = 24,000 psi

- Strength and Elastic Modulus — Reference
  - http://www.makeitfrom.com/material-properties/toughened-tempered-soda-lime-glass/

Loads and Boundary Conditions

- Structural Analysis of the roof was performed.
- An impact force was applied to a localized area on the top of the roof.
- Loads were applied to evaluate windshield breaking load and load required to deform the roof approximately 3 inches.
- Outer perimeters of the roof were fixed, including both windshields where they meet the hood and trunk of the car.

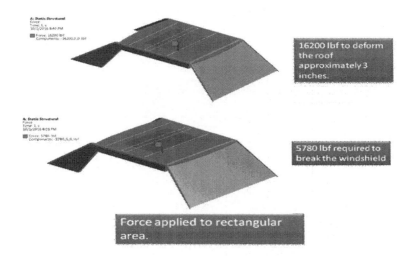

16200 lbf to deform the roof approximately 3 inches.

5780 lbf required to break the windshield

Force applied to rectangular area.

Boundary Condition

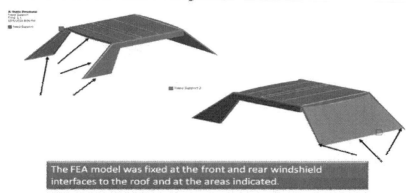

The FEA model was fixed at the front and rear windshield interfaces to the roof and at the areas indicated.

FEA Model

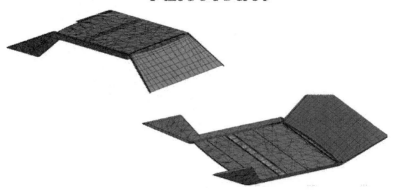

FEA Model

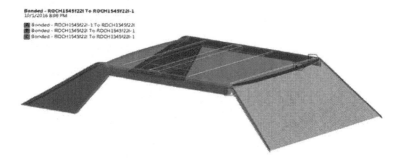

Windshield was bonded to roof as shown.

Displacement Results

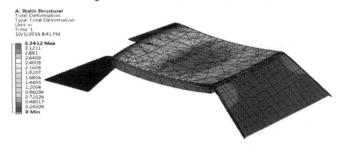

16200 lb load will deform the top of roof 3.36 inches.

Windshield Breaking Load

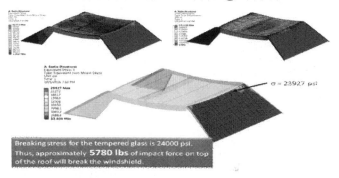

$\sigma = 23927$ psi

Breaking stress for the tempered glass is 24000 psi.
Thus, approximately **5780 lbs** of impact force on top
of the roof will break the windshield.

LOAD CONDITIONS AT BRIM OF FRONT
WINDSHIELD, AND LOAD APPLIED TO ENTIRE
SURFACE OF ROOF

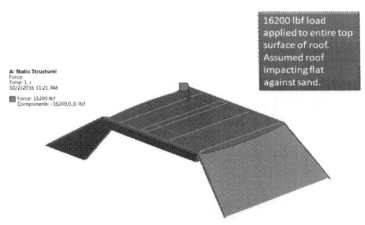

16200 lbf load
applied to entire top
surface of roof.
Assumed roof
impacting flat
against sand.

Displacement Results – Load on Entire Roof Surface

A 16200 lb load will deform the top of roof 1.93 inches. Thus, a localized force will deform the roof more than if the entire surface was impacted

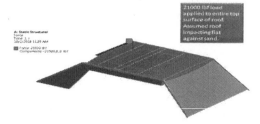

21000 lbf load applied to entire top surface of roof. Assumed roof impacting flat against sand.

Displacement Results – Load on Entire Roof Surface

21000 lb load will deform the top of roof 3.19 inches. This is for case when entire roof surface is impacted.

Windshield Load at Front

Load near front Windshield

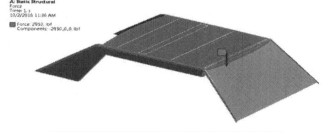

2950 lb load applied at front.

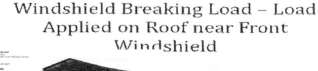

Windshield Breaking Load – Load Applied on Roof near Front Windshield

$\sigma = 24030$ psi

Breaking stress for the tempered glass is 24000 psi. Thus, approximately **2950 lbs** of impact force on top near the front of the windshield will fracture the windshield.

Summary

- Structural analysis performed using Finite Element Analysis Method.
- The analysis provided was performed with an approximate roof panel design made of cold-rolled steel.
- Loads were applied to identify the impact force that would create an approximate 3-inch dent on the top of the roof.
- Cold-rolled steel with a Yield Strength of approximately 44,962 psi was considered.
- The nonlinear stress strain curve created for the nonlinear structural analysis was assumed to be bilinear after the steel's Yield Point (44,962). This assumption approximates the behavior after the material yields.
- Analysis shows that an impact force of 16,200 lbs. would create a displacement of 3.36 inches on the roof panel.
- A 21,000 lb. load applied to the entire roof surface will deform the roof 3.19 inches.
- In addition, a load of 5,780 lbs. applied to the top of the roof will shatter the windshield.
- In my opinion this high of a force was the result of an impact with solid ground/dirt/sand from a crash event. This damage was not a result of extracting the car from the water.

INDEX

A

A&E Investigative Reports Chappaquiddick. See Brtitish Broadcasting Corporation (BBC)
Ahlbum, Jon, iii, 43, 297
alcohol, 26, 28–29, 63, 65, 99, 124, 131, 305, 321, 338, 364
Anderson, Jack, 23
Arena, Police Chief Dominick, i, ii, v, 6–8, 15, 19–21, 26, 36, 52, 53, 54, 58, 74, 76–81, 90, 101, 104, 109, 117, 119, 121, 127, 128, 135, 152, 157–68, 199, 204, 210, 218, 222, 249–57, 266, 273, 274, 287, 288, 318, 337, 341, 352, 360, 363, 364
Arthur D. Little Company, 127, 142, 296
Aspen, Colorado, 42
Associated Press (AP), 281
Average Citizen, 360

B

Baker, Bobby, 66
Ballou, Pussy, wife of Todd, 11
Ballou, Todd, iii, 10–12, 198, 214, 237, 246, 308, 315, 320, 347
Batten, Douglas, iii, 43, 98, 99, 193
Benzidine test, 18, 94–96, 202
Bettencourt, Edna, wife of Tony, 251
Bettencourt, Skip, son of Tony, 251
Bettencourt, Tony, ii, 1, 4, 15, 16, 32, 212, 226, 228, 251, 274, 288, 311, 317
Billings, Lamoyne, 318
blood, 17–19, 29, 36, 37, 90, 91, 94–102, 193, 194, 201–4, 227, 259, 260, 286, 302, 304, 315, 320, 329, 332, 339, 343, 344–47
Boiler Room Girls, iii, 1, 4, 13, 14, 20, 68, 96, 199, 203, 206, 217–19, 222–26, 241, 244, 259, 261, 281, 283, 305, 317, 338, 340, 346–48, 355, 356
Boston, 265
Boston Globe, 248, 326, 327, 353, 364
Boston Herald Traveler, 19, 106, 194, 195, 200, 214, 265, 296, 329
Boston Neurological Laboratory, 326
Boston Record-American, 91
Bowman, Patricia, 359
Boyle, Judge James, i, ii, v, 25, 28, 58, 106, 194, 200, 201, 220, 228, 229, 230, 231, 240, 243, 267, 280, 295–97, 311, 318, 333, 362–63
British Broadcasting Corporation (BBC), 7, 15, 16, 18, 20, 30, 31, 36, 37, 61, 84, 88, 91, 97, 102, 104, 105, 117, 118, 121, 129, 134, 154, 161, 168, 214, 217, 222, 223, 226, 234, 252, 256, 266, 275, 285–90, 294, 297, 304, 310, 320, 322, 327, 332–35, 338, 345, 356, 359, 360, 361
Theory, 57
Brominski, Judge Bernard, i, ii, v, 318
Brooklin, Maine, 293
Brougham, Dr. Milton, 326
Brougier, Robert, 4, 8, 9, 15
Brower, Brock, 250, 256, 263
Bruno, Hal, 13
Buick Mercury, 63, 223, 317
Burke, David, ii, 16, 282, 318
Burke, Richard, 21
Burns, Lansing, iv, 11, 198, 308, 315, 347

C

Cacciatore, Guglielmo, 148, 190–94
Cape Cod Hospital, 326
Cape Cod Today, 336
Cape Poge, 10, 73, 83, 246
Cappavella, Joseph, 4

carbon monoxide, 29, 30, 99, 193, 203, 234, 302, 305, 314, 320, 347

Casey, Chris, 38

Cemetery Road, 8, 59, 106, 199, 207, 208, 217, 246, 306

Chappaquiddick Beach Club, 11, 23, 198, 308, 315

Chogin, 277

Ciesbrecht, Professor Cordon, 120

Clark, Robert, 317

Clark, Robert, III, 317

Clifford, Ralph L., 22, 196

Colonial Inn, 14, 343

Concordia Boat Yard, 10, 11, 308

Constantino, Linda, 50

Crandall, Jim, 75, 136, 140, 144

Crimmins, Dorothy, v

Crimmins, John, iii, 29, 197, 210, 221, 229, 240–44, 259, 289

Croly, Herbert, 362

Cross, Dr. Rod, 68, 108, 109, 116–19, 169, 190, 193–95, 284, 286, 367

   Chapters, 132–89

Culver, John, 317

Cushing, Cardinal, 18, 58, 352

Cutler, Robert, iv, 31, 34, 65, 72, 73, 226, 285–86, 288, 297, 302, 340, 341, 342

   Theory, 64–65

D

Daily Sitka Sentinel, 281

Daley, Dan, 219, 318, 329

Damore, Leo, iv, vi, 9, 10, 12, 16, 19–24, 28, 31, 98, 99, 117, 206–7, 215, 218, 219, 223, 232, 233, 241, 243, 251, 252–53, 256, 257, 262, 273, 282–83, 289, 294–97, 302, 305, 308, 316, 328, 329, 331, 347, 351, 360, 363

Davis, John, 62

Denison, John, 325

DeWitt, Katherine, iv, 74, 82, 95, 258, 316, 360, 363

   Theory, 58

Dinis, Edward, ii, v, 18, 19, 37, 94, 122, 194, 205, 224, 233, 257, 267, 284, 296, 329, 333, 364

Donahue, Scott, 38, 39

Donovan, Paul, 281

Driscoll, John, 318

Dubois, Robert, ii, 104, 105, 117, 288

Dunn, John, 14, 15, 30, 31, 209

Duxbury, Massachusetts, 25

Dyke House, ii, 1, 4, 7, 23, 216, 251, 252, 255, 257–58, 260, 261, 262, 263, 303, 307, 341, 353

E

Edgartown Regatta, ii, 1, 343

Edgartown Yacht Club, 7, 10, 42, 343

Egan, Arthur, 10, 21, 249

Esquire, 91

Evening Standard, 200

Ewing, Steve, iii, 16, 30, 31, 32, 42, 43, 104

F

Farrar, John, ii, vi, 4, 15, 17, 19, 34–36, 43, 54, 68, 70, 71, 73–85, 88, 90–96, 97, 100, 103, 105, 107, 111, 115, 121–25, 131, 150, 168, 190, 192, 193, 195, 199, 201, 204, 235, 265, 286, 289, 335, 344, 345, 346, 350, 356, 357, 365

Feldman, Dr. Robert, 326

Ferguson, Ed. *See* Ulasewicz, Tony

Fernandes, Armand, ii, 31, 106, 107, 165, 168, 194, 200, 296, 297

Fischer, William, ii, 88, 97, 104–5, 107, 110, 117, 123, 127, 129, 130, 134, 135, 146, 149, 161, 169, 173, 178, 285–88, 294, 297, 338

   Speed Estimate, 152–54

Flanagan, Joseph, ii, 95, 97, 168, 280, 302

Floyd, Ann, 12, 157

Flynn, Bernie, ii, v, 58, 226, 248, 257, 262, 288–90, 312, 331–35, 361

Forago, Ladislas, 59

Frieh, Eugene, ii, 17, 18, 29, 36, 90, 91, 94, 96, 102, 104, 119, 201, 321

G

Galbraith, John Kenneth, 318

Gargan, Joseph, iii, vi, 4–6, 9, 12–14, 19, 20, 22–27, 30–31, 57–60, 63, 64, 66, 67, 76, 95, 99–101, 123, 165, 196–99, 205–47, 252, 253, 254, 256–57, 261–62, 266–68, 271, 278, 282–85, 301, 304–18, 320, 321, 322, 324–35, 337, 339, 340, 344–56, 360–64

Gautreau, J.E., 10, 52

Gentle, Steve, 197

Gifford, Dun, ii, 15–18, 215, 226, 227, 228, 253, 255–56, 272, 285, 288, 290, 310, 317, 321, 322, 332, 333, 340, 364

Gilmartin, James, 21

Goodwin, Richard, 317

Gostenhofer, David, viii

Grant, Jared, ii, 28, 265, 268

Guay, David, 18, 91, 102

Gwirtzman, Milton, 318

H

Hackett, David, 318

Hanify, Edward, 21, 62, 318

Harbor View Hotel, 1, 270

Harborside Inn, 10, 343

Hastings, Don, iv, 10, 23, 24, 74, 246, 248

Hatton, Joyce, 42

Hell-Ville, Madagascar, 276

Herald News, viii, 54

Hersh, Burton, iii, iv, viii, 16, 22, 213, 243, 266, 267, 298, 322, 324, 326, 341

Hewitt, Richard, ii, 32, 100, 265

Hoar, Roddy, iii, 11, 12, 157, 198, 214, 306

Hoover, J. Edgar, 66

Hubbard, Jack, 45, 86, 112, 115, 135, 140, 142, 152, 157–61, 162, 165, 166, 178

Hyannis Port, ii, viii, 11, 15, 41, 196, 254, 314, 340

J

Jacoby, Jeff, 364, 365

Jeffers, Jerry, vii, 7, 258, 288

Joesten, Joachim. *See* Cutler, Robert

Jones, Barton, brother of Carol, 61

Jones, Carol, iii, viii, 2, 12, 44, 45, 52–56, 60–61, 66–68, 106, 194, 197, 198, 199, 203, 211–27, 237, 242–45, 253, 255, 260–62, 264, 272, 284, 288, 291, 292, 299, 301, 302, 311–14, 328, 332, 335, 340, 343–44, 346, 347, 356, 361–63

Encounter, 38–44

Jones, Curry, father of Carol, 55, 291

Jones, Gerald, 48

Jones, Hugh, 124

Jones, Jane, sister of Carol, 341

Jones, Maryann, sister of Carol, viii

Jones, Peggy, mother of Carol, 61

Jones, Penn, 67

Jones, Peter, brother of Carol, 12, 61

K

Kappel, Kenneth, iv, 64, 65, 67, 68, 100, 106, 114, 124, 195, 198–99, 202, 214, 217, 258, 260, 281, 287–88, 292, 298, 302, 328, 331, 345

Theory, 62–64

Katama Bay, 27, 28, 248, 268

Katama Shores Motel, 1, 20, 66, 205, 206, 212, 218, 223, 224, 233, 253, 308, 317

Katsas, Dr. George, 37, 205

Kelley, Gerald, 278

Kennedy, Joan, wife of Edward, 23

Kennedy, John John, son of President Jack, 42

Kennedy, Joseph, son of Robert, ii, 59, 343

Kennedy, President Jack, 23, 66, 196

Kennedy, Registry Inspector George, ii, 100, 101, 126–28, 135, 136, 142, 152, 154, 157–66, 178, 250, 252–57

Kennedy, Robert, brother of Edward, 1, 2, 28, 66, 259

Keough, Rosemary, iii, 20, 21, 59, 199, 200, 228, 232–34, 239–43, 247, 288–90, 304, 305, 308, 315–17, 320, 322, 329–30, 336, 344, 350, 356

Kielty, John, 17

Kielty-Moran Funeral Home. *See* Kielty, John

Killen, George, ii, 18, 29, 248, 262, 280, 289, 297, 302

King, Martin Luther, 67

Knight, Laura, 310

Kopechne, Gwen, mother of Mary Jo, 19, 278, 281

Kopechne, Joseph, father of Mary Jo, 19, 279, 281

Kurtis, Bill, 285, 289, 290

L

l'étoile restaurant, 61, 67

Ladies Home Journal, 281

Lange, James, iv, 74, 82, 95, 97, 114, 211, 258, 316, 360, 361, 363

Theory, 58

Lardner, George, 195

Larksville, Pennsylvania, i, 279

LaRosa, Ray, iii, 2, 13, 20, 26, 29, 63, 64, 209, 216, 221–24, 229, 233–39, 241–44, 304, 314, 317, 325, 327, 329–30

Lawrence Cottage, i, ii, 1, 2, 4, 13, 14, 17, 20–23, 26, 43, 44, 57, 60, 68, 123, 124, 195–99, 209, 212, 218–20, 223, 226, 227, 228–29, 232–37, 241, 242, 244–

49, 256, 260, 261, 262, 264, 272, 283, 299, 303–5, 308, 313–17, 321, 324, 325, 327, 330, 340, 343, 345–47, 350, 355, 362, 364

Lawrence, Sydney, ii, 22, 195–97

Leland, Leslie, i, ii, iv, v, vi, 29, 52–54, 194, 266, 278, 281, 283, 284, 289, 323, 333, 357

LeMehaute, Bernard, 26

Life magazine, 23, 256, 257, 263

Look, Christopher "Huck", ii, vi, 7–10, 24, 25, 42–44, 46, 50–60, 63, 64, 66–68, 84, 105–6, 123, 193, 195, 198–201, 207–15, 217, 218, 220, 222, 226, 227, 229, 233–47, 254, 256–57, 260, 272, 276, 282, 288–92, 299, 302, 306, 311, 314, 323, 340, 344–47, 356, 357, 361–62, 364

Look, Christopher, son of Huck, 52, 291

Los Angeles Times, 359

Lowry, Joseph, 248

luminol. *See* Benzidine test

Lyons, Mary Ellen, sister of Nance, iii, 20, 198, 205, 206, 229, 238–43, 330, 350, 356

Lyons, Nance, sister of Mary Ellen, iii, 101, 198, 199, 205, 206, 210, 238, 241–43, 329, 330, 344, 350, 356

M

Maddox, David, 46, 291

Maeso, Dr., 119

Malm, Mrs. Pierre, 6–7, 23, 26, 204, 216, 250–51, 254, 256, 257, 260, 262, 341

Malm, Sylvia, daughter of Mrs. Pierre, ii, 7, 60, 215, 216, 251–60, 262, 289, 303, 305, 341, 345

Mankiewiez, Frank, 318

Manual of Physiology, 320, 321

Markham, Paul, iii, 4–6, 9, 13, 14, 19, 20, 22, 24, 26, 27, 30–31, 57, 58, 60, 63,

64, 67, 76, 100–101, 104, 123, 165, 196–99, 206, 209–44, 247, 252, 254, 256–57, 307–35, 266–68, 271, 278, 282, 283, 285, 301, 305, 306, 307–35, 337, 339, 340, 342–44, 347, 350, 353–56, 360–64

Marshall, Breck, 11

Marshall, Burke, 6, 11, 23, 196, 310, 313, 315, 317, 361

Martha's Vineyard Airport, 32

Martha's Vineyard Hospital, 102

Martha's Vineyard Shipyard, 12

Martin House, 38, 39, 41, 42, 46, 305

Martinez, Dr., 119

McCall's magazine, 9, 17, 19, 258, 265, 279, 280, 284, 356, 357

McCarron, Richard, 294, 318

McCormack, Mike, 52, 291

McDonald, Nancy, iii, 10, 220, 306, 345, 347

McHenry, Raymond, 129, 135, 173

McHugh, Dr. John, ii, 18, 29, 30, 94, 95–99, 106, 118, 142, 194, 201, 202, 259, 296, 302, 329

McLaughlin, Walter, 280

McNamara, Robert, 317

Memorial Wharf, 12, 27, 55, 198, 268, 309, 315

Mercier. Laurence, 4, 15

Midlothian Mirror, 67

Midwest Association of Technical Accident Investigators (MATAI), 97, 104, 110, 117, 123, 130, 134, 135, 154

Miller, Jack, 318

Mills, Dr. Donald, ii, 17, 18, 29, 30, 36–37, 58, 90, 91, 92–97, 102, 119, 201, 205, 275–76, 295, 297–98, 321, 352

Molla, Robert, 126, 152, 157–59, 178

Moore, Stan, ii, 6, 14, 22, 31, 228, 290, 313, 316, 347, 358

Morrissey, Judge Francis X., 358

Mountain Lakes, New Jersey, 38

Mudd, Roger, 359

Mytoi Gardens, 124, 304, 314

N

Nader, Ralph, 58

National Enquirer, 9

National Oceanographic and Atmospheric Administration (NOAA), 27, 72, 74, 75, 122

Nelson, Donald, iv, v, 59, 115, 123, 129, 297, 338

Theory, 59

Nevin, Dr. Robert, ii, 275, 276

New Bedford Standard-Times, 360

New England Telephone Company, 21, 318

New York Graphic, 21–23, 196, 310, 316, 361

New York Post, 23

New York Times, 15, 21, 106, 263

Newberg, Esther, iii, 96, 101, 195, 197, 205, 212, 223, 224, 231–33, 240–45, 246, 253, 254, 308, 315, 317, 329–32, 350, 351, 356

Newsweek, 13, 28, 359

Nixon, President Richard, 195, 248

Norton Point, 27, 28

O

O'Connor, Frank, 318

O'Donnell, Kenneth, 318

Ochoa, Raul, 108, 109, 148, 150, 190, 194

Oldsmobile 98, 128

Oldsmobile Cutlass, 128

Oldsmobile Delta 88, 89

Oldsmobile Toronado, 128

Olsen, Jack, iv, vii, viii, 18, 32, 42, 55–57, 62, 63, 76, 77, 98, 193, 218, 222, 223, 226, 247, 251, 252, 253, 256–57, 263, 264, 316, 331, 333, 358, 363

Theory, 59–60

Orlando Sentinel, 281

P

Padanaram, Massachusetts, 10, 11
Paquet, Judge Wilfred, i, ii, v, 318, 362, 365
Parker, Alan, v, 14
Peachey, Russell, ii, 4, 214, 272, 315, 324, 347
Philadelphia Bulletin, 248
Physics Teacher, 132, 169
Pimpneymouse Farm, 44, 225
Pinney, Andrew, 260
Pinney, Raquel, 61
Plymouth Valiant, 2, 4, 39, 42–43, 45, 50, 57, 60, 63–66, 67, 68, 197–99, 203, 211–13, 216, 219–22, 228, 236–42, 252, 253, 257, 260, 299, 305, 306, 308, 311–15, 322, 325, 330, 331, 332, 340, 343–46, 362, 364
Plymouth, Massachusetts, 63
Poe, Edgar Allen, 267
Post Standard, 23
Poucha Pond, i, 8, 26, 32, 57, 74, 78, 124, 178, 234, 248, 251, 264, 295, 303, 345

R

Reader's Digest, 26, 129, 135, 154
Redman, Paul, 318
relay, 2, 236–40, 242, 244–45, 327, 331, 349
Resolute, 343
Reston, James, 58
Reybold, Malcolm, iv, 2, 236, 331
    Theory, 57
Ribicoff, Abraham, 318
Richards, Marilyn, wife of Ross, 6, 14, 30–31, 226, 228, 316, 347
Richards, Ross, ii, 6, 14, 15, 22, 30–31, 209, 226–28, 310, 316, 333, 347, 350
Roberts, Bruce, 335
    Theory, 58
Rochester, iii, 273, 274

Rock, Wilfred, ii, 15, 16, 332, 347
Rust, Zad, iv, 10, 74, 106, 200, 222, 234, 265, 294, 335, 360
    Theory, 58

S

Samuel, Robert, 4
Schlesinger, Arthur, 318
Seafood Shanty Restaurant, 12
Shaffer, J. B., iv, 74
Sherrill, Robert, iv, 19, 219, 243, 295, 296, 328, 331
Shriver, Sargent, 318
Silva, Dodie, wife of Foster, 14, 23, 247–49, 264
Silva, Foster, ii, 14, 23, 26, 202, 247–49, 264, 324, 347
Silva, John, son of Foster, 14
Silva, Tony, 15
Slade, Nika, daughter of Carol Jones, 61
Smith, David, 26
Smith, James, 62, 318
Smith, Jean, wife of Stephen, 22
Smith, Stephen, ii, 6, 22–23, 227, 307, 313, 315–18
Smith, William, 359
Sorensen, Theodore, 23, 196, 314–17, 341
Spitz, Dr. Werner, ii, 36, 37, 294
Spy (New York monthly), 20
St. Andrew's Episcopal Church, 55
Steele, Walter, ii, v, 52, 53, 54, 318, 364
Stephens, Liz, 39, 311
Stephenson, Gertrude, 44
Stewart, Mrs., 22, 316
Storer, Mary, 124
Sumatra, 10, 11
Summit, New Jersey, 38
Swift, Sally, 336
Sydney University, 129, 132, 157, 178

T

Tannenbaum, Susan, iii, 218, 219, 223–24, 228–34, 238, 241, 243, 247, 283, 315–17, 350
Taylor, Marvin, 251
Tedrow, Richard and Thomas, iv, 11, 24, 25, 28, 29, 91, 92, 94, 103, 217, 258, 276, 298, 318, 336, 343, 345, 346, 355
Theory, 59–60
Tilghman, Rev. Hal, 157
Time magazine, 9, 20, 325, 336, 359
Toliver, Clarence, son of Lula, 38, 44, 225
Tolliver, Lula, 38, 41, 42, 44, 46, 50, 215, 255, 311
Tom's Neck Farm, 157, 262
Topjian, Dr. Melvin, 18, 97, 98
Tretter, Charles, iii, 6, 14, 20, 21, 31, 209, 210, 218–25, 228, 232–34, 238, 239–43, 247, 305, 308, 313, 315–17, 320, 324, 329–30, 344, 347, 348, 350
True Forensics, 37
Trustees of Reservations, 124, 248
Tunney, John, 318
Turf 'n' Tackle, 293, 294
Turnbull, Dorothy, grandmother of Carol Jones, 38
Tyler, Nancy, 66, 67

U

Ulasewicz, Tony, iv, 11, 21, 195, 196, 197, 248–50, 254–56, 257, 321
Union Leader, 10, 21, 196, 249, 361

University of Texas Medical Branch, 119
University of Virginia, 24

V

Victura, 1, 198, 308
Vineyard Gazette, 58, 72, 257, 289
Virgin Islands Daily News, 356
VW bus, 38–39, 40, 41, 45, 54, 211, 212, 214, 216, 305, 311, 344, 356

W

Wagner, Helga, 21–23, 196, 197, 227, 305, 316, 326, 332, 341, 361
Wakeman, Mary. *See* Storer, Mary
Ward, Fred, 133, 135, 138, 140, 146, 164–66, 287
Washington Post, 195
Washington Star, 27
Wasque Farm, 38, 48
Wasque, Chappaquiddick, 8, 40, 63, 341, 344
Watt, Dr. Robert, 289, 290, 325, 326
*Web*MD, 90, 102, 203, 295
Welansky decision, 204
Wentworth, Mary, 336
Wikipedia, 35, 87, 90, 124, 207
Wilkes-Barre, Pennsylvania, 18, 36, 61, 91
Willis, Larryann, iv, 57, 88, 95, 97, 294, 331, 334, 335
Theory, 57
Witten, Thomas, 24
Woods Hole, Massachusetts, 20, 63, 317